SCREENING PRECARITY

Screening Precarity

Hindi Cinema and Neoliberal Crisis in Twenty-First Century India

Megha Anwer and Anupama Arora

UNIVERSITY OF MICHIGAN PRESS Ann Arbor

Published in the United States of America by the
University of Michigan Press
First published September 2025

A CIP catalog record for this book is available from the British Library.

Library of Congress Cataloging-in-Publication data has been applied for.

ISBN 978-0-472-07764-9 (hardcover : alk. paper)
ISBN 978-0-472-05764-1 (paper : alk. paper)
ISBN 978-0-472-90523-2 (open access ebook)

DOI: https://doi.org/10.3998/mpub.12771973

The University of Michigan Press's open access publishing program is made possible thanks to additional funding from the University of Michigan Office of the Provost and the generous support of contributing libraries.

Authorized Representative: Easy Access System Europe, Mustamäe tee 50, 10621 Tallinn, Estonia, gpsr.requests@easproject.com

Contents

Digital materials related to this title can be found on the Fulcrum platform via the following citable URL: https://doi.org/10.3998/mpub.12771973

Acknowledgments

This book emerges from our previous and ongoing research projects, conversations, and collaborations on popular Indian cinema. So we begin by vehemently and profusely thanking each other. We met in January 2018 at the annual Modern Language Association conference, and since that moment there has been no turning back. In many ways, our friendship and collaborations have sustained us in impossible times. The daily, multihour Zoom calls, weekend marathon virtual coworking sessions that entailed reading, writing, lunching, and gossiping together, albeit on camera while in different geographies, might well have saved us both. This book would be unimaginable without each other. We consider ourselves blessed that a chance encounter has yielded a lifetime of companionship built around a shared exploration of life's endless travails and many pleasures. This is why we dedicate this book to each other, and to the fount of prolific productivity and laughter we stumbled onto together. *Saranghae* forever!

We would also like to thank the anonymous reviewers for the care they took in reading our manuscript and for their thoughtful questions, which have helped us revise and refine our project and ideas. Thanks are also due to our editor Sara Jo Cohen, whose enthusiasm and encouragement for the project has meant so much to us. Haley Winkle, who stepped in to take over from Sara after her well-deserved promotion to editorial director, has made the transition feel seamless, and we're lucky to have our book in her hands. We consider ourselves lucky to be in conversation with the dynamic scholars of Hindi cinema. Their work, peppered across our bibliography, not only shapes our own, but it also animates our commitment as scholars and teachers to continue to invest in culture as a site of resistance even in times when hope is hard to marshal.

Megha Anwer

I am very lucky to be embedded within a vibrant community of friends who have sustained me through the thick and thin of writing this book and living life. Anish Vanaik, Deepasri Baul, Vrinda Marwah, Kriti Budhiraja, Lindsay Weinberg, Puja Sen, and Niyati Sharma have recommended readings and theoretical frameworks that changed, for the better, the contours and coherence of my research. Their (sometimes brutally) piquant feedback on chapter drafts was always necessary and always generously delivered. At every turn, they have weathered my elations and doldrums with timely laughter, eyerolls, encouragement, and indulgence. Their commitment to intellectual and political honesty, their challenge to "keep it real," to "not miss the woods for the trees," have been inspiring and invaluable guidelines on the road to completion of this book. They have willingly watched and discussed the best and the worst of Bollywood films with me, and without their shared love and curiosity for Hindi films, I might not have powered through many of the films we engage here. In a whole host of ways, their imprint is discernible in every fiber of this book. There are friends who propelled this project in other ways: Anna Monical, coparent to Buffy, Rocky, and Ursa (our irrepressibly rambunctious cats), in the past decade has come to be the closest I have to family in this town. Her bravery, beauty, gentle yet irreverent wit, compassion, and integrity have taught me so much about how it is possible to be fully decent even while living a precarious life. Her joyful willingness to hold down the cat fort every time I travel has allowed me to enjoy a mobility I couldn't otherwise imagine. Jason Filer has alerted my mind to life's many miracles (our friendship being one of the biggest and rarest ones). His signature one-liners ("we'll talk again") and our idiosyncratic, collaboratively curated rituals enshrine the promise of happy days, full of electrifying (often difficult) conversations, music, food, fake fights, and the Divine. Rambling walks and interminable conversations in state parks and coffee shops with Muiris MacGiollabhui sustained me in my most trying moments. I will always remember our chat in the parking lot of our favorite joint in town on that fortuitous night in November 2023. So much changed for the better that day, and in no small part, it was thanks to him. Without these friends, it would be quite impossible to write a good book, let alone live a good life. That the book culminates with Deepasri's move to within driving distance in the Midwest, Kriti's relocation to an even closer town in the Midwest, and Lindsay's return from her fellowship in Denmark, could not make for a more auspicious beginning of a new chapter. Anish's brilliance, generosity, unyielding love and support have breathed life into this project, much like with everything else I have done or will ever do. I am so grateful that his partnership continues to be one of life's greatest blessings. From my parents, Ahmer and Pamela, I have received not only unconditional love, but also a lifelong love of sensorial delights. Very early in life, they introduced me to the best of cinema, music, art, literature, and theater, and ways of thinking about them with care and criticality. I hope this book accurately reflects and does justice to everything I learned from them.

The intellectual and professional support that my friends and colleagues at Purdue's John Martinson Honors College have offered in my nearly decade-long stint here has made a workplace feel more like a community. Natasha Duncan, Liz Brite, Dwaine Jengelley, Adam Watkins, Jason Ware, Lindsay Weinberg, Zahra Tehrani, Katie Jarriel, Pete Moore, Anish Vanaik, Nathan Swanson, Muiris MacGiollabhui, Ashima Krishna, Temi Adeoye, and Emily Allen have offered critical moments of mirth, mentorship, and solidarity. Their interdisciplinary expertise as scholar-teachers continues to inspire me every day, and I am incredibly thankful to be able to work alongside them. At multiple junctures and through a variety of ways, Jenna Rickus, Natasha Duncan, and Kris Bross's support of this project went a long way in getting me to the finish line. Sarah Vaughn, Mariah Mendoza, Priyanka Brunese, Chaonan Liu, Tracy Hieatt, Jess Ramsey, and the team of advisors (Dani Parsons, Onyx Uzomah, Mike Morton, Phelan Tinsley, Jasmine Pruitt, Emily Sheetz, Alyssa Wagner, and Andrew Archey) perform absolute magic at work. I learn so much from their tireless commitment to work, to our students, and to having fun. I am especially grateful to Kris Bross, associate dean for research, Karen Plaut, executive vice president for research, and Purdue's Office of Research for supporting the writing of this book with the "Elevating Visibility of Research" award (2023).

Anupama Arora

I am grateful to my family for their love, and for their faith in me to complete this project. My parents, Akshey Kumar and Sudarshan Arora, offer unwavering support even as I am relieved that I won't have to fend off my dad's weekly query about the book's progress (is it done yet?). My younger siblings Aradhana and Vaibhav are the sweetest and kindest people whose patience and love sustains me. I am grateful to them for not just bringing my brother-in-law Pradeep and sister-in-law Prabhjot into our lives, but for bringing into the world my nieces who rule my heart: Tanishi, Kavisha, Kaashvi, and Ridhvi. Friends in Providence—too many to name—provide a welcoming and nourishing community. Most of all, Gautam: *Seni seviyorum*. Thank you for feeding me, making me laugh, putting up with my (mostly reasonable) demands, and for reminding me of the stuff that really matters when the going gets tough. Thank you for being my rock and my companion in life's many adventures including the writing of this book.

I also owe a huge debt of gratitude to my undergraduate and graduate professors at Sri Venkateswara College and Jawaharlal Nehru University for being inspiring teachers, scholars, and mentors and for making me a better writer and reader of texts and the world. I am equally grateful to my dear friends and formidable scholars Veena Hariharan, Sandrine Sanos, and Gohar Siddiqui for their intellectual generosity, warmth, and humor; over the years, they have given me generous feedback on my work and have been constant sources of conviviality, advice, and good *gupshup*. At the University of Massachusetts Dartmouth, I am grateful for the intellectual community and friendship of my colleagues in the English and Communication, and Women's and Gender Studies Departments. I would also like to acknowledge that work on this book was supported by the Provost Fellows Program Grant and the Dean's Publication Support Grant at UMass Dartmouth.

Sections of individual chapters have appeared previously. We thank the publishers for permission to reprint. Parts of chapter 4 first appeared in "Love, Interrupted: Caste and Couple-Formation in New Bollywood," *Quarterly Review of Film and Video* 39, no. 3 (2021): 615–43; the journal's website is https://www.tandfonline.com/. A part of chapter 5 was first published in "#ImNotAChick-Flick: Neoliberalism and Postfeminism in *Veere Di Wedding* (My Friend's Wedding, 2018)," *Bioscope: South Asian Screen Studies* 11, no. 2 (2021): 146–68; DOI: https://doi.org/10.1177/09749276211992595. A part of chapter 6, "Khakee Encounters: New Bollywood's Cop-Films and Political Agency in the Age of Precarity," was first published in *Jump Cut* 63 (2025). A part of the epilogue was first published in "*Pathaan*, Precarity, and the Muslim Question in Neoliberal India," *New Cinemas: New Cinemas: Journal of Contemporary Film 21, no. 1 (June 2023): 133–39.*

1: "Our Vulnerable Broken Nation"

Constructing Precarity in Hindi Cinema

On February 2, 2021, pop superstar Rihanna tweeted about an ongoing mass mobilization of farmers in Delhi, asking, "Why aren't we talking about this?! #FarmersProtest."[1] Bollywood actor Kangana Ranaut, in her rapid response, declared the protestors "terrorists . . . trying to divide India, so that China can take over our vulnerable broken nation and make it a Chinese colony much like USA."[2] The next twist was supplied by the ruling Indian government's prompt and aggressive rejoinder to Rihanna's tweet. Prime Minister Narendra Modi's right-hand man and home minister of India, Amit Shah, declared that Rihanna and Greta Thunberg (who had also tweeted the *CNN* article about the farmers' protest in India) were part of a "motivated campaign" to deter India's unity and progress.[3] Senior government officials urged their social media followers to "push back" and stand "united" against this "propaganda." Almost like clockwork, and with an eerie homogeneity, an array of Bollywood stars like Akshay Kumar, Ajay Devgn, and Karan Johar—occupants of the very highest echelons of *célébrité*—condemned foreign interference aimed at dividing the nation and promoting anarchy.[4] While Rihanna and Thunberg popularized the #FarmersProtest, Indian politicians and celebrities worked overtime to make the hashtags #IndiaTogether and #IndiaAgainstPropaganda go viral, as they tried to contain the damage done to the nation's reputation. There are many things to unpack about this episode. The apparent lockstep of a section of Bollywood and the ruling regime is one. Even more puzzling, however, are the terms of their shared response: the anxiety about India as a precarious nation.

At the heart of this social media controversy is a contestation over the reality and meaning of India as a precarious nation or, in the words of Kangana Ranaut, a "vulnerable broken nation." On the one hand, the rhetorical escalation in Ranaut's reaction to Rihanna's tweet and her disparaging language (she called Rihanna a "fool" from the land of "dummies") can be easily dismissed as the actor's individual eccentricity and virulent nationalist jingoism; she has gained immense notoriety on both counts. The breadth of actors joining the response, however, reveals a far more widely shared anxiety about India's status as a global power and a desperate desire to manage how domestic political ruptures and internal vulnerabilities are perceived and narrated abroad. At the same time, these responses also articulate an overcompensatory vehemence in their denial of India's precarity. In some ways, then, Rihanna's tweet unleashed such passions because it simultaneously tapped into a pervasive discourse of India's precarity, as well as the absence of consensus over what the grounds for India's precarity really are and ambiguity over who counts as the truly precarious.

For Rihanna, Thunberg, and Indian actors like Swara Bhaskar and Richa Chadha who applauded Rihanna's original tweet, it was the farmers who were vulnerable because of the Indian government's neoliberal revamping of the agricultural sector and the removal of the state protections they had enjoyed before. And it was once again farmers who were the real victims, as they were arrested and their civil rights suspended under the guise of maintaining public safety. Ranaut, the other celebrity superstars, and government officials, on the other hand, posited India as a sabotaged nation, compromised both by the terroristic protests of illiterate farmers who didn't understand the value of privatization and liberalization, as well as by the social media war orchestrated by foreign interests trying to disrupt national integrity. In this complex rhetorical maneuver, India was simultaneously a beleaguered nation and a global power that the rest of world dare not mess with.

The episode also threw open the question of who is entitled to naming and calling out India's precarities. In other words, it crystallizes contestations over what constitutes a legitimate political voice in, and about, India. The ease with which Ranaut's tweet ascribed terroristic motivations to farmers is indicative of the sleight of hand by which political positions are rendered illegitimate, especially when they threaten the current government. All it takes is a casual equation with terrorism, or a loaded invocation of China's economic imperialism, to delegitimize political protests by farmers adversely affected by the neoliberal commercialization of agricultural processes.

And finally, that a transcontinental social media row between celebrities sent the Indian government's PR machinery into overdrive, calling upon Bollywood celebrities to defend the Indian state, draws attention to Bollywood's recruitment and embedding in global power networks that are as much about state power as they are about star power. This moment reveals the role that Hindi cinema plays in the etiology and grammar of precarity in India today. This is why we offer an exploration of the celluloid configurations of precarity. We study how precarity is mediated by the film form in India and what that mediation reveals both about the contemporary Indian polity and what Sangita Gopal calls "the social life of the movies."[5]

Postindependence Hindi cinema has always represented *precariousness.* Arguably, ontological and material vulnerability have concertedly constituted the heart of this cinema.[6] The majority of the films, from those in the so-called golden era of Bombay cinema (the 1950s–1960s), all the way up to the 1990s, when India underwent liberalization, either directly or implicitly posited themselves as cinematic redressals of the vulnerabilities that abounded in a newly postcolonial nation.[7] This is because the project of reconstructing a nation recovering from colonial plundering, from dire inequities of class, gender, caste, and the trauma of Partition, necessitated a proactive engagement with the its real, material insecurities, and the conjuring of imagined deflections, distorted anxieties, projected enmities, and fantastical solutions. In other words, popular Hindi cinema has always converted national insecurities into cinematically fecund territories.

In this book, we move away from the history of Hindi cinema's articulation of precariousness and examine instead filmic renditions of *precarity*[8], a distinct and historically contingent condition produced by neoliberalism.[9] In doing so, we offer an analysis of what constitutes "the cinema of precarity" in India today. We study a range of postmillennial Hindi films, primarily those released in the first two decades of the twenty-first century, for how they interpret, obscure, distort, and accommodate neoliberal precarity and the "offending conditions"[10] it produces. The films may be thought of as contentious cinematic terrains that record India's transition from the glee and gusto of liberalization in the 1990s to a nation contending with the failures and inadequacies of neoliberalism's promises and the ascendency of the material-affective redressals offered by Hindutva. The book is also an intervention in the politics of representation, particularly of how marginal identities are shaped, scripted, and screened, when neoliberalism and authoritarianism enmesh.

This is not to suggest a neat or linear changeover in the tenor of the films that began at some precise moment or in any particular year of the twenty-first century. On the contrary, it is worth acknowledging that even the early years after liberalization were marked by doubts in cinematic rendition. Even before the Great Recession struck the American economy in 2008 (one of the reasons for our periodization), an event which had global reverberations, films from the 1990s offered stark reminders that all was not well in the period of neoliberal jubilation. In particular, the gangster genre of films set within metropolitan and small-town *mofussil* ecologies—*Satya* (Truth, Ram Gopal Verma, 1998), *Company* (Ram Gopal Verma, 2002)—and films like *Oye Lucky! Lucky Oye!* (Dibakar Banerjee, 2008), *Luck by Chance* (Zoya Akhtar, 2009) expressed the dark undercurrents of postliberalization aspiration in middle- and working-class settings. And, since the 2010s, films such as *LSD: Love, Sex, aur Dhokha* (Love, Sex, and Betrayal, Dibakar Bannerjee, 2010), *Peepli Live* (Anusha Rizvi, 2010), *Gangs of*

Wasseypur (Anurag Kashyap, 2012), and *Titli* (Butterfly, Kanu Behl, 2014) continued this trend, fueling anxieties about neoliberal fantasies of abundance. Contrarily, even as reservations about neoliberal precarity have gained prominence, there continues to be a subset of films that celebrates the lives of those for whom neoliberalism has fulfilled its promises. Sleeper hits like *Band Baaja Baaraat* (Wedding Procession, Maneesh Sharma, 2010), and *Sui Dhaaga: Made in India* (Needle and Thread, Sharat Katariya, 2018) are a testament to the persistence of neoliberal dreams, even when little material reality bears them out.[11] Our periodization, then, registers a substantial shift in tone and emphasis of Hindi cinema's output rather than a sharp break.

The films we study in this book are also visual invitations to participate in configurations of precarity that have emerged and developed in response to a "crisis ordinariness"[12] that pervades the Indian polity. This crisis ordinariness is not the result of a sharp, datable moment of disjuncture but is born out of a relentless, strategically paced series of ruptures manufactured by the Indian state: from (most recently) the disastrous mismanagement of the COVID-19 health crisis, to the ruling Bharatiya Janata Party (BJP) government's attempts to rewrite—both constitutionally and culturally—India's "identity" within national and global discourses. We argue that the barrage of crises is no accident. Rather it is a symptom of an ideological congruence between neoliberal economics and a neoliberal Hindutva state, the two working in tandem to produce what Melinda Cooper suggests is neoliberalism's dictate: "the necessity for continual crisis."[13]

Postmillennial Hindi Cinema: A Cinema of Precarity

We treat the Hindi films discussed here as responses to a state of *continual crisis* that India has experienced in the first two decades of the twenty-first century. This state of crisis, as we have suggested above, is as much the outcome of a landscape of material deprivation as it is the result of the political narratives manufactured about it. The films, in this context, are both depictions of an ongoing sense of crisis as well as narratological contributors to it. This interweaving—of reality and narrative—is at the heart of what Henry A. Giroux calls the "cultural politics" of neoliberalism.[14]

We study these films for how they perpetuate neoliberal logics of precarity and can operate as the Indian state's instruments of domination. We search these films for how they absorb and exude ideology and normativity, to appear as hegemonic accounts of the present and of history in the making. In that sense, these films function as modes of address that make demands upon us for how we respond to crises that are both born out of and reproduce precarity. Often these films make us feel the crisis and the cruelty of neoliberalism without letting us diagnose it or hold it accountable for our personal and collective suffering. We show how, in this way, these films craft our will about which precarities we accept and which we exaggerate; they press us to consent to certain configurations of moral, political, affective authority, while dismissing as illegitimate or faux other ethical obligations. The broad swath and spectrum of precarities that postmillennial Hindi cinema represents can thus help us understand the boundaries, ranges, and intensities of precarity. We come to recognize how contemporary Hindi cinema constructs certain precarities as ineluctable and others as autonomously fixable. We learn about which precarities are deemed extreme and explicit and which are cast aside as ineffable or immemorable.

As a universal condition, precarity refers to the insecurity, uncertainty, and instability connected to employment prospects and professional trajectories, and to the general transformation in the nature of jobs, produced across classes under neoliberalism. This class-professional insecurity, however, impacts the precarious subject's physical and psychological well-being too, producing a distinctly neoliberal subjectivity. Scholars have noted how "a sense of precarity . . . haunts the vast majority of Indians" and "that there is no invulnerable life, there is no guaranteed safety."[15] In the context of India, the neoliberal subject's material and affective precarities intersect with pre-existing social vulnerabilities of religion, caste, gender, and sexuality mobilized in unprecedented ways by Hindutva. Bollywood's cinema of precarity enables us to recognize the universal, indiscriminate violence of neoliberal precarity, but also to register the disparate and differential consequences of that violence for marginalized groups: the poor, Dalits, Muslims, women, migrant workers, slum dwellers, etc. The precarious subjects of the films we study are caught in a maelstrom of contradictory impulses and politically dubious predilections. They are desperate to feel entrepreneurial-agentic in a world that is vehemently apathetic and resistant to even imagining, let alone crafting, alternative political visions for a less precarious world. The result is a festering of aspirational ressentiment, which not only fails to alleviate the precarious subject's suffering, but instead scapegoats other, even more, precarious bodies in an attempt to keep alive the cruel optimism and eternally deferred entry into the pleasures of neoliberalism.

In a different register, we explore how contemporary Hindi cinema constructs and articulates precarities in ways that are surprising within, and resistant to, a dominant right-wing national schema. Here we rely on Francesco Sticchi's analysis of films as "experiential constructions" that "set concrete spatial and temporal dynamics to interact with."[16] Working with the Bakhtinian concepts of dialogism and heteroglossia, Sticchi rejects the idea of films as producing static or monologic meaning. Instead, he encourages us to take stock of the "intrinsically manifold and unresolved" discourses and aesthetic utterances that "interrelate in unpredictable ways," not only within the film but also between the film and its viewer(s). This "ontological polyphony" of interaction between the characters of the film, and through the viewer's affective-somatic interaction with them, entails engaging with films not as predetermined semiotic codes but as dynamic relational systems in which the spectator operates as a "co-creator reinventing her/his own polyphonic subjectivity while exploring an artistic ecology."[17] The films we study here are, therefore, not treated as pure vessels of dominant ideology, explicitly commissioned by the state to do its bidding through the promotion of certain films and genres.[18] We view them more as structures of negotiation that continuously explore, elaborate, distort, disassemble, and reassemble the national and global networks in which they are embedded and that explore the relationship between narrative and reality. And, crucially, they do so in ways that exceed the desires and logic of state-generated commandments.

Films in India are being produced in a climate of overt, covert, and self-censorship. While many films serve a clear propagandist function, others encode a critique of neoliberal Hindutva within their narratives in a subtle and obscure fashion. This is why, even though we highlight how these films proactively promote precarity, and sometimes practice self-censorship to navigate the dictates of neoliberal Hindutva, we also study the alternatives and resistance to precarity proposed by Hindi films. In some cases, these films are direct responses to, or at least make tangential (albeit recognizable) references to, contemporary social movements protesting state-manufactured precarities and precarities borne out of the cultural marginalization of women and minorities. We pay attention to the moments in which characters disrupt the neoliberal logic of precarity: when they opt out of "forms of individualization";[19] when they invest in relationships of care, in shared intimacies and dependencies, and thereby reimagine "new openings of how to live."[20] In order to recover the understated resistances of the films we study here, we try to historicize their visual vocabulary, read against the grain of their apparent meaning, and embed them within the political economies in which they are produced.

In this book, we track precarity at work, in both formal and informal sites of labor: government jobs; corporate offices; factory settings; contractual work; self-employed struggling artists, including actors in the film industry. We draw attention to the precarious subjectivities and psyches produced as counterparts and coping mechanism to precarious material existence. Several scholars of precarity have remarked on the psychological strain that relentless insecurity imposes on neoliberal subjects. Lisa Rofel, for instance, suggests that neoliberal discourse penetrates "into the sinews of our bodies and the machinations of our hearts";[21] Guy Standing argues that it generates personalities characterized by anger, anomie, anxiety, alienation, passive-aggressive frustrations, and chronic uncertainty; others focus on the vulnerability, hyperactivity, restlessness, affective exhaustion, and compulsive hustling of the precariat.[22] We track the visual, spatial, somatic, and verbal manifestation of these psychological traits in the central and marginal fictional characters that appear in these films.

The cinematic ecologies of these films also occasion insight into the shifting terrain of India's relationship to its Muslim and Dalit citizens (see chapters 3 and 4). These films both record and normalize the dominant configurations (including the denial) of religious and caste precarity, often by superseding their vulnerability with constructions of the nation as the uber-precarized entity. The economic-political-cultural-existential precarity of marginalized communities is thus placed in competition with national insecurity, the only precarity that's made to count. We also study the gendered dimensions of precarity by casting an intersectional lens upon its functioning. Thus we reject essentialist predictions of how vulnerability circulates and is distributed by registering the real precarity of poor, Muslim, and Dalit men and women and upper-class-caste women's complicity in the precarization of others.

Just as importantly, therefore, we study these films for their representations of nonprecarious lives and ask what the visual markers of nonprecarity, of economic-political-cultural security, are. At the same time, we also take note of how these films conjure precarities of the elite. What, we ask, is the grammar of suffering and vulnerability when one's ontological and material existence are not in jeopardy? In doing so, we draw out the narratological maneuvers by which these films draw affective investment in the lives of neoliberalism's beneficiaries, even as they render ungrievable[23] and invisible its victims. As a result, we also assess precarities that emerge from a clash between those with extreme class-caste-religious privilege, looking to protect their hegemony of security, and the precariat, jadedly trying to achieve the blueprint of a fantasy that is no longer sustainable or achievable.

We engage with these films as symptoms of *shared*, not solitary, affective environments, of the crumbling of collective fantasies and promises of a "good life" that were never truly collective or universally realizable to begin with. In most instances, therefore, the affective-aesthetic cinematic ecologies of these films acknowledge the failures, evoke the contradictions, the ellipses, and the lapses that constitute the differentially shared and unevenly distributed precarities. They give an account of the toll that neoliberal precarity takes in terms of the anxiety, depression, and subjectivities it produces.[24] None of these films simply accommodate a neoliberal right-wing worldview without pushback or without reframing and buffing its most jagged edges. They do not trick audiences into investing in neoliberal ideology by masking its cruelties. Instead, the films often address neoliberal cruelty head on, and then offer outcomes that function as object lessons in "how to" navigate and negotiate a neoliberal ethos and landscape. Surviving neoliberal precarities requires leaps of faith and the chasing of impossible dreams in increasingly unsustainable material conditions. These films don't withhold objections to this reality; they reveal the hollowness of the promises that are fulfilled and give audiences enough to experience the different textures of dissatisfaction with, and disaffection for, neoliberalism. In doing so they arrive at the verge of challenging the system's acceptability. At the critical moment, however, these films typically loop instances and forms of resistance to precarity back into adjustment to and appeasement of neoliberal right-wing demands. Here we examine how political articulations and actions are often realigned and appropriated for cinematic consumption. And we therefore ask: What are the cruel optimisms that these films resort to; what are the individual and collective adjustments they compel?

We find that in many instances, the tussle between exposing and accommodating neoliberalism's crises and precarities, across the breadth of the films examined here, are never definitively resolved in any one direction; they yield an oscillation between deplored affective breakdown and meek resolution to crisis. We argue that this yo-yo-ing typifies the cinema of precarity today.

In investigating postmillennial Bollywood films primarily produced since the second decade of the twenty-first century, we take our cue from Berlant to ask how cinematic genres adjust and improvise in response to the manufactured precarities of contemporary India. Therefore, we are interested not only in the internal schemas of precarity that unfold within the films—those experienced by the characters or those that determine the plot—but also the formal schemas of adjustment performed by the film genres themselves. What we suggest is that, on the one hand, in formal terms and as modes of address, these films enact a distancing from a proximate past.

In a sense, they bow out of a post-1990s euphoria that had congealed through the last decade of the twentieth century and the first few years of the twenty-first. Gone is the easy ubiquity of big weddings, uncomplicated aspirations for globe-trotting, and relentlessly successful entrepreneurialism. The slow-leak dissipation of postliberalization euphoria enacted by these films finds expression in their affective materiality. Their protagonists manically alternate between high-energy celebrations and melancholic self-destruction enacted across global landscapes. The films proffer a more direct and angry articulation of frustration, and their climaxes are often inconclusive and open-ended. And, most significantly, precarities of neoliberalism erupt to the surface, and the narratological maneuvers by which they are deflected or distorted are exposed as futile efforts at a return to "normalcy."

On the other hand, these films also enact a harking back and a turn to older genres and structures of feeling that were associated with and emerged in the postindependent, preliberalization era of the Hindi film industry. This "return" of older genres is not marked by a temporal-spatial nostalgia for a time or national geography that has disappeared, since many of these films represent an ideological contradistinction to much of the shifting politics espoused between the 1950s and the 1980s. The "return" to older genres, then, conveys more a sense of formal borrowing, a recovery of forms and genres that belonged to preliberalization India. But they are deracinated from their original context of emergence, discombobulated, and then reanchored through a reassembly to fit the current moment. In different chapters of this book, we therefore track how past genres are invoked and reworked, simultaneously borrowed and disaggregated through their application to the present conjuncture.

These "adjustments" in Bollywood's genres may be understood, then, in terms of Raymond Williams's idea that at any given moment, culture is constituted by the interaction and competition between its "residual," "dominant," and "emergent" elements. Here we add that the present moment is configured not only by these competing strands of becoming, but also by the impasse produced by the extended crises that have marked the past decade of the Indian polity. Cinema archives, as Berlant suggests, show not only "what is being lost" but also "track(s) what happens in the time that we inhabit before new forms make it possible to relocate within conventions the fantasy of sovereign life unfolding from actions."[25]

We treat the cinematic genres that have (re)emerged, in the past decade and half, as a congealing of past genres but also as interregnums or as stopgaps that are waiting and watching for what the future holds. What is common to these films is that, for the most part, they are strident articulations of the precarities—whether real or imagined—that define the present, without being able to offer radical or realizable solutions or escapes, even as they scramble for them. This capacity to name the precarious present without laying a stake or direction for a secure future, is also a defining feature of Bollywood's "cinema of precarity."

How We Got Here: A History of Neoliberal Precarity

The story of economic precarity is not new. For the vast majority of workers under capitalism, survival has always been precarious. Wedded to maximum extraction of labor and profit making, capitalism's politicoeconomic modality has been characterized by insecurity of employment, paltry wages, the danger of fatal injuries, and endless hours of factory work that brutalize and alienate laboring masses, disaggregating their ability to build a life of security. Jan Breman[26] goes as far as to say that in the nineteenth century, precariousness of labor was the "defining condition of proletarianization."[27]

By the 1950s, however, organized labor and its political allies had struggled long and hard against the human cost of capitalism, and they pushed wealthier capitalist countries in the West to incorporate techniques and institutions of social protection against unemployment, illness, accident, social insecurity, and exclusion.[28] The next two decades of Fordist economics marked an aberrant phase in the history of capitalism and its relationship to precarity, in that there was actual material improvement in the conditions of laborers. These years saw the rise of stable, full-time jobs, regulated working hours, recuperation time for workers, and a de-escalation of hostility toward unions.[29] In contrast to the abysmal work conditions of the nineteenth century, this period witnessed a new phenomenon: "an affluent and even happy worker, who is so content with his life that he gives up on political struggle."[30]

Several historians and Marxist-cultural theorists argue, however, that even this ostensible reprieve from relentless exploitation under capitalism must be assessed as ultimately profitable for capitalism itself. The reorganizing of work along Taylorist lines increased worker productivity by breaking up the work process into a set of discrete, calculable tasks. As Richard Seymour writes, "The expertise of the craft worker was replaced by the predictable, routinized tasks of the industrial worker."[31] In this context, the managerial class's function cohered around maintaining pressure on workers to remain loyal, productive, and submissive. It is erroneous, therefore, to imagine that the primary goal of the social security net and institutions of the welfare state was to ensure the security and protection of the workers. On the contrary, worker security was granted in exchange for reneging on organized workers' rights. This is why, as Isabelle Lorey suggests, welfare systems were geared toward supporting those who were "obedient and cautious citizens":[32] committed to self-government techniques that confirmed economic productivity, and willing to ensure themselves against the precarization of others. This process enabled capitalism's reconfiguration and reclamation to strike again, when workers were least prepared for its full-throttle resurgence.[33]

By the 1970s, these labor wins proved inadequate in the face of the free market's counterreactionary will to reassert its dominance. Welfare mechanisms were systematically dismantled as obstacles and rigidities that impeded the labor market. The economy was transformed on a global scale to make way for the "more frictionless flow of capital across national boundaries, buttressed by neoliberal policies and dogma."[34] This Thatcherite-Reagan backlash against the welfare state produced what Berlant calls "the neoliberal feedback loop":[35] a reorganization of capitalism that rejected outright "jobs for life" in favor of the flexibility of labor[36] and the "financialization of daily life."[37] It was no longer the production of commodities that governed the economy, but the expansion and remodulation of financial fluxes, "whereby money became the main object of the productive process."[38] Even the public sector was expected to turn productive and managed as a business enterprise through private loans, debts, and insurance.[39] This was, therefore, an even more strident return to nineteenth-century principles of the free market, with newer technologies at capital's command to increase its mobility and power to exploit human labor.[40]

David Harvey has argued that while capitalism's destabilizing and destructive propensities have always prevailed, neoliberal economic practices harness this insatiability in unprecedented ways.[41] Neoliberalism has produced precarity that is both broad and deep, as the ranks of those suffering and alienated has expanded dramatically. While precarity was originally associated with the lives of people ridden by poverty,[42] today it denotes a generalized vulnerability to unemployment. And while this was once a hallmark of the proletarian condition, today the threat of losing one's employment status plagues managers and white-collar professionals as well.[43] Lorey identifies this as the normalization and democratization of neoliberal precarization.[44] If Fordist capitalism governed through the promise of (social) security, in the neoliberal regime the threat of insecurity is now deployed not only against the marginal, recalcitrant other, but as the very basis of ordering the bourgeois center. Neoliberalism's targets are no longer just the poorest, migrants, the shrinking manual workforce, women workers, or racial minorities; rather its disciplinary effects are experienced by those who previously belonged to the upper rungs of the class stratification: public sector workers, civil servants, managers, etc.[45]

The global dimensions of this economic order mean that not only has neoliberal insecurity permeated through classes, but also across transnational contexts and politics. Neoliberalism's ravaging success is tied up with the ease with which capital can abandon challenging labor conditions and shift production to national territories where regulation is laxer, labor cheaper, and ethical obligations void. Gilles Deleuze and Félix Guattari term the contemporary economic political system "integrated world capitalism," whose destruction plays out across geographies, in both amorphous but also in hyperdifferentiated and ultralocal ways. After all, capitalism operates through inclusion that is simultaneously differential.[46] The state of precarity, then, entails a play between the universalizing impulse of neoliberalism and its peculiarly local-individualized manifestations. Breman suggests that until the 1970s, the dominant development paradigm presumed that the processes of industrialization and urbanization would bring the "underdeveloped world" closer to the experience of the advanced economies characterized by growing employment in manufacturing, rising living standards, and mass consumption. The informal sector was expected to be a "zone of transition" that would eventually be absorbed by the growing formal economy. Not only did this development fantasy never materialize, it also collapsed in North America, Europe, and Japan. The hollowing out of trade unions, factory relocation and robotization of the workforce, and expansion of the nonunionized service sector and low-paid workers into the global labor market had disastrous consequences for wages and work conditions, even in the West.

The move from the Fordist model of capitalism to neoliberal globalization has resulted in a fundamental worldwide transformation of work, its meaning, its forms, and its boundaries. Under the guise of flexibility but ultimately driven by capital's quest to cheapen labor, neoliberal capitalism has led to widespread precarity through a growing casualization or deregularization of work. What is called "irregular work" by the International Labor Organization (ILO) comprises most of the work in countries of the Global South; for instance, "88% in the informal sector in the case of India" where "two-thirds of workers . . . are in casual work."[47] In any case, "flexploitation" or "new modes of exploitation" rooted in independent employment, part-time, temporary, and projects-related jobs[48] have increasingly become the norm. These are "denoted by a family of terms such as 'McJobs,' 'junk jobs,' 'flexiworking.'"[49] Fordist securities, at least for some, in the industrialized Global North—defined by long-term employment, well-paying unionized jobs, incentives to create corporate loyalty and cohesion, and sense of work-based class solidarities—have given way to more transient jobs with few prospects of career progression. What we have now is a "gig economy" and a perpetual looming threat of unemployment, volatile contracts, lack of a secure work-based identity or belonging to a solidaristic labor community.[50] These are features of precarious work that have slowly become commonplace in many sectors and across classes, sparing not even skilled workers or educated professionals.

While always characterized by uncertainty, unpredictability, and riskiness, precarious work manifests itself variously. If jobs become less secure, stable, and fulfilling, then "work regimes become subject to speed-ups and enhanced surveillance, and demand intensified effort."[51] This further exacerbates "the already unequal balance of power between capital and labor." Labor now expands outside the usual sites of the office or the factory and gets turned into "twenty-four seven activity."[52] In some senses, the distinction between work and life, between work and nonworking life, disappears as most of our everyday life activities are transformed into productive operations.

The individual too is transformed into "human capital," a subject who "operates on her/himself by accepting the continuous process of selection, judgement, and evaluation;" "who commits to perpetual training and self-improvement."[53] Even so, the perpetual training, acquisition of skills, and productivity provide only slight protection against the vicissitudes of neoliberal precarity. Since their goal is to work in capital's favor and produce a more "tractable and subservient" workforce,[54] ultimately all these individualized, self-managing tactics leave the unskilled and low-wage workers disproportionately more vulnerable to dispensability. Likewise, regular or skilled workers with relatively secure jobs might supervise poorly paid contract workers without benefits, but they live in constant anxiety about being replaced by them.

Perhaps the most efficient guarantee of neoliberalism's persistence, and even more dangerous than neoliberalism's economic crisis, is the crisis of politics and the collapse of resistance it has induced. Neoliberalism's ubiquity, its spaceless-nameless quality (Monbiot), the acceptance and normalization of its dictate that "there is no alternative" have produced a logic whereby, as Frederic Jameson argues, "it is easier to imagine the end of the world than to imagine the end of capitalism."[55] Its adaptive, co-optive capacity makes it impossible to know when we are being "resistant, co-opted, or complicit."[56] This is because neoliberalism commands not only the market but also insists that a market rationality govern all aspects of life: politics, citizenship, social relations, identities, and subjectivities are all subject to the survival of the fittest ethic. The possessive individual and consumer citizen are held up the exemplars of neoliberal modality.[57] Neoliberal ideology convinces us that the "sense of insecurity, perpetual competition and individual isolation" are natural; this is what life is really like.[58]

It's also hard to conjure resistance to this world order because, as Byung-Chul Han suggests, unlike in industrial capitalism's system of oppression, where "both the oppressors and the oppressed were visible,"[59] neoliberalism is preserved not through repression, but through seduction; prohibition and privation are replaced by the goals of pleasure and fulfillment. Once the oppressed worker is converted into a "free contractor," a self-exploiting "entrepreneur," the class struggle is easily obfuscated. People start to "see themselves, not society, as the problem." A combination of factors—the systematic dismantling of unions; the high rates of unemployment; precarious employment; huge debt; the threat of state violence; the expansion of the surveillance state; and the "emergence of apocalyptic narratives in which the future appears indeterminate, bleak, and insecure"[60]—have resulted in a generation that is despairing, resigned, burnt out, and withdrawn from the political arena. In other words, people recognize that there is little they can do as individuals. All significant gains made in workers' rights were a consequence of collective action, revolutions, strikes. Under neoliberalism this kind of political agency feels like a thing of the past; the working class is too heterogeneous and fragmented, and it lacks a work-based identity and solidaristic labor community[61] to be able to sustain any collective action. Precarity imposes social withdrawal and political disengagement; it corrodes collective identification.

And yet protests by the discontented precariat have erupted globally in response to neoliberal's parasitic policies and the pervasiveness of precarity they have produced. While the concepts of precarity and the precariat were originally deployed in proximity to protests in Europe against labor insecurities (*précarité* in France; *il precariato* in Italy), they have gained polemical strength and have broadened into a slogan, a rallying cry to mobilize and connect movements involving workers' rights, citizenship, migration, and prodemocracy activists. Some of these include, for instance, MayDay protests throughout Europe (the 2001 Milan MayDay protest and subsequent EuroMayday protests starting in 2005, which Guy Standing refers to as the "first stirrings of the global precariat"); 2001 protests against the G8 in Genoa, Italy; civil demonstrations in London in 2011; worker agitations against austerity policies in Athens in 2010; Arab Spring protests (in Tunisia, Egypt, Syria, etc.) in 2010; Occupy Wall Street in the United States in 2011; antiausterity movements like the Spanish 15-M in 2011 and 2012; Gezi Park protests in Istanbul, Turkey, in 2013; anticitizenship bill protests in India in 2019; and farmer agitation in India in 2020. These protests also highlight alliances that have formed between otherwise seemingly heterogeneous constituencies such as "cultural producers, knowledge workers, migrants, autonomists, unemployed, trade unions, radical leftist unions, and organizations of irregular people."[62]

These demonstrations and social movements encapsulate the resistance of the precarious who refuse to be cast off as dead and disposable by governments oriented to the finance market. Comprising those "who refuse to be governed through insecurity," these protests and the forms they have taken can be viewed as an assertion of "democratic principles" which counter the hierarchies and disparities engendered within post-Fordist capitalism. They are resilient reminders that the project of neoliberalism is on a rickety wicket. For Judith Butler, the obdurate and persisting bodily presence of those protesting links precarity with "forms of social and political agency." Lorey similarly sees the Occupy Movement's camps and assemblies as examples of new forms of democracy that have arisen in response to the democratization of precarization. Theorists like Ernesto Laclau and Chantal Mouffe also celebrate the resurgence of a left populism—the "multitude"—with its horizontal forms of collaboration, political participation, communities of support, dialogue, and exchange in its search of a new politics. Michael Hardt and Antonio Negri champion the Occupy Movement as an opportunity for "the political power of the citizen worker"[63] to be regained. They treat these populist upheavals as a "scaffolding" that lays the groundwork for a more radical break that can enable the building of a new society.[64]

There is, however, a contestation over the efficacy and durability of these social movements. Scholars have warned against an overenthusiastic response to these populist uprisings, even where their espoused politics are more radical than anything seen on a mass scale in a long time. With the Occupy Movement itself, for instance, the very reasons for its success were also what led to its splintering and dissipation. As Sarah Jaffee has argued, while its leaderless structuring and absence of concrete demands about how to dismantle the power of the elite one percent attracted a wide swath of protesters, the idea of leaderlessness also masked how power actually operated in the movement. And the lack of a political strategy for moving forward "wound up as a refusal, oftentimes, to deal at all with existing systems."[65] As a result, a politics of the 99 percent ultimately got reduced to "signs without organization."[66]

The ideas of community and sharing forwarded by these open-structured movements are themselves all too easily neutralized by appropriation by neoliberal discourse. As Chul suggests, while sharing is supposed to replace the economy of property and possession, the truth is that a sharing economy is still inaccessible to people without resources. And in any case, the demand of moving from owning to access still does not address the structural inequities of capitalism. Instead, it has led to a "total commercialization of life" such that every car is a cab in a rideshare system and every home is an Airbnb hotel in a digital marketplace. Similarly, every corporate work culture has usurped slogans like "Community First," and these communist principles have themselves evolved into commodities.

Even though many of these social movements have found resonances across the globe, they remain fragmented around race, ethnicity, gender, class, and sexuality. For Laclau and Mouffe, the construction of a "people" through these disaggregated popular identities against the establishment offers the most adequate way to recover and constitute democracy, and it ought to be the main task of radical politics. And while it is certainly true that these left populist movements have given people on the margins their voice back, what must be acknowledged alongside this is that the identity-centered politics, and a media-centered strategy for political action, runs the risk of reducing resistance to discourse and to a fight for representation. In other words, what ought to be starting points of resistance become the struggle's endpoints. In that sense, these popular movements are as much a symptom of neoliberalism at work, a sign of the postpolitics it avows, rather than a real engagement with its overhauling.[67] What stands before those of us invested in combating neoliberal precarity is to have a comprehensive conceptualization of what it takes to convert these protest movements into sustained challenges to state power, to transform "revolutionary situations" into revolutionary "outcomes."[68] This requires not the "idealization of the revolutionary tendencies of actual movements" but a clear-eyed assessment of lessons learned from their collapse.

Theorizing Precarity

That precarity is built into neoliberal capitalism is the starting point for precarity studies and for Guy Standing's influential work, *The Precariat*.[69] Standing's work emphasizes primarily the socioeconomic dimension of precarity. Standing contends that neoliberal policies have led to the creation of a distinctive socioeconomic group, the precariat, which counts among its members "many millions around the world without an anchor of stability."[70] The precariat, a neologism that combines "precarious" and "proletariat," describes a class-in-the-making that occupies the bottom of the new tiered class system, and, as Standing suggests, better explains class relations in the contemporary global market. This pyramid consists of the elite or plutocrats at the top followed by the salariat, proficians (professional + technicians), manual employees (or the old working class/proletariat), and the precariat and the unemployed or lumpen precariat at the base.[71] While the precariat is heterogeneous, those in its ranks share in common "a sense that their labour is instrumental (to live), opportunistic (taking what comes) and precarious (insecure)."[72] Lacking labor-related security or feeling of belonging to a solidaristic labor community, the precariat is a "dangerous class" as it experiences "anger, anomie, anxiety and alienation," which makes it susceptible to "populist politicians and neo-fascist messages."[73]

For Standing, the precariat is a distinctive and peculiar social class in many ways, and it does not map neatly onto older notions of class, status, or occupation. For example, unlike the salariat or proletariat of yore, the precariat lacks labor security and stable full-time employment and attached benefits. In terms of status, which was traditionally seen as being tied to a person's occupation, the precariat has "truncated status" and experiences "status discord," that is, those in its ranks feel that their high educational qualifications are incommensurate with their job or income.[74] As a result of feeling the pressure to answer to market forces and be "infinitely adaptable"[75] in order to ward off precarity, the precariat is under time stress and "wired into job-performing lifestyles."[76] Stuck in jobs that are static and going nowhere, those who are precarized might experience "uptitling" or "fictitious occupational mobility" as they are given high-sounding epithets meant to conceal their disposability.[77] Thus, for Standing, precarity is related primarily to the chronic uncertainty regarding jobs or work and employment under neoliberal's economic regime.

Lorey engages precarity as a new form of regulation and power under neoliberalism. Neoliberal governing, Lorey argues, works by normalizing precarization and turning it into an "instrument of government"[78] that serves the purposes of capitalist accumulation and social regulation. If, previously, governments legitimized their control by constructing precarity as confined to nonhegemonic others at the fringes of society, now they manage populations through inducing insecurity "as a mode of life."[79] Thus precarity now moves to the middle as it becomes "democratized" or normalized, and the state of insecurity and crisis becomes the state of everyday existence as individuals come to be governed through instability.

Living in this constant state of insecurity, individuals self-govern and self-discipline. "Biopolitical governmental self-governing"[80] or "self-precarization," as Lorey puts it, requires that individuals actively modulate themselves and "arrange their lives on the basis of a repeatedly lowered minimum of safeguarding, thus making themselves governable."[81] Individuals come to perceive social conditions responsible for their precarity as capable of being treated or managed through self-responsibilizing techniques, by being entrepreneurial, by taking risks, and through self-empowerment strategies. The constant regulation of one's conduct allows for "imaginary self-sovereignizing" and fosters "fantasies of mastering" one's own precariousness.[82] Within this new state rhetoric of empowerment, "insecurity becomes recast as freedom, self-exploitation reframed as 'being your own boss.'"[83] The government of the precarious thus creates biopolitical subjects out of entire populations who internalize and accept the conditions of insecurity.

Where Lorey analyzes precarization as the hegemonic organizing principle by which we are governed and govern ourselves, Lauren Berlant conceptualizes precarity in terms of the disorganization it causes. Berlant turns to the affective field precarity produces, which, in turn, is also what sustains and reproduces precarity. In exposing the "emotional underpinnings of the economy,"[84] Berlant offers a critical understanding of how and why our individual and collective emotional registers come in the way of toppling systems that perpetuate precarity and compromise our well-being. Berlant describes the present moment as an intensification of precarity; precarity has spread across class and localities and now envelops even the formerly protected classes: unionized populations, entrepreneurs, small property owners, and the professional managerial class, what Giorgio Agamben calls the "planetary petty bourgeoisie."[85] As a result, precarity has morphed from an economic condition to an affective environment that frames the dominant structure and experience of the present.[86]

Berlant suggests that the precariat, as an affective class, is distinguished by "cruel optimism," a perverse and compulsive adherence to the fantasy of a "good life" that is no longer attainable in the present world order. No matter how hard we slog and do everything right, there are no guarantees that things will get better or that our neoliberal aspirations will be realized. In fact, Berlant goes a step further to argue that cruel optimism "exists when something you desire is actually an obstacle to your flourishing."[87] It is, therefore, precisely our addiction to neoliberalism's phantasmic ambitions that ensure that we continue in a state of precarity, instead of opting, for instance, for an alternative route such as undertaking a struggle for a more secure world.

Cruel optimism, then, refers also to the personal and communal "logic of adjustment,"[88] the coping mechanisms that allow us to withstand the cruel contradictoriness of the present moment. These techniques and skills of management make it possible for us navigate what's overwhelming; comfort us through an existence that is "painful, costly and obsolete";[89] and help bridge the gaping chasm between life and fantasy. Importantly, these "affective rhythms of survival"[90] that emerge when we're confronted with the attrition of the neoliberal fantasy, find articulation in the aesthetic conventions and genres of the moment, and contribute to producing a whole new precarious public sphere. This is why Berlant studies affective responses not as solitary utterances but as symptoms of shared emotional atmospheres.

Like Lorey, for Berlant too, precarity must be understood in de-exceptionalizing terms, not as a singular catastrophe, traumatic event, or shock-inducing loss, but as "crisis ordinariness," a "process that is embedded in the ordinary," that pervades the everyday, and produces ongoing, generic adaptations to it. In fact, the trick of precarity is that it distorts what is normal to seem shocking. This is why, rejecting trauma theory, Berlant insists that we categorize the present moment as an "impasse," marked not by slammed-door departures or drowning, but by the elongated durée, the nondrama of treading water. Berlant also compares the impasse of the present moment to a cul-de-sac, in which, paradoxically, movement returns you to the same space. This getting nowhere, in spite of all the "dogpaddling around," produces anxiety and demands activity: "gestures of composure, of mannerly transaction, of being-with in the world as well as of rejection, refusal, detachment, psychosis, and all kinds of radical negation."[91] These overcompensatory somatic articulations, facial expressions, and psychological somersaults, then, are the language, the visual vocabulary of neoliberal precarity.

Standing, Lorey, and Berlant, then, all explain precarity as a theoretical category through which to understand the shifts in material existence, processes of subjectivization, and shared affective atmospheres, brought about by neoliberalism. All three theorists of precarity emphasize the expansion of precarity under neoliberalism from a condition that once affected only the working class to one that now envelops all classes except the very elite. If precarity's movement from the margin to the center is one dimension of its hegemony, then the internalization of precarity by neoliberal subjects as a new normal is its second defining characteristic. An articulation of a neoliberal ethic-aesthetic or a coping mechanism to survive its cruelties, the precise function that reproduces the logic of neoliberalism, is also ensuring its tenacious continuance.

It is important to note that Butler engages with precarity differently from Standing, Lorey, and Berlant, in that she treats it not so much as a function of neoliberalism but as an ontological presupposition that lies at the very heart of what it means to be human and count as such. For Butler, our shared corporeal vulnerability, or precariousness, is the basis for how we recognize and acknowledge the intertwined materiality of our existence and approach our place in the world as always already dependent on others. Our bodily needs are indebted to the care and protection that others, in many instances, "anonymous others"[92] extend to us; this is not a condition we can will away "without ceasing to be human."[93] And thus, our precariousness makes a "tenuous 'we' of us all."[94] Contradictorily, the vulnerability of our bodies—to injury and exposure—which makes us relational and dependent on others, is also what further exacerbates precarity. Our skin and flesh expose us to the gaze, touch, and violence perpetuated by others; at the same time our bodies also become instruments for committing harm to others as well. This is why, even when we struggle for the security and rights of our own bodies, "the very bodies for which we struggle are not quite ever only our own. The body has its invariably public dimension."[95] Thus the mythologies of "self-sufficiency and unbridled sovereignty" are necessarily disrupted the moment we take stock of our shared, interdependent precarity and contend with the larger global process that constitute us and the world.

In this book, however, we rely on Butler not so much for how she treats precariousness as an a priori condition of being, but for her insistence that our shared precarity must always be attuned and attend to the differential forms of allocation of vulnerability that have a direct bearing on "who counts as human," "whose lives count as lives," and "what makes for a grievable life."[96] Lives, after all, as Butler reminds us, are "supported and maintained differently'; while certain lives are highly protected, others are subjected to incommensurate forms of violence. This is why "precarity is indissociable from that dimension of politics that addresses the organization and protection of bodily needs" and may, in fact, be thought of as the "social condition of political life."[97] Here, then, in Butler's formulation, the ubiquitous precariousness of life gives way to the processes of precaritization that manufacture precarity as a politically induced condition; "Precaritization allows us to think about the slow death that happens to targeted or neglected populations over time and space."[98] Additionally, Butler is useful for thinking about neoliberal precarity in its striated global distribution. Butler encourages us to remember how neo-imperial networks render the lives of people in other parts of the world inordinately more precarity-ridden.

In this project, we treat precarity as a phenomenon produced by neoliberalism's precarizing impulse, as it acts upon a general state of precariousness. Precarity, differently from precariousness, is a politically induced condition, which renders certain populations more vulnerable, excluded, and exposed to injury, violence, and death. And we embed precarity as it has emerged in contemporary India within larger global economic and cultural networks of capitalism and nationalism.

India's Story of Liberalization: 1990s and Bollywood

The story of contemporary neoliberal Hindutva and its intimate imbrication with popular Hindi cinema begins decades earlier and can be traced back to the economic reforms of the late 1980s and early 1990s, which led to profound and far-reaching political, socioeconomic, and cultural changes that transformed the fabric of postcolonial India.[99]

In 1991, after four decades of Nehruvian socialism, of planned economy and state control, India opened its borders to foreign investment. Economic liberalization "introduced market forces into areas of the economy controlled by the state. It facilitated foreign direct investment and trade, freed business firms from the license-permit raj, and eased banking regulations to increase consumer credit and encourage spending."[100] What was seen as the cumbersome developmental and protectionist state of the postcolonial decades gave way to the state's withdrawal from socialized spaces of consumption—education, health care, public health, energy, and transport, for example—coinciding with the elimination of bureaucratic red tape restricting imports of foreign commodities. Suddenly, the Indian market was flooded with the irresistible charisma of consumer goods, designer labels, and a hundred television channels.

As we discuss in our introduction to *Bollywood's New Woman: Liberalization, Liberation, and Contested Bodies*, while the nation's economic transformation was undoubtedly radical, even more dramatic and unprecedented still was the resultant impact on the social and cultural milieu of India. Among other scholars, Leela Fernandes and Rupal Oza[101] have described in great depth the sociocultural repercussions of liberalization in India. What occurred in the decades following liberalization was an economic but no less a discursive reconstruction of the nation as "New India," "India Rising," or "India Shining." It was an abrupt transformational imagistic makeover of the hitherto ascetically pious and austere, frugally and virtuously "simple" Gandhian nation to a sizzling new frisson of speed, shine, and excitement, at the center of which lay the power of commodity culture and a fetishistic preference for foreign technology, international travel, and global brands. The model citizens of this accelerated economic "revolution" were no longer rural farmers on state television network Doordarshan's *Krishi Darshan* or the unionized working class of a Nehruvian social narrative as seen in the older idea of the "*Naya Daur*" (new era). In fact, more and more the state enacted a "growing amnesia"[102] toward its disenfranchised populations, which got disowned as irrelevant spaces of poverty and insufficiency. In their place, a confident, aggressively self-celebrative (and predominantly Hindu) middle class gained ascendancy, consolidating its economic claims and moral authority as the rightful heirs of the burgeoning new India of liberalization. "This middle class would be the producer as well as the consumer driving the engine of economic growth and prosperity, a Fordist model of development re-engineered for India."[103] In this narrative, citizenship of Global India came to rest for successful self-actualization on conspicuous "acts of consumption, acquisition of goods [and] CEO lifestyles."[104]

If glitzy malls were one hypervisible outcome of the influx of global capital, then one accompanying symptom of the economic transformation was an acute and intensified experience of loss: loss of control, sovereignty, autonomy, and national culture. Oza contends that the evacuation of familiar cultural markers engenders a compensatory desire to fortify traditional identities.[105] It was in this context that the political party of Hindu nationalism, the BJP (founded in 1980), stepped in to usurp the terrain and present itself as "the force that could galvanize both the economy and the Hindu majority of the nation"[106] in contrast to the Congress Party (with roots in the Indian National Congress founded in 1885), which was aligned with the "past" of planned economy and stagnation and of secularist nationalist politics. In the wake of globalization, the Indian state, following the policy of widespread disinvestment in its functions, faced a real crisis of legitimation. In contrast, the BJP's investment in the concept of ethnocultural nationalism took "the lead in resuscitating the concept of nation."[107] The period from the late 1980s onward through the 1990s into the new millennium came to be marked by a free-market ethos along with a rise in the fortunes of the aggressively Hindu chauvinist BJP and the concomitant spread of fundamentalist politics, persecution of religious minorities, muscular-masculinist nationalism, and hawkish, jingoist rhetoric in the national public sphere. This "Hindutva-liberalization dyad" or the "political alliance between Hindu nationalism and neoliberal forces reshaped the perceptions of social life, and this shift in points of reference and transformations of sensibilities is visible in the popular Hindi cinema of the 1990s."[108]

Indeed, popular Hindi cinema came to play an overcompensatory role in responding to the seismic shifts of liberalization by offsetting consumerism and neoliberal mobility aspirations with the visual codification of brahmanical-patriarchal hierarchies for coping with cultural changes brought upon by neoliberal globalization. Hindi cinema, often seen as an important bearer of national identity or a repository of national-cultural value since Independence, became the site where both the euphoria and anxieties, the aspirations and crises, surrounding the liberalization of the Indian economy have played out.[109]

As many scholars have examined, the 1990s mark a crucial turning point for popular Hindi cinema as a result of liberalization. The Hindi film industry, which was finally granted "industry status" in 1998, underwent a dramatic overhaul, a process that has been described as a "Bollywoodization of Indian cinema"[110] or "gentrification,"[111] wherein classic Hindi cinema gave way to "New Bollywood."[112] Aspects of the new milieu included the corporatization and centralization of film production in Mumbai, the rise of multiplex exhibition, investment of astronomical sums of finance capital, a worldwide distribution network, and an accompanying premium on glitzy "showbiz" and grand "production values." Visually lush, replete, smooth, tight, and pacey, the films no longer looked like unfinished products from an economy of poverty and chronic underdevelopment. Simultaneously and crucially, "Bollywoodization" manifested as the dramatically changed outlook and reworked thematic priorities of popular cinema, the iconography of Global Bollywood or New Bollywood films implicitly manufacturing consent for post-1990s neoliberal values.

The most popular big-budget films dedicated their narrative focus to the lives of the extreme rich. Gone were the iconic templates of the everyman exemplified in figures like the naive indigent played by actors like Raj Kapoor in films like *Shri 420* (Raj Kapoor, 1955) and *Awaara* (Vagabond, Raj Kapoor, 1951), or the 1970s figure of the angry young man railing against a corrupt state and its dysfunctions, played by Amitabh Bachchan in *Zanjeer* (Chains, Prakash Mehra, 1973) and *Deewar* (Wall, Yash Chopra, 1975). Their postcolonial cinematic embodiments were replaced in the 1990s by the grotesquely lavish, decorative lifestyles of industrialist joint families (*Maine Pyar Kiya*, I've Loved Someone, Sooraj Barjatya, 1989; *Hum Aapke Hain Koun . . !*, Who Am I to You, Sooraj Barjatya, 1994; *Kuch Kuch Hota Hai*, Something Is Happening, Karan Johar, 1998; *Hum Saath Saath Hain*, We Are Together, 1999; *Kabhi Khushi Kabhi Gham*, Sometimes Happiness, Sometimes Sadness, Karan Johar, 2001; *Vivah*, Wedding, Sooraj Barjatya, 2006) and diasporic business tycoons (*Dilwale Dulhania Le Jayenge*, The Braveheart Will Get the Bride, Aditya Chopra, 1995; *Pardes*, Foreign Land, Subhash Ghai, 1997). For film audiences of the 1990s and early 2000s, class elites and their unabashed cultures of consumption represented a new aspirational goal as well as a new universal norm. The values, rituals, anxieties, and preoccupations of the nouveau riche were the subjects of national-cultural mythologization. Globe-trotting, factory-running, convertible-driving protagonists (*Dil Chahta Hai*, What the Heart Desires, Farhan Akhtar, 2001;*Zindagi Na Milegi Dobara*, You Only Live Once, Zoya Akhtar, 2011) were insignias of Indian liberalization's success story. They showcased the privileges afforded to those who were willing inductees into neoliberal ideology and protocols.

Most critically, it was many of these films' capacity to revive a fetishistic traditionalism and reconcile it with unrepentant luxuriating in international brands that turned the characters into India's new ideal consumer-citizens with cross-class, mass appeal. It's no wonder then that the BJP—the party that granted industry status to the film sector in order to variously capitalize on, and exert control over, it[113]—patronized and promoted the popular genre of the 1990s "family melodrama" films since they provided an effective platform to disseminate their own ideological agenda on different fronts. Many scholars[114] have commented on the conservative tendencies informing the "family entertainer" or "the designer romance-NRI" films that came to valorize well-to-do Hindu authoritarian-patriarch-led feudal families and sexually chaste Hindu women observing archaic Hindu rituals as exemplifying superior family values and (Hindu) Indian culture and tradition. These films—which affirmed "India's moral foundations by representing its 'traditions' and announce India's triumphant entry into the global market by managing to persistently include a wide array of multinational brand names in its narratives"[115]—illustrated the cozy alignment between the Indian state and the film industry as they both aggressively courted a transnational audience and the wealthy Indian diaspora to tap into global capital or the potential for earning foreign revenue that the free market enabled.

As neoliberalism's promises went unfulfilled and the optimistic mood of the 1990s gave way to uncertainty and insecurity by the 2010s, this short-lived love affair between the state and the film industry also soured and, in some ways, proved a Faustian bargain for the industry as the Hindu Right has "come for Bollywood" in its relentless zealous march to colonize and saffronize the cultural domain. A volatility defines the current relationship; and with its savvy understanding and mobilization of the power of media, the Hindu nationalist government continues to tighten its tentacles around the film industry and its cultural workers. We return to this discussion toward the end of this chapter as well as in subsequent chapters in the book.

Hindutva Neoliberalism: Crisis and Precarity in India Today

Neoliberalism's trajectory in India, at least at the start, looked a little different, and it presented a more complex picture from its European and US counterparts. While neoliberal policies in the Global North amounted to waging war on the poor, in India liberalization reduced the percentage of people living below the poverty line.[116] The Indian middle class, unlike in Europe, grew as a result of neoliberal reforms.[117] And, as Jisha Menon points out, India "took pride in its transition from a socialist style economy to a liberalized one without damaging its democratic institutions."[118] Perhaps this explains 1990s Bollywood's gung-ho assimilation into and perpetuation of neoliberal worldviews. By the end of the second decade of the twenty-first century, however, the promises of neoliberalism and the aggressively self-celebrative mood of the 1990s had waned. The country's postliberalization economy has gone from boom to bust, and with it the possibilities of the good life ("*achhe din*"—good days) have collapsed for the majority.

The most important development in the political sphere has been the election and re-election of the Narendra Modi-led Hindu right-wing nationalist party BJP as the single-majority party in the 2014 and 2019 general elections. Hindutva under Modi's leadership differs from Hindu nationalism of the 1990s, sometimes in degree and other times in kind. There has been, for instance, a mainstreaming and sharp ascendance of Hindutva neoliberal political power, and an accelerated "saffronization of the public sphere."[119] There is a banalization of Hindu nationalism that is increasingly permeating every aspect of life, and the forms of discrimination against religious minorities, especially Muslims, that were always present but to a lesser extent, are expressed more openly. "Simultaneously brazen but concealed, nebulous and mainstreamed, militant yet normalized,"[120] Hindutva has now infiltrated into new spaces as a result of the cozy and tight relationship between the ruling right-wing nationalist BJP and its ideological fountainhead, the RSS (Rashtriya Swayamsevak Sangh) and its affiliates (part of the Sangh Parivar or family). What were previously fringe elements (belligerent, militant, and vigilante Hindu leaders or right-wing militia groups such as the Bajrang Dal or Ranvir Sena, for instance) are now not just accommodated but celebrated and protected by the power of the state. And while violence against caste- and religious- minorities or sexual violence or state repression of dissent are not a recent occurrence in India,[121] what is remarkable is the multiplication, systematization, casualization, and normalization of myriad forms of violence and abuse of political power in the past decade. This perpetual state of crisis has been the hallmark of the neoliberal Hindutva state.

This historical moment has also been marked by a litany of real, imagined, and manufactured disasters, a sign of "India Drowning" rather than "India Shining."[122] The country's ruling right-wing party has deployed these crises as a tool of governance—creating and feeding off an endless loop of insecurities and anxieties, an "infinite paranoia"[123]—to manage the populace. In this prevailing modus operandi of what Lorey would classify as "governing through insecurity,"[124] the BJP has opportunistically inculcated a sense of national victimhood among the country's religious majority to deflect attention away from the failures of its market-oriented governmentality. Thus, as neoliberalism's chickens have come home to roost with massive protests and unrest rocking the decade, the Indian state has self-servingly perfected a template, one that contrives precarities, stoking a sense of loss and of a (Hindu) nation under siege. Simultaneously, it has willfully ignored the very real economic, human, and environmental wreckage caused by its neoliberal economic policies on those at the margins of society.

In fact, the state's violence exceeds the crime of negligence, as it proactively declares as "antinational" those who protest and dissent against this devastation. The self-serving divisive rhetoric and policies of the majoritarian government manage to both weaponize the nation-in-peril discourse to its advantage and shift the blame of fomenting social turbulence to those who dissent against its program, while presenting itself as the promoter of a united and strong India.

The utter disregard with which millions of internal labor migrants were cut loose by the government in the wake of the abruptly declared national lockdown in the face of COVID-19 (in March 2020) is only the latest episode in a series of market-oriented neoliberal policies that have decimated the poor and working classes in postliberalization India. Geared toward supporting the interests of neoliberal corporate capital, a string of policies has created widespread vulnerability and accelerated inequality. For example, the arbitrary and autocratic way in which the currency was "demonetized" in 2016 disproportionately impacted wage laborers and small traders while ultimately proving unsuccessful in its ostensible goal of conquering corruption. The 2017 implementation of the GST (goods and services tax) overtaxed the poor while protecting the elite. The new farm bills (2020) threatened to aggravate agrarian distress by exacerbating the vulnerability of small farmers and leaving them exposed to the vicissitudes of the market.[125] The privatization or continuing push to privatize essential services (such as health, sanitation, education, energy, water), the focus on a consumption-oriented economy, the growing financialization of the economy, the steady dismantling of state-sponsored social welfare programs and reduction of public welfare expenditure,[126] and the defanging or coopting of unions have wreaked havoc on the lives of millions of poor and lower-middle classes.

At the same time, a general state-corporate nexus has protected the oligarchs or billionaire industrialists who continue to reap profits from free market capitalism (by one estimate, the richest 1 percent have accrued 73 percent of the wealth created in India). Furthermore, market pressures and imperatives have led to even more informalization and casualization of labor. Increasingly, even the middle classes experience conditions of job insecurity, whether in the form of unemployment or diminished opportunities for occupational mobility. The dispersion of vulnerability on an unprecedented scale, the resultant multiplication in the ranks of the precarious, and the disaffection these have festered have created a fertile breeding ground for mass mobilization in the cause of Hindutva as a panacea for the nation; in the bargain, it has yielded an intensification of gendered, communal, and caste violence.

Scholars have especially noted the emergence of right-wing populism and "neo-Hindutva" or new forms of Hindu nationalism in twenty-first-century India. The Hindu Right has made hay of panics engendered in the wake of globalization, targeting and mobilizing them to fortify traditional identities. Here the concept of "ressentiment" provides a useful lens to understand the workings of neoliberalism in tandem with Hindutva. As Ajay Gudavarthy has written, the idea of ressentiment has come to mark the everyday idea of social life in India, a "combination of resentment and sentiment—which, in a sense, is a mix of envy, humiliation, and powerlessness."[127] This idea helps to explain both the entrepreneurial aspirations produced by neoliberalism as well as the weaponization of the failure of those aspirations by the politics of Hindu nationalism. Priya Chacko refers to BJP's political project as one of "Marketized Hindutva," "a melding of neoliberal economic approaches and Hindu nationalism that is driven by a populist politics of resentful aspiration."[128] Thus ressentiment provides the affective foundation of reactionary forms of populism.[129] Deprived of "the good life" to which they feel entitled, and unable to fulfill these aspirations, individuals and groups harbor ressentiment and seek to regain by force the power they see as rightfully theirs.

Indeed, a key trope in "neo-Hindutva"[130] is the generation and exploitation of a feeling of injury or victimhood among the Hindu majority and the creation of scapegoats toward whom to direct that fear and anger: an ever-shifting, proliferating, overlapping Other (the Muslim, the migrant, the secularist, the English-speaking liberal elite, the Dalit, the pub-going woman, the student activist, the Christian missionary, etc.). To keep the hurt or injury current, right-wing groups relentlessly hatch "causes"—against Valentine's Day; the "beef ban" and related "*gau rakshaks*" (cow protection vigilantism); "Love Jihad"; "*ghar wapsi*"; "triple talaq"[131]—many of which mobilize "outrage and offence" to "challenge and regulate voices deemed to compromise Hindutva visions of Indian society."[132]

The notion of the embattled (Hindu) nation and the need for "self-defense" becomes the rallying cry behind which the warriors of Hindutva line up in hate. Whether they are protecting their sacred cows or their women, these "angry young men" who feel irrelevant, who feel that economic liberalization has left them behind, find a sense of renewed identity, vigor, and purpose in Hindutva.[133] While they constitute the mobilizational force of right-wing expansion, neoliberalism's beneficiaries—the elite and middle classes—not only endorse this mobilization but also serve as its ideological architects and defenders. In this environment, panic reigns supreme; the specter of the existential threat posed by the Other, Islamophobia, and anti-Dalit violence become banalized or normalized.[134] This, in turn, makes it easier for civil liberties to be readily suspended in the name of shoring up the sovereign state. The dehumanization or derealization justifies "violence on the Other whose life, because not considered human is not grievable."[135] Thus Muslims and Dalits can be attacked with frightening frequency and without impunity so much so that the word lynching itself has come to acquire a "domestic familiarity" and "mundane inevitability,"[136] and even the pretense of a commitment to secularism enshrined in the Indian constitution has been abandoned.

According to the National Crime Records Bureau, the crimes registered under the Prevention of Atrocities Act increased by 176 percent between 2012–2013 and 2015–2016 (ten times more than crimes in general).[137] Caste-based violence against Dalits and overall harassment—itself a response to Dalit assertion of the past few decades—is at an all-time high as evident in incidents such as the suicide of the Dalit student Rohit Vemula (2016), anti-Dalit violence at Saharanpur (2017) or Bhima Koregaon (2018), or the casualization of the lynching of Dalit men and gang-rape of Dalit women. At the same time, Dalits are managed through an inclusion-exclusion model, coerced, or coopted into the majoritarian Hindu nation, as "the Hindutva-isation and securitization of Adivasis and Dalits through their violent incorporation into Hinduism"[138] is continuously attempted.

Within escalating Hindutva, Muslims become second-class citizens and experience what Banki identifies as "precarity of place":[139] their right to remain in their country of residence is imperiled as their homes, lives, and livelihoods are systematically attacked. In addition to casual everyday discrimination (in housing, education, employment, etc.), this is evident in a series of incidents targeting Muslims over the past few years: the large-scale disenfranchisement of (largely poor) Muslims through the 2019 Citizenship (Amendment) Act (CAA) and National Registry of Citizens (NRC);[140] the hounding of Muslim student activists and Muslim universities (such as Aligarh Muslim University or Jamia-Millia Islamia); the pro-Hindu 2019 Ayodhya verdict about the construction of the Ram Temple. The disputed construction site had seen some of the deadliest Hindu-Muslim riots in 1992 after the demolition of the Babri Masjid (mosque) by activists belonging to the Hindu right-wing organization, the Vishva Hindu Parishad. The open complicity of the state apparatus in violence toward Muslims is apparent in many instances, including the 2013 Muzaffarnagar (Uttar

Pradesh) and the 2020 northeast Delhi riots. The Indian state's move of abrogating Article 370, which had granted special status to the Muslim-dominated state of Kashmir (2019), and continuation of the ruthless suspension of civil liberties in the state stand out as acts of hostility by the neo-Hindutva toward its Muslim citizens.[141]

Similarly, a series of high-profile verdicts and decisions in the judicial and legislative sphere, the appointment of Hindutva leaders into prominent political positions, and the less transparently "political" but equally insidious changes in the public sphere (in education and media, for instance) leave no doubt about India's grim and determined march toward becoming a Hindu Rashtra (Nation).[142] The ruling party bears all the hallmarks of right-wing populist politics: a charismatic leader, scapegoating of marginalized groups, nativism, jingoism, religious ethnocentrism, conspiracy-mongering, all in the service of furthering a majoritarian agenda and simultaneously deflecting attention from the massive socioeconomic failures.

Feminist scholars have especially noted the increased precarity of women within the convergence of neoliberal logics with Hindutva. Gendered bodies develop into embattled moral terrain, especially during periods of major sociocultural upheaval, and since the 1990s, women's bodies have become sites on which anxieties around national culture in the face of rapid globalization have been articulated. The newly liberalizing economy both recruited and celebrated the middle-class Indian woman to measure and celebrate India's participation in global networks, while closely scrutinizing the liberated woman for her deracination; and apprehensions over open economic and national borders are transcribed as moral anxiety about this new Indian woman's "openness" and potential for gender or sexual transgression.[143] Thus, on neoliberal India's New Woman's shoulders is placed the impossible burden of being the icon of a liberated new India of seemingly endless choices while preserving national-cultural identity in the face of foreign influences. Within this context, patriarchal structures have tenaciously reinvented themselves and a toxic masculinity has reared its head. It operates hand in glove with Hindu muscular nationalism as it increasingly polices Hindu women and disciplines minority women.

The horrific fatal sexual assault of Jyoti Pandey on December 16, 2012, in south Delhi, which sparked mass outrage and protests, might be read as an instance of the clash between what Tithi Bhattacharya calls "neoliberalism's dreams and the nightmare of violence" that neoliberalism itself produces. Bhattacharya locates the incident within the histories of domestic migration from rural to urban centers prompted by economic reforms and in the failure of the "dreams of improvement" promised by these reforms. "While it may seem like an obscene exercise," Bhattacharya urges us to comprehend the economic-cultural precarity shared between the rapists and their victim, to acknowledge the "deep, anomic rage that a section of the working class has against everything that neoliberalism promised would be theirs and then put tantalizingly beyond their reach."[144] Sexual violence against women, then, is not a carryover of traditional feudal-patriarchal lineages, nor is it merely a backlash against permissive possibilities available to women as a result of liberalization's modernizing impulses. On the contrary, the escalation in the violence against women must be treated as the result of neoliberalism's very operation, which manages sexuality and labor in innovative and violent ways and which encourages the deflection of frustrations of one oppressed group upon another precarious segment of the population. This is how the vulnerabilities produced under one regime of government become the grounds of recruitment into another regime that compensates with the illusion of dominance.

The Hindu Right has also made concerted attempts to coopt even the vocabulary of "women's empowerment" and aggressively recruit women; it counts within its ranks firebrand female Hindutva leaders (Uma Bharati, Sadhvi Rithambara, Sadhvi Pragya Thakur) and has established militant organizations such as the Durga Vahini, Hindutva training camps for women. These organizations openly preach hate and violence toward the non-Hindu Other in the guise of self-protection and national honor while simultaneously encouraging Hindu women to embrace their roles as wives and mothers to produce sons for the nation. In more recent years, regressive patriarchal institutions such as Khap Panchayats, steeped in caste supremacism, have felt empowered with the blessings of the ruling right-wing government. All these developments have led to an overall extension, intensification, and mobilization of forms of gendered violence for the project of Hindutva.[145] For instance, not a day goes by without news of "honor killings" of interfaith or intercaste couples or violence against minority men and women.

The increasingly repressive measures and precarities of the majoritarian state have, however, not gone unchallenged and have given rise to organic alliances among the precarious, as shown by recent protests against the CAA-NRC or the new farm laws. Muslims, Dalits, women, peasants, and students—in a recognition of the tenuous and fortuitous quality of one's supposed well-being—have gathered in solidarity to express discontent with the neoliberal state's divisive policies and politics of dispossession. The security state has responded with draconian measures: intimidation, censorship, and imprisonment of activists, journalists, students, and ordinary citizens have become the order of the day in a repressive regime that rules through generating and instrumentalizing instability and insecurity.[146]

We must ask then, along with Wendy Brown, about the extent of the success of neoliberalism's "stealth revolution" in "undoing of the demos."[147] In some ways, the protests that bookend the second decade of the twenty-first century—the 2020–2021 anti-Citizenship Act Amendment (CAA) and farmer protests, juxtaposed against the 2011 anticorruption campaign and the protests that followed in the wake of the 2012 Delhi rape—allow for a reflection on the manifestations of populism in response to the construction of real and perceived precarity in India, the possibilities and limits of reimagining political action under neoliberalism's onslaught of the social contract.

Earlier in this section, we discussed the rise of right-wing populist politics in India that seek to "take back the nation" and Make India Great Again, fueled and managed by the ruling government through its divisive policies of cultural nationalism and religious majoritarianism that promise security in the face of precarity. As elsewhere in the world, however, twenty-first-century India has also seen other forms of social populism on the rise with mass mobilization that articulates discontent around a range of issues: corruption, women's safety, sexual harassment, LGTBQIA+ representation, repression of civil liberties, Dalit rights, and ecological concerns, to name a few. Even as these contest the hegemony of right-wing populism in India, the difficulties of sustaining these protests, or the compromised politics of these movements, are a symptom and result of the weakening of the social order and dismantling of avenues for democratic processes.

Let's look, for instance, at a movement that captured the nation's attention at the beginning of the second decade of the twenty-first century. In 2011, the "India Against Corruption" (IAC) campaign, led by the seventy-four-old year-old Anna Hazare, galvanized the youth and resulted in the quick emergence and stunning success of a self-proclaimed antiestablishment new political party, the Aam Aadmi Party (Common Man Party) or AAP, under the leadership of Arvind Kejriwal. While Team Anna split from Team Kejriwal quickly, both had the same support base and the same ideology of those who had hopped on the neoliberal train: aspirational lower- and middle-class, upper-caste, urban, and English-educated Indian youth who were frustrated by their inability to access fully the fruits of the postliberalization economy. The campaign promised graft-free politics and better governance. But, as commentators such as Arundhati Roy and Anand Teltumbde have pointed out, the campaign was not interested in structural change or in addressing and overhauling societal hierarchies in an egregiously unequal society.[148] Not only were the campaign's leaders beholden to big corporate interests who were beneficiaries of the postliberalization economy, the campaign was also infused with a majoritarian, upper-caste, and "aggressively nationalist" sentiment.

In the case of Kejriwal and AAP, these soft majoritarian impulses have found bolder expression over the decade that cannot be excused as "instrumental electoral reasoning" (doing Hindu-style *puja* before elections or invoking Hindu gods and visiting Hindu temples, especially the disputed Ayodhya site; distancing itself from the Muslim-women-led anti-CAA protests; turning a blind eye to the annihilation of Muslim lives and livelihoods in Delhi riots in 2015 and 2020).[149] Thus AAP's campaign of "the people" did not address the precarities created and aggravated by the "corruption" generated by neoliberal policies (land grabs, scams, rising unemployment, and inflation). Instead, the movement "steered clear of the root causes of the disease of corruption and pitched its prescriptions around corruption as symptom."[150] Not surprisingly, then, neoliberal politicians got behind this campaign, seeing the potential of these protests: a "safety valve" for a certain group of people to let off steam while ultimately supporting the neoliberal logic for the continued withdrawal of the state from the public sphere.

Like the anticorruption protests, the 2012 antirape protests (and the 2018 "me too" protests) in India are other examples of what might be considered middle-class populism organized around single-issue platforms. Centered around the vulnerability of women to sexual violence, populist rage erupted in the wake of the gruesome rape and death of Pandey in 2012. Why did this singular case get outsized attention when little attention is paid to poor, rural, Adivasi, Dalit, and Muslim women who have disproportionately been on the receiving end of state-sanctioned sexual violence for decades? This case generated so much sympathy because Pandey and her upwardly mobile family (migrants from rural to urban India, working-class father, college-educated daughter as the primary breadwinner) represented aspirational New (Hindu) India. They demonstrate how the process of "relative mobility" and "incremental" benefits leads to the creation of a neoliberal consensus across social groups while making the work of forging coalitions across them especially hard.

In this context, the broad solidarities across people from different social groups that emerged in the "Shaheen Bagh" movement led by Muslim women against the right-wing "legislative populism,"[151] enacted through exclusionary acts such as the CAA-NRC, provided "a glimpse of what a reimagined politics might look like."[152] These countrywide protests were celebrated as "India's first mass movement since the movement for national Independence."[153] Similarly, the 2021 farmers' protests (that Rihanna tweeted about), which represented a "popular upsurge against neoliberal arithmetic in India,"[154] provide an example of how new expressions of democratic dissent are being articulated in India today.

But even as these solidarities of the precarious promise momentary hope, their fragile coalitions face formidable challenges against a repressive majoritarian regime that has instrumentalized neoliberal precarity by engaging in "complex inclusion-exclusion" politics—where some groups are conditionally welcomed into the fold at the expense of others—which serves as roadblock to sustained, progressive, and transformative political action.[155] The "Hinduization" of Dalits, for instance, speaks to their tenuous inclusion within the nation-state, effected on the backs of the exclusion of Muslims from the national arena. Politics are messier on the ground and dissolve into "a jumble of competing discourses"[156] as minority religious groups, rather than being a homogeneous group, also divide along class or caste lines (upper-class or lower-caste Muslims or Sikhs or Christians, for instance). The seductive promise of neoliberalism to provide relative dignity and mobility, the incremental and sporadic spread of inequality and the crushing of fraternity, alongside the claims of cultural majoritarianism to "foster a sense of community," all do "not allow for easy political alternatives to emerge."[157]

Structure of the Book

While all the films we examine are Hindi-language films, there is some diversity in the films in terms of their production or industrial contexts and narrative forms or aesthetics. Some are smaller-budget films that cater to a more niche audience and might be termed multiplex films. Others are produced by well-established studios, feature superstars of the industry, and received big theatrical releases. Two films are "shorts," part of Netflix film anthologies, and one is an independent film. By cutting across genre and industrial contexts and by grouping films that might be studied separately, we highlight how neoliberal precarity undergirds the narratives of these films.

In analyzing these films, we examine how neoliberalism and Hindutva work together, how the vulnerabilities produced by one create the fertile grounds for recruitment into the logic of the other. In doing this, we try to show how neoliberalism and Hindu nationalism marshal together their differently resonant narratives about precarity. This also allows us to trace the wide variety in the narratives of precarity itself, which nevertheless cohere to produce a shared condition in contemporary India.

Our chapters are organized around class, religious, caste, gender, and political precarity in contemporary India, and in each chapter we study their varied intersections as imagined and represented in cinema. The divergences in precarity are a result of the unpredictable and variegated ways in which these precarities combine, intersect, and overlay one another. In mapping the cinematic renditions of class, caste, religious, gender, and political precarity, each chapter focuses on three facets of how precarity operates. First, we explore the affective, emotional worlds and psychologies that precarity produces. Second, we attend to the spatialization of precarity: the real and imagined geographies produced by precarity but which also undergird how precarity permeates and manifests. We emphasize mise-en-scène as a continuous thread across the chapters, especially because mise-en-scène is critical to describing how precarity is spatialized and how space is precarized. Finally, we study the (often desperate) attempts by cinematic characters to escape precarity and the desultory consequences of the exercise of agency in the absence of an explicit antineoliberal and anti-Hindutva political vision.

In doing so, we demonstrate the different evocations of a precarious subjectivity in and of itself, but also in relation to other precarious subjects. Our composite conceptualization of precarity, therefore, considers the hierarchies within which precarities are located, as well as how precarious subjects constantly navigate and negotiate these hierarchies. A precarious subject/subjectivity is never one thing alone; it morphs in relation to the other nodes of power, privilege, and disenfranchisement that it encounters and engages. This is why the various permutations and combinations of precarities are so important to our project. That is what allows us to observe which bodies, communities, and political visions are rendered precarious, and under which conditions, in the pursuit of ethnocentric authoritarianism.

What we find is that there is no one template for how each film engages precarity, Hindutva, or the enmeshment between the two. Neither is there a categorically confirmational or conflictual relationship between Hindi cinema and the Indian state. In fact, some of what we try to extract in our readings are the inconsistencies, the dissonances that accompany the overlaps and resonances as these films grapple with the uncertainties of neoliberal precarity and the zeal of ethnonationalist imperatives. In fact, the pleasure that many of these films offer the spectator comes from the fact that they escape and exceed a totalizing ideological culpability governed by the demands of a draconian state.

Our second chapter, "The Crisis of Entrepreneurialism and Hindu Masculinity," tracks the ways in which the sociocultural forces of Hindutva and the waning of entrepreneurial enthusiasm, the latter associated with the first two decades of liberalization, have produced a new articulation of Hindu masculinity. In many ways, the masculine protagonists we study in films like *Luck by Chance* (2009), *Tamasha* (Spectacle/Performance, Imtiaz Ali, 2015), *Sui Dhaaga: Made in India* (2018), and *Eeb Allay Ooo!* (Prateek Vats, 2020) are an amalgam of two distinct masculinities that have, until now, dominated celluloid configurations of Indian modernity. On the one hand, the heroes of these films channel the angry young man (1970s)—a character and aesthetic type that expressed discontentment and semisuccessful attempts at claiming dignity and grabbing power—in historical contexts marked by overwhelming, disenfranchising transitions, especially for the economically vulnerable. On the other hand, the Hindu men discussed in this chapter are the (almost) failed equivalents of male protagonists that peppered Hindi films between the 1990s and early 2000s, whose defining trait was their commitment to entrepreneurial success. The entrepreneurial heroes that emerged in the 1990s marked a distinct break not just from the angry young man, but also his on-screen predecessor, the "five-year plan" hero, the idealistic and prostatist Nehruvian hero who articulated the ideological concerns of the period. As Sanjay Shrivastava[158] and Sudesh Mishra suggest, these heroes—often engineers, scientists, doctors, or bureaucrats—embodied "the Nehruvian ideals of masculinity" as they combined "social dedication, as it pertain[ed] to national progress and development, with poetic sensitivity and the attributes of fidelity and self-sacrifice."[159] According to Shrivastava, this hero was "both an instrument of change as well as its personification"[160] as he helped usher in the *naya daur* (new era) of modernization and improvement by putting his faith in the "intentions and capacities"[161] (such as the five-year plans for economic development) of the postcolonial nation-state to work toward the national good.

The films discussed in this chapter instead give us men who exude the markers of a precarious subjectivity and help us define the language of precarity: gross deference and opportunistic scheming; endless anxiety about success; repressed anger that bursts forth in episodes of untrammeled rage; schizoid personalities that negate the possibility of an anchored, certain self. The psychosomatic compilation of these men, then, may be read as cinematic renditions of precarity that cuts across class. We study upper-middle-class men trying to climb the corporate ladder or trying to make it as actors in the film industry. And we engage the representation of working-class men, ground down between the miseries of their impoverished families and the need to innovate ways to make a living in a world that is impossibly hostile to the poor. We identify these men as "almost successful," not because they never achieve their goals, but because these films go out of their way to reveal the element of fantasy involved in doing so. And because these films spend substantial time in letting their protagonists and audiences confront the cruelty that injects the optimism required for entrepreneurial ambitions, even on the rare occasions when it does arrive, it is left terribly wanting. Finally, we highlight the Hindu identity of these men (unlike the implicit Hinduness of their cinematic antecedents) to register the subtle ways in which these films construct a Hindu, petit bourgeois, masculinity in crisis.

In the next chapter, "Spatial Precarization of Muslim Men," we turn our attention to the precarity of Muslim men in neoliberal, Hindutva-embracing India. The vulnerability of Muslims in both the Indian nation and in popular Hindi cinema is not new. Despite India's self-avowed status as a secular state, the trauma of Partition resulted in not just territorial-national bifurcation, it led to the displacement of fifteen million people, many of whom undertook the perilous journey as impoverished migrants across the border between India and Pakistan, and it led to the death of two million people as a result of communal violence. It also produced a need for the Indian state to work overtime to "manage" its strained relationship with its Muslim subjects. Muslims who had refused to leave India for Pakistan, on the one hand, represented the promise of India's success as a secular nation. On the other hand, they embodied slippery citizenship, unreliable subjecthood that threatened defection and national treachery at all times. Muslims were thus marked, symbolically, as the "enemy within," permanently and potentially haunting the integrity of Indian state as well as the security of its Hindu majority. A part of the postcolonial Indian national project, then, was to cultivate, in its newly independent citizenry, patriotism for its unique though tenuous secular fabric (as distinct from Pakistan's denominational national identity). Equally critical to the national project was an ostensible re-establishing of trust between its religious communities. Crucially, Hindi films played an integral role in this discursive goal, constantly redrafting the ever-shifting contours of this agenda, as we will discuss in an overview in chapter 3.

In chapter 3, through our analysis of *Black Friday* (2004), *Aamir* (2008), *Raees* (Rich, 2017), and *Gully Boy* (Zoya Akhtar, 2019), we examine the precarity experienced by religious minorities in India today. We argue that contemporary Bollywood films tend to conflate slums and Muslims, two distinct social entities, one spatial and the other a religious identity. In doing so, Bollywood compounds xenophobic paranoias about national precarity with elite frustrations about urban working-class tenements. This produces a doubly inflected nightmare of slums crawling with and controlled by morally bankrupt and innately criminalized Muslims. Many things go into the making of this new doubled copula Muslim/slum, Muslim-in-slum: a long sequence of discursive and generic developments that in turn correspond to a range of sociological, legal, and attitudinal changes in the societal fabric of urban India. Although nearly all scholarship on the "Muslim question" has noted the emergence and prevalence of the "Muslim = terrorist" configuration in Hindi films of the moment, the *spatial coordinates of such an equivalence* remain the missing term in the equation. A key intervention in this chapter is the unearthing of cinema's complicity in the generalization of poor Muslim slums as inevitable terrorist dens and hideouts, a damning social identification achieved via the shorthand of the cinematic image. What results is, simultaneously, an evocation of literal terrorism or symbolic terroristic-ness that masquerades as poverty, and a political narrative of the poor that views them as dangerous and threatening. As a result, these films allow for a right-wing synergy whereby a sectarian response to Indian Muslims can join forces with neoliberal fanaticism about ensuring a disappearance, not so much of poverty as of India's urban poor themselves. Such a program thus subtly advocates, at a single stroke, ridding the urban national-social space of both undesirables and menaces: the urban poor and the terroristic Muslim. In focusing closely on the cinematic transformation of slums into what Aravind Unni calls a "Muslim Space,"[162] we undertake a careful visual examination of the imagistic terms by which Muslim NRIs, terrorists, criminals, gangsters, and even artists navigate, inhabit, and populate the slum. We also study how the spatial matrices of the slum in turn envelop, facilitate, and provide asylum to the "conspiratorial" machinations of its Islamic inhabitants, resulting in a double dynamic, what might be termed "*the terrorist in the slum, the slum in the terrorist.*" And consequently, a realist aesthetic long associated in popular Hindi cinema with the representation of subalternity, is marshaled to produce a conservative outcome.

While the figure of the Muslim, and the anxieties their religious identity produce, have a long-standing history of management in popular Hindi cinema, the film industry has more or less elided caste and Dalit identities with alarming insistence. This is a conspicuous absence since Dalits form approximately 16.6 percent (or two hundred million) of India's total population, according to the 2011 census.[163] The elision or evasion of caste is effected through a variety of narrative maneuvers and contortions. The ubiquity of the upper-caste-ness of the characters, and the actors who play them, goes onto normalize the processes by which cinematic realities double upper-caste hegemony. In some films, caste is subsumed within class precariousness.[164] Or caste is named only to reference the lives and bodies of those that lie outside the privileges of upper-casteness, never to call attention to the automated Brahmanism of its protagonists. Caste also hovers on the margins through the everyday use of caste-based slurs; untouchability, after all, is the worst condemnation in a casteist order. In some ways, then, caste has been paradoxically hypervisible and invisible in Hindi cinema. It exists in the realm of the unnamed, and in rare instances in the realm of injury and oppression, to be alleviated at the erratic benevolence of upper-caste saviors. There are a few exceptions: in some postindependence Hindi films (popular, middle, and parallel cinema), caste made an appearance whether through some oft-repeated and interrelated tropes, such as intercaste marriage (*Sujata*, 1959), the exploited Dalit woman (*Ankur*, The Seedling, Shyam Benegal, 1974; *Lajja*, Shame, Rajkumar Santoshi, 2001; *Bandit Queen*, Shekhar Kapur, 1994), the downtrodden Dalit or Untouchable (*Lagaan*, Land Tax, Ashutosh Gowariker, 2001; *Swades*, Homeland, Ashutosh Gowariker, 2004), or caste-based reservations (*Aarakshan*, Reservation, Prakash Jha, 2011). For the most part, though, the willful caste-blindness of Hindi cinema (at least popular cinema) dictates that the normative cinematic Indian citizen-subject is mostly an upper-caste, middle-upper-class Indian (male), and upper-caste Hindu brahmanical traditions and customs masquerade as quintessentially and totalizingly Indian ones. By some estimates, India produces between 1,500 and 2,500 films in forty to fifty languages, but in this sheer volume of films, a Dalit-Bahujan protagonist still remains rare.

Three postmillennial New Bollywood films—Dalit director Neeraj Ghaywan's *Masaan* (Crematorium, 2015), Anubhav Sinha's *Article 15* (2019), and Ghaywan's *Geeli Pucchi* (Sloppy Kiss, 2020)—mark a distinct break in mainstream Hindi cinema's long history of silence around, and invisibilization of, caste. In chapter 4, "Love in the Time of Precarity: Caste and the Collapse of Romantic Love," we examine these films not only for their engagement with caste precarity, but also for the ways in which they compel a reconfiguration of Bollywood's most cherished narrative templates of romantic love and coupledom. When the hierarchies and oppressions of caste are forefronted, these films allow us to track the interconnections between caste precarity and the precarization of the couple form, unveiling coupledom as the ultimate expression of inequitably distributed privilege. As the films interrupt the fantasy of the Bollywood romance, they suggest how the relentless repetition of this fantasy—especially celebrated through a big, fat, lavish "designer" Indian wedding in postliberalization films—is a sign of the brahmanical patriarchal violence integral to heteronormative romance and matrimony. And yet even while the films under consideration in this chapter explode this fantasy as they present caste as a structural impediment to love and coupledom, we see how the films participate in a "cruel optimism" that holds on to a faith in romance and to the good life. These fantasies work through the prospective promise of a caste-transgressive coupledom, or of personal liberation from the repressiveness of caste regimes, or the possibility of building an alliance with others who exist in structures of palimpsestic vulnerability. Ultimately, we suggest that the couples-in-crisis found in these films are symptomatic of a neoliberal nation struggling with its legacies of caste without being able to offer radical solutions for an equitable future.

Chapter 5, "Sexual Precarity, Class Divides and Neoliberal Feminism," examines the exclusions performed by neoliberal feminism. We study the on-screen encounters between women from different socioeconomic classes in *Veere Di Wedding* (My Friend's Wedding, Shashanka Ghosh, 2018), *Lust Stories* (Zoya Akhtar, 2018), and *Is Love Enough? Sir* (Rohena Gera, 2018). These films showcase the "New Woman," the predominant model of empowered womanhood that Bollywood cinema has resorted to since liberalization. This figure is characterized by a neoliberal postfeminist subjectivity, geographical mobility, a reliance on consumerism to articulate her entrepreneurialism, and sexual autonomy. Of course, within mainstream representations of the New Woman, the poor or the working-class or lower-middle-class women usually remain on the outskirts of this category of newness. Here, through our reading of moments of interclass interactions between and among elite and nonelite women, we reinsert class precarity as a critical lens to understand contemporary Bollywood's engagement with gender. We argue that the female domestic workers, immigrant laborers, and aspirational lower-middle-class young women in these films interrupt and reconfigure the easy narratives of pleasure, mobility, autonomy, choice, and sexual desire that are ordinarily associated with the elite New Woman. We study how these films attend to the interior lives of nonelite women and ask whether these neoliberal forms are even capable of rendering class-gender precarity that does not resort to the usual cliches: romanticizing the working class or sexualizing women on screen. We pay special attention to the ways in which the discourse of sexual precarity—as the primary source of vulnerability for women—invariably frames women's gendered precarity and sidelines class-based considerations of structural inequalities. This narratological and ideological fixation on women's bodily-sexual precarity ignores the ways in which nonelite or working-class women are exposed not only to the dangers of sexual harassment by upper-class men, but also to violence, marginalization, and exploitation by their elite female counterparts.

In chapter 6, titled "Politics and Political Agency in the Age of Precarity," we close with an exploration of political agency in the age of precarity through examining postmillennial "cop films" (*Simmba*, Lion, Rohit Shetty, 2018; and *Sooryavanshi*, Rohit Shetty, 2021) and films about middle-class political awakening (*No One Killed Jessica*, Raj Kumar Gupta, 2011; and *Shanghai*, Dibakar Banerjee, 2012). Even as neoliberalism disrupts both the possibility and success of collective mobilizations, it generates fantasies of agentic social intervention. Neoliberalism's political crisis encourages the proliferation of individuated solutions rooted in the valorization of violent masculinities and middle-class activism. For instance, the promotion of vigilante justice, extrajudicial processes, and regressive populist solutions (kill the rapists!) in "cop films" both articulates the disappearing act of the neoliberal state from providing solutions, while simultaneously legitimizing and normalizing its draconian measures and disregard of democratic processes. Thus in this final chapter we focus on the genre of cop films and films that encapsulate middle-class and elite responses of outrage to complex political questions and phenomena. We study these films for how they identify precarity, for who they spotlight and construct as the precarious subject. How do these films, we ask, conceive of shared precarities, insecurities that have become pervasive across disparate groups and can become grounds for rallying together? And what solutions do these films proffer as resistant responses against the condition of precarity? We track who the agents of change condoned or condemned by these films are. What tenor of politics is given a free rein and whose political agency is validated? Or which grammar of politics is stringently contained in and by these films?

We also want to note that while it is not the central thrust of this project, what undergirds the study of these films is an acknowledgment of the ways in which the Bollywood-ization of the Hindi film industry—its revamping under the auspices of globalization—is itself mired in systems that produce and perpetuate inequities and insecurities. In that sense, we turn to Bollywood, not just as a site of representation, but as an economic-cultural vector in its own right, whose representational productions are themselves results of the precarities manufactured by and sustained within the industry itself. For instance, we recognize the economic precarity and professional insecurity that haunts the lives of new actors, a reality that came to a head after actor Sushant Singh Rajput's suicide. The cacophonic debate about "nepotism" that Rajput's death stirred in the film industry in the midst of the pandemic in 2020 signaled a bitter competition for narrow opportunities controlled by feudal norms that gave entitled star kids a leg up, while outsiders struggle to build their film careers on merit, talent, and grit.[165] The debate resonated in the public sphere because Indian institutions, most visibly politics and film, are dominated by dynastic families who strenuously argue that their survival in fact depends on democratic norms, the people's will, and winning the popular vote. Kangana Ranaut had led the charge against cronyism in the film industry before she waded into polarizing political discourse at the forefront of right-wing culture wars.[166]

At the same time, a consideration of the privileges and struggles faced by actors does not even begin to encapsulate the challenges faced by the industry's behind-the-scenes freelance talent, as well as its itinerant skilled and unskilled labor that perpetually incurs the threat of unemployment, underemployment, sexual exploitation, and cruel work hours and that enjoys zero security even under "normal" work conditions, let alone during crises of the kind prompted by COVID-19, when the entire industry came to a grinding halt. We also take stock of the eternal copresence of precarity in the industry through the dramatic ebbs and flows in celebrity popularity, in the ineffable ways in which changing political landscapes map onto the emergence, sustenance, and waning of star power.

Aatish Taseer has argued that precisely because Bollywood has stood for and been celebrated as a microcosm of pluralistic India, it has emerged as a prime target of the Modi government and its social media trolls.[167] We read political anxiety and precarity in both the implicit and blatant demands placed upon actors, directors, and other film industry personnel by the Indian state to fall in line with its politics, and the hurry with which they oblige. The state's increasing surveillance of content on streaming platforms such as Netflix and Amazon Prime Video has had a chilling effect on filmmakers and actors. Some filmmakers have embraced "genres that match the BJP's tastes: dubious historical epics that glorify bygone Hindu kings; action films about the Indian Army; political dramas and bio-pics, dutifully skewed. These productions all draw from the BJP's roster of stock villains: medieval Muslim rulers, Pakistan, Islamist terrorists, leftists, opposition parties like the Indian National Congress."[168] In 2019, a group of A-list Bollywood celebrities were brought in on a private plane to Delhi to meet prime minister Modi, and they were encouraged to post the group selfies they took with him. For Swapnil Rai, this selfie "is emblematic of the power of the state, the deliberate harnessing of 'star power,' and Bollywood's affective brand association to relationally and osmotically create affect for the Indian national leader, Modi."[169] Critically, as Taseer notes, not a single Muslim actor or director was included in this photo-op. The wide grins and the general atmosphere of bonhomie between a Hindu-supremacist political leader and the industry's young celebrities may be read not only as a publicity stunt aimed at increasing Modi's popularity among the millennials, but also as an indication of powerful celebrities falling in line and aligning themselves with the reconfiguration of the film industry along communal lines. Some celebrities like Kangana Ranaut have willingly and gladly emerged as champions of the Hindutva brigade, as defenders of Modi's vision, and they see their tirades against the nepotistic libtards[170] of Bollywood as very much in keeping with the agenda to promote and safeguard India as a Hindu nation.

Actors like Akshay Kumar, Ajay Devgn, and Ranveer Singh have been touted as (Hindu) actors who finally broke the "Khan monopoly"[171] (of Muslim Indian actors and superstars—Aamir, Salman, and Shah Rukh Khan) that had ruled the industry since the 1990s. Bhavya Dore has written about Akshay Kumar's ingenious dabbling in right-wing political visions by modeling himself as a nationalist hero, championing the BJP government's Brahmanical, patriarchal, protectionist policies, and in the process setting himself up as a Hindu alternative to the three big "Khans" in the industry. Radhika Raghav unpacks the star text of another Hindu superstar, Ranveer Singh, to suggest that despite modeling himself as a fashion rebel through his iconoclastic, bohemian, and contrarian sartorial choices, he participates in "normalizing Hindu gender ideologies" that confirm that status quo.[172] His corporate-managed persona only strengthens normative cultural politics and millennials' values around gender, caste, class, and religion. In another context, Kuhu Tanvir writes about live performances at prestigious award ceremonies by Bollywood actors like Hrithik Roshan and the late Sushant Singh Rajput as "visible evidence of the masculinization" of the Hindu nation. Their dance choreographies, she argues, are reminiscent of an angry lord Shiva's Tandav, their bodies marked by signs of their Hinduness (forehead *tilak*), and the stage backdrop flush with signifiers of an aggressive Hindu politics: images of fire and red flags that invoke the "lasting vision of the demolished Babri Masjid."[173]

Another related point to note here is the way in which Hindu actors in Bollywood today harness their masculinity and a politics of Hindutva to fashion themselves as entrepreneurial icons, a discussion also of relevance to chapter 2. Put another way, a key element of the process by which Bollywood has been Hindutva-ized is the way in which A-list male actors have enlisted their varied masculinities in the service of establishing Hindu hegemony within the film industry and have simultaneously emerged as exemplars of Hindu-Indian entrepreneurialism. The grandest story of entrepreneurial persistence is offered by Amitabh Bachchan, whose hypervirile masculinity, as Sreya Mitra[174] suggests, has long served multiple purposes. He has represented everything from embodying a national frustration at political ineptitude in the 1970s to the millionaire Hindu benevolent patriarch blessing the conjoining of Hindu traditions with neoliberal desires. In his personal life, his endless reinvention of himself is predicated on the abdication of a secular politics for the prioritization of consumerism, regardless of its complicity with a Hindutva-forwarding agenda. This is evident in his choice to be Gujarat's brand ambassador despite the state's notoriously criminal endorsement of Islamophobic and communal politics.

If celebrities don't line up behind or are not quiescent with the Hindutva agenda, they risk not just virulent social media attacks by the champions of Hindu nationalism, but harassment in different forms. For instance, while Swara Bhaskar is continuously subjected to social media trolling for her critique of patriarchal Hindutva politics, others are subject to unwarranted tax raids and investigations (Anurag Kashyap and Taapsee Pannu, known for their critique of the government's policies, were subject to arbitrary hounding by the Income Tax Department).[175] There's also intimidation and harassment for depicting Hindus or Hinduism in contexts deemed inappropriate or simply for naming their children after historical Muslim figures despised by the Hindu Right.[176] And there are trumped-up accusations. During the investigation of an actor's death, Deepika Padukone, Sara Ali Khan, and Shraddha Kapoor were questioned by India's narcotics board for using recreational drugs.[177]

In October 2021, the harassment of Aryan Khan—the son of Shah Rukh Khan (SRK)—on false drug possession charges, revealed yet again the ruthless single-mindedness with which the ruling right-wing government is tightening its vindictive grasp on the dominant media institution and culture industry in the country and demanding complete obedience to the state's majoritarian agenda. As commentators have noted, SRK's "powerfully attractive image of Indian Muslimness is also inherently threatening to the Hindu Right,"[178] and thus his "public humiliation" panders to appease the "insecurity of the Hindutva mindset."[179] Not only is SRK one of Bollywood's most successful and respected Muslim Indian actors, but he has served as an embodiment of a pluralistic and secular India through his personal (interfaith marriage) and professional life and film roles. Paromita Vohra writes, "SRK's persona evokes the kind of Indianness that defies categorization into singular, exclusive identities."[180] That is the threat posed by SRK and by extension the industry that he represents. It is perhaps tragically suitable that a hero whose heterogeneous roles helped middle-class Indians navigate the possibilities and promises of 1990s liberalization now becomes a scapegoat to conceal the failures of those promises and the precarities they yield.

2: The Crisis of Entrepreneurialism and Hindu Masculinity

In postliberalization India, the entrepreneurial ethic codified itself around the economic and political commitment to finally free the nation and its citizens from the constraints of government control and bureaucratic corruption. Nandini Gooptu,[1] in her study of enterprise culture, offers a discursive analysis of the language of aspiration that pervades political, corporate speeches and media campaigns of the 1990s and early 2000s. What's palpable in these texts is the desire to "fly," "lead," and "do" whatever it takes to become a global superpower. Gooptu's study reveals a collective vocabulary and mindset determined to shake off the conception of India as a "sleeping," "emerging" economy and fulfill its potential as a nation of aspirants, innovators, and entrepreneurs. And, in keeping with neoliberal logics, this idea of Indians as "doers," unfazed by absent infrastructures and egregious inequities, gains pertinence beyond the domain of economics. It becomes a universal guiding impulse, an infinitely portable ethos, a circulating ideology that applies to everything. Thus the figure of the entrepreneur morphs into a metaphor for an ever-expanding array of social practices[2] that cut across class.

The "neo-subjects" of entrepreneurial India, as Peirre Dardot and Christian Laval[3] would call them, are distinguished by their initiative and risk-taking capacities. They emerge as self-maximizing, self-reliant, self-disciplined, autonomous citizens who, through the choices they make, take responsibility for their own well-being and success in every facet of their life. Entrepreneurialism is not only "established as an objective fact" of postmillennial India, it is, as Thomas Martilla argues, also "disseminated across different social sectors."[4] Whether it is in private or public spaces, in intimate or work contexts, in educational or leisure pursuits, neoliberal subjects reject passivity, conducting themselves as agents of change for the nation and for themselves. And, as Colin Gordon[5] and others have shown, the ultimate entrepreneurial maneuver under neoliberalism is to convert the self itself into a site of enterprise. In a context of professional and interpersonal precarity, to become an entrepreneur of oneself is to always remain employed.

The male protagonists of *Luck by Chance, Tamasha, Sui Dhaaga: Made in India*, and *Eeb Allay Ooo!*—Vikram, Ved, Mauji and Anjani, respectively—allow us to grasp neoliberalism's regime of subjectification geared toward producing entrepreneurial subjects.[6] They offer insights into what Christina Scharff calls the "psychic life of neoliberalism"[7] and the psychological impact of precarity on entrepreneurs struggling, albeit differently, to fulfill the neoliberal ideal. In fact, the variance in how these characters internalize and enact entrepreneurship creates space to study the divergences in Hindi cinema's engagement with enterprise culture. Each of these characters exemplifies different trajectories of entrepreneurship, reminding us that enterprise culture's ubiquity is not a marker of its uniformity.[8] Even as these films explore the Hindu male's profound investment in the idea of entrepreneurialism, they also give expression to the heterogeneity of its application across class and professional contexts. There is no singular entrepreneurial subject; in these films the male entrepreneur is always "refracted" through the particularities of his class, profession, urban spatiality, and the relational matrix within which he is located.[9]

These films also capture a range of how contemporary Hindi cinema interrogates the crises that entrepreneurialism addresses and produces. In other words, the films differ on whether they treat entrepreneurialism as a pathway to success and a solution to neoliberal precarity or whether they blame entrepreneurialism, or at least dominant versions of it, for generating social and psychological fractures and worsening precarity. We use these four films, therefore, to register Hindi cinema's polyvalent partiality to enterprise over the course of a decade (2009–2019), and we track the hopes and hazards, escapes, and dead ends of neoliberalism, cinematically conceived. Together, these films communicate a yo-yo effect in Hindi cinema's relationship to India's enterprise culture. They don't offer a linear, temporally progressing narrative of enterprise or its critique. We cannot say that these films illustrate either an intensification of a positive investment in enterprise culture or a loss of faith in it. *Luck by Chance*, released in 2009, is a mainstream film of a first-time director and in some ways marks a more strident critique of enterprise than any film before or after it. It offers a variant of enterprise culture, where a privileged man performs vulnerability as a form of entrepreneurialism. In comparison, *Sui Dhaaga*, released almost a decade later in 2018, reinstates the most basic, uncritical template of entrepreneurialism, the kind associated with films like *Wake Up Sid* (Ayan Mukerji, 2009), *Rocket Singh* (Shimit Amin, 2009), and *Guru* (Mani Ratnam, 2007). Likewise, if *Luck by Chance* and *Tamasha* distinguish between toxic enterprise and its sustainable variants, *Eeb Allay Ooo!*, an indie film from 2019, categorically dismantles enterprise altogether as a violent, faulty, and unattainable goal. The films sometimes crack the code of enterprise, and at other times they shed light on how the code itself is cracked, exposing the epistemic, ontological fault lines within it. What they give us, then, is not a neat cinematic map to track the nation's adherence to or disenchantment with entrepreneurialism. Instead, these films trace a compulsive circling back to enterprise as a narrative fount, and a simultaneous dissatisfaction with it. They encapsulate Hindi cinema's repetitive, ad nauseum, desperate explorations of enterprise that interrogate the ideal just as fervently as they paper over the lies and the damages caused by its mythos.

In this chapter, we also turn to masculinities under neoliberalism and the politics of neoliberal Hindutva, as shared frameworks or cohering schemes through which to think jointly about the four male entrepreneurs in the films and study their relationship to themselves and their worlds. In her book, *The Stories That Bind*, Madhavi Murty notes that "the story of the intersection of neoliberalism with Hindu nationalism is a story about masculinity—aggrieved, obstructed, incomplete, aggressive, and on the move—spectacularized into authority."[10] In our discussion, we show how the films' male protagonists are exemplars that record the degree of reciprocal enmeshment between neoliberal enterprise, masculinity, and Hindu hegemony. This embroilment is pervasive.

Several scholars have theorized neoliberalism's impact on masculinity as a social organization; as an affective, aspirational state; as a form of attachment and belonging to the world; as a mode of dominance in the world; and as a node of intersection with class, religion, caste, sexuality. Neoliberalism has transfigured every dimension of masculinity, understood as "socially produced but embodied ways of being male,"[11] and "doing gender, in relation to, and in tandem with, other individuals in particular spaces and social settings."[12] *Luck by Chance* and *Tamasha* offer us insight into the fate of hegemonic masculinity in neoliberal India's urban settings and its cultural-cinematic and corporate industries. In contrast, *Sui Dhaaga* and *Eeb Allay Ooo!* situate subaltern men within a set of aspirations and expectations that are becoming ever more difficult for them to fulfill in the contemporary economy.

Historically, hegemonic masculinity is left unmarked and seems to pass without a history.[13] Its entrepreneurialism is construed as a given, not entrepreneurialism at all, but an automated rite of passage into success and successful masculinity. By contrast, it is usually the styles, modalities, and practices of subaltern men that are explicitly and palpably cast as entrepreneurial and masculine. Neoliberalism, however, disrupts the seamless segues of dominant masculinity. This is because even dominant forms of masculinity are not exempt from the uncertainties and crises that characterize neoliberal governance. Through

Vikram and Ved, then, we can observe these disruptions and understand how neoliberalism condemns to precarity, contingency, and desperateness even those who occupy hegemonic status. Or, in other words, *Luck by Chance* and *Tamasha* help us observe how even the privileged must enter into structures of negotiation with the insecurities they encounter, albeit from positions of authority. If Vikram and Ved represent a reconfiguration of elite and upper-middle-class Hindu masculinity, they also articulate the mobility and contingency of both masculinity and hegemony. They help us recognize the new hierarchies of masculinity at play, as well as the new ploys by which dominant masculinity re-establishes its authority and power over nonhegemonic others.

These men from varied economic classes, thus, help us decipher the "uneven effects" of neoliberalism on different groups, even while tracking the pervasiveness of neoliberalism's debilitating impact.[14] For some of the men like Mauji and Anjani in *Sui Dhaaga* and *Eeb Allay Ooo!*, their very survival is at risk. For others, their psychic coherence is jeopardized by neoliberalism's differential operations. These impacts are not the same and must not be equated. Nevertheless, it is important to recognize them both as outcomes of the same world order where one's well-being and flourishing are indefinitely postponed, where everyone's future is cast into uncertainty and the present thrust into interminable crisis. The difference is that while some have the hope and can exercise the agency to find affective and material escapes, others are doomed to hopelessness and failure. Even so, finding the conjoined inheritance of these varied crises offers the basis of imagining and building solidarities that can resist the imperatives of neoliberal precarity.

Middle-Class Entrepreneurialism

Following Purnima Mankekar,[15] we too read *Luck by Chance* (henceforth *LBC*) and *Tamasha* for what they reveal about the "structures of feeling"[16] that are embedded within enterprise culture. Differently from her, though, we find that these two films attempt a critique of the fantasy of entrepreneurialism in which capital, romance, professional success, and personal success can all comfortably accommodate and even productively coconstitute each other (as in *Band Baaja Baaraat*, Maneesh Sharma, 2010). This coconstitution is considered variously untenable by both films. Instead of bolstering such an integrative vision, *LBC* and *Tamasha* disaggregate the entrepreneurial ethic to expose its dark side and sharp limits in terms of the interpersonal violence it unleashes and psychosomatic schisms it produces. In doing so, these films distance themselves from mainstream entrepreneurialism, especially its masculinist dimensions of *jugaad* (frugal innovation) and relentless corporate drudgery. In contrast, the films articulate alternative entrepreneurial modalities for how to survive and succeed in a neoliberal world.

Unfortunately, even the countermodalities that promise a more ethical and less self-subjugating practice of entrepreneurialism are really fantasies of escape, complicit in ensuring neoliberalism's tenacity. This delusion of being able to better navigate neoliberalism, and being able to opt out of its toxic, masculinist cut-throat-ism and ritualized mediocrity, is part and parcel of the current order's cruel optimism. It permits a world full of disappointment, betrayal, and hopelessness to be more durable. The many-splendored variations of enterprise culture are precisely what anchor its resilience. Critically, then, both the critique and the alternatives proposed by these two films demonstrate neoliberal's solipsism: that "there are very few clean dividing lines between [the neoliberal project] and its 'other.'"[17] A critique of the "wrong kind" of entrepreneurialism and the propping up of palatable variants expose the techniques of legitimacy by which neoliberalism re-entrenches its permanence and ubiquity.

With liberalization, the new urban middle classes emerged as the early adopters and champions of "entrepreneurial citizenship," zealously internalizing the idea that "citizens can construct markets, produce value and do nation building all at the same time."[18] In demographic terms, it was also the nation's youth who represented the "untapped" potential of neoliberal India. In many ways, then, Vikram and Ved, the two young male, upper-caste Hindu, upper-middle-class protagonists of *LBC* and *Tamasha*, respectively, present as the ideal embodiments of the entrepreneurial ethos that gripped India in the 1990s. Working with Michel Foucault's understanding of "ethos," we can say that Vikram and Ved's mode of relating to the world and the people in it, their choices, thoughts and affective range, actions, and behaviors are regulated by, responding to, or performing the entrepreneurial imperative.[19] And their social coordinates—of gender, caste, class, age—constitute the model configuration for guaranteeing entrepreneurial success.

As it turns out, however, there is a critical gap between the ideal and material reality. The "specter of entrepreneurship"[20] haunts Vikram and Ved differently; the two men bear its weight differently, and ultimately, even their (almost) success as entrepreneurs is dissimilar and carries contradictory meanings. In some ways, both films show us the place of culture industries and cultural workers in the entrepreneurial imagination and worldview, even as they represent opposite ends of the spectrum. At one end, with *Tamasha* we see the romanticization of the performing arts. Here the creative entrepreneurialism of the artistic genius is pitched as markedly superior to the slog of corporate enterprise. Artists, storytellers, and theater crystallize the best of entrepreneurial culture. At the other end of the spectrum is *LBC*'s trenchant foray into the inner workings of Bollywood: its nepotism, vacuity, chanciness, self-exploitation, manipulative climbing of the success ladder. There is no rose-tinted treatment of artists, actors, directors, or even their cinematic outputs. In fact, the industry's successful cultural workers epitomize enterprise culture's most unflattering dimensions.

Luck by Chance

Vikram, in *LBC*, is an upper-middle-class young man who comes to Bombay (Mumbai) from Delhi to become an actor in the Hindi film industry. He has no godfathers to ease his way into Bollywood. He does have a couple of friends and acquaintances who are tangentially connected to the industry's B-circuit networks. His childhood friend Abhi is a theater actor with some TV experience; Abhi's roommate Samir is an assistant director for a major Bollywood-family-owned production house; their neighbor-friend Sona is a starlet who's done a few regional films and played minor roles in a handful of mainstream Hindi films. Vikram lives with an aunt but spends a lot of his time with Samir, Abhi, and Sona, when he's not working zealously to accrue acting chops and ingratiating himself with people and into spaces that wouldn't ordinarily be accessible to an "outsider" like him. Despite his own class privilege, it is his outsider status in the film industry that propels a need for entrepreneurial innovativeness.

Early on in the film, we notice the synapses of his brain working overtime to absorb everything that could have even the remotest implication for his entrepreneurial journey to stardom. He enrolls at the Nand Kishore Acting School, a B-grade enterprise run by an older character actor known for playing stereotypical, secondary, comic-goon roles in Hindi films. In the acting classes, Vikram is like a human sponge, imbibing every bit of information, stockpiling every half-baked, third-rate advice shared with the fledgling actors. Here Vikram learns the inchoate and polyvalent skills needed to become a Bollywood actor: everything from riding horses, wielding swords, dancing, building muscle, and developing his acting portfolio with awkwardly posed professional headshots. No matter how farcical and absurd the lessons, Vikram listens and learns intently. His commitment to the process, to extrapolating everything he can from this opportunity, never flags.

He is dedicated, patient, and hardworking even in a milieu where he very clearly has more talent and elite social capital than most others around him. This is because he understands that the value of the acting school experience extends beyond just a credential he can tout during auditions. It also gives him the opportunity to practice the all-important soft skill of *appearing sincere* amid absurdity and mediocrity, a skill that comes in handy as he makes inroads into the film industry. During the graduation ceremony, his instructor reminds the class that in addition to "talent, you also need luck." The key, ostensibly is that "you must be in the right place at the right time." Given his entrepreneurial commitment, Vikram doesn't just internalize the text; he also pays close attention to the subtext, which is to leave nothing to luck. Vikram learns that he must convert every exchange, encounter, and interaction into tools in his entrepreneurial arsenal and use them like chess pieces to maneuver himself into all the right places, to constantly put himself in luck's path. Only then will luck not elude him. This is the most important lesson he refines as a "struggling actor": to leave no stone unturned and remain committed, above all else, to his own enterprise. The focus on "luck" isn't about hard work; it's about keeping his eye on the prize and letting nothing stand in his way, not friends, romantic loyalty, petty taunts, paternalistically exploitive directors, or ditsy star kids who have a nepotistic advantage in the industry. There are no ethics too absolute, no relationships too sacrosanct that Vikram won't breach to meet his end goal.

He stashes away Abhi's philosophy about the power of theater, and during a film audition expediently offers it up as his own, thus stealing his friend's ideas and experiences to fashion his own persona as a thinking, serious actor. On another occasion, he binge watches all the old movies of a 1980s heroine Nina Walia, mentally hording away visual snapshots of what sari she wore during an iconic song sequence, and he casually slips it into a conversation with her to feed her vanity and implant himself in her memory. When Vikram helps friends, it is strategically to initiate a reciprocity of favors from them. For instance, he procures a "grandfather clock" that Samir urgently needs as a prop for a film set. Samir, who until that moment had rebuffed all of Vikram's requests to introduce him to directors, now out of gratitude invites Vikram to a Bollywood party, where Vikram meets and flatters Nikki Walia (Nina's daughter), a chance encounter that serves him exceedingly well later. The grandfather clock belongs to his aunt's deceased husband. Vikram takes it from her house in the wee hours of the morning, leaving behind a note to let her know that he's taking his uncle's memorabilia to get it polished, hoping she'll accept it a gesture of gratitude for letting him stay with her. It costs him nothing to get it polished, of course; Samir gladly takes care of it for free on the film set. These minor, subtle sequences do the work of establishing Vikram's opportunism, his willingness to go the extra mile to enculturate himself to others, to people please, to be spontaneously strategic and extractive in his relationships. Vikram's workaday unscrupulousness is symptomatic of the normalization of individualization, self-responsibilization, and competitiveness in the entrepreneurial subject.

But *LBC* does not confuse Vikram's single-mindedness with crass, unfeeling ruthlessness. His precarity-induced interiority (resulting from the genuine disadvantages he suffers as an industry outsider) also makes room for genuine emotions, camaraderie, and empathy. Vikram feels the intensity and authenticity of his own emotions. He feels real hurt, shame, embarrassment, anxiety that make him human and relatable. When Abhi (jealous about Vikram and Samir's growing closeness) insults his headshots, humiliates him for borrowing money from friends, and declares him talentless, Vikram feels deep, legitimate anger, fragility, insecurity, and a sense of betrayal. We also see him express true excitement and joy for others. For a moment, when it looks like Sona will finally get her big break as a lead heroine, his happiness for her is sincere, his congratulations heartfelt, and his expression of love for her earnest. When Sona finally learns that the producer she's been sleeping with for three years has no intention of casting her in his corporate-financed film, Vikram shows up for her, offering her emotional sustenance and a confidence boost that have a lasting impact on her ability to navigate her professional-sexual precarity.

The film's ingenuity lies very much in its capaciously compassionate rendition of each of its characters, their idiosyncrasies, the film-industry typologies they represent, but also the real-life Bollywood celebrities they gesture at (so many celebrities cameo as themselves and lean into the star persona they're associated with off-screen). One might even argue that the film is peppered with illustrations of precarity that cut across class. It gives us the ridiculous but sympathy-inducing precarities of the industry elite: their financial struggles in securing funding for their films, particularly in the context of Bollywood's corporatization and the influx of international capital; the fickleness of directorial and actorly fortunes; the intergenerational sexual precarity of women actors, no matter their class origins and how illustrious their careers. On the other hand, its opening credits song sequence is dedicated to the movie business's working-class precariat, the noncelebrity personnel who work tirelessly behind the scenes of moviemaking. We get stunning portraits of dressmakers, makeup artists, unnamed extras, security guards, clapboard loaders, stuntmen, background dancers, technicians, film ticket sellers, woodworkers, poster printers, and makers of hoardings. It is their precarious, mostly informal sector work that allows celebrityhood to persist and filmmaking to continue glitch-free. The song shows us tableaus of their unglamorous labor, recognizing it as the foundation for the glitz we encounter through the film. In nearly every tableau, these workers stare at the camera, inviting the audience to notice their smiles, their boredom, their exhaustion, the precision of their work. Their gaze compels us to confront their precarious presence. Each shot in this image sequence carries affective power. They make us realize that Bollywood cameras are rarely interested in these behind-the-scenes men and women. In lovingly creating these insistent and unsanitized portraits of them at work, *LBC* interrupts their disappearance from the screen.

The film's focus on upper-middle-class precarity comes to us through Vikram's experiences. Even as someone from a privileged background in terms of his caste-class-religious identity, Vikram finds it hard to make it in a nepotistic profession that rarely opens its doors to outsiders. He lives in Bombay on borrowed money from his father, aunt, and friends. His class background entitles him to look around for acting jobs, make routine trips to production houses to drop off his portfolio, take acting lessons, and spend the rest of his unemployed days hanging out with friends. And yet we feel his precarity acutely: in the subtle jibes he endures for his "vagrancy," when his aunt tells him to stop wasting time and return to Delhi and work in his father's shop. We register how much harder he works than his star kid costar Nikki Walia (Nina's daughter), and how much less he gets paid than her even though it's a launch film for both. We recognize, too, that strategic maneuverings and shenanigans are very much the name of the game in elite Bollywood circles. In this, they are no different from the conniving, premeditated calculations and the self-aggrandizing strategies that Vikram deploys. The difference is that while Vikram must fend for himself entirely, the big directors and film stars have a whole panoply of human and capital resources they set into motion to assist them in their wheeling and dealing. A whole spate of secretaries, wives, agents, celebrity mothers, brothers, private financiers, and designers descend to manage tricky situations, smooth over conflicts, find new talent, make sure that films get funded, assuage diva egos, and prioritize celebrity self-interest.

Two things confirm Vikram's precarity but also his hard-nosed entrepreneurialism. The first is his eerie ability to ration his emotions and seamlessly segue between genuine feelings and performed affect. In one scene, his aunt passive-aggressively humiliates him for asking for money and demands to know how much longer he plans to stay with her. Vikram looks humiliated and teary-eyed at his aunt's barb. In the next moment, he pockets the money she gives him, leaves the house, and simply shrugs off the interaction, as though he was faking the emotional injury. In an instant, and very discernibly, he switches on a different body language; pulling his shoulders back, he puts on his sunglasses and struts off with a smug, cool expression. It's impossible to tell which of his two responses is authentic. Does he let his aunt's humiliation wear off because he wasn't affected by it to begin with, or must he set it aside to get on with proving her wrong? Understood differently, this moment helps us recognize that both the vulnerability of precarity as well as the sociopathy of resiliency—a cynical detachment—that it demands, are real and copresent in the entrepreneurial citizen.

The second marker of his precarity, and his entrepreneurialism, is Vikram's ability to leverage his relative class privilege against the other much more precarious bodies he encounters. The melancholic and dreary audition scene is telling. It simultaneously showcases Vikram's panic response rooted in his precarity—in being one among thousands trying to make it in an industry that barely makes room for newcomers—as well as his entrepreneurial agility to focus and sift through his competitors. In doing so, he quickly realizes that most of them are not real contenders because they carry none of the signifiers of social, cultural, linguistic, and educational capital that he embodies. He knows only too well that in neoliberal India, a Bollywood star can only be someone whose precarity is situational, not structural.

At first glance, the cold industrial vibe of the dreary room that Vikram enters, when he's called into audition for Romy-Rolly's new production, is flooded with dozens of indistinguishable men, all tall, lean, dressed in jeans and T-shirts, nervously scouring the script, memorizing their lines. The camera, following Vikram's gaze, takes in the panoramic view of the room, scanning the sheer scale of his competition. As he continues to take in the visual information, he does a quick, slight head nod, once again "switching on" his entrepreneurial mode. The nod is his cue to snap out of being overwhelmed. If a dialogue had accompanied it, we might have heard Vikram say something like "If this is what I'm up against, then so be it." He continues the perusal of his contenders, this time not with panic but with motive, with the intent to isolate his real competition. He has looked around enough to know that most of the men reek of desperation; their tattered shoes give away their dire straits. Some of them don't even know enough English to fill out the registration form. His assessment is corroborated by the auditions of these men that intercut the scene. We, like Vikram, know soon enough that most of these men have little chance of success; they are ineligible candidates for this role, and their lack of self-awareness of their own class limits is a dead giveaway. Vikram has nothing to worry about with them. So much so that he even helps a couple of them fill out their form. His only real challenger is a tall, good-looking man who moves with ease and carries himself with the confidence of a class compatriot. Expectedly, he, along with Vikram, are the final contenders for the role. Vikram moves fast, neutralizing the threat he poses in the next round of auditions by feeding him erroneous information, encouraging him to play up his brawny, aggressive masculinity, thus ensuring that he bombs his interaction with the director, who rejects him for being too arrogant.

Vikram is astute enough to understand that Bollywood's script for masculinity has diversified: the corporeal command that actors like Amitabh Bachchan exuded in their "angry young man" persona has given way to the gentler, charming masculinities of actors like Shah Rukh Khan, actors who are equally beloved by provincial and multiplex audiences. But he also understands that it's a question of how masculinity intersects with status. As an interloper to the industry, he cannot afford the luxury of entitlement. He knows the tricky balance he must perform. He needs to appear comfortable in his own skin when surrounded by stardom, while still expressing sufficient gratitude, flattery, and servility. Aggressive, arrogant masculinity is the prerogative of industry insiders. Cumulatively, these tactics of success are also what Jeremy Vachet[21] would call Vikram's coping strategies in a precarious culture industry.

What Vikram teaches us in *LBC* is that the precarious self always coexists with the entrepreneurial self. In fact, entrepreneurial fantasies are what the precarious self relies on to keep going. Vikram's pep talk when Sona is in a precarity-induced crisis, perfectly condenses not just the crux of his entrepreneurial ideology, but also its heady appeal and power. Vikram finds Sona, weeping and despairing about her hopes of becoming a movie star: "Maybe it's not in my fate." He sits down across from her, insisting that she look at him and offers her a provocation: "What is destiny? This word exists only for people who don't have the courage to make their own life." Sona protests: she has shown strength . . . and after three years of waiting, all she's got is her producer-mentor-predator's rejection, telling her that she doesn't have what it takes to become a lead in a big-budget film. Vikram does not abide her desolation: "You cannot let a bastard decide who you can be. You didn't come here to do Chowdhary's film. You came here to act. For too long you've trusted someone else. Now, trust yourself. Success doesn't come to us. We must go to it. Keep walking on your path . . . Slowly, the whole world will follow." Vikram's words do the trick and spark the resilience she needs to stick it out in the industry. And although she never makes it as a movie star and her relationship with Vikram predictably disintegrates the moment he joins Bollywood's big league, she holds onto the lesson he teaches her: to refuse the victim narrative, chart her own course, and define her own successes.

At the end of the film, in an interview, Sona credits her accomplishments to Vikram, the person who taught her that "we choose our own success and failure." By this time, she has become a well-known TV celebrity for her role in *K-Serials* (the epithet given to the extremely popular, long-running Hindu family dramas produced by Ekta Kapoor). If neoliberal class privilege allows Vikram to perform vulnerability and climb the ranks, for Sona, cultural precarity pushes her to take recourse to the Hindutva cultural landscape through acting in TV serials imbued with a Hindu consciousness. Even so, she's the only financially independent woman in her family, an accomplishment that feels as meaningful to her as the pleasure she gains from doing this work. In a precarious world, few people can boast of either privilege. This is why she cannot feel sad about not being a big movie star: "I feel happy that I am an actress who is doing decent work and earning enough. I've decided to stay happy." The film confirms for us that Sona has, indeed, "found [her] place," not only in the industry but also in the city. Her responses to the interviewer's questions morph into a voice-over, as we see her hailing a cab and heading to Film City for another satisfying day of work. The voice-over stops, and the credits start to roll. The camera, however, stays with Sona for an inordinately long time, watching her look out of the taxi, giving us a closeup of her purposeful, contented, confident and dignified face. She's come a long way from young girl we met at the film's opening: full of naive delusions, imagining herself to be superior to the extras on the set, rejecting roles she considered beneath her, and relying on the false promises of exploitive, narcissistic men.

Even though *LBC* follows Vikram's journey into stardom, it is Sona's story that bookends the film's opening and close. And by the end, it appears as though the film passes the entrepreneurial mantel from Vikram to Sona. It is not just her decision to "stay happy" that certifies her rightful place within the neoliberal ethic. It is also that she comes to represent a more ethical mode of inhabiting and enacting the entrepreneurial spirit. She maximizes her potential, overcomes debilitating forms of vulnerability without losing her integrity. She gains a thick skin without losing her heart.

In her essay on the 2010 hit film *Band Baaja Baaraat*, Mankekar argues that the phrase "we are like this only," which became a popular postliberalization mantra in the 1990s, "emblematized the brash self-confidence" of lower-middle-class youth in urban India.[22] It captured their unapologetic air about their lack of fluency in English and their insistence on partaking in neoliberal aspirations. *LBC*, we might argue, heralds a new phrase for a new conjuncture.

After a series of experiences that force Vikram to introspect, he apologizes to Sona for lying to her and for his selfishness, and he pleads with her to return to him. She is, after all, the one who supported him more than his own family. He could, without fear of judgment, be himself with her, and he needs her as his anchor and support. She scoffs at his words, not because she doesn't believe him, but because she knows he believes himself, a little too readily. She sees through the "structure of feelings" that constitute him as an entrepreneurial man. His emotions are real but transitory, inconsistent, and relevant only in the moment. The realness of his emotions doesn't guarantee their endurance. Moreover, as Sona continues to explain, even in offering a sincere apology and baring his vulnerabilities, he cannot help but expose his self-referentiality: "I was listening to you carefully, about how I was a part of your life, how I showed you support, how I can still be a support and anchor for you. But all of this is about you. Where is there any mention of me and my life?" She knows all too well that it's only a matter of time before another distraction rears its head and he'll disappear in its pursuit. She walks over to a crestfallen Vikram, standing across her, his head bent in shame at the accuracy of Sona's insight. She takes his hand and offers a devastating placation: "This is not your fault. You can't do anything about it. *Some people are like this only*" (emphasis added).

This shift from "We are like this only" to "Some people are like this only" marks an important transition. If the first articulates a doggedness by the class precariat to participate as themselves, along with everyone else, in the singular fantasy that neoliberalism conjures, then Sona's words mark a distinction between divergent versions of the neoliberal enterprise. Her path to self-actualization is qualitatively and morally different from Vikram's. While "some people" can't help but succumb to the worst of what entrepreneurialism demands—shady, scheming, unscrupulous tactics—the real entrepreneurs are those, like her, who survive these very tactics without losing their core values of decency and carve out alternative pathways to success, even if it means modifying their ambitions. This is why, the last sight we have of Sona is as a flesh-and-blood character, whose development is somatically discernible and whose words and wisdom linger into the film's final shot. Vikram, by contrast, loses his embodied presence and is reduced to cheesy taglines ("I don't believe in destiny, I believe in me") and glossy photos on magazine covers and giant billboards in the Mumbai skyline. He looms large but is distant and two-dimensional.

Zoya Akhtar's love letter to Bollywood is then also a neoliberal feminist promise, a testament to women's capacity to explore and execute an entrepreneurial modality that matches men's resoluteness without internalizing their manipulativeness. Ironically, though, in swapping out her erstwhile gullibility for the fantasy of an ethical entrepreneurialism, Sona and the film participate in concocting a dangerous lie about neoliberal worksites: that, here, "no one asks about your caste" and knowing and doing your job well is enough to see you through to success. In a sense, Vikram's hawk-eyed study of other people's weaknesses is at least a more honest account of what entrepreneurialism entails: exploiting women's sexualized training to seek male attention; pandering to familial sentimentality; catering to buffoonish, powerful men looking for obsequiousness from younger good-looking male protégés; sizing up competition by mapping other men's class through their threadbare shoes, fluency in English, and provincial accents. Ultimately, even as *LBC* distances itself from Vikram's loathsome enterprise, it commits a dangerous disingenuity on two counts: it poses women's neoliberal adventures and trajectories as the solution to men's "bad" enterprise. And it suggests that "good" entrepreneurialism is agnostic about social inequities of caste and class. In chapter 5, we study other films to further examine the fate of this false promise resurrected by *LBC* and the sharp limits of such a gender-essentialist and class- and caste- blind idea of entrepreneurialism and version of feminism.

Tamasha

Tamasha also posits two entrepreneurial modes, putting its weight behind one and rejecting the other as corporate grind. Unlike *LBC*, though, instead of distributing the two versions across different characters, in *Tamasha* they are practiced by the same person, Ved. The plot revolves around his challenging journey from the soul-crushing slog of the business world to one of artistry and creative innovativeness.

We first meet Ved on a holiday in Corsica, France, when he helps Tara, another *desi*, stranded there after her passport and wallet are stolen. Ved offers his phone for her to use to call home and make the necessary arrangements to have money wired and a new passport issued. Predictably enough, romantic sparks fly, as the two gush about their mutual love of Asterix comics, especially their childhood favorite "Asterix in Corsica," the reason they chose Corsica as the destination for their respective solo vacations. The two start to share lodgings, flirt with each other, take long drives in a convertible, do hikes, crash parties, take on pretend personae of yesteryear actors and characters from older Hindi films, a sex worker and her client etc.

There is, however, a catch. At Ved's behest, they decide not to exchange any real-world information about themselves: no names, no cities of origin, not what they do, no friends in common. They decide to tell each other only lies. The rationale? This holiday marks a break from the banality of the everyday. They don't want to be tied down by the conventions of compulsive heteronormativity: the man pathetically trying to impress the woman with his "*ghisay pitay*" (lackluster) jokes and feeling bogged down by demands of propriety and compelled to "behave decently." That would be a waste of this trip. Ved has worked too hard to come here, where no one knows him, where he can be anyone, do anything; why tarnish this temporary neoliberal utopia where nothing is prohibited with the expectations and protocols of hegemonic behavior? And, correspondingly, to liberate Tara from proprietorial injunctions that would compel her to play "Miss Touch Me Not" in response to his sexual overtures, he promises to "keep a safe distance" and "not make a move" on her. Vegas rules apply, of course: "Whatever happens in Corsica, stays in Corsica." After their adventure is over, they'll disappear from each other's lives.

Things don't remain quite as neat and compartmentalized as they imagined. Ved keeps his word, but at the last minute, right before her departure, Tara decides to initiate sex. She wakes up a sleeping Ved, kisses him, and slips into bed with him. The next scene has her getting into a taxi, heading to the airport. She scrunches her face, perhaps in disbelief or semiregret about her decision to break their pact. Or, as we discover very soon, perhaps because she's cheated on her boyfriend back in India. Her boyfriend is at the Kolkata airport to receive her, and we see right away that she's lost interest in him. The folk-inspired song "*Heer toh badi sad hai*" starts playing to a series of montage shots spanning a period of four years. In this time frame, she breaks up with her boyfriend, starts a coffee business with her father, saunters through the streets of Kolkata by herself, rebuffs the advances of other men interested in her, dances alone in her apartment, becomes increasingly isolated and disaffected so much that she celebrates her birthday by herself. Her disconnection from the world, from work, and from other relationships indicate that there's been no return to normalcy after Corsica. Nothing compares to the pleasure, intensity, and intimacy she experienced there with Ved. At the end of this four-year period, she relocates to Delhi, when her father gifts her a business of her own.

In the nation's capital, she starts frequenting "Social," a working studio and coffee shop she recognizes from the stamp on a book that Ved was reading in Corsica. Eventually, she sees him there and pretends to bump into him. But she cannot sustain the pretense long; she lets Ved know right away that their meeting is not a coincidence, that she's been hoping to find him. "I kept waiting for it to 'become okay' . . . but it's been four years and I still feel the same." Tara tries to contain her intensity, but her body and words betray just how consumed she has been by thoughts of Ved. She worries about sounding like a "crazy stalker" and promises that she won't "pile on": "I know you have your own life and might have a girlfriend." Ved clarifies immediately that he doesn't have a girlfriend. The relief and joy that wash over her are tangible.

Alas, in all the excitement and anxiety of seeing him, she doesn't quite register just how different he is from the man she met in Corsica. He looks older, certainly, thanks to the French beard he's grown since they last met, but also temperamentally subdued. He exudes none of the vivacity, electrified energy, bohemian mannerisms, and cavalier disposition we associated with his Corsica self. He seems glad that she found him but offers no other response to the torrential outpouring of her forceful, passionate declarations. He smiles indulgently and tells her not to worry or apologize, but there is an unnerving docility to his gestures, words, and movements. Clearly, he's no longer a vibrant yuppie on a holiday, but a painfully polite, deferential cog in the corporate machine. And so, what ought to have been the climactic happy ending to a love affair that began four years ago in a foreign land becomes a painful discovery of the false promise that Ved-in-Corsica represented. The entrepreneurial man turns out to be the Marcusian "one-dimensional man."[23]

This is where *Tamasha* perpetuates its sleight of hand: It postulates that *true enterprise* is distinct from, and must break with, dominant articulations of *enterprise culture* as codified within mainstream sites, spaces, and relationships hijacked by capitalism. It suggests that Ved has misunderstood the real neoliberal memo, or at least its true spirit most generously defined, by living not the life enterprise culture promises, but its defunct double. He has internalized his Partition-traumatized father's script that adulthood, professionalism, and success require the quelling of individuality, desire, and play. Instead of playful *jugaad*, he coerces himself to perform oversincerity. He mistakes hard work for toiling joylessly. He gives up self-exploration for self-exploitation, relinquishes his love of storytelling, epic sagas, and theater, and forces himself to embrace the uncreative engineering-MBA lifepath. As a result, he becomes the quintessentially dolorous dude who confuses entrepreneurialism with being the "company man," loyal to the corporate enterprise. Instead of letting his abundant life and dynamic personality infuse his work—what visionary entrepreneur artists ought to do—Ved lets work overtake his life. His sense of self is entirely derived from work. His job title as "product manager" becomes definitive of his entire personality. His conversations revolve around rankings of restaurants and marveling at how "countries are the latest companies and companies are the latest countries." He is grossly sycophantic toward his abusive, patronizing boss, praising him to Tara as his "guru" and the "one-man army" who changed the face of Indian telecom. His boss, in turn, addresses Ved with the diminutive "boy" and humiliates him for nervously stuttering during presentations. This over-the-top submissiveness and toadying behavior are the script he imagines he must follow to fulfill his father's expectations and climb the corporate ladder.

Fascinatingly, what scholars of neoliberal enterprise[24] would have described as prototypically representative features of entrepreneurial psychology in Ved, the film turns into deviations resulting from the entrepreneurial man not following his heart. The problem is not with enterprise culture, it is with going off-rail, misdirecting, and wasting one's exceptional, innovative entrepreneurialism in the wrong profession.

In some ways, Ved is like Subodh from *Dil Chahta Hai* (Farhan Akhtar, 2001), but on steroids. They are both "timetable men," but they have dissimilar worlds and worldviews. Subodh mind-numbingly and tediously clocks everything: the exact date and time of every dull incident (where and when he first met Pooja, where and when they ate ice cream). Worse, he monotonously shares these doleful details indiscriminately with everyone, and he uncritically performs the most infantile, cliched rituals of love (every day buying a heart-shaped balloon for his girlfriend). These are obvious signs of his uncoolness. He is not like the three hip main leads of *Dil Chahta Hai*, who epitomize the arrival of postliberalization economy, globality, and sexuality. Subodh, by contrast, is too "uncle-like" and lives by a basic, preliberalization code of consumerism, communication, and romance.

In *Tamasha*, by contrast, Ved's hyperritualized and overprogrammed functioning is his coping mechanism for being ground down and for losing his sense of self. His psychology is thus a testimony to the failure of neoliberal fantasies and the deformities of enterprise culture. His self-regimentation and life-on-repeat existence is about being engulfed by the pervasive strands of the neoliberal ethic, rather than, as with Subodh, being on the outside of it. Ved's morning alarm, hyperpunctuality, and compulsive time checking—even at the end of a date with his girlfriend—are signs of being literally and metaphorically always on-the-clock: nothing spontaneous, no surprises, always time-bound, rehearsed, and mechanical. We may read the time lag between Subodh's character and Ved's, and the shift in tenor in how their typology is understood and treated—from a joke to an ontological threat—as a symptom of postmillennial India's changing relationship to neoliberalism and enterprise culture.

In "Unbecoming Men," Sonal Jha has argued that neoliberalism produces a masculinity framed in terms of "dislocatedness, precarity, and disappointment,"[25] and we see this play out with Ved. Quashing his own desires produces a cognitive dissonance that turns into a full-blown mental-corporeal schism when Tara rejects his marriage proposal because he's not the man she fell in love with. Ved is heartbroken by her rejection and disavowal of the flesh-and-blood man he is in favor of the fantasy she's conjured: "That is no one. That's only in your head. You've been imagining that's who I am but the real me is the one standing in front of you." Being forced to confront his hollow, dissatisfying, and inauthentic life takes a psychological toll that spills out in half-formed sentences, word salad speeches, a lot of berating self-talk with his mirror reflection, a feverish recommitment to his daily rituals that become increasingly unsustainable, and erratic, crazed behavior that freaks out his colleagues, friends, and boss who unceremoniously throws him out of his job.

Like Vikram in *LBC* who, when confronted with his precarity, directs his rage at Sona and Nikki, the two women in his life, Ved too hurls the cumulative weight of his childhood trauma at his father's hands, his professional humiliation, and sense of inadequacy, at Tara. He blames her for his manic behavior. He deliberately misconstrues her reasons for abandoning him (he's too "ordinary," and not the right "level" in status) and aggressively defies her description of his true self as wild, fearless, bohemian, and not the role of the "unthinking" "regular man" he's been playacting at work. "I *am* ordinary, I *am* average," he insists, comparing himself to the briefcase-carrying, faceless men hurtling through crowds.

A chance encounter with an autorickshaw driver who aspired to become a singer in Bollywood but never made it there because of usual life constraints—parents' expectations, wife's demands, children's education, pressure to earn a living—makes Ved come to grips with the ubiquity of self-repression and the hiding away of dreams and desires in the current sociocultural-economic dispensation. This interaction, and losing Tara and the job, also prompt him to choose differently. He slowly starts to build his identity and reputation as a bard, orating poetic fragments and stories to the nocturnal guests of a roadside *dhaaba*. For a couple of years, he slowly builds his fan base until he has his very own, full-fledged theatrical production that plays to packed audiences. The journey to resuscitate his artistic genius and creative entrepreneurship entails, of course, healing his familial and romantic wounds. He must convince his father to let him pursue his own artistic journey rather than replicate his father's Fordist ambitions of secure employment through STEM education. And, once he's built his career around his artistic passions, he seeks out Tara, this time as his erstwhile Corsica self: playing cute hide-and-seek games, leaving little mysterious notes for her to find, and playacting at a Bollywood character, a globetrotting "Don."

In the end, then, the spirited young man, with a zest for life, has come full circle and blossomed into the promised face of enterprise: not a slave to regimented time, but the quintessence of pioneering, artistic masculinity and flexible, precarious employment associated with freelancers and self-employed people. Like the ideal entrepreneurial subject, striving for self-responsibility, for determining the fate of his own happiness and well-being, is what enables Ved to thrive; he makes autonomous choices that turn the self-making process into work and make work pleasurable. And best of all, his entrepreneurialism is edificatory for others. His lessons in striking out, breaking the rigmarole of dreary, uninspired work, now crafted into a large-scale Broadway-style production, can inspire other Indian youth to internalize the right type of enterprise as they enter the political regime of "entrepreneurial citizenship."[26] In this he represents what Lilly Irani, Thomas Martilla, and Nandini Gooptu, among others, call the ultimate goal of enterprise ethic: the betterment of self and nation by producing "value with social surplus" that benefits an extensive social body. Through his art, Ved not only makes his own future, but he also generates the possibility of progressive futures for others. Artists as entrepreneurs, the film convinces us, are not workers; they are change agents and nation builders.

Tamasha's closing fantasy conceals far more than it reveals about enterprise culture. It scapegoats as "bad" the most dominant version of enterprise, the kind that is accessible to and defines the lives of most educated, urbane, upper-middle-classes Indians like Ved. In the guise of critiquing it, the film resurrects all the myths and mythological aura of entrepreneurial discourse perpetuated by neoliberal ideology.

It sets up true enterprise as that which is emancipatory. Ved's job loss, a classic sign of precarity, when even the salaried are vulnerable to unemployment, is turned into an opportunity to reinvent and rediscover his lost self. Helen C. Williams et al. trace the history of the idea of "enterpreneuring-as-emancipation" to demonstrate that this hope has long served as an essential component of neoliberal subjectification.[27] The truth, however, is far from gratifying: On the ground, the entrepreneur's existence is rife with uncertainty, instability, stress, anxiety, depression; the dream is never realized. The entrepreneur symbolizes what Vachet sees as the contradiction at the heart of neoliberal precarity: "nothing is prohibited," but "nothing is achievable."[28] It's not surprising, then, that hardly any films spend plot time exploring the afterlife of entrepreneurial success. To become an entrepreneur marks the narratological limit of most contemporary Bollywood cinema.

Tamasha, unlike *LBC*, eclipses the social, cultural, and economic privilege that enables entrepreneurial success. It sidesteps the question of intergenerational wealth altogether and pretends that Ved's and the autorickshaw driver's stories are akin and their fates conjoined. In studying the philanthropic developmentalism of enterprise culture, Irani describes how entrepreneurs treat the poor as resource-rich terrain for the implementation of entrepreneurial practices. Poverty becomes not a class category to resist and abolish, but a diverse site upon which to innovate. That Ved recruits the working-class aspirant as a singer in his production reiterates the equivalence in their fortunes. Here the film, like much of enterprise culture, promises those who are at the margins that social mobility is possible and just around the corner. It also reiterates the idea that Ved's entrepreneurialism isn't just about him but is expansive and creates opportunities for others. In this, the film also subtly (because the side plot is so minor and innocuous) but poignantly makes a distinction between innovators and their "Others." As Irani reminds us, in the way that entrepreneurial discourse circulates in India, everyone is celebrated as a "potential entrepreneur," but not everyone is seen as capable or deserving of it.

Together, Vikram and Ved are thus a different articulation of the crisis of masculinity under neoliberalism. Their uber-urbane, upper-class, and caste identities internalize neoliberal predicaments less in their physiology, or as bodily crisis, and more as particular psychic arrangements produced by neoliberal ideology. In this, Vikram and Ved are different from the men that Jha discusses in her work on "the new Indie" films that emerged in the 2010s. The male protagonists of films like *Bala* (Amar Kaushik, 2019) and *Dum Laga ke Haisha* (2015) are a far cry from the exceptional, assertive masculinities that have traditionally dominated Hindi cinema. If the "angry young man" and the "five year plan hero" were cinematic embodiments of agency, ability, resistance, and control through the 1960s and 1970s, then these neoliberal protagonists, plagued by "emasculating afflictions" like sexual dysfunction and alopecia, challenge the very idea of the "hero" in traditional terms. Instead, they give expression to the small-town, micro- and minority stories of nonexceptional masculinities. For these male protagonists that Jha discusses, the loss of corporeal reliability and normativity becomes an occasion to reassess their otherwise dominant place within the neoliberal order. With Vikram and Ved, it is precisely their dominance within this order that yields, respectively, manipulative and dissonant emotional landscapes and attempts to secure their power.

Even so, together these men give expression to the collapse of a secure, triumphal, hypernationalist, imposing masculinity[29] that emerged in the first two decades after liberalization. In 1990s and early 2000s, a confident, globally mobile, buoyantly consumerist masculinity represented the arrival of India on the international stage as a neoliberal economy and nuclear power. Around the 2010s, however, neoliberalism's "dismal record" became apparent,[30] making it clear that it was only the country's ruling classes that had benefited from liberalization. While the films that Jha discusses offer an insight into the lives of "neoliberalism's Others," as Paunksnis calls those left behind by neoliberal India,[31] *LBC* and *Tamasha* demonstrate the toll that neoliberalism extracts from those it favors and the anxious masculinity[32] it yields even among those who are economically secure.

On the face of it, *LBC* and *Tamasha* also articulate a distant, amorphous, and opaque relationship between the politics of Hindutva and neoliberal polity. Ved and Vikram are far from practicing Hindus; nothing about their worldview expresses a reliance on hegemonic Hindutva and its traditionalist accoutrements. And yet in both films, an overtly Hinduized public sphere is a persistent, even if marginal, presence. In fact, the two films give us a glimpse into the cultural and mediatized methods that Hinduized the nation's imagistic, iconographic landscape, paving the way for the normalization, ascendency, and omnipresence of Hindutva ideology.

At the end of *LBC*, the TV series that gives Sona regular acting employment is based on actual domestic dramas, colloquially called *Saas-Bahu/K-Serial*. As a phenomenon, these television series played a critical role in accelerating and solidifying the saffronization of the middle-class domestic sphere, particularly in North India. Targeting women as their primary audience, these shows weaponized gendered, familial relations[33] in the project of "remaking the Indian nation under the ideology of Hindutva, creating not just a Hindu nation but a Brahmanical nation."[34] In doing so, they successfully redirected political stakes onto the cultural sphere, and connected the "micropolitics of gender" and with the "macropolitics of [reconfiguring] national identity."

It is telling, then, that while Vikram's privilege gives him the leeway to participate in the elite, unmarked, cosmopolitan circuits of the film industry, it falls to Sona to find recourse to cultural practices and media spheres that fast-track Hindutva's political-cultural agenda. It is a pity that a young woman who lives such a nonnormative life, who runs away from home, escapes an arranged marriage, alienates her parents, and fends for herself to build a career in an impossibly competitive profession, must participate in regressive narratologies and conservative mediatized cultures that promote the very undoing of everything she has strived for. The woman entrepreneur is recruited into and assigned the work of preserving and reconstituting the nation's identity through cultural work that generates affective and ideological investment in the morals and practices of traditional, patriarchal, Hindu domesticity. The male Hindu entrepreneur, on the other hand, is set free to explore the elite echelons of the film industry and its world of high fashion, big capital, celebrity dynasties, and global mobility.

Similarly, in *Tamasha*, Ved's childhood is determined by the power of stories that infuse his social milieu. In prolonged flashback sequences, we see him voraciously and indiscriminately consuming epic tales: in temples, churches, classrooms, at school plays, through street theater and religious festivals. He also visits a local fakir in Shimla and begs to be regaled by the infinite repository of stories he knows. The old man slips seamlessly between the story of Sita from the *Ramayana* and Helen from *The Iliad*, insisting there is no difference: "a story is a story and it's the same everywhere, across time." Laila and Majnu and Romeo and Juliet are interchangeable. Jesus could just as easily be called Isa, and Brahma Ibrahim. The young Ved protests, wanting his stories to be clearly demarcated and distinguished from one another. What is evident about Ved's childhood fascination with publicly performed stories is the preponderance of Hindu epics and mythology and a distinct marginality and near absence of stories from Islamic traditions. Somehow, Islam is exempt from the logic of universality applied to narrative templates. We see Ved imbibe European—Greek and Renaissance—influences, but often, in Ved's childhood imagination, even these become occasions for him to fantasize about Hindu icons. During Mass at a church, his imagination conjures the scene of marriage between Prithviraj Chauhan and Sanjukta. In his childish worldview, Hindu texts are the ur-texts, and Hindu tales are the main story. And, importantly, the formation of his unmarked, Hinduness coproduces his dominant masculinity. All his favorite stories are told by, and center on, powerful men who protect, save, chase women that are invariably weeping, melancholic, suffering; their sole purpose is to inspire Hindu gods and kings to action and to bring them back to life. No surprise then that decades later, in adulthood, Tara is both the recipient of his rage and the fount of his inspiration to recover his artistic, entrepreneurial self.

In the next chapter, with *Gully Boy*, we revisit the figure of the artistic entrepreneur, this time, socially and religiously constituted as a Muslim man who inhabits spaces of indigence. Here we study how a lower-class Muslim masculinity navigates the national neoliberal pressures to innovate in the age of Hindutva.

Precarity and the Entrepreneurial Poor

In contrast to *Tamasha* and *LBC*, *Sui Dhaaga* and *Eeb Allay Ooo!* turn their attention to "neoliberalism's others,"[35] that is, subaltern men from lower-middle-class and poor backgrounds. Both films are peopled with protagonists and other characters who belong to the large, expanding informal labor sector in India. This sector accommodates the majority of the manual workforce and has experienced an intensification of precarity under the neoliberal regime. The discourse of entrepreneurship interpellates populations from socioeconomically disadvantaged groups, encouraging them to internalize to various degrees an entrepreneurial ethos—active, self-reliant, taking initiative, risk taking, self-improvement—as the solution to navigate their class precarity and derive masculine self-worth. Rendered entrepreneurial, the indigent Hindu male protagonists of both films make concerted attempts, that strain their sanity, to self-responsibilize and launch themselves out of poverty and fulfill their potential through their own endeavors, resulting in success for one and failure for the other. Through this narrative arc, one film reinvests in the entrepreneurial fantasy to escape precarity, while the other shows the cracks and contradictions of entrepreneurial ideology, revealing it to be a construct that serves the interests of the neoliberal ruling classes and state.

Sui Dhaaga and *Eeb Allay Ooo!* also offer insight into subordinated masculinities under neoliberal Hindutva. The films show us that its subaltern Hindu male protagonists, Mauji and Anjani, might benefit, however unevenly, from the "patriarchal dividend"[36] as well as their dominant religious or caste identities, which grants them limited power over marginalized or multiply precarious others (whether non-Hindu men or women or Dalits). As economically disadvantaged men, however, they also suffer "disproportionately the costs of existing gender regimes." And we see how they struggle to adapt to the changing labor markets as well as the pressures of entrepreneurial self-making under neoliberalism.[37]

Both films allow us to see a different strand of the entanglement between neoliberalism, masculinity, and Hindu nationalism in twenty-first-century Hindi cinema: while in *Eeb Allay Ooo!* the central character is drawn into a Hindu religious parade after neoliberalism fails him, *Sui Dhaaga* serves as propaganda for "marketized Hindutva" through its celebration of the Hindu male entrepreneur's self-reliance.

Sui Dhaaga

Sui Dhaaga revolves around Mauji's journey as he quits his humiliating dead-end job as an errand boy to become a successful fashion entrepreneur who starts and runs his own garment business. Mauji is a young North Indian Hindu man; he lives with his wife and parents in a cramped house a few hours outside New Delhi. When the film begins, we find out that Mauji comes from a family of artisans (his grandfather and father were both tailors), and has become part of the informal urban service sector after the government shut down the *Shilpgram* (village of skilled artisans and rural arts and crafts) that employed him and other artisans. As a result, he and his family have moved from the village to a town near the capital city in search of employment. He now works as an errand boy to a retailer of sewing machines, Bansal-ji, much like the other displaced artisans who too have found sundry jobs in the city. Mauji, however, does not resent or blame the neoliberal state for exacerbating his precarity. His voice-over, with which the film opens, establishes him as possessing the right kind of attitude and sensibility required of an entrepreneur: "All is well. Here in the city and at home. The rooms are few, but there are so many stars in the sky that one can easily spend the night counting them." He translates problems into opportunities; he is a dreamer, and he does not suffer from a failure of imagination.

Mauji's mantra "sab badiya hai" (all is well) harks back to the mantra "Aal Izz Well" from *3 Idiots* (Rajkumar Hirani, 2009), a popular film that sells the neoliberal entrepreneurial fantasy where a servant's child (Rancho/Phunsukh) becomes a celebrated inventor with multiple patents to his name. Moreover, like Mauji, Rancho/Phunsukh (played by Aamir Khan) is a socially conscious and patriotic entrepreneur whose inventions (involving solar power) serve India's needs, as opposed to his aspirational nemesis who has migrated to Silicon Valley in the United States and is only interested in generating economic wealth for himself. Released almost a decade later, *Sui Dhaaga* holds on to this discourse of enterprise.

At the same time, the film does not shy away from presenting how economic precarity adversely impacts the physical well-being of the poor. We witness the bodily vulnerability of Mauji and his family, whether it is through images of the constant casual verbal and physical abuse that Mauji endures from the shopkeeper's son; or Mauji riding his bicycle in the scorching heat and dust, nursing a bleeding foot and limping to claim a free sewing machine; or his mother's stress-induced heart attack and father's hair loss. And yet it offers a straightforward and ringing endorsement of enterprise as the answer to this precarity. It promulgates an optimistic vision that even when the odds are stacked against you, you can rise above your circumstances and overcome adversity by relying on nothing but your own talent, resourcefulness, and resilience. It valorizes the work ethic, originality, spirit of risk taking, and ingenuity of its poor protagonists as they successfully pull themselves up from their bootstraps and roll up their sleeves and achieve success. The poor are thus "projected as entrepreneurial assets of the nation."[38] To show how the film perpetuates the promise of entrepreneurship, we draw upon the concepts of what Irani refers to as "'rendering entrepreneurial' to explain how the state goes beyond the management of poverty to the proliferation of enterprise around poverty." The state's reliance on "entrepreneurial citizenship" positions entrepreneurship "not just an economic activity but as a nation-building one."[39]

Indeed, Mauji understands his duty to contribute to his country through his enterprise. When Mauji's father expresses defeatist sentiments—"first Chinese ready-made garments ruined us; now, Chinese machines will ruin us/defeat us"—Mauji responds confidently to his father with "well, the machines might be Chinese but the hands are *Hindustani haath* [Indian hands]." He goes on to marshal support from his fellow artisans, addressing them as "Sipahi" (soldiers) who respond in unison, with fervor, as they get ready to model the fashion collection. Mauji understands himself not as much as a "bearer of rights," but as the bearer of responsibility. Meanwhile, his fellow workers/soldiers become the "beneficiary others" of his enterprise.[40] So not only do the "poor entrepreneurs" become ideal neoliberal subjects as they self-responsibilize and take charge as autonomous individuals, but they also generate additional value in society.[41]

In the film, poverty is turned into enterprise, and the poor are shown to be skilled at devising creative coping strategies in the face of adversity and endemic deprivation.[42] Anthropologist Ravinder Kaur has argued that the *jugaad* innovation narrative "offers an uplifting, potentially emancipatory discourse of mobility in a setting where even after two decades of economic reforms, wealth gap and poverty stubbornly persist."[43] The celebration of *jugaad* allows the neoliberal state to turn "its own failure to deliver public goods effectively to all its citizens . . . into a rich opportunity."[44] The film feeds into this ideology that narrates poor people's *jugaad* as creativity, promise, and a vehicle for mobility. For example, Mauji and Mamta improvise and use old bedsheets to make a maxi for his mother to wear in the hospital. In another scene, when the fashion competition judges rightly worry that while the poor dreamers (Mauji and Mamta) have talent, they might not have adequate capital ("investment, infrastructure . . . manpower") required to produce an entire collection, Mamta shows how poor people can hustle and gather resources: "In our *mohalla*, there are a lot of artisans and craftsmen who left *shilpgram* and do menial jobs now. We'll ask them to join hands with us." While sentimentally inspiring, this solution sidesteps the wide socioeconomic gaps that exist in terms of access to privilege and to financial or cultural capital or to formal knowledge. Differential oppressions are problems to be overcome by resourcefulness and passion.

The ability to generate economic value while addressing poverty becomes a key distinguishing feature of the right kind of entrepreneurialism, the good enterprise. And this is where the contrast with the bad enterprise of upper-middle-class businesswoman-entrepreneur Harleen Bedi makes Mauji and Mamta's entrepreneurialism shine in an even more positive light. Bedi runs a garment factory, Bedi Fashions, that she took over after her father's successful "tailoring business was wiped out by Chinese ready-made garments." She sacrificed the completion of her fashion design education in the United States and returned to manage her father's ailing business, turning it around into a successful venture. This successful enterprise, however, is built on several corrupt practices. When Mauji and Mamta end up in her factory after the hospital maxi they make for Mauji's mother and other patients is a runaway success, Bedi is shown to be an exploitative opportunist who preys on the vulnerability of the poor; with a shrewd glance she sizes them up and smells both their creativity and their need. She refuses to see Mauji and Mamta as equals—or as entrepreneurs in their own right—perfunctorily addressing Mamta when she tries to suggest that their situation was like hers since their family of tailors had also suffered from the flooding of the market with foreign-made clothes. She extracts their skills and ingenious ideas, stealing them and marketing them as her own. And since her approach is businesslike and utilitarian, geared toward maximization of production and profit, she strips the maxi they'd made of any individuality to make it plain and easily reproducible. She's canny enough, however, to recognize the value of their creative work and saves the "embroidery design" from the gown to use in her own fashion fund application.

Bedi's modus operandi and hypocrisy are further revealed in a phone call where she tries to use her connections to rig the process and get her designs shortlisted for the Raymond Fashion Fund competition: "I've gone to small towns and remote areas and picked out beautiful things. We have such talented, gifted artisans in our country. They deserve a platform. Please get us shortlisted." Similarly, she takes a photo of herself with the factory workers as PR material for her application for the competition: "They should know that I'm not alone. The entire country is with me." This is deeply disingenuous because neither is she "with the country" nor is "the country with her" as she not only exploits and abuses the poor artisans in need, but also because her factory sells clothes with a "Made in China" label. Guddu, the middleman, tells a disconcerted Mauji that this is because no one would buy clothes made in "Ghaziabad" (i.e., made in the regional backwaters). When Mauji questions this practice, Guddu mocks him as a "*desh-bhakt*" (patriot). But, as the film shows us, Mauji's patriotism is what aligns him with the right kind of enterprise. He uses enterprise to generate pride and profit for the country, and he comes to represent the entrepreneur as national hero.

The film ends with Mauji's voice-over narration that reinforces the promise of entrepreneurial citizenship to enable social mobility for all. "It wasn't just a win for Sui Dhaaga. It was a win for the art/artisans (*kala*)." As truly entrepreneurial citizens, Mamta and Mauji start a sewing and tailoring school with the express purpose "to make other fighters like us self-reliant," an echo of the entrepreneurs-as-soldiers idea articulated in the film. These fearless and confident entrepreneurial citizens welcome the idea of competition, which assumes, as a virtue, that everyone has equal opportunity at the outset. Mauji simply states, "There's many talented people all over India competing with us. They're all mad in India." The film uses the mad/made wordplay to celebrate the "insane" innate spirit of innovation in every Indian to perpetuate the idea that India is a land of mad, crazy dreamers full of potential to become successful entrepreneurs based on sheer grit. We see that their products sell on Amazon with the tag "Made in India. Sell locally and globally." Mauji showcases not just the entrepreneur's ability to dream, but to "articulate those dreams in language that validates global capital."[45]

It is ironic and telling that a transnational corporation like Amazon—with its exploitative labor practices that intensify precarity for small businesses and workers in India and worldwide—is presented as a liberatory force while China is demonized in the film.[46] Incidentally, this moment also marks a new trend in product placement, which became ubiquitous in popular Hindi cinema since the 1990s and with the genre of the family entertainers. *Sui Dhaaga* was released on Amazon Prime Video. The film as commodity, and the commodities produced within the film, both belong and pay obeisance to the most mammoth global conglomerate, which is the very antithesis of the domestic "made in India" ethos.

Importantly, Hindutva ideology posits India's religious culture, and Hinduism in particular, as uniquely and ontologically hospitable to enterprise.[47] In this discourse, the hallmark of Indian selfhood is, and always has been, "inventiveness, ingenuity, tenacity, resourcefulness, self-reliance, resilience, risk-taking, initiative, innovation, adaptability, flexibility, pragmatism, ingenuity, and a strategic and tactical approach to problem solving."[48] Enterprise is thus essentially Indian, and Indians are seen as distinctively positioned to become self-reliant entrepreneurs. The special place of *jugaad* in Indian culture and capitalism,[49] and as a unique concept that India has given to the rest of the entrepreneurial world, further confirms the inherent salience of the intimacy between Hindu identity and enterprise culture. In fact, as Gooptu goes onto show, contemporary manifestations and practices of Hindu spiritualism borrow heavily from components of enterprise culture: they advocate aspiration and action, self-knowing and soul realization; utilize self-help language and managerial practices; and offer lifestyle packages, armed with "the sacral power of Hindu religious systems," to improve mental and physical well-being.[50]

In *Sui Dhaaga*, the entrepreneurial masculine citizenship celebrated is also overtly entangled with Hindutva logics. In its ideological leaning, the film, whose subtitle is "Made in India" (a phrase that's also repeated in the film), presents itself as an unapologetic public relations advertisement for the ruling right-wing government's neoliberal policies, such as the "Make in India" initiative and the "Atmanirbhar Bharat Abhiyan." Launched in 2014, Make in India's goal was to make India into a manufacturing hub by enabling greater foreign direct investment in some key sectors of the economy, with the state falling back into the role of facilitator in this task of creating more openings for global capital. A different version of this initiative was the "Atmanirbhar Bharat Abhiyan" (Self-Reliant India Mission—ABA) announced in 2020.[51] Political scientist Priya Chacko discusses the "Atmanirbhar Bharat" scheme, which "has been particularly identified with a reorientation in economic policy to move India from 'reliance to self-reliance' through manufacturing-led, export-driven growth to generate mass employment."[52] Chacko argues that ABA is an example of how "a neo-liberal–Hindutva civilizational paternalist political rationality is shaping economic policy in India."[53] She notes that while neoliberal paternalism disciplines individuals and businesses into becoming "market actors," Hindutva paternalism builds "societal conformity with the reactionary identity politics of Hindutva civilizationalism."[54]

In the film, not only do we see how Mauji, the Hindu male entrepreneurial citizen, self-disciplines as a market actor, he simultaneously displays a logic of Hindu paternalism and reactionary politics that promote discipline, duties over rights, traditional gender-based hierarchies, and the idea that India is in a struggle against foreign domination (China).[55]

The film gives us the habitus of the Hindu precariat in contemporary India through Mauji's Hindu household and social milieu. He and the other laid-off *shilpgram* workers are all Hindus, who contentedly chant "Radhe Radhe Japo Chale Aayenge Bihari," a Hindu *bhajan* (devotional song), on the bus on their way to their jobs in the city. After her return from the hospital, his mother wants to organize a *kirtan* (an event of Hindu devotional singing) at home to allay her uneasiness. Before Mauji and Mamta leave the house to present their designs for the contest, the mother bids them off with a prayer and a *tilak* on their foreheads to wish them success. And successful they are! When Mauji prepares the collection for the fashion competition, he asks his mother to pray for his success, and she happily obliges with chanting "Jai Siya Ram" on her prayer beads. Prayer to the gods will, and does, no doubt ensure success, regardless of structural disadvantages.

It becomes clear that the entrepreneurial leader and citizen that the film valorizes is a Hindu man, not the Muslim man or even the Hindu woman. So even though we see another minor character, a poor Muslim man named Naushad, engaging in enterprise, it is presented as the wrong kind of enterprise. Naushad is involved in a racket of buying sewing machines, the ones the government provides to the poor for free, on the black market to supply them to Bansal-ji. He also bribes the cops to look the other way. When Bansal-ji tries to shortchange Naushad and pay him less, Mauji intervenes. Here Mauji's Hindu identity and vocabulary facilitates his intervention with his Hindu boss (who has a little corner shrine with figurines of Hindu gods in his shop and is frequently seen praying to these gods) on Naushad's behalf: he asks the boss to do "*punya ka kaam*," a holy deed. Even though both Mauji and Naushad might be similarly class precarious, Mauji's hegemonic religious identity gives him some limited access to power. Mauji appeals to Bansal-ji by saying that Naushad's job is "risky" and he could end up in jail without bail. Thus, even though Naushad has many of the markers of an entrepreneur—he takes risk, is resourceful, gathers information through his networks, identifies opportunity, adapts himself to the "market," and so on—his entrepreneurial aspirations are tinged with corruption. But he is given a chance to redeem himself. When Mauji needs space to manufacture clothes for the fashion show collection, he, in true entrepreneurial fashion, recognizes and leverages this old acquaintance with Naushad, recognizing it as a terrain of potential, and seeks his help in securing an abandoned factory. Even though Naushad is the one who provides the required critical resource, it is Mauji who is presented as the benefactor, leader, and employer when he offers Naushad an opportunity to "invest" in the good kind of enterprise by being part of the team.

Similarly, Mamta (the Hindu woman) is accommodated as an entrepreneur through a companionate marriage. The film offers a celebration of enterprise wherein capital, couple formation, and citizenship are all coarticulated. As we noted earlier, Mankekar has written about the "the co-implication of enterprise culture and specific structures of feeling" in films such as *Band Baaja Baaraat*. We see this in *Sui Dhaaga* through a "discursive co-production" or the mutual dependence of enterprise and coupledom. From the opening sequence, we sense Mauji's dissatisfaction with his relationship with his wife; he feels that there's a "wall" between them because they've not been able to connect as she's buried under household chores and taking care of his elderly parents. It is after they win the fashion fund competition that Mauji tells his parents, "I held her hand for the first time today. I held her hand because, for the first time, I felt worthy of her." Couple formation and intimacy are forged in the crucible of aspiration. The film's invocation of this metaphor of holding hands celebrates the "ethos of entreprendre (the root of the word 'enterprise'), which means 'to take in hand, to take hold of.'"[56] The couple is fused with their enterprise, as *sui* (needle) and *dhaaga* (thread).

If one looks closely, however, it is really Mamta who exudes the true entrepreneurial spirit: she is the one who dares to dream and seek opportunity. She first plants in Mauji's head the idea of setting up their own business. "Do something of your own. Start your own business. You are so talented," she tells him. And later, after they are humiliated by Bedi, it is she who suggests that they apply for the fashion competition: "If we want our dignity back, then we will also participate in the fashion competition. We'll put our own name on our products and sell them." Her role, however, is as a helpmate to her husband, the Hindu male entrepreneur, and to help establish or prop up his masculinity through successful entrepreneurialism.

Mauji's anxious masculinity is on display throughout the film. It is a result of Mauji's investment in, and inability to fulfill, hegemonic capitalist masculine ideals such as being the primary breadwinner or protector of his family in the context of shifts in the labor market. In this, Mauji resembles the hero of Katariya's first film, *Dum Laga ke Haisha* (2015), a small-town precariat male who struggles with feelings of inadequacy. Mauji's material precarity and the concomitant effects of this relentless insecurity on his subjectivity are revealed through his volatile outbursts that punctuate the film. At various moments where he feels powerless or useless, he seems to be on the verge of a breakdown and capable of exploding into violence (in Bansal-ji's shop, at the dispensary, in Bedi's factory, with his brother). His fraught interactions belie his claim that "sab badiya hai" (all is well) and betrays the barely concealed repression that this optimistic refrain is built upon. While Mauji is never physically abusive toward Mamta, he does silence her in public (as in the confrontation with Bedi) and does not always acknowledge her hard work and contribution to their collective entrepreneurial endeavors. In another scene, he accuses his brother of being his "wife's parrot" or his "wife's "lapdog" partly since the brother has moved in with his wife's family in opposition to traditional expectations. We can see that his sense of diminished masculinity has also led to the inability to create a family with his wife (they don't share intimacy; they have no children). Similarly, while Mauji himself endures daily humiliations as errand boy in Bansal-ji's shop, he only finally loses his calm when he feels that Prashant, Bansal-ji's son, has spoken disrespectfully of his wife and their (sexual) relations. Entrepreneurship, then, is presented as subsuming these frustrations and modulating his sense of emasculation.

Mauji displays aspects of what Sanjay Shrivastava has called "Modi-masculinity," a "reformulation of older versions of Indian masculinist discourse" combined with "the new forms of subjectivities (e.g., individualism) within existing social structures."[57] In the film, Mauji defers to his parents even as he assimilates himself to newer political economies of neoliberalism. He is an individualized subject who makes his own enterprise, "though not exactly as he pleases but, rather, through the dictates of social structures, such as family and kin networks."[58] Mauji's sense of masculinity is attached to the performance of filial piety. As Mamta tells Bedi when she encourages Mamta to leave Mauji, "He rides his bike in the hot sun instead of taking a bus so that he can save bus fare just so that he can buy his father a *paan* [betel leaf]." It is no surprise then that after their entrepreneurial success, we do not see Mauji and Mamta embarking on global tourism. Instead, it is the aging parents who partake in the joys of consumer citizenship as we see happy postcard photos of them at the leaning tower of Pisa. This is the kind of "moral consumption" seen as "'appropriate' to the Indian cultural context."[59]

Eeb Allay Ooo!

The story's protagonist is a poor young male migrant from Bihar, Anjani Prasad, in search of employment opportunities. Anjani moves in with his sister and brother-in-law, who live in a *basti* (a squatter settlement) on the outskirts of Delhi. The film revolves around his unsuccessful stint as a "monkey repeller," a job he struggles to do and is eventually fired from. The film's onomatopoeic title refers to the guttural calls made by men hired to repel monkeys by mimicking the sounds of a langur (a large monkey with a black face framed by white fur) to scare away rhesus monkeys who have overtaken residential neighborhoods in Delhi. Directed by Prateek Vats, *Eeb Allay Ooo!* has won many awards and garnered much recognition: it won the Golden Gateway Award and the Special Jury Mention in the India Gold section of the 2019 Mumbai Film Festival; it was selected in the competitive section of the Pingyao International Film Festival (China) and for the Panorama Section at the 2020 Berlin International Film Festival. In contrast to other more mainstream films in this chapter that depict enterprise culture as offering a fantasy of escape or success to varying degrees, this indie Hindi film confronts us with the unmitigated consequences of neoliberal economics and exposes the limits of the promise of enterprise to "manage" poverty and achieve socioeconomic mobility.

Economic precarity is ubiquitous in this film: Anjani and his family and fellow workers are all a part of the sizeable unorganized sector in India, who struggle with insecure or unstable employment, temporary contracts, lack of prospects, low wages, random firings and layoffs, little autonomy or control over their time, abuse, and strict surveillance by their employers. The film offers insight into the ways in which privatization of the public sector has resulted in the casualization of labor and distinctly precarious working conditions for those in the lower-middle or working classes. In the new contractual economy, the government outsources its job to private contractors and subcontractors who hire workers such as Anjani for low-grade temporary work like keeping monkeys from wreaking havoc around important government buildings in Lutyens' Delhi. As director Prateek Vats explains, "These people might work for the government, but they are not recognized as government employees, and they don't get a pension or other benefits. You can get them to do anything. No strict qualifications are needed for the job. It depends on how much you can bend and accommodate."[60]

Thus, while Shashi, Anjani's sister, might willingly delude herself, as a coping mechanism, into believing that Anjani has a "*sarkari naukri*" (government job), he knows and articulates the difference; "It's not a government job; it's contractual," he insistently reminds her. Meanwhile, optimistic but savvy Shashi understands that Anjani has limited options in a city with "30 million jobs" but no job vacancies for someone with such few qualifications: he barely completed high school, he can't drive, he can't cook, he doesn't know any electrical or plumbing work, he doesn't know English, and he is not tech-savvy. Of course, Anjani is confronted with this harsh truth once he loses this wretched job.

Anjani's situation is paralleled by that of his brother-in-law, and the film's editing constantly invites us to make connections in their precarious work situations. Like Anjani's job, the brother-in-law is also a contractual worker working the night shift as a security guard in an amusement park. His vulnerability is evident in the interactions between him and the middleman manager, which cut to scenes between Anjani and his contractor, Narayan. The manager uses corporate-speak to announce to the workers that they will have to start carrying a gun as an "on-site requirement" to manage the worsening "law and order" situation. Here, rather than empowering them or making them feel secure, the manager weaponizes the insecurity of the poor by requiring them to do something that they are visibly uneasy about. When the brother-in-law timidly dares to ask if carrying the gun is a "requirement," the manager silences him with a simple rejoinder, "a job isn't a requirement either." The brother-in-law's manager deals the final cruel blow by telling him that while he can't be sure that the management team will entertain his request to not carry a gun, what is certain is that the promised "increment will be cut." Similarly, Narayan, in response to Anjani's protestations about the impossibility of managing hundreds of monkeys, simply tells him, "Then don't do it. Don't do it. It's my fault that I gave you a job." The middlemen know fully well that their poor employees can scarcely afford to lose their jobs, even as they know that their own job security will be in peril if they don't achieve outcomes. The middle management's precarity is brought home when a government bureaucrat threatens Narayan, "Keep your boys in check, otherwise I will terminate your contract." This is what Lorey describes as governing through insecurity, where the erstwhile "relation of opposition" between "the precarious and the immune, insecurity and security/protection" increasingly take on a graded relationship."[61] While different social groups are unevenly exposed to the vicissitudes of neoliberal capitalism, insecurity permeates all nodes of the employment continuum. Almost no one is exempt.

These employment-related insecurities spill over into sociocultural-psychological insecurities, producing "precarized minds" and volatile subjects in distress, as evidenced by the psychosomatic symptoms displayed by his brother-in-law. In the face of insecurity in the workplace, the brother-in-law's affective landscape is characterized by what Standing has called "the 'four As': anger, anomie, anxiety, alienation."[62] We sense his trepidation throughout the film, manifested in facial expressions of despair and helplessness. In one scene, he throws up; in another, when he bikes back home with the gun that's weighing heavily on his shoulder and mind, he is drenched in sweat and out of breath with exertion and fear. We see how these feelings of frustration and powerlessness accumulate, and he erupts in anger, pointing the gun at the petty businessman–small-time trader who taunts and harasses his pregnant wife to work faster. Through an edit, this scene is connected to Anjani's feelings about the "catapult." Like the gun, Anjani is given the catapult at his job and told to carry it only "as a show, to induce fear in the monkeys" but not to use it. Predictably, he does use it. He had prefigured the tragedy when he told Mahender that "If I have it, I will use it." The gun and the catapult become emblematic of the uselessness of safety paraphernalia given to precarious workers.

The multiple psychological as well as physical manifestations of precarity are also evident in Anjani's arc through the film. The film begins with a monkey repeller warning the new recruits that he's training that the job is "very dangerous; there is risk of physical harm. Bruises, broken bones." We see the physical toll that the job takes on Anjani as he shivers in fear as monkeys grimace and lunge at him. Similarly, as he tries to learn to mimic the langur's call properly, he complains to his fellow co-worker Mahender: "My lungs will explode if I push anymore." Throughout the film, many closeups of Anjani's contorted face reveal his frustration and desperate exertions to make the guttural call.

The psychosocial impact of precarity is evident in the interpersonal dynamics between Anjani and his insecure fellow workers, a tension that finds release in acts of casual and understated bullying and harassment. In a scene that registers the disturbing and violent aspect of the struggle for economic survival (and in some ways, prefigures Mahender's lynching by a mob), these workers, in jest, surround Anjani around the cage in which he gets accidentally locked in while setting it up with banana bait to trap monkeys. These workers tease and jeer at Anjani—"Today, you're our monkey"—and ask him to mimic a monkey (screech and eat a banana) before he can be let out, while he gets increasingly terrified and agitated, pleading, "Let me out. I can't breathe." This is a poignant scene that captures Anjani's feelings of entrapment in a job he doesn't like but that he desperately needs; and more broadly, the feeling of being in a cage resonates as a metaphor in the film for the situation of the precariat or the urban poor, whether the claustrophobic physical spaces they call home or the general socioeconomic spaces of inequality they traverse. In a thoughtful piece on the film, Megnaa Mehtta notes that "Migrants in most cities are dispensable, and even if Anjani acts for a few hours as the predator, he and others like him remain the quintessential prey."[63] Thus this scene also redirects attention to the larger provocative question raised by the film about exactly who occupies the place of prey and predator in a world that sets up oppressive hierarchies between humans and enacts horrific violence against both marginalized humans and animals.

The film is not interested in setting up or reinforcing species hierarchy between man and monkey; that is, it does not say that humans are "reduced" to the level of nonhuman animals or even that animals are treated better than human beings. Instead, the film alerts viewers to think about the entanglement between different beings or creatures where they contemporaneously face the brutal impact of, and are vulnerable to, neoliberal capitalism. After all, the nonhuman animals (monkeys) and human animals (migrants) leave their natural habitats (whether forests or villages) to come to the city in search of "food," as their homes or habitats are encroached upon as a result of uneven development, urbanization, resource extraction, or ecological devastation wreaked under neoliberalism.[64] Eschewing the human-animal hierarchy, the film instead seeks to shed light on how the culture of neoliberal Hindutva distorts and weaponizes species hierarchy to biopolitical ends, as we return to discuss later in this chapter.

It is not just precarity but attempts to manage precarity through enterprise that produce psychosomatic symptoms. As we see, not only does enterprise not benefit Anjani, it also worsens his precarity. We see how Anjani takes initiative and risks and demonstrates adaptability and resourcefulness, as he makes concerted efforts to achieve success at his job. Realizing that he can't make the guttural sounds, his *jugaad* is to come up with creative alternatives to attain success at his job. For example, he prints out and puts up large posters of langurs around the government buildings. He paints his face black and dresses up like a langur, which not only helps to keep the monkeys away but also allows him to make some extra cash from posing for photos with tourists. In a middle-class neighborhood, when he comes across an automated machine that emits langur sounds, he has the idea to record his friend Mahender's guttural calls on his phone to use that to scare monkeys away. None of this "creativity" of the poor is rewarded though; in fact, he is punished for his entrepreneurial actions as he is physically abused by the contractor—who yanks his hair and ears, making him wince and cry in pain—and is eventually fired from his job.

Anjani's subaltern ingenuity cannot be recognized within the middle-class valorization of enterprise culture. It points to the limits or "fractured nature of 'enterprise culture' in the city"[65] and who can lay claim to urban space. This also becomes a commentary on the politics of urban space; as Vats, the director of the film, says in an interview, he wanted to show what "the seat of power" of the world's "largest democracy" looks like from "a migrant working-class gaze."[66]

In fact, Vats credits Mahender (Nath), who plays himself since he comes from a community of people who have worked with langurs for generations and whose real-life work is that of a money repeller, for being the "window for understanding this world better."[67] The use of a nonprofessional actor to play an important character conveys the film's realist aesthetic as well as indie status and ethos. In fact, the film privileges his perspective, as Mahender's is the first voice and face, in closeup, that we hear and see in the film. Additionally, we see the area of Raisina Hill and its environs (where all the important government buildings are located in New Delhi) from the eyes of the precariat: the monkey repeller, the sweeper, the balloon seller, the tea-shack vendor. Mahender and Anjani as entrepreneurial subject are "refracted through the particularities of the city's spatial politics." We come to see the "city street as an embodied public sphere, a contested terrain where middle-class aesthetics and politics contend with the unruliness of species, social groups, and a well-organized web of illegalities that links the state to the citizens."[68] Thus, even as the migrants' "labor" is needed to maintain the important buildings and posh neighborhoods, their "lives" are not, and they themselves constitute an unseemly and undesirable presence that does not belong in these spaces of power and are banished to the margins of the city. This spatial apartheid is visible as the film contrasts the wide open and clean spaces of Raisina Hill with the crowded squatter settlement beyond the railway tracks where Anjani lives and from where he takes the long journey to work every day. But by placing and centering the precariat in spaces where they are not supposed to be seen, whether for pleasure or work, the film registers their claim to the city. Migrants like Anjani seem to confront the postliberalization state—"we are here because you were there"—and become spectral reminders and remainders of the costs of neoliberal policies that have led to their displacement. Like the trapped monkeys left on the edges of the city who will eventually find their way back again to the same spaces from which the humans want to expel them, and of which they were the original inhabitants, the presence of these disposable human bodies speaks to a reclaiming and haunting of the center by those the neoliberal state would rather invisibilize and marginalize or wish away.

In contrast to *Sui Dhaaga*, where the successful performance of subaltern Hindu masculinity through entrepreneurialism is valorized, *Eeb Allay Ooo!* exposes the lie and limits of enterprise. Its cruel promise creates and compounds the crisis of masculinity under neoliberal Hindutva. Through Anjani's portrayal, we get the economic and affective contours of nonhegemonic masculinities under neoliberalism. He is a young man who has migrated from the village to the city in the hope of securing a decent job, only to find himself in *narak* (hell) as he refers to his precarious employment situation. He finds no self-worth from the job in which he is constantly berated by the contractor and hazed and mocked by his coworkers. At home, a one-room living space that he shares with his pregnant sister and brother-in-law, he is reminded by them, even if kindly, that he should be a "grateful migrant" and suck it up since they've run from pillar to post to obtain this contractual job for him.

In addition, Anjani constantly feels his authority undermined by Kumudh—his educated, confident, and pragmatic girlfriend—who works as a doctor's assistant. Unlike *Sui Dhaaga, Eeb Allay Ooo!* refuses to mobilize coupledom or couple intimacy in aid of enterprise, instead depicting how the couple-in-progress disintegrates under the pressure of a precarious existence. We see how the tech-savvy Kumudh tries to help Anjani by making him listen to langur sounds on headphones so that he can immerse himself and better reproduce the call. Later, when he is fired from the job, she browses the internet for jobs for him. Anjani, however, comes to resent her, especially when she advises him to take up any job, including that of a "sweeper." As an upper-caste Hindu man, he doesn't see this job as befitting him. As the relationship between the abject Anjani and the aspirational Kumudh fizzles out, he drifts rudderless, battling feelings of displacement and failure.

Neoliberal Hindutva's promises, nonetheless, pervade the film's landscape. Anjani's sister holds on to the good life fantasy and tries to convince her frustrated brother (and herself) that he will flourish in spite of this job that's clearly physically and mentally wearing him down. "Try to put your heart in the job and work hard," she tells him. "Once you're steady on your feet, you can do what you feel like." In another scene, we see Anjani's sister in a temple, praying in front of an idol of the Hindu monkey deity, Hanuman, a devotee of the Hindu deity Ram from the *Ramayana*. She asks the priest a critical question: "God says that you should keep praying, and '*Achhe Din*' will follow. But when [will they come]?" Her invocation of "*Achhe Din*" [good days] is a direct reference to the Hindu nationalist BJP party's election marketing slogan in 2014, which suggested that its election would mean a prosperous future for everyone in the nation.

As scholars have noted, Modi "successfully harnessed the dream of 'good times' to the vehicle of Hindu nationalism and . . . instrumentalized the neoliberal formula of economic growth towards the making of a strong Hindu nation."[69] The BJP's promise of a rosy future might have convinced the Indian voter in 2014, but in the years that have followed, growth was lower than expected and the country faced the highest unemployment rate in forty-five years.[70] The promise of "good days" has been replaced by the aggressive mobilization of Hindu nationalist pride. In the film, as India's Republic Day—January 26—approaches, we see how citizens are inundated with nationalist messaging on media and in public spaces with loudspeakers blaring, "Nationalism should fill our hearts. We should all pray that our nation becomes powerful and successful." The sound of patriotic songs of sacrifice—such as "*Ae Mere Watan Ke Logon*" (O, people of my country), a song that was originally performed at India's Republic Day in 1963 to commemorate the martyr soldiers of the 1962 Sino-Indian War—fills the air. So, even as Anjani's family is in the throes of increasing economic and emotional insecurity, they are urged to think about Hindu or national pride and honor and to keep praying and making sacrifices for the success of the (Hindu) nation.

As we see in the film, however, religion ends up aggravating Anjani's material precarity even as Hindu nationalism holds out the promise of mitigating the feelings of displacement and failure that come from having no authority in a neoliberal economy.

Toward the beginning of the film, the monkey repellers watch an informational documentary as part of the new employee onboarding. In it, the monkey-god Hanuman is being worshipped in a temple. The voice-over narrates: "Because they [the monkeys] are treated as gods, they are given food, they are corrupted . . . they are made to think that they don't need to forage anymore, so they become bold. They start entering, they start demanding. Then the gods become pests." This reverence accredited to animals does indeed become pestilential, not just for Anjani but also for his comrade Mahender, leading to one man's loss of livelihood and the other man's loss of life.

We see how Anjani's job is made impossible by observant Hindus who feed the sacred monkeys and thus aggravate the "monkey menace" in neighborhoods. More than once, Anjani asks a middle-class Hindu bureaucrat not to feed the monkeys. The man insists that "sharing [his] hard-earned money with Hanuman-ji" is his right. At another moment, when Anjani confronts this official—sporting a *tilak* on his forehead, chanting a Hindu mantra to invite a monkey that he's anthropomorphized as "Sonu"—for feeding a banana to a monkey, Anjani is chastised in English and put in his place. "Who are you?," the man rhetorically inquires to let him know that he's a nobody, and he threatens to talk to Anjani's contractor. Not content with this power move, this same man complains to the contractor when he sees Anjani dressed in a langur costume, which ultimately leads to Anjani's firing. We don't know quite what the middle-class Hindu man's objection is. Does he find Anjani, a poor man's enterprise, threatening, or are his bourgeois aesthetic sensibilities injured by large posters of langurs around stately buildings, or is he offended by the fact that Anjani is scaring his beloved monkey-gods? In any case, what becomes clear is that both anthropomorphism and neoliberal Hindutva value certain humans and certain nonhuman animals more. This becomes tragically clear when Mahender is lynched by a presumably upper-caste Hindu mob for killing a monkey. It's a world, as the film's director puts it, "which is increasingly becoming hard to make sense of . . . a world where being a monkey is far more liberating than being human."[71]

The film features three deaths, two nonhuman animals and one human, and thus speaks to the intertwined reciprocal vulnerability of multiple species in an atmosphere of violence and precarity. Anjani kills a monkey with the catapult in response to feeling increasingly vulnerable and agitated by his inability to do his desperately needed job. Mahender also kills a monkey by mistake in self-protection and, in turn, becomes a victim of violence from a mob whose religious sentiments are incensed. These multiple deaths bring attention not only to the conjoined fates and dispensability of unwanted lives, human and nonhuman animal alike, under neoliberal Hindutva that governs through insecurity, but also to the distortions created under this regime where the nonhuman animal becomes the pretext for oppression of the human.

Mahender's "ungrievable" death sheds light on how Hindutva's Brahmanical and authoritarian logics, its oppressive politics of humanist differentiation and exclusion, prioritize animals more than some humans. In contrast to the monkey that Anjani kills, which with its open eyes appears uncannily alive on the morgue table, we do not see Mahender's dead body. Through his violent and abrupt expulsion from the narrative, the film makes its point about how little "value" the lives or deaths of some human beings are accorded. By mourning and remembering his friend's "unclaimed" body, however, Anjani refuses to let him become an uncounted, unregarded, or ungrieved life or death. Judith Butler notes that the "differential allocation of grievability that decides what kind of subject is and must be grieved, and which kind of subject must not, operates to produce and maintain certain exclusionary acts of nation-building."[72] In the film and in contemporary India, a "differential allocation of grievability" supports the exclusions of Hindu nationalism. Mahender's lynching by a mob recalls the chilling and ubiquitous stories of escalating violence from Hindu vigilantes policing the various elements of a Hindu social world.

The film brings attention to the mobilization or politicization and weaponization of the animal (cow, monkey, elephant) and meat eating in contemporary India where, in the name of animal rights, Hindu nationalists have hounded minorities, especially threatening the lives and livelihoods of Dalits and Muslims. In the name of cow protection and welfare, cow vigilantes harass and maim those they see as desecrating the sacred "Hindu mother cow," and these acts are either ignored or condoned and enforced by various right-wing state governments through beef consumption bans, cow slaughter bans, shutting down of slaughterhouses, setting up of cow shelters, promoting vegetarianism, and so on. Multiple scholars have studied the socioeconomic politics around meat in Modi's India—as we will also discuss in chapter 3—whether to show how Hindu vegetarianism is built around casteist beliefs or how the closing of slaughterhouses and beef bans have hurt the informal sector (composed of poor and rural Dalits and Muslims) that caters to domestic needs while enriching the corporate (Hindutva-affiliated) players involved in the export of beef.[73] Thus, far from being about animal welfare, many of the vigilante and legislative actions serve as a tool in the ruling Hindu right-wing government's authoritarian populist project. *Eeb Allay Ooo!* provides a commentary on how human and nonhuman precarity of existence is intertwined and contorted in the service of violent majoritarian politics. Thus, as Yamini Narayanan has argued, "the fullest extent of anti-casteist and anti-fascist politics in India, must then also compose an *anti-anthropocentric anti-Hindutva resistance*."[74]

The climax of the film leaves Anjani poised between a crisis-ridden present and an uncertain future. In this last scene, an unemployed Anjani, aimlessly roaming the streets of Delhi, is pulled into a Hindu religious procession. The palimpsestic mise-en-scène is suffused with meaning. Hindu visual and aural signifiers—saffron flag, Hindu mantras from a loudspeaker, the blowing of a conch shell—saturate the scene as Anjani joins the multitude of poor people who've gathered for free food that is being supplied as part of some Hindu religious event. A feverish energy characterizes the scene as the procession appears, probably a "Ramlila" enactment during the festival of Dussehra. There are actors on horses and floats dressed up in costumes as "Mother India" and as mythological Hindu deities (Ram and Shiva, painted in blue to echo a traditional iconography). Other actors, men dressed up as Hanuman and as monkeys and langurs, dance aggressively, staking a claim to the streets. These men conjure for audiences the image of the "Bajranj Dal," a militant Hindu right organization, named after "Hanuman's troops" or Ram's monkey army. They might also remind viewers of the "Angry Hanuman" image that has become ubiquitous in India since 2015, an image that transforms Hanuman into a belligerent and scowling figure much like the Hindu nationalist makeover of the Hindu deity Ram into a fearsome warrior, speaking both to the hypermasculinization-muscularization of Hindu deities and the unabated saffronization of urban and rural landscapes. In the scene, men in saffron—Hindu priests—with prominent forehead *tilaks* stand by and chant Hindu mantras. As someone "blackens" Anjani's face with paint to make it look like a langur's, Anjani dances frenetically as if possessed and becomes one with this crowd. In closeups and in slow motion, men in painted faces smile meaningfully and mysteriously at the camera before the film closes with a shot of a maniacally smiling Anjani.

The director explains how this ending "can mean many things—Has Anjani gone mad? Has everyone else around him gone mad? Is he defeated? Is he empowered? Is he dangerous now? Is it an impression of hope? Or an expression of hopelessness? To me, any of these (and more) are valid interpretations. The question is not really what it means but rather what one feels at the end of it."[75]

We read Anjani's cathartic bodily release as a critique of enterprise and the damage caused by its promise and relentless demands—of self-discipline, self-regulation, self-responsibilization—as a way to conquer socioeconomic precarity. This Anjani is Mad(e) in India; his "insanity" is manufactured in India, a product of the unbearable heaviness of life under the neoliberal economic order. Equally, the ending also reveals the kinds of politics—of right-wing populism—that the feeling of structural irrelevance, or irrelevance in the workplace, might create that would attract young and disenfranchised men like Anjani.[76] Hindu nationalist hegemonic masculinity holds out the promise of (homosocial) belonging to subaltern men like Anjani. What, indeed, is the meaning of the mysterious smiles of the men who look into the camera? Is it the smile of the insane precariat? Is it a knowing and victorious smile that shows how and why men like Anjani become recruited and baptized as foot soldiers for Hindutva's cause? We are confronted with this important question as the film nudges us to pay urgent heed to the toll that neoliberalism-induced precarities, and the accompanying grievances, are taking on subaltern men and the costs that society might pay by refusing to recognize and address them.[77]

Anjani's gravitation toward this religious procession is not exceptional, as it resonates with the ways in which unemployed male youth of India are constantly mobilized (literally made mobile) in the cause of religious pilgrimages. For example, the annual processions taken by *kanwariyas* have become India's largest religious gathering in the past few years (with an estimated twenty million participants). Historically, *kanwariyas*, devotees of the god Shiva, conduct a *yatra* or pilgrimage carrying a *kanwar*—a bamboo pole with water from the Ganga hanging from a brass container at each end—to a Shiv temple during the monsoon season in July. Commentators have noted many changes in the style and scale of this pilgrimage—and more generally the proliferating number and magnitude of Hindu religious celebrations—in the past decade and connected them to the workings of neoliberal Hindutva. Sociologist Vikash Singh, who has written a book[78] on the *kanwariyas*, argues that religion "seems to offer the only alternative to market fundamentalism and instrumental rationality; but it also sprouts in the same social field and hence is always already blended with the same forces of neoliberalism and jingoistic nationalism." The *kanwariya* pilgrimage, for instance, is increasingly dominated by precariously employed or unemployed aggressive young Hindu men (from all castes) who display muscular Hindu nationalism as they carry hockey sticks and fly the national flag. The *yatra* makes these otherwise powerless and prospectless men feel embattled, worthy, entitled, and empowered all at the same time. Snigdha Poonam writes that for the young men who participate in these pilgrimages, it offers them a brief "escape from the uncertainties of their daily lives" and becomes "their one chance to prove their talents—physical strength, resourcefulness, wit—without being faced with market realities."[79] In the film, the procession that Anjani joins seems composed of a similar demographic, of ordinary and poorly educated or underemployed or unemployed men on the move, primed to serve as Hindutva's warriors.

In this chapter, we have examined the convergence of Hindutva and neoliberalism through the ubiquitous discourse of entrepreneurialism that perpetuates and manages the crisis within hegemonic and subaltern Hindu masculinity. While all four films resonate in showing how the precarities created by Hindutva become the basis for recruitment by neoliberalism or vice versa for the protagonists, the films diverge in the intensity of their critique of enterprise as the passage out of precarity, a consequence also of their distinct status as mainstream, multiplex, or independent films. In the next chapter, we turn our attention to the spatial precarization of Muslims as we study the political reverberation of a range of films featuring Muslims and slums as these two "entities" are collapsed within the spatial politics of neoliberal capitalism and Hindu nationalism to support a chauvinist state's ethnonationalist agenda.

3: Spatial Precarization of Muslim Men

In the last two decades or so, the intensification of precarity experienced by religious minorities in India has expressed itself in and through Bollywood films predominantly as the Muslim=terrorist configuration. The threatening new avatar of the necessarily *Muslim* terrorist was not born overnight. Many things went into the making of this new filmic phenomenon. He (this menace of our times is almost invariably male) is the final expression of a long sequence of discursive and generic developments that in turn correspond to a range of sociological, legal, and attitudinal changes in the societal fabric of urban India. And, although nearly all scholarship on the "Muslim question" has noted the emergence and prevalence of the Muslim-as-terrorist configuration in many Hindi films, the spatial coordinates of such an equivalence remain the missing piece in the equation.

We draw attention to a different tendency in postmillennial films that address the "Muslim question" by studying the *spatial coordinates* of the Muslim=terrorist *equivalence* and by analyzing films that conflate slums and Muslims, two distinct social entities, one spatial and the other a religious identity. This produces a doubly inflected nightmare: slums crawling with, and controlled by, morally bankrupt and innately criminalized Muslims. A key intervention in this chapter is the unearthing of postmillennial cinema's complicity in authorizing a generalization of poor Muslim habitation in slums as inevitable terrorist dens and hideouts, a damning social identification achieved via the shorthand of the cinematic image.

What results is, simultaneously, an evocation of literal terrorism or symbolic terroristic-ness that masquerades as poverty, and a political narratology of the poor that views them as dangerous and threatening. Thus, films like *Black Friday* (2004), *Aamir* (2008), and even *Raees* (2017) allow for a right-wing synergy whereby a sectarian response to Indian Muslims can join forces with elite frustration about working-class tenements. The films, then, either overtly or suggestively, legitimate discourses that advocate, at a single stroke, for ridding the urban national-social space of both menaces: the urban poor and the terroristic criminal Muslim. In a film like *Gully Boy* (2018), however, the maneuver to delegitimate Muslims through an association with poverty and slums, and vice versa, follows a less xenophobic, totalitarian route. The solution there is bound up with the romanticization of neoliberal ethics. Precarity, in *Gully Boy*, is less the grounds for eviction—from the city and the nation—and more the inroad to assimilation and success. While all four films feature Muslims in slums, they do not engage in a similar vilifying or demonizing of Muslims and in some cases even present sympathetic portraits of Muslim protagonists, giving the films the potential to subtextually subvert Islamophobic right-wing Hindu nationalist discourse. Nonetheless, collectively, the films make accommodations with neoliberal Hindutva and feed into the dangerous othering of Muslims through the invisibilization, normalization, and obfuscation of the volatile intersectional precarization of the religious minority in postmillennial India.

Cumulatively, the cinematic transformation of slums into what Aravind Unni calls a "Muslim space"[1] enables us to register the imagistic terms from which no Muslim is exempt: NRIs, terrorists, criminals, gangsters, and even artists navigate, inhabit, and populate the slum. We also study how the spatial matrices of the slum in turn envelop, facilitate, and provide asylum to the "conspiratorial" machinations of its Islamic inhabitants, resulting in a double dynamic: what might be termed "*Muslim in the slum, the slum in the Muslim.*" By entwining the cinematic history of the slum with the evolving figure of the Muslim in Bollywood—trajectories that scholarship to date has seen as running parallel to each other—this chapter unearths Bollywood's efforts to locate the terrorist (the primary ethnoprofile stereotype of a Muslim in much post-1990s Hindi cinema) in a *spatial* way.

It is important to recall that in the history of popular Hindi cinema, neither the indigent nor the Muslim have always been stationary or cosubstitutable categories, nor automatic recipients of derision and fear. On the contrary, even a quick retrospective of the cinematic depiction of slums and Muslims down the decades makes clear a richly variegated history. We find a range of sometimes microscopic and at other times dramatic shifts that annotate the onscreen history of these respectively spatial and denominational entities. Indeed, in order to fully grasp the magnitude and repercussions of this new doubled copula—Muslim-and-slum, Muslim-in-slum—we must contend with each constituent of the couple in turn. A substantial portion of this chapter will be concerned with charting these distinct and independent dual histories—of the filmic slum and the changing figure of the Muslim in Bombay cinema—in the hope of arriving at some exegetical accounting of when, how, and why the two converged in the form of a highly value-laden coupling.

This fusing of the histories, respectively, of the slum and of Muslims in Hindi films isn't something fortuitous. It corresponds, even if tenuously and tangentially, to the sociopolitical and cultural discourses articulated by the state, affirmed by the legal machinery, trumpeted by the media, and regurgitated by informal channels of knowledge dissemination and rumor circulation, the various strands that ostensibly cohere the nation. Thus, the film texts under consideration in this chapter manifest the nation's shifting lenses toward certain designated spaces and communities. Given that such films variously observe, endorse, and dismantle the nation as an "imagined community," we might then usefully think of Hindi cinema as bearing witness to the continuously altering, tumultuous, and even violent relationship between the "nation and its fragments."[2] And yet these films do more than just mimetically reflect; they also proactively narrativize and semantically emplot violent events and histories spawned by both the state and citizens. In so doing, they perform and participate in a precarity production of their own.

Slums on Screen: Sites and Sights of Poverty[3]

Igor Krstić's *Slums on Screen: World Cinema and the Planet of Slums* (2016) offers a rare articulation of the role that indigent spaces have played in the representation of the cinematic city. Krstić's critical contribution lies in demonstrating that slums never appear as value-neutral spaces; the aesthetics of their spatialization is "indissolubly entangled" with political and ethical concerns.[4] India has the largest slum population in the world; unsurprisingly then, the slum city has always gripped popular Hindi cinema's imagination. The constant flow of migrants in search of work and prospects from the rural hinterland into urban centers inevitably rewrote India's urban map. Certain parts of the city morphed to accommodate new hopefuls who arrived here without work or shelter, in search of both, convinced that the city alone could guarantee their hopes of upward mobility. Discussing Calcutta and Bombay, Partha Chatterjee describes the preliberalization city as one that, however grudgingly, accommodated the poor into its sociopolitical contours through informal techniques, thus acknowledging that the city's economy could not subsist without their precarious labor and services.[5] There was a recognition that though the poor were the effluvia—the excess and waste—of modernity and urbanism and that they produced an "unintended city—the city that was never a part of the formal 'master plan' but was always implicit in it"—they nevertheless formed the constructivist bedrock without which the planned "official city" could never exist or survive, let alone thrive.[6]

In the early decades after Independence, popular Hindi films did not shy away from foraying into the disenfranchised spaces of the city. It was perhaps a result of its embracing of the Nehruvian socialist vision that it recorded the informal techniques that wove the poor into the city's landscape. The postcolonial Indian city, then, in actuality and in Hindi cinema, made room—within an urban and cinematic geography—for the city's poor, their necessities, and their residential territories.

Ashis Nandy proposes a possible explanation for the natural affinity, in the decades following Independence, between Hindi films and the "unintended city." The "urban slum," he suggests, is the most apt "metaphor" for popular Hindi cinema because both display the "same impassioned negotiation with everyday survival, combined with the same intense effort to forget that negotiation."[7] He extends the analogous relationship between slum and film by suggesting that popular cinema, because of its "stress on lower-middle-class sensibilities," is "the slum's point of view of Indian politics and society, and for that matter, the world."[8] Indeed, right up to the 1990s, the overall political and aesthetic vision of popular Hindi cinema was closely tied up with the nation's class subalterns. That figurative analogy aside, it is arguable that through its constant reiteration of the existence of the poor, cinema helped empower, through spotlighting, the "discarded and obsolete population that inhabits the unintended city." A population encouraged by official intent to "bow out of history" thus returns, like the Freudian uncanny, to "occupy a large space in the public domain, geographically and psychologically."[9] Popular cinema thus mediated the return of a banished underclass into the Indian city's imagination of itself.

Popular Hindi cinema's willingness, eagerness even, to record the lives of slum and *chawl*-dwellers[10] in turn produced a fascination with non-built-up, unofficial spaces of the city: the streets, the sidewalks, and footpaths, the sundry sites and improvised places of itinerant squatting that welcomed people who may have arrived in the city physically but hadn't quite "arrived" within its chimeral habitus. The footpath leitmotif allowed films from the 1950s through the 1970s to sketch memorable and indeed archetypal filmic vignettes of unskilled migrant workers and industrial laborers gathering together to recreate a village-like communitarian existence on the city's marginal outdoor locales. The "footpath" as generic topos thus blended traditional forms of village-square familiality with the more clearly "modern" cosmopolitanism of the city street.[11]

This dual and contradictory nature of the cityscape (urban/rural, modern/traditional, developed/underdeveloped) contoured the affective and ideological framing of first-generation post-Independence cinema. The enthusiastic desire for a propulsive march toward modernization, cosmopolitanism, and technological advancement went hand in hand with considerable ambiguity and anxiety. The violence of modernity, its frenzied pace, its deracinating strain, the tenuous anomie of urban life, the rigors and uncertainties of urban joblessness and poverty: such breaks in the bright, smooth map of progress did not entirely cancel the newly independent nation's ringing affirmation of its developmental promise. But the less-than-savory actualities of metropolitan existence did cast a shadow of dubiety upon any too pat and easy celebratory narrative of the postcolonial nation and its rapidly burgeoning cities.

Films such as *Shri 420* and *Deewar* (the latter featuring Amitabh Bachchan in his trademark "angry young man" avatar), although separated in time by some two decades (and certainly miles apart in political tenor and aesthetic style), do nonetheless share in common Hindi cinema's will to archive and harvest the traumas of urban alienation. Such landmark films thus set the stage for a spatial-ideological dialogue between the "city of the rich" and "the city of the poor," often weighing in morally in favor of the latter's claims. Even though the films did not offer a problem-free or viable solution to the social and spatial challenges of inhabitancy faced by the poor, they gave narrative expression to a political need to grapple with the implicated social concerns: basic housing for the poor, the manipulative ploys and cruelty of the rich, the ineffectiveness of bourgeois law in taking on the blights of social inequity and exclusion, the role of protests and struggles by disenfranchised groups to partly restore the balance and retrieve some claim to a share in a city which they, the working poor, after all helped build.

In the scholarship on Indian films, two studies in particular stand out for their serious attempt at tracing a history of slums on the screen. Amrit Gangar explores in some depth the cinematic history of slums, or *chawls*. Gangar discusses eight *chawl* films (from the 1960s to 2003) to argue that most of them, despite their documentation of the workaday facts of quotidian existence, end up romanticizing the *chawl* as a cosmopolitan utopia.[12] He lays out a systematic typology of *chawls* most commonly seen in such films:

> [They] evocatively capture the chawl space and spirit; the way human beings manoeuvre and negotiate in quest of their own aspirations. The chawl is a place where everyone knows everyone else; it is a huge extended family in comparison to the bungalows and villas of the rich: the spaces generally stereotyped as sources of corruption and immorality. *Space* then acquires an ethical dimension, glorifying poverty, and privileging the size of space inside the "dil" (heart) and not the physical space outside.[13]

Moreover, the "generous use of extras,"[14] "privacy obliterating" openness,[15] and a self-conscious construction of "chawl-chalgat" create a framework whereby multiple storylines can coexist in the film. As a result, the narrative form of these films duplicates the spatial parallelism and interwovenness that characterizes the physical and architectural organization of the *chawl* itself. What seems missing from Gangar's analysis, though, is any accounting of the sharp fall in the *chawl*'s presence in Bombay films since the onset of liberalization, or, at the very least, a dramatic alteration in its mode of depiction.

This is a dimension identified and extensively discussed by Ranjani Mazumdar. Following the ascendancy of the liberalized global economic arrangement, Mazumdar argues, Bollywood became invested in depicting "consumer-oriented families . . . geared to global mobility."[16] Postliberalization cinema was defined by a preoccupation with a "panoramic interior,"[17] "commodity display," "the aestheticization of streets through the spread of visual signage and surfaces," and an "individualized and depoliticized subjectivity,"[18] together constituting the "urban delirium" of a thriving and posh megacity.[19] This cinematic "city of spectacle"[20] assiduously distances itself from unsettling encounters with the face of poverty and propels "the fantasy of a lifestyle unblemished by the chaos and poverty that exists all around."[21]

Cinema's growing disengagement from India's indigenous poor and its ignoring of nonelite audiences in favor of pandering to diasporic ambitions and international patronage is no accident. It is part and parcel of a major attitudinal shift in urban India's discursive, juridical, and policy-making response to the country's disadvantaged populations. This change may indeed be traced within a larger global context, best captured by the UN's 1999 "cities without slums" initiative. Revisiting the nineteenth-century etymological roots and political associations of the word "slum," Alan Gilbert argues that by reviving the highly emotive and connotatively charged word, the UN initiative resurrects old myths about the poor as disease-ridden criminals, in the bargain confusing the dilapidated quality of housing cities have to offer the poor with the moral characteristics of the people living in them. As a result, "Slums and slum dwellers are viewed as constituting one undifferentiated problem."[22]

Scholars of contemporary Indian cities suggest that this intolerance toward the poor is a postliberalization phenomenon and bespeaks tacitly announced changes in the conception of citizenship today. In the early decades of postcolonial India, state socialist ideologies tended to depict workers or rural villagers in idealizing terms, as the archetypal citizens.[23] By contrast, since the 1990s, the "mainstream national political discourses increasingly depict the middle classes as the representative citizens of liberalising India."[24] What this has manufactured is "consumer citizenship,"[25] or what Ghertner would term "property citizenship," a model of citizenship where those with purchasing power and private property get enfranchised as eligible citizens with rights to public land and facilities (manicured parks with jogging tracks, malls), while "squatters" or those living in informal settlements are excluded from any such consideration.[26]

Through a meticulous study of judicial documents, Ghertner, Kalyani

Menon-Sen, and Gautam Bhan traced a changing attitude on the part of courts and justice delivery agencies toward poverty and slums to demonstrate that, more than ever before, courts have made aggressive interventionist judgments that delegitimize working-class colonies as "illegal."[27] The antipoor judgments made by the courts conflate slum dwellers with the "garbage and solid waste" and "muck and debris" that slums produce,[28] dehumanising the spaces of the poor and thus the poor themselves by deploying the word "slum" as an adjective and verb rather than a noun, transforming it from a "place" to a "disease and condition."[29] In the end this paradigmatic and discursive shift is due to a radical reimagining of urban sociospatial aesthetics per se and to the desire to transform "walled cities"[30] into "world cities."[31] Unlike the preliberalization postcolonial city, the neoliberal city is impatient with all that cannot fit into a slicked up and marketable version of itself. The dream project then is to build what Solomon J. Greene calls "staged cities" whose geographies are strategically redesigned—by concealing the misfit landscapes of the poor and by a state-sanctioned policy of displacement—to host international "mega-events."[32] Thus, among the frightening consequences of this politics of "spatial purification"[33] is that it exalts slum clearance into a "just and ethical" enterprise of "good governance," rather than recognizing forcible relocation as an act of violence committed by the state against the city's most vulnerable demographic segments.[34]

This ongoing "politics of forgetting"[35] and growing spatial-cultural "amnesia"[36] toward the poor rooted in a fantasy of "cities without slums" translates into the cinematic practice of producing "films without slums." Slums now feature in films primarily when violence and terror have to be shown.[37] At the same time, even as post-1990s Hindi films typically distance themselves from cartographies and thematic renditions of indigence and deprivation, preferring to luxuriate wholesale in the glitzy bourgeois city with its sanitized spaces of consumption, there are some exceptions to the rule. In "Cinematic Clearances,"[38] Megha Anwer studies two box-office hits from the first decade of the twenty-first century, *Kabhi Khushi Kabhi Gham* and *3 Idiots*, to argue that even such cult films, despite their primary focus on and identification with the city's successful and slick spaces, can include some attempts, albeit equivocal and ambivalent, to incorporate the poorer urbanites within their filmic economy. She demonstrates that rather than simply disappearing the poor, what transpires in such films is a more insidious process. The films integrate the slum in their city landscape only to neutralize its dangers aesthetically by excising unsavory "scenes of poverty." Or they render poverty something ludicrous and farcical, a subject for poor jokes and bathos, and thus a phenomenon politically inconsequential and not worth bothering about. Thanks to this presentational legerdemain, even if depicted as nonviolent and inoffensive, even perhaps quirkily lovable, the locales of poverty come through as innocuous, unsustainable, and above all uninhabitable by "real" people, that is, people who matter.

From Nawab to Gangster, Poet to Gunman: The Muslim's Journey in Hindi Cinema

Several studies have charted the on-screen career of Muslims in popular Hindi cinema. Commentators have identified the Muslim figure's fluctuating presence on screen, the shifts and changes of this image evolving in tandem with different cinematic genres and styles. Importantly, such modulations in representation have been taken as symptomatic of a continuously morphing relationship between the nation and its principal religious minority. Of particular interest in this context are the effects of the increasingly assertive majoritarian politics that in the past few decades—especially since 2014—have been aggressively embraced by Hindu right-wing outfits. Inevitably, the primary object of their vituperative attacks—the Muslim—has endured the consequences of such a polarizing and precarizing politics.

Commentators such as Mukul Kesavan, Ira Bhaskar, and Richard Allen have undertaken extensive examinations of what they respectively designate as the "Islamicate" roots and "cultures" of Bombay cinema.[39] Focusing on films of the 1950s and 1960s, Mukul Kesavan grapples with the irony of a cinematic tradition emerging out of a predominantly Hindu cultural ambience that, notwithstanding the official fostering of a rapidly Sanskritized public sphere, in films stayed loyal to its reliance on Urdu (the refined and elegant language identified with North Indian Muslims) and deeply embedded in an aesthetic of "Muslimness."[40] The genre of films termed "Muslim Socials" in the decades immediately following independence is a notable case in point. In these films (such as *Mere Mehboob*, My Beloved, H. S. Rawail, 1963) the speech, dress, social mannerisms and milieu, and certainly the poetical Urdu lyrics of Bombay films' beloved set piece songs, were for the most part Islamic.[41] At one level, these films humanized and normalized the minority community by pitching their lives within that staple of mainstream cinema: a romantic plot. At the same time, however, the nostalgic idealization of Muslims in the Muslim Social fixed the Muslims in a premodern world, and the lack of any real engagement with the community's post-Partition socioeconomic realities, or the contemporary challenges facing them, tended to derealize the Muslim.[42]

Outside of the Muslim Social genre, the most familiar typology of Muslim characters in films of the 1950s and 1960s was a safe one: that of the "hero's" best buddy. This would be an amusing and witty (or less flatteringly a buffoonish) figure who often featured in the comic subplot of the film. It was a choice of safety because alongside interfaith friendship, a desired ideal and image of *domination-subordination* was encapsulated here in an inoffensive mode so one could laugh indulgently with (at?) the lovelorn Urdu *shair* (poet) played by prize comedienne Johnny Walker.[43] At the same time, on a kindlier reading, the camaraderie between the hero and his Muslim *yaar* (pal) allegorized the wish for close bonds of friendship between the two communities in Nehru's India, signifying triumph over the lingering disaffections of the Partition, as long as the proper hierarchies of the relationship were not forgotten.

With the decline of the Muslim Social genre in the 1970s we find an accelerated "disappearance" and "marginalization" of Muslims in Bollywood cinema[44] as these characters get reduced entirely to a "supporting capacity."[45] And even though these adjunct characters, now playing necessary second fiddle to the Hindu protagonist, were more ordinary, "everyday people," they continued to be delineated as stereotyped abstractions (sporting skull caps, offering *namaz*), even as individualizing details of their social backgrounds, class positions, and personal dispositions and histories—and certainly any elements of inner complexity or psychological depth—were glossed over and ignored.[46] By entirely tokenizing their presence, Bollywood's latter-day Muslim portrayals thus succumbed even more to what Maidul Islam calls a "hegemonic majoritarianism."[47]

By the 1990s, however, the friendly if yokelish stereotype of the Muslim more or less vanished, giving way to an entirely different typology. The fanatical "terrorist" with his unbridled aggression, the mobster, the pimping nasty, the trigger-happy hit man, the maniacal and psychopathic patriarch,[48] these were (and remain) the face of the Muslim in the Bollywood film. Behind the change of image lay key revisions in societal perception. The relentless rise of Hindu right-wing political forces since the late 1980s, the sectarian polarization created by the Ram Janmabhoomi movement and the post-Ayodhya riots of 1992–1993,[49] and the global context of America's "War on Terror" in the aftermath of 9/11, may be seen as multiple and convulsive politico-historical nodal points that directly contribute to the revamping of Muslims in films as the radically evil "demonised Other."[50] As it is, Muslims have carried the burden of a double stigma: they are accused of being antinationals or what Sumita Chakravarty calls the "undecidable"[51]—people whose loyalty to the nation cannot be counted on—and at the same time as a pampered minority that, in the Hindu imaginary, is constantly appeased by Indian politicians as part of a vote-bank politics.

The cumulative endpoint of these multiple factors and lines of development both onscreen and off has meant that Bollywood's Muslim has by now morphed from the fumbling-bumbling but basically benign and unoffending "hero's companion" figure of yesteryear, to the living avatar of the archetypal archenemy. The nongangster Muslim, the average local workshop "*mian-bhai*," the socially assimilated "normal" citizen next door who happens to bear an Islamic name, these comfortable memorials from a bygone filmography have now become dispensable presences, increasingly extinct. Even when they do make a token appearance once in a while—as in *Sarfarosh* (Martyr, 1999) or *Mission Kashmir* (2000) (both of which have Muslim police officers willing to die a martyr's death for the nation)—the "good" Indian Muslim must labor under a special pressure to endlessly "prove" himself loyal and "against" the evil Muslim "out there" who is the eerie figure of wickedness that remains more compelling, more tangible, and more recognizably and "truly" Muslim.[52]

It is along these two different axes that Bollywood constructs and categorizes the "bad" and "good" Muslim. First of all, these categories gain meaning from the Muslim's understood role of affiliation or disloyalty vis-à-vis the Indian nation. The second and more tricky, oblique way in which this categorization works is by a dialectic of required opposition: Here the "good" Muslim must constantly labor to "prove" that he *is not* the "bad" Other. Acceptable Indian Muslims must now don fatigues as steely-eyed military or police personnel whose raison d'etre must be to hunt down the "bad" *mozzies*.[53] This is more than a mere job or professional assignment. In the Muslims' case it is *the* existential choice for them: to face and overcome the temptation to join "that side," and only thus (perhaps) wipe off the stigma of ignominy for "their" part in the 1947 Partition. Nothing less than to unmake *mozzie* Pakistan is what it takes to prove oneself loyal to India.[54] Unsurprisingly, a concomitant development in Indian cinema since the 1990s has been an upsurge of "cine-patriotism."[55] The hallmark of this subgenre is its uninhibitedly jingoistic movie discourse, or more exactly a raging tirade directed against the neighboring nation. The name "Pakistan" functions here as a sort of elaborate code word that allows intense Islamophobic sentiments to be legitimately aroused in the contemplation of large Muslim demographic concentrations in one politico-geographic space. The unspoken tacit innuendo here is that all Muslims are by association Pakistanis.[56]

Barring a few films, postmillennial cinema continues to peddle in representations of Muslims as terrorists or criminals. For instance, a subgenre of Bollywood films are set against the global context of America's "War on Terror" in the aftermath of 9/11: *Kurbaan* (Sacrifice, Rensil D'Silva, 2009), *New York* (Kabir Khan, 2009), and *My Name Is Khan* (Karan Johar, 2010). In these films, a peculiar side effect of diasporic ambitions seeking eagerly to accommodate themselves within a post-9/11 Islamophobic ethos is that the good South Asian Muslim asserts their loyalty not so much to the Indian nation but to the United States of America, the *Ur*-nation that all the more stringently demands anti-Islamist loyalty as its pound of welcome flesh from its immigrant population. In such films as *New York* and *My Name Is Khan*, "good" Muslim protagonists struggle to disavow a conservative, reactionary Islamism that villainously identifies itself as critical of America's neoimperialist geopolitics. And while Muslims as ordinary human beings, as regular Indian citizens, as not terrorists or defined always by their relationship of loyalty to the nation, do exist in films of the past decade (such as Zoya Akhtar, *Dil Dhadakne Do*, 2015; *Zindagi Na Milegi Dobara*, 2011; Gauri Shinde, *Dear Zindagi*, 2017), these representations unfortunately remain few and far between.[57]

"Outsiders" in Urban Crevices: The Muslim and the Cinematic Slum

It is within this larger cinematic context that the figure of the Islamic terrorist harboring in the city slum reappears repeatedly in the postmillennial Hindi film. It creates a two-track vilifying genealogy—of marked city spaces as well as religious minority populations—in suspect identification. Notably, this is a conjuncture that is formulated in contrast to and reversion of past avatars assumed by the Muslim onscreen. The convergence and coupling onscreen of a criminalized urban space (the slum) and a putatively nefarious religious group (Muslims) serves to articulate and indeed purposively whip up a whole new set of insecurities and modes of tackling them.

A common connecting thread in these twin discourses—the one centered on the perception of an "Islamist threat," the other on the unhygienic and disorderly state of slum dwellers—is the convenient construction of both as "outsiders." So the Muslim gets positioned as "alien" to the nation, just as the slum is an indigestible alien ("foreign") presence in the slicked-up postmodern city.[58] As cities (whether Delhi, Bangalore, Mumbai, Calcutta, and others) continue to eradicate spaces of poverty to fit a globalized neoliberal aesthetic, and urban space is increasingly reorganized along religious lines, scholars who study spatiality in contemporary India have suggested how slum demolitions neatly tie together the current government's neoliberal and Hindutva ambitions.[59] There are unmistakable parallels between the judicial vocabulary invoked to justify the evacuation and demolition of slums and the chauvinistic rhetoric of majoritarian political formations like the BJP and the Shiv Sena. The homologies of thinking and attitude articulate a spatial and communal cleansing intention.

On the one hand, courts put their legal weight against slum populations by making judgments that warn the urban poor against staking spurious claim to city spaces and amenities, since "nobody forced [them] to come" to the city.[60] On the other hand, government-run initiatives such as "Operation Pushback"—a program started in Delhi during the 1990s aimed at ridding the city of allegedly illegal Bangladeshi immigrants[61]—read non grata Muslims—index a new and totalized urban intolerance for those who cannot be taken as "official" denizens of the metropolis: that is, the rich, the propertied, and the well-accoutred. In fact, the initiative's nomenclature blatantly converts the populations who inhabit slums (since Bangladeshi migrants are reputed to be primarily slum dwellers) into "infiltrators," a contaminative national threat that demands a militaristic "pushback." At a stroke, bulldozers that mow down poor housing tenements, and state-sponsored armed interventions that stave off insidious threats to national security, become parallel and equally permissible and desirable safety measures, coterminous in their search for safety and homogeneity. In fact, in contemporary India, bulldozers have emerged as a Hindu nationalist symbol, as they have become an extrajudicial tool wielded by right-wing Hindu politicians to quell dissent and administer instant mob justice by demolishing poor Muslim homes, businesses, and places of worship with imputiny.[62]

Tellingly, the word "operation," with efficient techno-logistical neutrality, straddles the domains of medicine, military strategizing, and administrative planning. And yet the "will to eviction" to which the term "operation" accords a techno-legal rationality is the very mentalité that resounds through the hate-inciting demagogy resorted to by sectarian inciters. It isn't surprising then that, in 1984, the Shiv Sena supremo Bal Thackeray had deployed this very word ("operation") in the context of Muslim bashing in Bombay. Declaring Muslims to be "a cancer on this country," he urged Hindus to take up arms and perform the "only cure" possible—an "operation"—to "remove this cancer from its very roots."[63] The doubly surgical-military metaphor is thus the go-to rhetorical device to excise the city and nation of "rats," "poisonous snakes," "traitors," derogatory words, unmistakably reminiscent of Nazi rants against Jews and gypsies, and used here by Thackeray for India's Muslims.[64] Such biopolitical metaphors not only play upon the imputed treachery of the nation's Muslims (evoked here as the "*aasteen ka saanp*"/the snake that roosts concealed in one's sleeve, waiting for the chance to bite and inject its toxin into the political body), they also "slummify" Muslim populations by aligning them in their lack of privilege with the image of poor hygiene and subhuman, slushy, roach-ridden living conditions associated with the city's poor.

Most of the films we study that are located in India's film and commercial capital of Bombay (renamed Mumbai in 1995) offer a variant on this *will to conflation*, a conjuncture in which the very identity of the Muslim becomes inextricably intertwined with the spatial topography, but also the negative "moral economy" associations of the slum. The upshot of such a twin-pronged evocation is that both entities stand communalized: The films render the Muslim slum dweller indistinguishable from a terrorist villain, and by the same token the *slum* becomes instantly identifiable in the popular imaginary of cine-audiences as *that place where terrorists hide out.* Read another way, there is no such thing as a poor Muslim, only a terrorist wearing poverty as camouflage. It follows that the urgent need to eradicate one entails, necessarily, eradication of the other. Space-linked identity becomes the premise and rationale for the will to expel.

It is not coincidental that in most of these films, it is especially the city of Bombay that furnishes the locus for such an identity-spatiality merging. In a sense, the postcolonial history of the city incorporates the origins of such a potential conflation. Several scholars have discussed at length the cultural transformation that Bombay has undergone: the collapse of its textile industry and its subsequent deindustrialization in the 1980s, and the city's transformation into the finance capital of India. On the sociocultural and ideological front this finds reflection in a rapid embracing of sectarian violence and a nativist assignation of "ownership" of the city. In Thackeray's "sons of the soil" vision a once cosmopolitan and vibrantly heterogeneous Bombay, in its new avatar as "Mumbai," is claimed solely for native Maharashtrians.

This process, culminating in the 1992–1993 riots in the aftermath of the demolition of a historic mosque in Ayodhya and the city's renaming as "Mumbai" in 1995, results in the city's progressive "decosmopolitanization,"[65] or, in Rashmi Varma's phrasing of the matter, in Bombay's growing "provincialization,"[66] which has resulted in increasing precarization of the Muslim/poor. Arjun Appadurai masterfully lays out the linkages between Bombay's housing crisis and its "ethnic mobilization"[67] that invites charismatic attraction to a "public spectacle of violence."[68] The unglamorous real situation of Bombay—a swollen megacity bursting at the seams with its ever-proliferating *chawls*, skyrocketing real estate prices, and a frightening space crunch—can easily be turned by the master magician's touch into a fantasy of "cleansed space, a space without Muslim bodies." The insecurity around urban space is transformed into a state-sanctioned precarization of Muslims. And the hope is presented as realizable through the unleashing of large-scale riots designed to rescript an "urban nightmare" into a "national dream."[69] Interestingly, the reclaiming of Bombay's public space within a sacred Hindu national cartography from which Muslims have been expurgated has not meant that the city turns its back on the other dream: capitalist modernity and high-finance affluence. On the contrary, Bombay, once styled a maritime "gateway to India," today aspires to be India's "gateway to the world." In fact, the procedure of ethnic cleansing, depopulating Muslim homes, and the creation of a Muslim-free society begins to be touted as a "bizarre utopia of urban renewal," the very means through which a crisis-ridden cityscape can resurrect itself to enter the hallowed glories of international markets and neoliberal economic prosperity.

Our contention here is that Bollywood films, by their obsession with "dangerous" Muslims harboring in slums, enacts and helps instate precisely this sinister urban fantasy. The films discussed in this chapter allow us to identify the process by which Muslims dwelling in "spectral housing" (slums) are recast as "spectral citizens," beings at once amorphous, incubus-like, and dangerous. Precarious spaces and precarious social identities are forced into a convergence. As a nation bent on cleansing itself of "illegally" infiltrative Muslims continues with its "war on terror," and as cities continue to undergo gentrification through the eradication of slums, Bollywood converts this two-pronged problem, viz. the dual "problem" of slums and Muslims, into a single one: that of *Muslims-in-slums*, thus manufacturing a simultaneously classed and communalist "solution" for the city's greatest menaces. The resulting "final solution" thus becomes a wonderfully simple and manageable "operation." Removing the poor and hunting down Muslim dons and extremists, in screen time, become one and the same action and strategy. Getting rid of one automatically rids us of the other; the old proverbial logic comes in handy: two birds, one stone.

From Topophilia to Terror-Phobia: Mumbai's Generic Landscape and the Slum as Terrorist Shelter in *Black Friday*

Anurag Kashyap's 2004 film *Black Friday* recounts the story of the 1993 bomb blasts in Bombay. In the aftermath of the demolition of the Babri mosque in Ayodhya by Hindu right cadres and leaders on December 6, 1992, different parts of India flared up in communal riots. Bombay was among the major cities devastatingly affected. For weeks the city blazed. Conservative estimates put the death toll at about 900 (two-thirds of casualties were Muslims). "[M]ore than 150,000, mainly Muslims, fled the city; and more than 100,000 took shelter in hastily erected refugee camps in Muslim areas in central Bombay."[70] The city's law-and-order machinery—under unofficial orders from Shiv Sena leader Bal Thackeray, then in power at the state center—adopted an openly Muslim-baiting attitude, often aiding Hindu rioters while turning a blind eye to Muslim localities that needed protection and using excessive violence against minority citizens. A few months later, in March 1993, several bomb blasts, planned and orchestrated by the Muslim underworld—the head honcho of which, Dawood Ibrahim, operates out of Dubai—brought the city to a standstill. Most accounts of the blasts read them as avenging the murder, rape, and humiliation of Muslims during the infamous Bombay riots.

Kashyap's *Black Friday* opens seismically with the blast detonations, and the rest of the film recounts the means by which the police pieced together the terrorist conspiracy and arrested the culprits. We are led through an itinerary based on the unsparing rounding up of suspects, brutal interrogation tactics, and reliance on the police's widely cast net of informers. The sheer number of phone calls made in this film—not only between the conspirators planning the blasts but also between the police agencies and their army of informants—opens up an astounding new dimension in the classic police drama: what we might term an informational panopticon of surveillance tactics. An endless number of scenes reference utterly marginal characters (who never again appear in the film) pick up a phone, dial a number, and pass on some detail as to the supposed whereabouts of suspects.[71]

Noteworthy here is the insistent, nearly machinic repetitiveness of these scenes, as though these were well-rehearsed set routines out of some investigation manual. The effect is to blur out the actual words spoken during these telephonic conversations; after the first few times we barely even register the actual information relayed. The phone call instead begins to function as a cinematic trope, a metonymic stand-in for everything that must follow: a cat-and-mouse chase between police and suspects, then a gruesome and viscerally violent interrogation scene, in turn followed by more of the same based on new information garnered from the detainee . . . ad infinitum, ad nauseum. Our relationship with terror, and thus with Muslims, unfolds completely predictably, as a tedium of the extreme.

Interestingly though, *Black Friday* never seeks recourse to a euphemistic visual vocabulary. Declining to bypass the spelling out of details of a police roundup, it never compresses or foreshortens the long hunt for terrorists, choosing instead to replay the same saga over and over in all its excruciating detail and by now recognizable minutiae. Eventually, the rhetorical power of the film's repetition trope converts what is otherwise a haphazard game of random coincidences, chance encounters, unspecific backdoor exchanges, and gossipy information circulation into a well-oiled drill that appears set in stone: rigorous, protocoled, calculated to achieve efficiently predictable results. Of all the hundreds of Muslims arrested in the film, not one, miraculously, is a wrongful arrest,[72] and not one fails to produce the desired result, whether in the form of a confession, further information, or simply strategic humiliation and demoralization of the conspirators. And quite ingeniously, once the bar for what is to be achieved from the interrogations is set so low, or rather spread so thin that merely the "terrorization of the terrorist" is a good enough agenda and end objective, then any "result" of the inquisition—even a terrified Muslim face—automatically notches as an investigational "success" for the police. This explains why the police never face a moment of hesitation or frustration nor come up against a single dead end in their case. Everything yields something.

Black Friday is an unmistakably urban film. Almost compulsively, like a murderer returning to the scene of crime, the terrorists return to Bombay even after they've been given strict instructions from the high command (Tiger Memon and Dawood Ibrahim) to leave the city and go underground. Seemingly desperate, drawn like a moth to the flame, they come back from their outstation hideouts only to be caught by the police inevitably. One can never be sure what it is about Bombay that magnetizes them back to their doom: Is it simply the impossibility of getting on elsewhere? A sense of outsider-ness in their ancestral villages? Paranoia about being hunted down no matter where they go? Or is it the itinerant jobs and worried families that await them in Bombay? No one really knows. And yet it is this very absence of a clear-cut explanation that makes the auratic power of Bombay even more compelling.

Even then, there is no easy way to suggest that *Black Friday* is a topophilic film that revels in its locus-love for Bombay. Quite the contrary: the cinematic methods of mapping the city reveal little commitment to exploring the "specificities" of Bombay.[73] What we find instead is a deployment of puerile and formulaic scenes of crowds, packed *mohallas*, predictable set shots of the faithful offering namaz in mosques, prison cells overrun with inmates, and the concluding final detail of the "routine" inside filthy interrogation rooms where cowering detainees are stripped down and tortured.

The purposive repetitiveness of the film mentioned earlier, combines with the hurtling speed at which locations change: the Bombay stock exchange quickly gives way to bylanes in lower-class residential colonies, garages where bombs are manufactured, warehouses where raw materials for bombs are stockpiled, ports where this material lands easily. Such predictable yet random impressions blend into one another; homes of individual terrorists and the slums where they hide out are made indistinguishable from one another. If, as Teresa Castro argues, cinema is a means of "territorializing" space, giving it an identity and meaning, structuring our geographical imagination that affects how we understand cities and act upon them,[74] then *Black Friday*'s rendition of Bombay—hotels in which terrorists congregate or plant bombs, airports they travel through, main roads they drive down—produces a kind of reverse topophilia: an apathetic inchoateness, a blur of sensory impressions, and, mood-wise, a strangely inconsolable disenchantment with urban inhabitancy. Overall, the sense persists of a distinct inability to reproduce on screen what, to borrow Giuliana Bruno's phrase, one might call Bombay's "intimate geography."[75]

To this extent, there is a dramatic disjunction between the terroristic conception of Bombay's strategic import and uniqueness and the film's own aleatory treatment of the cityscape. At the end of the film, which chronologically marks the beginning of events, we witness the moment when the plan for the bomb blasts was hatched. A group of five to six Muslim males are engaged in a heated discussion about how to avenge the demolition of the Babri Masjid and destruction of Muslim life and property during the riots following and how to bring "Hindu rule and Hindus to their knees." Tiger Memon addresses these men in an emphatic, sonorous voice, rendering a one-word answer to all their questions: "Bombay." When asked what he means, he elaborates: "Bombay! It is India's financial capital. If we declare war on Bombay, the whole world will take notice." Instantaneously, his terrorist comrades sit up, alert, excited, as the comprehension of Bombay's symbolic status dawns on them.

The film, by contrast, shows us nothing of this Bombay, the Hindu-bourgeois city that the conspirators refer to. In a remarkable exclusion of all the conventional tropes of India's economic boom, *Black Friday* diligently and singularly focuses on the lower-class decrepitude that abounds in the city. As a matter of fact, the film's insistent use of a red and blue filter to shoot large parts of the film make it impossible to distinguish lower-class Muslim dwellings from clearly middle-class ones. One-room lodgings in congested slums, because of the "psychedelic" lighting, are made to appear gaudy, and, conversely, luxuriant bourgeois living rooms become easily interchangeable with darkened underground conspiratorial dens and dungeons. Additionally, the seamless ease with which poor Muslims congregate in the homes of their wealthier counterparts, and the nonchalance with which affluent Muslims navigate slums, further erases the boundaries between bourgeois city and slum city, adding to the overwhelming sense of Bombay's shabbiness, its despairing, collapsing topography seeping into the rest of the city. This produces something more than simply a sense of the ubiquity of the Muslim terrorist or the familiar hypervigilant belief that they are everywhere.[76] Visually, this collapse of topographical and class distinctions and borders, abetted by the terrorists' facility in donning an open-ended class persona, highlights a fundamental indecipherability, an un-pindown-able alterity at the heart of Muslim identity.

Even though the film registers this ambiguity about the terrorist—who the hell *is* he? An irate businessman? A smuggler? An unemployed urban bum? What are his class and social antecedents? Where exactly does he "normally" live (a mansion in Dubai? A *chawl* in Mumbai)?—it nevertheless tells us exactly where to *find* him: *in the slum.*[77] After the police spread the word, using their informants, that they are looking for the men involved in the blasts and receive a whole host of tip-offs, they make a massive round of arrests. The viewer is found facing a police station hallway thronging with people: about thirty men (and four women) stand in circular formation, with a constable in the middle, his hands on his waist, inspecting the melange of people arrested as suspects. The irony of the situation is that the men and women he scrutinizes hardly constitute a blend of different people. Rather, they all look alike: dressed in raggedy clothes (vests, *dhotis*, unironed shirts with buttons undone). An unshaven, unkempt look dominates, as does the skullcap, a part of traditional Muslim attire. As the camera's gaze swivels around the room we find more of the same: men dressed as laborers, waistcloths tied around their foreheads (as laborers often do while working under the hot sun), their grimy vests peeking from under their half-buttoned shirts. This group of suspects is never again shown or even referred to in the rest of the film, but this moment goes a long way in consolidating a visual repertoire on which we can always rely to identify or define a terrorist, a poor man with a skull cap.

Immediately following this scene, we see the deputy commissioner of police, Rakesh Maria, who's in charge of the bomb blast case, walk through the corridors of the police station. His path is obstructed by a group of men and women—families of the arrested men—protesting the police's brutality and begging for the freedom of their sons. The commissioner's expression and demeanor with this crowd—his pursed, slightly puckered lips; the movement of his head from side to side as he observes the supplicants; the mildly annoyed, mildly exhausted expression in his eyes that nevertheless remain aloof—might be seen as a moment of his dumbfoundedness, the silent admission that he has nothing to say, no explanation to give for the police violence.[78] The top cop's silence, on such a reading, might be construed as a moment of guilt, shame, or embarrassment, silent acknowledgment even. And yet a closer observation of his body language belies such an explanation. The actor playing the commissioner (Kay Kay Menon) towers over everyone else in the room. His herculean stature appears even more exaggerated because he seems to be holding himself above the people cowering and pleading "beneath" him. Shrinking away from his surroundings, he protects his body from touching anything. What Rakesh Maria cringes from is not just the stench of poverty but also the morally blameworthy indigence of terrorists. Conveniently, these men and their families subsume in themselves both forms of reprehensibility. The shower he takes immediately afterwards makes more sense in light of his need to wash himself clean of the malodor of Islamic poverty, that is, of something dirty, criminal, and terroristic.

But it is not simply that Muslims are associated with poverty—that in and of itself would hardly be wildly "off," given that a preponderant part of India's Muslim population is indeed economically depressed—but that their poverty is articulated as a condition of natural decrepitude into which they "must" fall when their Mafioso patron retracts his benevolence. The travels of one of the terrorists (Badshah Khan) from Bombay to Delhi, Uttar Pradesh to Rajasthan, thence to Calcutta, and then back to Bombay as he follows Tiger Memon's orders to evade the talons of the law, bring him to the brink of utter destitution. By the time he reaches Calcutta it has become clear that no one is going to send him money or a ticket to Dubai or Pakistan, that his bosses have dropped him like a hot potato. And it is only then, when he has run out of all money sent by his Mafia bosses and has finally lost hope, that he is reduced to finding a meager living accommodation: a bedless corner in a room shared by a dozen other working-class men. Deprived of power and money, the extremist in the end has returned to what he always was: destitute and Muslim, which is really the same thing.

Yet another distorted relationship posited between Muslims and poverty is that poverty is what shields them, is the cover behind which Muslims hide, not just as an ideological explanation or excuse for their misdeeds, but quite literally as a physical shelter to avoid capture. Poverty's spaces are what Muslims take recourse to in order to elude the law. Imtiaz Ghavate, another terrorist in the film, weaves in and out of a slum as he is pursued by the police; he emerges out of the slum every time he thinks the cops have lost his trail and then dashes back in whenever they track him down. The slum possesses a disorderly, porous spatiality with no clear entrance or exit gateways.

This long chase sequence is prolonged precisely by virtue of the slum's criminal-harboring potential. The camera, like the police, tries desperately to keep pace with Ghavate, but both are unable to weave quickly enough through the narrow, serpentine lanes of the slum as rapidly and adroitly as the quarry does: the terrorist Muslim is supremely "at home" in the slum milieu. As a result, there is a moment during the pursuit when the camera, unable to execute a nimble right turn, finds itself jammed up against an unpainted, craggy wall; the blurry blackness of the wall, then, is all that the camera—and we the audience—can surmise and take away from this unruly, rebellious, chaotically intractable space. The erratic layout of the slum yields up dark nooks and crannies where you might least expect them, making it impossible for the police to nab their suspect. Consequently, the slum is more than just an ordinary hideout. The slum is the getaway *zone of choice* for the terrorist on the run. Even when one of the constables can see Ghavate right before him—they are both precariously balanced on massive pipelines that run through the slum—the latter remains elusive, uncapturable.

The slum's cartography is thus ideally designed for the machinations and improvisatory hide-and-seek techniques in which the terrorists are well-versed. The police, on the other hand, in what is the only moment of humor in the entire film, find themselves completely out of their depth when traversing this landscape of poverty. Foolishly inept as they are, they talk to each other on their efficiency-pretending walkie-talkies, trying fruitlessly to pin down Ghavate's location, run parallel to him, and beg him to give up because there is no way they can reach him through the wide sewage drain that separates them. Exhausted and seeking consolation in long tea breaks as they lounge around on the sidewalks outside the slum and wait for him to emerge, the policemen seem silently to admit their limit in the mazes of the slum. This resistance to tracking inherent in the slum's spatial dispositions, and conversely the slum's ability to behave like a pulsating live organism that can curl in upon itself, contract its insides, conceal and protectively surround miscreants who hole up there, is what more than anything else defines what Unni terms the "Muslim space." One need only add that the Muslim space, in this case, is at the same time a space of poverty, and home to crime-as-terror.

A Terrorist for All Seasons: Full-Fledged/Itinerant, Poor/Middle-Class Ultras in *Aamir*

Raj Kumar Gupta's *Aamir* (2008) contains a fascinating rendition of a Muslim slum. The film's central character Aamir, a young middle-class doctor returning from London to visit his family, finds himself embroiled in a high-voltage terrorist drama as soon as he exits the airport in Bombay. In fact, even before he leaves the airport building, he has already become a terrorist suspect. At the immigration desk the officer on duty insists on triple-checking his documents and has his suitcase opened and examined for suspicious goods, and when an irate Aamir retorts, "Look, I'm not a terrorist," the officer replies, "How do I know that? It's not like it will be inscribed on your face." The irony of this moment is twofold. For one, Aamir does in fact become a terrorist (even if against his will) and the immigration officer's suspicions are therefore apparently ratified by the film's unfolding plot. To that extent Ananya J. Kabir is right in asserting that even when films like *Aamir, Kurbaan,* and *New York* present ostensibly sympathetic Muslim figures caught in the aftermath of 9/11, such supposedly nonhostile films, by the sheer fact of rehearsing the threat perceptions, effectively reconfirm and reinforce the conservative assumption that anyone who subscribes to the everyday tenets of Islam is, at the end of the day, automatically susceptible to terroristic ideologies.[79]

Secondly, inasmuch as all the Muslims that Aamir encounters in his *dérive*[80] through the city turn out to be terrorists (or accomplices in acts of terror) the question of who is a terrorist and who isn't, whose facial inscriptions reveal what, becomes redundant: they are *all* terrorists, active or prospective. Once *every* Muslim is recognized as a potential terrorist the guessing game can come to a halt. Since a name itself reveals all, faces need no longer be searched for telltale individual signs. In this film, literally everyone—from *paan-walas* to shanty restaurant owners and grungy motel managers, from local thieves to "friendly" neighborhood prostitutes, from public phone booth operators to small-time waiters—is in on the terrorist conspiracy. No matter where Aamir goes, men and women around him have a prescient knowledge of his arrival and they are all cued to give him information that will set rolling the next stage of the plot.

In fact, even Muslims and Muslim spaces that do not directly offer him additional clues are nevertheless made part of Aamir's sojourn and thus made complicit as silent yet crucial links within the amorphous terrorism chain that literally has no beginning and no end. As his first stop, Aamir has to visit the dilapidated yet buzzing "National Restaurant" in the Muslim-dominated area of Dongri in South Mumbai. Here he's seated at a table, which has been "risarvad" for him, is refused food and water, given deadly stares by the owner and waiter, and then asked to leave. He gleans no new information and learns nothing significant from this venue, and no explanation is given as to why Aamir is made to come here. As a result, from the point of the view of the terror plot, this sequence serves no useful purpose other than to prolong Aamir's confusion and torment, which in turn makes him a better candidate for blackmail and exploitation.

This moment and other such sequences (where nothing happens) also serve an additional function: they offer up excellent opportunities for the film to put on display the antediluvian ("backward") world of Muslims, where simple words like "reserved" and "restaurant" are misspelled and mispronounced in strange distortions. This is a world in which seeds of Islamic terrorism have universally permeated. There is no strict distinction between the nonterrorist Muslim who runs an ordinary business and the terrorist proper. The former, when necessary, can be rendered terrorizing, just as their business ventures can be made to serve as convenient rest stops for terrorists on the move. In effect, everyone is either a full-fledged terrorist or an itinerant, part-time one. In some ways the latter are even more dangerous because their workaday professional facade hides their more sinister deviancies.

Because of his entanglement in the terrorist plot, Aamir has to travel from the airport straight to the slum,[81] making his return home a characteristic *dérive*, which involves the abandoning of "predictable paths" and a jolting awareness of parts of an urban landscape thus far unknown.[82] Traversing these polarized spatialities—the world of the airport versus the bile-inducing filth of the "Muslim space"—opens up several political possibilities for a radical critique of urban poverty and the economic and cultural marginalization of religious minorities in India. Any such critique, however, is pre-emptively dismissed by the film because ideas to this effect are articulated by the terrorist mastermind, the anonymous bald man who orchestrates the terrorist plot and gives Aamir instructions on what to do and where to go.

This man (euphemistically called *bhai jaan*/older brother by an Islamist "brotherhood") is portrayed as a morally compromised specimen, not only because of his espousal of a violent religious fundamentalism, but also because every word he utters about Muslim misery and economic hardships is a piece of rationalizing shamelessly intoned as he chomps and burps through giant portions from bowlfuls that lie before him on a heavily laden table: large quantities of greasy curries, half-chewed chicken bones, gargantuan plates of rice become markers of the gluttonous hypocrisy of the Islamic terrorist and his community's grouses. Clearly, we surmise, this overendowed, overfed terrorist, being served hand and foot by his minions in a large, expansive house, has no business pontificating about the penury and wants of his Muslim brethren.[83]

In fact, the discourse of structural inequalities and discriminatory politics is categorically belied in the film by Aamir, who protests against *bhai jaan*'s behest that he go "see" how Muslims "really" live: like "insects"; they barely have a place to shit, let alone live. Even though Aamir has just walked up a completely ramshackle building with its "slum naturalism" visual aesthetics underscoring a broken facade, half-erect walls, a staircase in disrepair, and although he comes out of the place sweating, gagging, and regurgitating because of the stench from the refuse that streaks the floor and walls in the building's communal toilet, he puts up a valiant defense against *bhai jaan's* allegation that Muslims face discrimination. "Who has stopped them from doing anything? Nobody stopped me," he asserts angrily and self-vindicatingly. Invoking the familiar bourgeois, corporate rhetoric of hard work, merit and self-determination bringing forth deserved rewards, Aamir, in effect, holds responsible for their own plight the people whom he's just witnessed living in nauseatingly insalubrious conditions.

A dramatic, visually disjunctive montage impact is produced in the sequence as we watch a middle-class man, classily swathed in a Western suit and sporting no religious markers, sticking out like a sore thumb in a milieu that is so unmistakably South Asian/*Bambaiyya* "Muslim." This discordant juxtaposition is, however, the very effect the film wishes to produce: Aamir stands out as a misfit in the slum because he is meant to do so. He is different from all the poor Muslims who, by Aamir's own theory, in effect deserve their insect-like existence in slums. His middle-class personae and attitude demarcate him. Unlike "them" (the workaday poor Muslims) he has worked his way up, thus earning his right to a share in the riches of society. In the end, too, his choice to die a martyr—letting the bomb explode, and himself with it, not on a bus as planned, but in a hole in the ground where the devastation caused can be kept to a minimum—sets him apart from the "innate" terrorism of poor Muslims. While middle-class Muslims too may be susceptible to the pulls of radical Islam—films such *Aamir, Fiza, New York,* and *Kurbaan* work on this premise—their protagonists' radical turn is nevertheless provided a plausible context: trauma during riots, a family held hostage, brutality endured in American prisons post 9/11. Even more, these unlikely "ultras" are afforded a chance at repentance and moral self-restitution, often through a voluntary death that ultimately foils the terrorist plot or safeguards their loved ones. The poor in the urban slum by contrast are neither given a history nor a chance to redeem themselves. Lacking reason or causation for where they are, as the constitutionally undeserving, they also lack any justification whatsoever for their *ressentiment*, or their extremist solutions and are thus implicitly stuck in a time warp and quagmire of futility and terrorism from which there seems no escape, because, evidently, this is who they are.

Distorting Precarity: *Raees*

Released in 2017, Rahul Dholakia's *Raees*, set in the fictional town of Fatehpura in 1980s–1990s Gujarat, revolves around the eponymous Muslim bootlegger and gangster Raees Alam (played by Shah Rukh Khan/SRK), who rises to become the kingpin of the illicit liquor business and is pursued single-mindedly, and finally killed in an "encounter," by Jaideep Ambalal Mazumdar (played by Nawazuddin Siddiqui), an upright Hindu cop. *Raees*, which borrows elements of crime thriller and gangster films, was loosely inspired by the life of Abdul Latif, a notorious Muslim bootlegger and terrorist, who was one of India's most wanted men in the period in which the film is set. The filmmakers, to avoid legal complications of course, denied any connection with real-life characters and declared their film to be a work of "pure fiction."

Raees shares some broad similarities with a film such as *Aamir*: an act of terrorism is committed, Muslims are involved, the *mohalla* is implicated. Thus, to an extent, the film provides another iteration of the Bollywood stereotype of Muslim as gangster or mobster or terrorist. No wonder then that a reviewer complained that the film stood out "in its total exclusion of even a single positive Muslim character," where "all Muslim characters in the film, without any exception, are criminals."[84]

On the other hand, however, in some Hindu nationalist quarters, the film was accused of presenting a sympathetic portrait of the Muslim gangster—a likeable antihero—and, therefore guilty of having an "anti-national"[85] bent and an "astute communal flavouring" because its goal was the "unabashed wooing of the minority community."[86] What also fed into this perception of the film is that it was made by a director whose first feature was critical of the gruesome 2002 Gujarat pogrom against Muslims, for which it was banned in Gujarat: *Parzania* (2005) was inspired by the true story of a ten-year-old Parsi boy who disappeared from his housing society during the massacre. And, to be sure, unlike many post-1990s films that feature Muslim protagonists as aggressive or fanatical terrorists without compunction, *Raees* presents its audiences with a compassionate *surma*-sporting Muslim, "more populist do-gooder than villain, a man whose heart is mostly gold, tarnished but unmistakable."[87]

There is no doubt that *Raees* walks a tightrope in its portrayal of the sympathetic tragic Muslim gangster figure. The film's representational ambiguity or instability speaks to "a tension at work related to the censor board and the current culture of fear in Modi's India that the film industry operates under."[88] But it is precisely because of this context—the climate of dread and unrelenting violence against the Muslim minority—that the film's balancing act or its adjustments with neoliberal Hindutva must be contended with. We show how the film leans into and reinforces some of the threatening portrayals of Muslims in postliberalization films and distorts the contemporary reality of the high escalation and normalization of Muslim precarity under a Hindu majoritarian government. The film achieves this distortion and sidelining through a sometimes anachronistic, as well as selective and manipulative invocation of national events, and through engaging the star text of SRK, the film industry and country's most beloved and prominent Indian Muslim.

The film's protagonist is a Muslim gangster who grows up in the slum; it is no surprise, then, that the film traffics in the Muslim = slum/poor = criminal stereotype. Yet it is the subtle ways in which the film suggests these linkages that reveal the film's political unconscious. While Fatehpura is inhabited both by Hindu and Muslim bootleggers or "criminals," it is the *mohalla*'s Muslimness that stands out as a result of the town's Muslim name and the outsize presence of Raees. By association, the poverty and the unlawful activity of the *mohalla* are identified with Muslims. Furthermore, the film's set design of the *mohalla* contributes to the overwhelming sense of the *mohalla* as a Muslim location. There is an inordinate use of the color green in the film to leave no doubt in the audience's mind that we're immersed in a Muslim world. Whether it is the pastel green walls of the *mohalla* or of Raees's home, or Raees's clothes, or the green twinkle lights during Muharram (shown more than once in the film), or the architecture (pillars, arches, and minarets) in different scenes; cumulatively they leave no doubt about the Islamicate contours of the film's spatiality.

The opening few minutes of the film conflate Muslims, the poor, and their residential localities with illegality or criminality. The film opens on the outskirts of town with the Muslim bootlegger, Ilyas, making hooch (inferior quality local liquor) in unhygienic conditions; he recruits poor children (like Raees and his friend Sadiq) from the *mohalla* as his minions, initiating them into a life of petty crime. It is this army of little boys, led by Raees, that warn him as the police conducts a surprise raid on Ilyas's establishment. When a cop identifies Raees as the miscreant and slaps him, Raees's mother jumps to his defense, only to be criminalized by the cop. This prejudiced Hindu cop demands that Raees's poor mother, who does scrap business, reveal what's in her threadbare bag: "Dhandey ka saamaan hai ya dangey ka?" (Are these the tools of your trade or the tools that will cause riots?); he abuses and accuses her: "Niqaab ke aad mein ulteseedhey dhandhey karti hai" (your veil conceals your ill deeds). Poverty, illegality, Muslimness are conflated in this scene where the *mohalla* Muslims are seen as always already criminal, the garbs of their religion (*niqab*/veil) camouflaging their illegality. Toward the end of the film, ironically, Raees's "dhandey ka samaan" (the tools of his trade) does conceal "dangey ka samaan" (the tools that cause riots) as Raees inadvertently aids a Muslim don (Musa) in the smuggling of RDX material, which is used to make bombs that cause the deaths of innocents. The implication seems to be that some sort of criminality always follows or surrounds a Muslim; every Muslim should thus be treated as a suspect. Rather than delineating how Muslims are often harassed disproportionately on charges of antinationalism and terrorism, the film instead suggests that perhaps these allegations are not so far from the truth; petty illegality is only the stepping stone to the far more heinous form of criminality: antinational activity.

It is not that the film is blind to the economic precarity of the Muslim male. In fact, the film shows how Raees is entrapped—both by the Hindu gangster Jairaj within a condescending and humiliating patronage system within which he must remain Jairaj's "boy" or minion, as well as by underhanded politicians—which forces Raees to turn to Musa for capital. The film thus affectively reveals the precarity of the Muslim male who must survive without a security net, marginalized and criminalized by the state and manipulated, exploited, and humiliated by local power brokers. And yet every time class precarity is engaged explicitly in the film, it is presented primarily as the lot of indigent Hindu characters in the *mohalla* that distracts from the intersectional precarity of Muslims. The film shows that the *mohalla* is inhabited by people of all religious ilk—Hindus and Muslims, a kind Parsi doctor—engaged in different occupations (car mechanic, factory worker, seamstress, teacher, etc.). We never really see them struggling for basic necessities (food, clothes, housing). There is no filth or overcrowded housing or overflowing gutters or beggars. But on the rare occasions we do encounter poverty, it is mostly deflected onto Hindu characters. For instance, the group of struggling mill workers are Hindus, a sole old Muslim man in a skullcap among the crowd notwithstanding. And it is a debt-ridden Hindu mill worker who commits suicide after the mill shuts down and the corrupt owner refuses to give any compensation or pension to the workers' families.

Ironically, the film also diffuses precarity as it suggests that Hindus suffer the worst consequences of harsh antiterrorism laws. The police officer Mazumdar terrorizes the *mohalla* after the bomb blasts in which Raees is implicated by threatening to impose the antiterrorism law "TADA," or Terrorists and Disruptive Activities (Prevention) Act, on everyone. We see poor Hindu men being subjected to the cops' torture as they seek information of Raees's whereabouts. The irony here is that before it was repealed in 1995, TADA was routinely abused by the state's agents, resulting in unlawful detentions, convictions, and legitimization of violence against Muslims.[89]

The film deploys and throws its weight behind the good/bad Muslim typology, a schema that is both a product of, and further intensifies, the precarization of Muslims. *Raees* peddles in a dichotomy that reinforces the precarity of Muslims within an increasingly militantly Hindu majoritarian nation that demands complete obedience and obeisance from the religious minorities within its borders. The film takes pains to present the central character Raees as the good Muslim, emphasizing his goodness variously: he is a family man who romances his wife and cooks for her; he is a man of the people who truly cares about the well-being of the community; he has immaculate "secular" credentials; and through killing the Islamic arch-foe/the bad Muslim/the terrorist, Raees proves his ultimate allegiance to the people and the nation. Every one of the other minor Muslim characters in the film is either a good or bad Muslim; there is no room for grays, for subjective complexity. In contrast, meanwhile, even the "bad" Hindus (the corrupt politicians or the Hindu bootlegger) are "good," especially since they don't orchestrate *danga-fasaad* (riots) or feed communal frenzy or engage in bloody violence. In fact, they ironically hire Muslims to do their dirty work (for instance, the assassin that Jairaj hires to kill Raees is Muslim). For all of Jairaj's faults, the film shows that this Hindu bootlegger don is not "Yamraj" (Lord of Death). There is an imbalance in how the interactions and relationship between Raees and Musa, and Raees and Jairaj, play out, to emphasize Musa's cold villainy. Thus, even as a distraught Raees, feeling betrayed, pulls out an AK-47 to kill Jairaj, tears streaming down his *surma*-lined eyes, Raees remembers him almost as a surrogate father in a nostalgic flashback that harks back to the beginning of their relationship when Raees was only a child. No such sentimentality infuses Raees's relationship with, or killing of, Musa.

The film's main (Muslim) baddie is Musa-bhai, and he and his right-hand man, Nawab, are the agents of death. Musa's depravity resides primarily in his antinational terroristic activities. When a cash-strapped and desperate Raees approaches Musa for work toward the end of the film, Musa exploits Raees's vulnerability and deceives him into smuggling RDX material from Doha (Qatar) that is used to make bombs as an act of vengeance for the attack in India on the train with Muslim pilgrims returning from Hajj. Raees thus becomes an unwitting participant in a terrorist act (he naively thinks he's helping Musa to smuggle gold). When Raees discovers to his horror that he has been duped and has blood on his hands and accuses Musa of butchering innocents, Musa-bhai shows no compunction and smugly tells Raees that he will be rewarded with an afterlife in *jannat* (paradise) since he has done *nek kaam* (a good deed). The bad Muslim weaponizes religion and entangles *dhanda* (business) and *dharm* (religion), and his badness lies in his simultaneous lack of loyalty to the Indian nation and his primal devotion to his Muslim identity.

Importantly, Musa's ease with cold-blooded murder is suggested by his association with the meat market. His first appearance in the film is in a meat market, and importantly, the access to Musa's house seems to be through the meat market. This meat market, like the slum, is overcrowded, disgusting, and inhabited by frenzied urban poor (in this case, primarily poor Muslim butchers). The market thus serves as the portals of Hell that lead into Musa-the-butcher's abode. The meat market sequence in the film reinforces the oft-recruited trope synonymizing Muslims with barbaric butchery. In the film, a turf war breaks out in the meat market; an aspirational neoliberal subject, Raees, who is trying to sell goats—and raise some capital to start his own bootlegging business by selling goat meat at good prices on the eve of the Muslim festival of Bakr-Eid—is perceived as competition by other Muslim butchers who see him as encroaching on their business monopoly. A threatening atmosphere is evoked: chickens flutter in fear in their cages; dark skullcap-kohl-taveez-wearing Muslim butchers—at ease with the business of slaughtering—sharpen their cleavers. Thick and raw slabs of red meat hang in the stalls. In addition to knives, these slabs come to be wielded as weapons in the bloody brawl between Raees and the other poor Muslim butchers. The mise-en-scène leaves no doubt about the associations of Muslims with ruthless slaughter, as people who are inclined toward brutality, against human animal and nonhuman animal alike.

Moreover, the film suggests that it is not just the bad Muslim (Musa) who has a proclivity for violence, but we see how even the good Muslim (Raees) has a voracious appetite. Raees is shown as relishing meat (mutton) in a Muslim eatery, as he sucks the marrow out of a bone. While this way of consuming meat may well reinforce the authenticity of the character, it also leaves the audience to draw a connection between his physical courage (*mian-ki-daring*), his brawn and ingestion of meat, and his (genetic) predilection toward bloodshed.

These suggestions that gather around meat—its consumption and production—resonate beyond the confines of the film, as they tap into the insidious and messy politics of meat in Modi's India. Especially since 2014 after BJP came to power at the center, meat—especially beef—has been weaponized against Muslims, as they have come to be stigmatized and targeted both within discourse and policy.[90] The ban on slaughtering cows, the movement to ban consumption of beef and buffalo meat, the growing militant cow vigilantism, the recent decision to allow for the import of pork—all of these developments specifically target the Muslim minority and render it incessantly more precarious. As Sushmita Chatterjee has noted, the worst hit by the beef bans are Muslims, along with poor people and workers in slaughterhouses and leather factories. All kinds of violence have accompanied these beef bans, such as unemployment for workers from leather factories, harassment of Muslim families, Muslim people being driven out of villages, attacks against people suspected of eating beef, and other escalating forms of violence.[91] Thus, weaponizing meat has caused certain caste- and religion-identified human bodies (such as Dalits and Muslims) to be treated as meat: as "those without recognition as productive citizens," as those who are disposable.[92] The film leans into this loaded signifier of meat.

Most importantly, though, the film invokes some national events that post-date the film's chronological setting (the 2002 Gujarat riots) and obliquely presents others to downplay the precarization of Muslims. The presentation of these national events that involved sectarian violence mutes the aggressive and incendiary Hindu nationalist rhetoric that led to the riots while amplifying the Muslim = terrorist formulation, and it minimizes the vulnerability of, and violence against, Muslim bodies that preceded and followed the riots and bombings.

The film's primary setting in the western Indian state of Gujarat is of foremost importance. Gujarat was the site of the worst anti-Muslim pogrom in post-Independence India (Godhra riots, 2002), which occurred when Modi, India's current prime minister, was Gujarat's chief minister. Even before the 2002 riots, the state, like other parts of India, had seen its share of communal tensions in the post-Independence period. In fact, since the mid-1980s, when the BJP became the leading political force in Gujarat, the state "became a nerve center for the Hindu nationalist movement."[93] In her essay, "Bootlegging, Politics and Corruption: State Violence and the Routine Practices of Public Power in Gujarat (1985–2002)," Ornit Shani suggests that since the 1980s, the "practices of public power . . . infused by routine forms of corruption, became entwined with deepening ethno-Hindu politics and a strong anti-Muslim bent." The 2002 riots were thus an expected outcome of "the communal harnessing of state power."[94]

In *Raees*, however, Hindu-Muslim tensions do not exist in Gujarat; people go about doing their illicit liquor *dhanda* regardless of their *dharm*. In fact, one of the few times that we hear anyone express a sectarian sentiment, it is mouthed by a Muslim employee of Raees's who suggests stopping the supply of free food to Hindus as a way of cutting costs and easing financial challenges for Raees, which invokes Raees's ire and provides another opportunity for the film to cement his secularist credentials. On the whole, Hindu bootleggers like Jairaj exist more or less in harmony with their Muslim counterparts like Raees, or, at least, the Hindus don't mix *dhanda* and *dharm*, unlike Musa. Similarly, the Hindu politicians are "corrupt" (they look the other way while bootlegging thrives in the "dry state" as long as their palms are generously greased) but not communal. There is no communal inflection in their relationship or conflict with Raees. The sources of conflict are elsewhere, in either business competition or political power brokering.

This maneuver—of invisibilizing sectarian tensions and undertones that impact all aspects of Muslims' lives and livelihoods as a religious minority—effectively mutes and marginalizes the intense "precarity of place"[95] felt by Muslims who are treated as second-class citizens within the nation. In the film, the hypocritical politician, Pashabhai, who imbibes alcohol with pleasure while adopting prohibition as his political platform, decides to lead a "daru bandi yatra" (a journey to ban alcohol) through Raees's *mohalla* despite Raees's warning and plea that he change the route of the rally since it will damage his bootlegging business. This rath yatra unequivocally invites comparisons with L. K. Advani's notorious *Ram Rath Yatra* (Chariot Journey) in 1990, with its incendiary and militant communal rhetoric that caused Hindu-Muslim violence in its wake and ultimately led to the storming and attack by Hindu fundamentalists of the Babri Masjid. As we have mentioned before, this episode launched the Hindu Right to national prominence, led to bloody riots in Bombay in 1992 and 1993 (depicted in the 1995 hit film by Mani Ratnam, *Bombay*), which disproportionately targeted Muslims, and culminated in the 1993 Mumbai bomb blasts orchestrated by the Muslim underworld.

In the film's presentation, however, the rally is shorn of any communal motives even as the iconography surrounding the rally is unquestionably reminiscent of Advani's yatra.[96] In the film, a conch (considered auspicious in Hindu ceremonies) is blown to inaugurate the rally. Pashabhai and his followers—young Hindu men—wear red stoles and wave swords; they throw the provocation "*kaun mai ka laal hai*" (which mother's son has the guts to stop the rally!) as they begin their procession through the *mohalla*. And when the rally is derailed successfully by Raees and the people of his *mohalla*, we have the answer to the rhetorical question: It is the sons of Muslim mothers who have the guts, the *mian-ki-daring* to stop the rally. But instead of being an unequivocally good thing, it subconsciously reinforces the fear of Muslim strength that can make Hindus cower. The rath yatra scene ends in chaos and suggests that it is ultimately Muslims who are prone to *danga-fasaad* (riot), since it is Raees who first resorts to violence even as his actions are incited by the goading and the confrontational sword-wielding aggression and volatile environment created by Pashabhai and his men.

The Muharram scenes also contribute to the idea that Muslims are willing to accept suffering and martyrdom for the cause of their religion. On the surface, the masochistic self-flagellation and "war-cries" of red-blooded chest-beating young Muslim men in black kurta-salwar suggest the Muslim's capacity for bearing physical pain. What it invokes, subconsciously, is also their capacity for, and pleasure in, inflicting violence in general (as also reinforced in the film's meat market sequence). It is precisely this sort of paranoia surrounding Muslim virility and Hindu effeminacy that militant Hindu outfits such as the Vishwa Hindu

Parishad (VHP) exploit as they sponsor combat training camps that teach "vulnerable" Hindus to defend themselves against the religious enemy.

A similar distortion of representation, which becomes pregnant with meaning, occurs in the film's anachronistic summoning of the 2002 train-burning incident in Godhra, Gujarat. On February 27, 2002, fifty-nine passengers on an overcrowded train—including many Hindu activists returning from the holy site of Ayodhya—were burned to death in a fire after altercations between Hindus and Muslims. In the pogrom that followed, more than 1,000 Muslims were killed and more than 150,000 displaced.[97] Seeking revenge, mobs of Hindus destroyed Muslim lives and businesses; reports of egregious human rights violations against Muslims abounded. In the film, however, it is a train carrying Muslim Hajj pilgrims that is set on fire by some "rioters" (never named as Hindus, thus excusing them of culpability). This results in riots, which lead to curfews to maintain law and order throughout the country, including Fatehpura. The state's functionaries—Hindu politicians, high-ranking officials, police, lawyers, and judges—are not shown to be motivated by communal sentiment; none of them seem to unfairly target Muslims or participate in the violence. Through this, the film mutes the very real and proven complicity of the state in creating, participating in, and aggravating the vulnerability of Muslims to violence.

These subtextual invocations and intricacies aside, the film's politics and treatment of Muslims and the spaces they inhabit are intimately tied up with the actor who plays Raees. Any discussion of *Raees* would be incomplete without a consideration of SRK's star text, especially as the arc of his career—from playing Raj or Rahul to Raees—coincides with the India's neoliberal trajectory. As Paromita Vohra, Sudhavna Deshpande, and Praseeda Gopinath have noted, SRK came to embody the "consumable hero" of liberalizing India,[98] and his various morphing personas in the films—the yuppie in Gap and DKNY hoodies, the entrepreneurial and aspirational subject, the NRI-with-desi values, etc.—served up a rich and volatile iconography for neoliberal India. As SRK rose to stardom in the 1990s and 2000s, in film after film he played upper-class upper-caste cosmopolitan (Hindu) Indian characters with strident "Hindustani" values (*Dilwale Dulhania Le Jayenge*, Aditya Chopra, 1995; *Pardes*, Subhash Ghai, 1997; *Kuch Kuch Hota Hai*, Karan Johar, 1998; *Phir Bhi Dil Hai Hindustani*, Aziz Mirza, 2000; *Swades*, Ashutosh Gowariker, 2004; *Kabhi Khushi Kabhi Gham*, Karan Johar, 2001). His personal background—a regular middle-class (Muslim) guy from Delhi who made it big in the film industry where he had no connections; a successful interfaith marriage with his teenage sweetheart, a Hindu woman—allowed for the presentation of the "ultimate neoliberal individualist success story" unencumbered by structural constraints (of class or religion). Thus SRK's "roles and public persona naturalized Hindu neoliberal hegemony," and he "participated in and co-created the fiction of the deracinated, secular, good Muslim."[99] This is not to say that he ever "passed" for Hindu or underplayed his Muslimness. We come to this later; for the time being, we want to note that this myth that SRK embodied has become increasingly untenable, notwithstanding the spectacular success of his more recent release, *Pathaan* (2023), a film we revisit in our conclusion. The collapse of the aspirational template he represents is tied to the escalation of communal polarization and coincides with the growing visibility and recognition of the failures of neoliberal promises.

In 2010, the year *My Name Is Khan* (a film, set in the United States, that takes Islamophobia as its subject) was released, SRK could still claim in an NPR interview piece (directed at an American audience) that "As far as the public is concerned, India is amazingly secular. I am a Muslim, but I am a leading star for the last twenty years, so if you just go by that, there is no issue ever."[100] SRK would be hard-pressed to reiterate this sort of confidence in India's amazing secularism in the second decade of the twentieth-first century, as he and his family have faced the brunt of growing Hindu majoritarianism. In 2014, he faced the fury of Modi Bhakts (as worshippers of Prime Minister Modi are referred to) when he spoke of the "extreme intolerance" in India during a Twitter town hall; a BJP politician was quick to question SRK's patriotism, with the accusation that he may live in India, "but his heart is in Pakistan" (lending tragic irony to the actor's corpus, which consists of films such as *Phir bhi dil hai Hindustani*/For all that, my heart's still Hindustani/Indian). In 2022, SRK's son, Aryan Khan, was arrested and harassed on trumped-up drug possession charges in what was seen as a politically motivated public humiliation of India's most adored (Muslim) star. Other Muslim superstars such as Aamir Khan (and those who ally with them) have also been on the receiving end of virulent backlash when they have dared to comment on the "growing intolerance" against religious minorities in India.[101]

The majoritarian state's aggressive inroads into Bollywood that we've addressed in other chapters, and its attempt to reconfigure and police the industry along communal lines, are blatant. For example, before the release of *Raees*, SRK had to appease the Hindu far-right party (Maharashtra Navnirman Sena/MNS), led by Raj Thackeray, that Mahira Khan (the film's main female lead, who's a Pakistani actor and thus "the enemy") would not be involved in the publicity of the film and that SRK would not work with Pakistani actors again. In another instance, in a prime example of dog whistle politics, the BJP national general secretary Kailash Vijayvargiya's tweet on *Raees* linked illegality, criminality, and antinationalism to the Muslim while also simultaneously triggering the discourse of Hindu precarity.[102] Vijayvargiya mentioned how PM Modi's demonetization plan[103] had already reined in "raees" (rich) people who traded in black money. But, now, he wrote, it was the Indian public's time to do their bit. The tweet pitted *Raees* against *Kaabil* (with Hindu actor Hrithik Roshan as its main lead), on the eve of both the films' January 26 Indian Republic Day release. It exhorted the capable Indian public (*kaabil junta*) to not let "dishonest" (*baemaan*) *Raees* grab what "rightfully" belonged to the *deshbhakt* (patriotic) *Kaabil*, thus feeding into the discourse of the vulnerable Hindu, whose right (*haq*) is threatened by the Muslim.

Raees occupies a special place in the canon of SRK's films. This is particularly true in the context of the last decade and a half, in which he has played characters with Muslim names. While some reviewers saw *Raees* as the film in which SRK unambiguously "came out" and "became" a Muslim because it was no longer "possible for SRK to wear his Muslim-ness casually, without reflection, without torment, without rebellion,"[104] others saw SRK's decision to "play a Muslim in three simultaneous films" as a "brave . . . assertion of identity" that sent "a strong message to a country." We have to wonder if it was a deliberate decision on SRK's part to play Muslim roles, a choice exercised as a conscious intervention in the politics of representation, or who is represented, how, and by whom. Or are these roles a reflection of the flagging stardom of an aging celebrity who has less control than ever over the roles offered to him? *Raees* marks a break from films like *Chak De India* (Shimit Amin, 2007) and *My Name Is Khan* (Karan Johar, 2010), where SRK played the good or apologetic Muslim who invests time and incurs sacrifice to prove his loyalty to the nation. One might even add *Pathaan* to this list, where SRK plays a patriotic Indian, even as the religious identity of his character is ambiguous because he's an orphan. *Raees* is also distinct from films such as *Ae Dil Hai Mushkil* (Karan Johar, 2017) and *Dear Zindagi* (Gauri Shinde, 2016), where the Muslimness of the characters he plays is normalized to such an extent that it is made to mean nothing, in that it does not speak to a larger political landscape.

In contrast, *Raees* presents SRK as a Muslim gangster in a never-before-seen "visibly Muslim" avatar (*kajal*-lined eyes, wearing a *taweez* around his neck, sporting a Pathani kurta-salwar, offering namaz or mouthing Islamic verses, observing Muharram). As he plays a Muslim gangster, the film also marks a break from SRK's earlier political stance in which he had turned down stereotypical roles for Muslim characters (the terrorist) that his Muslim star counterparts had taken on: Aamir Khan (*Fanaa*, Kunal Kohli, 2006) or Saif Ali Khan (*Kurbaan*, Rensil D'Silva, 2009), for instance. *Raees* does not allow for an easy read; it cannot be seen simply as an instance of SRK's bravery or an act of compromise because he finally plays a Muslim criminal. Instead, what *Raees*, read alongside SRK's star text, allows for is a reflection on the ways in which real-world precarities induce pressures within the film industry. This can take the form of the paucity of roles available to Muslims actors or in the restrictedness of characters that can occupy the screenscape as Muslims. *Raees* opens us up to the recognition that no one, not even the most popular Muslim film star(s), is exempt or remains unscathed in the processes that render a whole religious community precarious. The processes of precarization run deep; its tentacles spread wide inside the entertainment industry that had until recently set its faith in a Muslim man, trusting him to guide a newly liberalized nation through the escapades of upward global mobility. In the new political landscape, the same industry and its icons must be disciplined and made to play handmaiden to Hindutva.[105]

This is not to say that resistance is futile, as signaled by the spectacular success of *Pathaan*, SRK's comeback film after a hiatus of four years. In spite of the calls by Hindu nationalists for the film's boycott for all sorts of spurious reasons, the film's phenomenal success has been seen as a pushback against hate, a resounding response by SRK's fans to the right wing's orchestrated attacks on him and his family. We return to a more detailed discussion of *Pathaan* in the book's conclusion to note that the film, more than a wholesale resistance to a dominant, right-wing national schema, articulates a structure of negotiation with that schema, the accommodation illustrating how a Muslim star and Bollywood might navigate the new normal as neoliberal Hindutva continues to tighten its stranglehold on the industry.[106]

What's Being Muslim Got to Do with It?: The Named and Unnamed Precarities in *Gully Boy*

Zoya Akhtar's *Gully Boy* (2019) is set in Mumbai's Dharavi, Asia's largest slum, which is home to more than an estimated million people (at least 40 percent of whom are Muslim). The film was nominated as India's entry to the Oscars, and even though it didn't win, it received high praise from domestic and international audiences for its raw delineation of the claustrophobia and repressions that mark the lives of its characters. *Gully Boy*'s novelty lies in that it is the first mainstream Bollywood film to introduce Hindi cinema's audiences to hip-hop subcultures originating from the slums of Mumbai.[107] The film is inspired by real-life rap artists Naezy and Divine, recast onscreen as Murad and MC Sher. Principally, the film follows Murad's coming-of-age trajectory, enabled by his peers—his coartist MC Sher, girlfriend Safeena, and other friends from his neighborhood—who step in at crucial junctures to aid Murad's drive toward artistic and lucrative success.

Precarity is writ large in *Gully's Boy*'s impoverished social milieu. The film is dominated by Muslim characters living in dilapidated, overcrowded, matchbox-sized homes. The neighborhood is a chaotic disarray of tin roofs, cacophonous quarrels that interrupt privacy, communal bathrooms in desperate need of rebuilding, a maze of electric wires, and *naalas* (gutters) overflowing with plastic. The young men have bleak professional prospects and spend long hours just hanging around in a dusty open field. Murad, despite a college degree, must choose between following his father's footsteps to become a driver for a wealthy family or join his bullying uncle's company as a low-ranking white-collar employee. His friend Moeen makes ends meet through car theft and getting street children to peddle drugs. When another friend Rishi manages to get a job as an assistant manager at a Benetton outlet, he is both celebrated for the feat but also teased for forgetting his friends. Likewise, the lives of the central women characters—Safeena and Murad's mother—are tarnished by a staple gendered precarity: financial dependence on the patriarch of the house; cruel disregard of their autonomy and desires; curbing of their sexuality, their right to education, and a dignified existence. It is precisely this hopelessly stunted and erratically violent habitus that Murad gives expression to in his poetry and rap.

We turn to *Gully Boy* to conclude this chapter because, unlike the other films examined as a part of contemporary Bollywood's "Muslim in the slum" rubric, it poses a fundamentally different problematic. For one, Murad—a poor Muslim and resident of a slum—is presented as a subject worthy of our positive affective investment. His class-spatial and religious minority status are not treated as grounds for delegitimizing either his right to life or his right to a good life. On the contrary, the film's sympathetic lens credentializes his artistic genius and endorses his poetic-political resistance. And, crucially, the film's capacity to do so relies precisely on a compassionate acknowledgment of Murad's vulnerability constituted by his double marginality. Murad's precarious subject position, like in so many rags-to-riches films that Bollywood produces, is what makes him a compelling character; it is what renders his humanity deserving of protection and his artistic genius worthy of cultivation.

Secondly, unlike the films discussed so far, neither terrorism nor criminality are rendered as the ontological core of Muslimness or poverty. The film, embedded in a milieu dominated by Muslim characters, categorically rejects the Muslim = terrorist cliché. Instead, it gives us a host of characters employed in occupations that, at worst, reek of desperate attempts at survival (Moeen's carjacking and drug peddling), but more often than not simply articulate the workaday mundanity of ordinary citizens going about their uninspiring professional routines, as drivers, mechanics, doctors, managers. In fact, rendering Muslims normal is a central achievement of the film. It de-exceptionalizes them by presenting them as human, not ideal, but not monstrous either. Even more, the film inserts Muslims into the larger category of the precariat, enduring the same plight, exuding the same herd mentality that, as Murad's voice-over tells us, all tired men on Mumbai's commuter trains suffer from and are guilty of. In that sense, the only "unforgivable" crime committed by the generic Muslim in *Gully Boy* is of being too normal; of walking the straight and narrow, overly trodden path; of living in fear of losing his job; of not dreaming boldly; of accepting his fate. The problematic presented by *Gully Boy*, then, is not one that, at least ostensibly, endorses a sectarian logic. Muslims in the film are not willy-nilly monstrous terrorists or grandiose dons, unworthy of our compassion or outside the horizon of relatability.

And yet what we demonstrate in our reading of the film is that this is not tantamount to an adequate political intervention to offset films that proactively legitimate the precarization of Muslims. Rather, *Gully Boy* opens up a new dimension of the "Muslim in the slum" framework, one that reveals the very entrenchment and inescapability of the communal logic asserted by films like *Black Friday*, *Aamir*, and *Raees*. Thus, even when *Gully Boy* gives us a sympathetic poor Muslim character, who is also granted freedom from terroristic determinism, the film nevertheless succumbs to painful narratological and ideological limits in representing the lives of Muslims. In fact, it is in the very process of normalizing the lives of Muslims that the film performs its most insidious maneuvers. And finally, because the film's solution to precarious existence hinges on a neoliberal articulation of individual exceptionalism, it renders not only its nonchalant secularism rickety and hollow, it also reduces the slum to a commodified object rather than a complex geography, a tool to enhance the performance of authenticity.

In order to rescue Muslims from the Islamophobic terrorist narratives that dominate Bollywood and present them instead as ordinary residents of a metropolitan geography, the film has to nevertheless establish the Muslimness of its characters. And this is where its strategy to construct Muslims as "normal" collapses upon itself. While the film takes recourse to the predictable plot device of a family crisis, the particular nature of the crisis—heralded by the father's bigamy—means that the film's strategy of normalization entails resorting to just another gamut of stereotypes that the Hindutva discourse uses to castigate Muslims. In other words, the film is compelled to reproduce and make concessions to sectarian iconographies that allow Muslims to be legible as Muslim. The very foundation of a sympathetic template of Muslimness that the film otherwise offers in Murad is predicated upon the stereotypes of Muslims as cruel men and on the suffering of the community's women.

There is, of course, Aftab (Murad's father), whose physical and emotional abuse of his first wife Razia (Murad's mother) induces the pinnacle of suffering in the film. He harangues and humiliates her, blaming her for his bigamy, for their son's disobedience. He expects her to slog for him, his mother, and his new wife, to sleep on the floor while he and his new wife take the bed. The film's atmospherics are held hostage by the unpredictable eruptions of his unprovoked rage. The intensity of Aftab's domestic violence marks him out as an extreme on the spectrum of Muslim men we encounter in the film. And yet he is by no means alone in embodying a toxic masculinity.

While Aftab's violence is rooted in the feudal mentality and class repressions he has internalized, which he projects as patriarchal violence against his first wife, the other older Muslim men we meet, who are successful, bourgeois counterparts of Aftab, all display a core conservatism in their relationship to women. Ateeq (Murad's uncle, Razia's brother), for instance, refuses to support his sister even when she's brutally beaten by her husband. When Razia goes to him for refuge, he's horrified that she wants to leave her husband and even more that she wants her brother to help her. In his worldview, a husband's entitlements trump a brother's obligations. In fact, Ateeq blames his nephew Murad for disobeying his father's prohibitions against pursuing rap and for defending his mother against his father's wrath. His empathies lie with Aftab, declaring, "anyone would lose their mind if their son behaves like this." And then there is Safeena's father—a doctor, a gentle, indulgent parent and husband—who nevertheless nearly endorses his wife's plan to stop Safeena's medical degree after the latter is caught sneaking out at night to meet her boyfriend and friends. It is only when, in a heart-rending scene, a hysterical Safeena desperately pleads with her father—"Abboo, please; you know I am a brilliant student; why are you making me give up college"—does he relent on the condition that her mobility will be monitored; he will drop her and pick her up from college every day.

It is true that the film does not expressly create an inevitable collapse between Muslimness and men's cruelty or women's suffering. Rather, the film attempts to pass these conflicts off as generalized, pervasive workings of patriarchal, feudal conservatism and intergenerational tussles that could be true within and across all communities. And yet there is no getting away from the fact that the xenophobic national climate in which the film was produced and released relies heavily on weaponizing the idea of Muslim backwardness and the oppression of Muslim women to pass laws, and launch discursive wars, aimed at disenfranchising and humiliating the Muslim minority in India. In this context, the fact that the film does not do more to distance itself from these predominant patterns that popular culture relies on to represent Muslims creates an undercurrent that undermines the film's overt messaging.

This brings us to the second and even more dangerous strategy that *Gully Boy* deploys to normalize Muslim characters on screen and within an urban landscape: it silences the national context within which the intersectional precarity of the film's characters is constituted. There is barely any mention of the systematic socioeconomic marginalization of Muslims, including and especially under the two stints of the Modi government. The National Sample Survey Office (NSSO) reported that Muslims face "a vicious circle of poverty," and that their economic condition has not shown any signs of improvement, even though India is touted as the fastest-growing large economy.[108] Maria Thomas, reporting on a working paper by Sam Asher, Paul Novosad, and Charlie Rafkin from the World Bank, Dartmouth College, and MIT, respectively, suggests that while historically marginalized groups like the scheduled castes (SCs) and scheduled tribes (STs) have witnessed a substantial rise in upward mobility—through reservations in educational institutions and jobs—Muslims have emerged as the "least upwardly mobile group in India."[109] Similarly, the United Nations Development Program (UNDP) and the Oxford Poverty and Human Development Initiative (OPHI) research shows that when considering religious groups, Muslims fare the worst in India's multidimensional poverty index.[110] In the last decade alone—as we also discuss in chapter 1—India has witnessed the Modi-led BJP government's move to limit Muslims' rights through the Citizen Amendment Act (CAA), the stripping of Kashmir's statehood and the constitutional privileges it enjoyed under Article 370, the rise of Hindu right-wing vigilante violence against Muslims, widespread impunity and police protection offered to Hindus involved in violence against Muslims,[111] the anti-Muslim riots in Delhi in 2020,[112] cow-protection laws and beef bans, official and unofficial bans against Muslims offering namaz in public spaces, and the passing of anticonversion laws. Together, these developments have tarnished India's secular credentials, consolidated religious polarization, and exacerbated the material and sociocultural and psychological precarity of Muslims in India.[113]

Gully Boy does not make much effort to contextualize either the long history of policies or the contemporary developments that frame the film's narrative or the lives of its characters. This glaring absence is gestured toward, and that too in hurried passing, only twice in the film. The first occurs during a conversation in which Murad's father, who has broken his leg, is talking to his first wife about why Murad should substitute for him at his job as a driver. All his reasons for why this is the best choice, even though his wife resists his decision, relate to economic and professional precarity: there are too many drivers buzzing around to take over his job, such jobs don't grow on trees, what if his employers like the new temporary driver more and retain him permanently? The employers are good people. And then, all of a sudden, he inserts another reason, almost as an after-thought: "Aur waise bhi; Mohammedan ko kaun poochta hai aaj kal" (in any case, it's hard for Muslims these days). For anyone paying attention, the tenor and heaviness of the moment shifts considerably. The conversation shifts from an assessment of what is professionally prudent to what is strategic as a religious minority. Of course, it is not a question of either/or, but of both modalities of vulnerability operating in tandem to push Murad into menial professions he despises.

And yet this moment stands out because it is the first time that a character demonstrates any kind of self-awareness of their status as belonging to a precarized religious minority. Even more, however, what is striking about this scene is that we never actually see this conversation transpire between Aftab and Razia. Instead, it is something we overhear from Murad's point of view. Murad sits in his grimy little corner of the house, looking sullen at the prospect of being expected to do his father's lowly job, as we hear Aftab's voice barging into the scene's soundscape. At first Murad sits still, listening to his father's rant, and then apathetically starts moving to put away the notebook in which he writes poetry. When we hear Aftab mention the plight of Muslims, we do not see even a hint of a reaction from Murad. And the scene cuts the very next moment. The temporal concision with which the Muslim question is raised and moved away from, the obvious singularity and brevity of the scene, combined with the visual dislodging of the character who brings it up, together produce an effect of dismissal and disengagement, a moment that pithily unravels the film's own discomfort with staying with the subject of Muslims in India.

The only other incident where Murad is made to feel his minority status is when he visits his rap mentor's tiny apartment. He walks in and is greeted my MC Sher, who tells the children he's playing with to say "hello to my friend Mr. Murad." MC Sher's father, grossly sprawled on the bed, who we subsequently learn is a dysfunctional drunk, interrupts the natural flow of the conversation with "Murad . . . where are you from?" And before Murad can respond, he answers his own question: "Bhendi Bazaar?" Bhendi Bazaar is a popular market in South Mumbai and a Muslim-dominated area. It is not a part of Dharavi, where Murad is actually from. This time we do detect a change in Murad's expression, which switches from a smiling, relaxed conviviality to an uncomfortable, terse silence. Evidently, he registers the communal undertone that laces the old man's inquisition and assumption, and he disengages from the sectarian logic that insists on spatially locating him within a religious ghetto. Quickly, Murad shifts gears and starts to admire MC Sher's collection of shoes that show pride of place in the tiny apartment. We never meet MC Sher's father again, and the film encourages us to dismiss him as a bigoted curmudgeon who has no capacity to appreciate even his own son's talent (he calls MC Sher a "bum").

In a more general sense, though, this moment reiterates the film's desire to relegate sectarianism and conservatism to a generational flaw. None of Murad's peers ever exhibit the crassness of unprogressive traditionalism; not one of them is orthodox with regard the mores of their own community or discriminatory in their interactions with members of another religion. There is always an easy bonhomie between Murad's circle of friends and MC Sher's crew, or even in the interclass interactions between Murad, MC Sher, Sky, and her friends. That religious difference is treated as a nonissue encourages us to believe that the younger generation is not governed by denominational pettiness. They are driven, instead, by their shared passion for music and by their dream of living a better life.

Importantly, though, the film is inaccurate in its characterization of young people in India. If the recent Pew Research Center's survey of religion across India is to be believed, then Indians are more religiously conformist than before. In the interview-based research done with thirty thousand Indians (2019–2020), the survey reveals that close to 65 percent of Hindus and Muslims think they do not have much in common with the other community. And a high majority in both groups is convinced that it is important to stop interfaith marriages. Forty-five percent of Hindus said they would not want Muslims as neighbors, while 64 percent of Hindus thought that being Hindu and speaking Hindi were integral to being "truly Indian." This data categorically belies the optimistic reality that *Gully Boy* would have its audiences subscribe to. And while, as an aspirational goal the film's subtextual message is a noble one, it presents this skewed reality not as something to work toward but something that already exists. And therefore the Muslim question, raised in passing, is converted into a nonissue, something that will invariably disappear as the younger generation takes over the world with their rap, their love for Adidas, and each other.

Ironically, then, in the name of "normalizing" its Muslim characters, the film de-exceptionalizes what is in fact a new moment in Indian polity in terms of the state's explicit adoption of a Hindutva-promoting agenda and its active flaming of anti-Muslim sentiment. In evacuating the references to these broader national trends and by assigning right-wing politics to the "old guard," the film poses disingenuous questions about, and solutions to, the Muslim question. There is a critical moment toward the end of the film when Murad finally challenges his father's worldview: "Abboo, have you considered that your thinking is wrong?" Aftab has been shuttling between berating Murad for quitting the job in his uncle's firm and pleading with him to remember that "people like us can't afford to have big dreams" and "must keep their head down and not be distracted by the world's promises." At first glance, Murad's pushback against his father's feudal fatalism seems to be a rejection of the latter's internalization of class oppression. There is, however, a simultaneous subtextual negation of the idea that Aftab had expressed earlier, that it's hard for Muslims in India today. When Murad prods his father to reconsider his deterministic, victimhood mentality, it is not only in relation to his status as a poor slum dweller, but also as a Muslim.

Neoliberal solutions are the answer to both faulty perspectives: poor people *and* Muslims can, indeed, change their reality and fulfill their dreams. All they need to do is change their "*soch*" (thinking). Therefore, although the film delivers a conjoined precarity, it mutes one, engages the other, and offers neoliberalism as the answer to both. That *Gully Boy* converts a religion and class precarity into a singular issue of class is reflected in Zoya Akhtar's interviews, where she repeatedly refers to the "class system" that colonizes people into believing that their lot is immutable.[114] Most critics too adhered to focus on class; few have drawn attention to the film's treatment of Muslimness, particularly to the ways in which the narrative of neoliberalism treats religious identities.

The film assiduously invests in the neoliberal myth of individual exceptionalism and in the idea that we can manifest success by the sheer tenacity of our passions. The big lesson that Murad learns from his relationship with Sky, the uber-elite woman learning music production in the United States, who also helps Murad record and create his first professional music video, is that "money follows passion." She delivers this crucial tutorial when he tells her that the need to "make a living" stands in the way of him pursuing rap. Later, when she tries to kiss him, he pulls away, asking why she's interested in him even though she knows where "he's from" (a euphemistic allusion to his spatial-class origins). Once again, Sky dismisses his misgivings by reminding him that "None of that matters—not where you're from or what you own" because he is an "artist." Artistic genius, then, is exempt from the laws of discrimination borne out of social hierarchies. Artists are worthy recipients of romantic *and* capital investment, the latter confirmed by the fact that the video she helps him produce goes viral. Murad himself comes to believe in the exempting and exceptionalizing power of his genius. In the song "Asli Hip Hop" (real hip-hop) he refers to it as his only "*dharm*" (religion); "he has no other "*jaat*" (status) other than of an "*kalaakar*" (artist) who can shape "*kal*" (tomorrow).

While the precarity of Muslimness in *Gully Boy* is never fully engaged with, and casually silenced, the treatment of the slum, as proxy for and doubling of class, follows a very different trajectory. The slum, as an impoverished geography, plays a crucial role in Murad's rap, and therefore is critical to the neoliberal escape route he charts out of poverty. Every rap battle victory he enjoys is predicated on proving his mettle against the monopoly of rich, classist men, dressed in elite global brands, who try to shame him for his poverty. To begin with, this doesn't come easily to him. In fact, the first time he's up against a contender who repeatedly calls him "fake" for wearing a knockoff Adidas T-shirt and tells him to scuttle away to his "gully," we see Murad lose confidence. He is unable to contest these accusations, and he retreats, allowing his opponent to declare it a "walkover." It takes MC Sher to show Murad that he must not let a sense of class inferiority silence him; if rappers coming from wealth have seen the world, then he too "knows a lot about the world from living in Dharavi." MC Sher teaches Murad to focus on what he has: hunger and pain, which is what it takes to be a great artist. Artists turn their "hunger into stories." All Murad has to do is to tell his story, in his own words, to let his words erupt and flow like lava.

The slum, then, is the gateway to Murad's success. In his early compositions, he writes about the slum in terms of the paucity and despair it represents. In "Doori" (distance), for instance, he talks about the contrast of a skyscraper against the hungry crying to a little girl, the small houses and empty kitchen utensils, his mother's silent tears. As his music evolves, however, he develops and articulates a much more complex relationship to his geographic identity. In his later songs, he starts referring to the slum as a microcosm of the city: "Poore shehar ki awaz mere gully mein" (the voice of the entire city is in my street), and while the houses in his *gully* might be "very small," the "people in them have big hearts." People here are always ready to help, they don't cheat, they don't bow their heads or lose heart. He calls the "chawl" (slum) Bombay's "*raunak*" (the life and soul of the city). And, finally, in "Asli Hip Hop" he refers to the "gully" as his "*mashooqa*" (lover). The slum offers Murad not only the substance of his poetry, but also a way for us to track his relationship to his own sociospatial identity. Even more, it is the strategic leverage he learns to use to his advantage, to signpost his "authenticity," his rightful entitlement to hip-hop. Damini Rajendra Kulkarni[115] offers a sharp analysis of the ways in which Murad's "emplaced and embodied expression of identity" is what grants him a unique, authentic voice that is worthy of being heard. Without this authenticity—that is at the core of hip-hop culture—he would be no different from the pseudo-rap-artists that he mocked at the start of the film who only know how to gloat about their cars, shoes, and women.

The subversive presence of the slum in Murad's poetry is matched by the visual aesthetics the film deploys to administer the slum. In that sense, *Gully Boy* actively participates in the long-standing debates that Krstić discusses in *Slums on Screen*, around the politics and ethics of depicting slums.[116] There are two distinct visual legacies of representing slums in cinema that are interrupted by *Gully Boy*. The first is the aerial view, or the "planetary view," as Ranjani Mazumdar[117] calls it. We get several shots of Dharavi, taken by drones, that give a scopic view of the slum—its tin roofs, crumbling bricks, walls with peeling paint—contrasted with the grandiosity of sleek, glass- and metal-framed skyscrapers in the background. In the history of cinema, such aerial shots have been used to produce a dual effect. The first is to establish an "essential interconnection between all mankind" and "foreground a shared vision of a united humanity."[118] Second, the aerial view manages to turn a vivid geography into an "abstraction" because the "high angle view" makes the "unruly appear tidy"; the dizzying, grimy maze is converted into a striking "spectacle" that reduces the "complex lived realities" into a "generalized notion of the universal."

The second template of the slum on the screen that *Gully Boy* incorporates with an element of meta-criticality is of "slum tourism." Here the film seems to align itself with the critics of *Slumdog Millionaire,* who accused the film of benefiting from glamorizing squalor and from depicting slums through classic archetypes of beggars, Mafiosi, and prostitutes. Quite ingeniously, *Gully Boy* incorporates a scene that perfectly captures the callous casualness entailed in slumming. We see a group of white tourists being led through the streets of Dharavi by an Indian guide, who encourages his clientele to take photographs, maximizing the angles made possible with their selfie sticks. The group barges into Murad's house, where his grandmother bargains with the guide to give her an extra five hundred rupees (even though, as the guide reminds her, their "right" to access her home is ostensibly built into the price of the ticket paid by the tourists). The tourists, entirely oblivious to these tricky negotiations that are transpiring, start walking around the house, gushing with admiration at how these poor people have managed to maximize every inch of their little shanty. We hear phrases like "it's incredible" and "I wasn't expecting," "it's crazy isn't it," and lots of laughter and chuckling in the background. The tourists barely pay any attention to the human beings in the house—the grandmother and Murad—even as they ask questions like "I wonder how many people live here." Murad, trying to get away from their ogling eyes, takes his plate of food to his bed, only to have one of the men come up after him. Murad addresses the stranger in his house to compliment his T-shirt. The tourist begins to tell him that it is Nas on his T-shirt—a famous American rapper—only to be confronted with a blank-faced Murad reciting Nas's poetry back to him. The man's response is mild surprise and a desire to a take a photograph of Murad, which he proceeds to do before Murad can give his consent. Murad blocks his face against the glare of the flash, but the man doesn't care or relent, says "Cool, lovely meeting you," and disappears. The vulgar extractiveness of the scene is blatant; it deftly expresses the film's condemnation of the pleasure that rich First Worlders derive from devouring Third World social misery.

Both the use of aerial shots and of slum tourism are incorporated, only to be rejected as ethical modalities for engaging and depicting the slum. The film attempts an alternative cinematic aesthetic that stands apart from politically dubious representations of the slum even as it tries to render and honor the slum as a complex spatiality, much like Murad's poetry does. This is best captured in the music video "Meri Gully Mein," a collaboration between Murad and MC Sher, shot in Murad's neighborhood. The song renders the slum as a dynamic, fluid, agile geography. The energetic movements of Murad and MC Sher's bodies, as they jump, swirl, and squeeze through tight spaces, converts the claustrophobia of the slum into a site that is rife for creative extrapolation, a site of joy, music, dance, authenticity, choreography, and innovative orchestrations. This sensual, energetic transposition of space is matched by the song's lyrics: the slum has "small houses but big hearts." The lyrics, in turn, are visually transcribed to produce a sense that these narrow *gullies* can enable, house, and materialize big movement, hypermobility. The winding, circling shooting of the video manufactures a head rush, a sense of the possibility of endless expansion of space, for the celebration of life and artistry. The frozen tableaus of Murad, MC Sher, and other working-class bodies posing like models in rags, insist on a type of pride and coolness in and of the slum. The way in which this song is filmed, therefore, torpedoes the ideological and topographical marginalization of slums and how such spaces are framed in dominant cinema and by the echelons of power.

And yet this is not the vision of the slum that the film ends with. The final image—and it is an image—of the slum comes to us as a backdrop for Murad's grand opening act for Nas. We never see the performance itself, but we see Murad walk out onto a stage, face a gargantuan-sized crowd wildly cheering for him. Among them, right at the front, are Safeena, MC Sher, and his overwhelmed, teary-eyed parents. And Murad is wide-eyed and nervous, in awe at the vision of adulation he beholds. What is important here, however, is that on stage behind him we see a large backdrop that is a blitz of LED, neon lights, that make up multiple, differently sized and variedly stacked rectangular boxes, a simulated structure. The techno effect is electrifying, like it's a large-scale circuit board, or a scaled-up microchip, something out of the Matrix. Suddenly the lights go out, and what emerges from behind the neon-lit grid is the façade of a slum: uneven, tiny houses, stacked upon each other, ladders going into rooms and rooftops. The image, now bathed in cool blues, although a stark contrast from the neon pink, white, and green of the grid, is still very much a hyperreal depiction of the slum. For one, the image, devoid of people, is alarmingly sanitized. None of the broken, peeling walls and untidy chaos of the original "infect" this image. The problem, as Roland Barthes would say, is not that this is an image of a slum. Rather, the issue is that what we have here is a slum reduced to an image: palatable, manageable, and consumable as a snapshot with a fixed meaning. The complex, realist rendition of the slum is traded in this last shot of the film for a glitzy, hyperstylized backdrop in a hypermediated event, where the slum acts as, and stands for, an electrified highway lighting up the pathway for cultures of hybridity to emerge. The Indian Slumdog is the opener for the American hip-hop artist, and his street roughness and poverty-induced earthiness are what got him there; his spatiality now constitutes his brand, and it is not a real geography that even needs the aesthetics of realism to refer to it.

And the same is true of his Muslimness. The *kajaled* eyes, the *pathani* kurta, and *taweez* tied around his neck are just mementos that commemorate his unique, exceptional individuality, cast and crafted under neoliberalism. The real question the film leaves us with is this: Who is the rightful heir of rap in India? Or, as Murad himself puts it, who will "introduce India" to "asli hip hop" (real hip-hop). The answer is clear: the neoliberal subject who is able to trade vulnerability for brandability.

4: Love in the Time of Precarity

Caste and the Collapse of Romantic Love

Heterosexual love and marriage, with different variations on the "boy meets girl" trope, dominate the majority of Indian films. Popular Hindi-language cinema, especially, has variously explored the trials and tribulations of love, and the obstacles that stand in true love's way are indeed many. They take the shape of feuding families (*Qayamat Se Qayamat Tak*, Mansoor Khan, 1988; *Goliyon Kee Rasleela Ram-Leela*, Sanjay Leela Bhansali, 2013), class divisions (*Bobby*, Raj Kapoor, 1973), linguistic and regional tensions (*Ek Duje Ke Liye*, K. Balachander, 1981), or religious or national differences (*Julie*, K. S. Sethumadhavan, 1975; *Bombay*, Mani Ratnam, 1995; *Veer-Zaara*, Yash Chopra, 2004; *Ishaqzaade*, Habib Faisal, 2012). This makes the silence around caste as a roadblock in romance especially conspicuous, mirroring the long history of the invisibility of caste in popular Hindi cinema.[1] In this chapter, we look at what happens to filmy love and coupledom when caste (and as it intersects with other vectors of class, gender, and sexuality) is forefronted as the central factor for precarity.

We examine three postmillennial Hindi films: Neeraj Ghaywan's *Masaan* (Crematorium, 2015), Anubhav Sinha's *Article 15* (2019), and *Geeli Pucchi* (Sloppy Kisses, 2020), as they provide an occasion to meditate on the (im)possibility of love in the context of casteist world.[2] We examine these films for their engagement with caste precarity and for the ways they compel a reconfiguration of popular Hindi cinema's most cherished narrative templates of romantic love and coupledom. When the hierarchies and oppressions of caste are forefronted, these films allow us to track the interconnections between caste precarity and the precarization of the couple form, unveiling coupledom as the ultimate expression of inequitably distributed privilege. As the films interrupt the fantasy of the Bollywood romance, they suggest how the relentless repetition of this fantasy is a sign of the brahmanical patriarchal violence integral to heteronormative romance and matrimony.

And yet, even while the films under consideration in this chapter explode this fantasy as they present caste as a structural impediment to love and coupledom, we see how the films participate in a "cruel optimism"[3] that invests faith in romance and the good life. These fantasies work through various prospective promises: of a caste-transgressive coupledom; or of personal, individual liberation from the repressiveness of caste regimes; or the possibility of building an allyship with others who exist within palimpsestic structures of vulnerability.

Since the 1990s and the liberalization of the Indian economy, the heterosexual romantic couple, located at the heart of Bollywood's cinematic enterprise, has followed two predominant trajectories. In the more mainstream, big-budget films directed by filmmakers such as Yash Chopra, Sooraj Barjatya, and Karan Johar, the couple's matrimonial union is unambiguously celebrated through a grotesquely lavish Indian wedding: the big fat Indian wedding (*Hum Aapke Hain Koun . . !*, 1994). The wedding, then, marks not only the film's temporal culmination, but also functions as the endpoint of a long litany of trials and tribulations. Jyotsna Kapur argues that this "contemporary big wedding phenomenon"[4] forms the ideological centerpiece of such films in that it amalgamates an upper-class, caste-based patriarchy with postliberalization politics of individuated choice, articulated most often through conspicuous consumption. Thus the very historical moment in which India emerges as a contender in the global economy is also reinvented as an occasion for the nation to reassert its ethnic identity, a coping strategy against the onslaught of cultural reconfigurations launched by economic reforms. And, crucially, the Hindu wedding—a site that readily conjoins the cornucopias of capitalism and traditionalism—is what enables this tricky, contradictory maneuver out of precarity into national superpower-dom.

While mainstream Bollywood films (and this includes preliberalization cinema) demonstrate a decided refusal to engage in the couple's transition from romance to the mundane normativity of domesticity, in postliberalization New Bollywood films (including those released on OTT streaming platforms), there is a deliberate attempt to imagine a postnuptial afterlife of the romantic couple. As David Shumway observes, romance is inevitably characterized by its inability to "tell the story of a marriage." This is why most Bollywood films culminate with the newlyweds "flanked on both sides"[5] by their familial clans, a sign that the romantic duo's "right to be" is finally legitimated. The sanctioning presence of the family confirms that the couple has been accommodated within the larger community collective and coopted into the nation-building project, of which the family is the mediating authority.

In contrast, however, as Sangita Gopal's groundbreaking work on love and marriage in New Bollywood's cinematic corpus shows, there's a postliberalization trend to imagine and represent the previously neglected terrain of marital life. In disavowing romance, these films replace "the problematic of romance with one concerned with intimacy."[6] It is the couple's "private space," their neoliberal subjectivities played out in the context of privatized, internal impediments and events—"miscommunication, distrust, extramarital attractions and affairs, nervous disorder, psychic possessions"—that come to dominate New Bollywood cinema, rather than the external challenges of "intolerant fathers, jealous rivals, conniving villains, dominant ideologies."[7]

This idea of romantic intrigue or postnuptial drama playing out in private spaces, however, is revealed to be a fantasy, a privilege, or a luxury when caste is centered as an analytic. Familial mores, community norms, societal imperatives, or those of the state loom large to render precarious intercaste love, as well as a Dalit couple's "right to be."

Thus, we contend that the films we examine here—*Masaan*, *Article 15*, and *Geeli Pucchi*—are strikingly different and represent what we argue is a new phase in Hindi cinema's romantic imagination. In none of these films is heterosexual couple formation or conjugality the central concern. None of the films have conventional happy endings. Neither do they have song-and-dance sequences—the site of expression of romance and desire and heterosexual couple formation in popular Hindi cinema—thus suggesting that intercaste love is impossible. In fact, the three films offer us either coupledom interrupted by betrayal or untimely death, or a heterosexual modality that neither culminates in conjugality nor luxuriates in a postnuptial aftermath. Even so, the films occasion an exposition of what we call the "crisis of coupledom" in contemporary India. We argue that prioritizing the couple form and romantic love as frameworks with which to read these films enables us to track New Bollywood's cinematic imagination of amorous desire, and its crises, when it intersects with caste and a provincial (small-town and rural) spatiality.

If, as Gopal suggests, "heterosexual couple-formation has always served as a site in which to imagine a model of the ideal citizen," then, we ask, what does the crisis of coupledom reveal about the ideal citizen in postmillennial India? Most importantly, in highlighting caste as the source of the collapse of, and rifts within, romantic love, we explore the ways in which New Bollywood has envisaged caste as a provocateur of a reformatted intimacy. In the films we examine, the simple act of falling in love takes on a political, radical dimension. Intercaste love especially triggers an upper-caste sense of precarity, which is swiftly and brutally managed through "honor killings," speaking to the violent tenacity of caste's endogamous imperative. By forefronting the inextricable entanglement of the logics of love and the logics of caste, these films recast(e) Indian cinema's dominant narratives of romance and coupledom.

Precarity and Privilege in *Masaan*

Neeraj Ghaywan's critically acclaimed *Masaan* (alternately titled "Fly Away Solo"), which won two awards at the Cannes film festival—FIPRESCI, International Jury of Film Critics prize, and Promising Future prize in the Un Certain Regard section—is set around the crematoriums of Varanasi and is constituted by two parallel plotlines. One revolves around Deepak Kumar, a college-educated Dalit man (from the Dom untouchable/Dalit community that prepares and cremates bodies) whose mutually reciprocated romantic relationship with upper-caste Shaalu Gupta remains unconsummated in marriage because she dies in a freak road accident. The film's other plotline focuses on Devi Pathak, the daughter of a Brahmin Hindu priest (Vidyadhar Pathak), both of whom are harassed by a corrupt cop who extorts them for money after the fallout of Devi's indiscreet sexual liaison: Devi's romantic interest (Piyush Agarwal) kills himself after being intimidated by the police. Thus both story arcs, which follow their own trajectories of conflict and resolution, feature "unconventional" couples who pursue forbidden love or transgressive desires outside of socially sanctioned norms. While the main characters inhabit the same milieu, the two plotlines develop independently of each other, only to intersect in the film's last scene. Devi and Deepak meet in the city of Allahabad, a city to which they've both moved to work for the Indian Railways, in an attempt to escape their hometown's stagnation and the hegemony of brahmanical patriarchy that impacts them both in distinctive and different ways.

In an attempt to create a broader audience for his film, *Masaan*'s director, Ghaywan, emphasized that the film wasn't a "multiplex film" or meant just for a "festival audience." In some ways, though, the film does fit the category of low-budget, nonformulaic, socially conscious, multiplex film, a New Bollywood film that eschews conventions of postliberalization popular Indian cinema.[8] Thus, for instance, there is no emphasis on stars or spectacle, lavish sets, song-and-dance sequences, upper-caste and upper-class protagonists in uber-urbane or transnational locales. In fact, *Masaan* shares the features of a "multiplot multiplex film" of the kind that Gopal discusses, a narrative form that consists of loosely allied story arcs, features pairs of heterosexual couples associated by place or circumstance, and deals with the vicissitudes of love and marriage.[9] Gopal argues that these second-generation, multiplot, multiplex films install new forms of conjugation and mark a break from the extreme experimentations with, and deformations of, the couple form in earlier multiplex films such as *Jism* (Body, 2003) and *Dansh* (Snake Bite, 2005) where sex and/or "strange and perverse relations" hijacked the entire domain of couple formation.[10]

Unlike the multiplot films that Gopal discusses, however, *Masaan* does not feature postnuptial heterosexual couples, nor does it really install new forms of conjugation, in that the film gives us only failed couplehood. Even so, its multiplot template serves some important and interlinked functions. First, by placing the two plotlines of interrupted couple formation adjacent to each other, it allows for a meditation on the intersectional workings of gender and caste in creating a crisis around coupling. The film alternates between the two narrative arcs to suggest the operations of brahmanical patriarchy in both, even as one plotline seemingly revolves around gender constraints as they relate to female sexuality and the other depicts a cross-caste romance. In most Indian films, caste is made invisible either through the presentation of upper-caste protagonists as caste-neutral or through other kinds of obfuscation, such as in *Toilet: Ek Prem Katha* (Toilet: A Love Story, Shree Narayan Singh, 2017), where the question of women's vulnerability distracts attention away from the reality of caste. In contrast, in *Masaan*, the parallel stories force the viewer to see the subtly interconnected technologies of gender-caste-class.

Second, and relatedly, all four young individuals that form the couples allow for a presentation of the internally diversified aspirational middle classes and its wide spectrum of subjectivities in small-town areas of neoliberal India. This enables the film to depict emerging urban areas as geographical sites with their own "dynamics and dialectics."[11] The film accommodates two upper-caste women, a Dalit, and an upper-caste man from a shared social and provincial milieu—even as they mostly inhabit different worlds within this milieu—as they navigate the vagaries of love and desire. This allows us to register both the differences and similarities—of gender, class, caste—that not only determine the characters' different struggles, but also come to represent the proliferating middle classes, who are precisely the targeted audiences in the new phase of multiplex expansion.[12]

The opening sequence of the film centers on Devi and Piyush's ill-fated dalliance. We see a shot of Devi watching porn on her cell phone, as a way to educate herself on sex before meeting Piyush. This scene articulates a sexual naiveté but also an open, frank approach to sex, a willingness to teach herself what her repressive milieu won't give her access to. In fact, *Masaan* works hard to normalize Devi and Piyush's physical intimacy. Later, when Devi's father asks her about Piyush and why she did something as outrageous as checking into a motel for a sexual rendezvous, Devi stands her ground to argue that her actions weren't all that outlandish: she and Piyush were friends, and she liked talking to him. Their sexual intimacy, then, is presented as harmless, a natural segue produced by, and within, everyday interactions that transpire in workplaces. Even in the opening scene, when Devi and Piyush touch each other hesitantly yet eagerly, the film extends a compassionate lens upon them, granting the couple both privacy and dignity.

An upper-caste, patriarchal state apparatus, however, sees things differently. The cops burst into the hotel room where Piyush and Devi are naked in bed and treat the couple as criminals indulging in depraved and illicit behavior. The pair is accused of having turned the hotel into a "bazaar" (brothel), and, of course, the stigma of the moment is projected onto Devi, her body simultaneously sexualized and racialized: Is she a "Nepali prostitute," the cops demand to know. Within seconds, the opening sequence's attempt at delineating a shyly adventurous, youthful encounter is violently disrupted by the literal and metaphorical "barging in" of state machinery, looking to discipline young people's socially unsanctioned desire.

In some ways, Devi doesn't have a linguistic, cognitive facility to explain what her actions mean, at least not in a way that is legible to a patriarchal state order. This is why Devi doesn't have a response to her father or the cop, both of whom demand to know what the endpoint of her pursuit of coupling outside the bounds of marriage was. When, for instance, her father says, "did you not for one moment ask yourself about what you're doing and why," her response is an ambiguous "pata nahin" [I don't know]. And yet she has a clear understanding and articulation of what her actions *do not mean*: a lack of honor, morality, or respectability. She is unequivocal in her insistence that her behavior is not deserving of revilement or shame. Devi refuses to be cast as the siren who led Piyush astray and is responsible for his death. So, when her coworker at the coaching center asks, "Didn't you feel any shame doing it?" and tries to browbeat her into feeling guilt that he died as a result of her indiscretion, Devi doesn't lose a moment in retaliating against his malicious insinuation: "Whatever it was, we were equally involved." Similarly, she rejects the cop and her father's narrative that casts her *izzat* (honor) as being jeopardized by her sexual "scandal." In that sense, her inability to "explain" her own actions is, in fact, the very means by which she rejects their appropriation by a patriarchal state that panics about and monitors women's sexuality.

And, most crucially, in doing so, not only does Devi counter Indian society and cinema's morally laden attitudes toward premarital sex, she, and through her the film, also espouses an alternative relationship to sexuality, one that is more interested in exploring the motivation, desire, and nature of coupling and intimacy rather than a teleological drive toward conjugality. This is why Devi's refutation of the men's characterization of her pursuit of sexual intimacy with Piyush as feminine deviancy, and her reframing of it within a narrative of "*jigyaasa*" (curiosity), is so important. This characterization stuns the men around her, especially because it articulates a female desire untrammeled by normative, repressive codes, and because it brazenly rejects the idea of a "sex scandal" as something that touches her interiority or sense of self. It certainly creates logistical impediments for her and her father, but it doesn't tarnish the validity of the gentle, tender encounter with Piyush and their mutual exploration of an affinity born out of the ephemeral and mundane.

It is true that the complications in Devi's story arc arise, for the most part, from her pursuit of premarital sex. At the same time, caste, and its intertwining with gender, play a significant role. For one, Devi's ability to indulge her sexual "*jigyaasa*" (curiosity) is tied to her caste-class privilege. Her upper-caste identity (irrespective of her lower-class status) grants her an easy mobility in Varanasi—a town marked by its hyperreligiosity—which, in turn, makes navigating the city to meet her lover a tad easier (albeit not without a fair share of tricky maneuvers). Furthermore, as the daughter of an educated Brahmin father, an erstwhile Sanskrit professor, she enjoys the privilege of being "treated like a boy," given an education and allowed to seek employment. Even here, though, the access afforded by her caste is interlinked with her dead mother's gendered suffering. Devi's father grants her so much agency because he carries guilt about letting his wife die when she was severely ill; instead of taking her to the doctor, in the classic vein of a patriarch who takes his labors too seriously and dismisses women's pain, he continued to grade his students' exams. The mother's death because of his negligence underpins the psychological motivations for the liberties he grants his daughter.

It is true that their upper-caste status doesn't protect Devi and her father from being blackmailed by the cop (he even turns a deaf ear to Devi's father's plea to spare them the exorbitant bribe since they hail from the same caste community). And Devi does suffer harsh consequences for exploring sexual intimacy outside of marriage. Still, her respectable upper-caste background protects her from the sort of harassment that a Dalit woman would have had to endure in the same situation. The cop is, after all, willing to extend a "second chance" to Devi, even if in exchange for a hefty lump sum; we can be quite sure that such a luxury would not be afforded to her Dalit counterpart.

Ultimately, Devi's sexual scandal is as much about patriarchal anxiety as it is about upper-caste anxiety; the two coproduce and undergird one another. Because it occurs outside the sanctity of caste-approved matrimony, Devi's violation of sexual protocol is potentially also a caste transgression. So, even though she and Piyush constitute an endogamous couple, marriage has not ratified their sexuality as caste-preserving and thus their liaison is threatening in all that it potentiates. Devi's sexual adventure and pursuit of premarital sexual intimacy, her defense of sexual curiosity, are thus not only a deliberate protest against the patriarchal regimentation of her feminine sexuality, but also an unwitting challenge to upper-caste control of women's bodies through marriage and the range of brahmanical, patriarchal norms that impose limits on women.

The film's editing nudges the viewer to make precisely these connections: that where gender is explicit, the operation of caste is just as vital; where caste is apparent, gender is also always in the fray.

This is why the opening sequence ends with Devi, sitting in the back of the police car, looking at Piyush's lifeless body in an ambulance, and bleeds into the next scene—also the film's other plotline—where we are introduced to Deepak. We see him with a backpack, returning home from the engineering polytechnic, where he's a student. This cut allows us to subliminally register several continuities between the first and the second sequence. For one, the backpack emerges as an integral part of the mise-en-scène in both; in Devi's case, her backpack, and the change of clothes she hides in it, symbolizes both her on-the-go, workaday persona as well as the sartorial secrets that enable her to quench her curiosity. The backpack, then, houses the technologies she uses to pursue a chance at a sexually fulfilling life, something not ordinarily afforded to her or most women, for that matter. In Deepak's case, his backpack identifies him as a student, pursuing higher education in a highly sought after field. His body, and its accoutrements—his backpack, the motorcycle—mark an anticaste disruption in an arena that has long stood as the preserve of the upper castes. The segue of Devi's story into Deepak's invites us to connect the yearnings and discontents of both of these young people, of different genders, from disparate castes and cultural milieus, who nevertheless share a geographical, spatial affinity to this small town.

Second, as the edit moves from a dead Piyush to Deepak, it invites us also to ascertain the similarities, as well as the differences, between them. They're both young men from small-town and second- and third-tier cities—precisely the new target audience of the multiplex—pursuing romance and desire and educational opportunities (in similar fields of study, engineering and computer science), and with aspirations of (upward) mobility. It is not too far-fetched to imagine that Devi could have met someone like Deepak in a chance encounter at a college or café, or through Facebook, an unsettling, nightmarish scenario for the keepers of caste laws and prohibitions, who find it increasingly impossible to keep at bay intermixing across caste divides, especially in contexts of mounting mobility.

If the opening sequence gives us the crisis in the romantic dyad of Devi-Piyush, the "intermission" of the film aptly marks the interruption in Deepak and Shaalu's couple formation. This occurs when Deepak reveals to Shaalu that he's from the lower-caste Dom community. Like Devi, the issue of caste is not even on Shaalu's horizon. This is very much in contrast to Deepak and his friends, who are hyperaware of caste markers (such as Shaalu's last name); Deepak, we learn, carries the secret "burden" of being lower-caste. Shaalu's caste privilege[13] makes her assume that Deepak is probably from the same caste-class as she is, as she jokes with him about his reluctance to not reveal anything about where he lives or introduce her to his family. Shaalu can be caste-blind in a way that Deepak cannot. A frustrated Deepak, who feels hemmed in by his caste, after revealing in vehement and horrifyingly descriptive language his family's occupation of preparing bodies for cremation, throws Shaalu a challenge: "Can you imagine [this life]? Do you still want to visit me, my family?"[14] His declaration is at once a reflection of his justified anger at the inequities of caste as well as an ultimatum to love, to withstand the process of making visible the materiality of untouchability. Remarkably, Shaalu rises to the challenge and shows herself willing to unlearn her privilege.

In another connection between the two plot threads, Shaalu's initial response to Deepak's offer of marriage is "pata nahin" (I don't know), which echoes verbatim Devi's response to her father when he had questioned her about her motives for being sexually involved with Piyush. It is significant, however, that this is Shaalu's response to Deepak *before* she knows that he's a Dalit. Her noncommittal response to Deepak might register her ambivalence, as a woman, about rushing into conjugality, or at least before ensuring and consolidating a more equitable relationship with him. In their "meet-cute," Deepak is attracted to Shaalu's feisty ragging of his friend, who has gifted her friend a giant stuffed teddy bear on her birthday without considering how she will take this home without being inquisitioned by her family. Shaalu's street-smart, practical gendered knowledge collides, in a sense, with Deepak and his friend's desire to participate in the upwardly mobile hallmark-ification of love. In comparison with Devi, Shaalu might appear virginal and less assertive of her desires. And yet she is not afraid to express her reciprocation of desire for Deepak. She calls him "cute" and kisses him back, is clear about why she likes him (his "honesty"), insists that he recognize and share in her interests (poetry), calls him out on his unwarranted sarcasm toward her, and mocks him for his chivalrous protectiveness of her. All these moments, even in the brief presence she occupies on screen, speak to Shaalu's desire for and pursuit of a nonhierarchical partnership with Deepak.

Her tentativeness toward Deepak, however, changes once he reveals his Dalit identity to her. As Shaalu confronts the reality of caste, now made so proximate through love, she undergoes a lesson in precarity and intersectionality, and she recalibrates the stakes of her romantic coupling with Deepak. While Shaalu is left speechless after Deepak issues the challenge to imagine his life, and by proxy her life with him, a subjective transformation ensues and she begins to overcome "something that might appear to be impossible."[15] Perhaps Shaalu's interest in antiauthoritarian and secular Indian, Muslim, Hindi/Urdu poets (such as Syed Akbar Allahabadi, Dushyant Kumar, Bashir Badr, Ghalib, Nida Fazli) anticipates her capacity to "experience the world on the basis of difference"[16] rather than an ideological investment in high brahmanical culture. Slowly, we observe her unpack her caste-blindness and caste-class privilege. When the bus that's taking Shaalu's family to a Hindu pilgrimage site stops by a roadside eatery, Shaalu hears her mother say that the food there is good because "the owner is from our caste." A sudden awakening to the reality of caste—thanks to her romantic intimacy with a Dalit man—now alerts her to the ubiquity of caste.

A perturbed Shaalu calls Deepak from outside the eatery and tells him that she's willing to marry him, and elope with him if necessary, because she knows that her parents "won't accept [him]." She describes them as being "stuck in the past, with their old-fashioned ideas." "But," she reassures him, "I'm with you. You just need to find a good job." Her decision to reject "safety-first love" and choose "risky love"[17] in her cross-caste desire for a subaltern man is a political and radical act that possesses the promise of personal transformation and carries the potential to unleash transgressive possibilities as it destabilizes the status quo of caste regimes built on the control of women's sexuality.

Shaalu's assertion that she is ready to elope with Deepak thus expresses a desire of conscious coupling and is a political act in defiance of the casteist order.[18] In this, she parallels Devi's own transgressions against brahmanical patriarchy. In a sense, Deepak and Shaalu's kiss, which, instead of the song-and-dance sequence of classic Hindi cinema, consolidates and seals their romantic relationship, is already loaded with anticaste potentiality, even before her formal decision. This forbidden kiss, depicted as tender and as the most natural thing—much like Piyush and Devi's lovemaking—is subversive in the face of the injunctions against touch, so central to the caste system. It challenges the rhetoric of intercaste desire as disgusting, criminal, and unnatural that is promoted by those who oppose it.

There is, however, another dimension to her declaration of romantic love and solidarity to Deepak. Lest we imagine that love has the power to evacuate caste, the language of her commitment to him remains, very much, embedded in the workings of caste. The very words that confirm the noncontingency of her desire—she loves him, no matter what his caste, and in fact goes a step further to commit to marrying him—nevertheless reveal the naiveté of even well-intentioned upper-caste people. Simultaneously, they give an account of the desperate, entrepreneurial routes Dalits search for in their attempts to escape the clutches of caste. Shaalu's naiveté in imagining that "things will get better later" (once the couple is married) is a symptom of the extent to which her caste has cocooned her from the reality of upper-caste violence, of families murdering young couples who dare commit the blasphemy of an intercaste marriage. Her hope, which Deepak echoes, that a "good job" will eventually make him palatable to her family, is another instance of this naiveté. They both assume that an aspirational middle-classness, achieved through professional means, will give him more leverage into "acceptability" in an upper-caste family.

There are, indeed, many moments in the film that suggest Deepak's absorption into a neoliberal modernity, that appears at first glance to be as accessible to Dalits as it is to upper-castes. This is why Deepak is able to deploy the technologies of a digital modernity and mobility (even if with a little help from his friends); internet cafes, Facebook apps, mix-tapes, a job in the railway, are ostensibly the scattered markings of the equalizing power of technological modernity. He is then, in many ways, a part of the "internet generation," which opens the possibility of a Dalit man pursuing an upper-caste woman without getting lynched for it.[19] He represents the newly emerging "middle class of educated-in-service Dalits,"[20] who shares with his father the belief that an education and employment will allow him, unlike his brother, to break from caste's curse of inheriting a profession. Here he is not wrong.

And yet, as we know, upward mobility through the prestige of a "good job" will not make Deepak any more desirable as a matrimonial candidate for an upper-caste woman; such is the indefatigable logic of caste. On the contrary, a socially mobile Dalit man further triggers upper-caste male anxiety and sense of insecurity in the face of Dalit assertion and rise to power; a Dalit man's access to an upper-caste woman aggravates the upper-castes' perception of loss of power, which they invariably retaliate against by punishing—with rape, lynching, flogging—caste-transgressive behavior. In addition, as Dalits continue to be subject to continuing socioeconomic precarities (e.g., discrimination in jobs), it becomes evident that, for Dalits then, the promises of neoliberal capitalism have been "unable to surmount the caste hegemony."[21]

Fascinatingly, *Masaan* does not explore the aftermath of what would happen were Deepak and Shaalu to get married. Shaalu's accidental death jeopardizes an easy promise or a simple confirmation of the fantasy's failure. Her death highlights the extreme unlikelihood of intercaste love coming to fruition, but it also keeps alive the hope of its possibility. In fact, in both story arcs, the couple formations are curtailed by accidental deaths. In the case of Devi and Piyush, it jarringly interrupts the natural flow of their upper-caste romance toward conjugality. That their story starts where most romantic adventures end—with sex and death—forces Devi to undergo a radical transformation, which takes her past an apolitical pursuit of sexual curiosity to a full-fledged contestation with brahmanical patriarchy, one which she, remarkably, wins.

The climactic concluding scene highlights the impossibility of regulating love and disciplining desire according to state or caste regimes, as the specter of intercaste union rears its head once again with Deepak and Devi's encounter in Allahabad. It is important that they meet on the *ghats*—the site where desire, death, and caste conflate—but not on the *ghats* of their small hometown, Varanasi.

Their meeting at the end of the film recalls a previous occasion, when they could have met but were kept apart by the intermeshed operations of caste and gender. Devi, in trying to find her father, tries to follow him to the *ghats* in Varanasi but is forbidden from going all the way because women aren't allowed near the morbid horrors of death. So she looks from above, and in the distance, on the *ghats*, we see Deepak working on cremation rituals. She doesn't know Deepak yet, but the site of Dalit labor, and its intimacy with the rituals of death maintained through centuries of caste coercion, overwhelm her and she starts to weep. Witnessing her lover slit his wrists and die out of fear of police violence and the loss of respectability produces an unspoken, unpredictable propinquity between a Dalit man and an upper-caste woman, characters out of two separate plots who don't know one another and yet share ineffable traumas resulting from precarities.

When they finally meet on the riverbanks in Allahabad, the scene creates a "sangam,"[22] as it were, not just of the two plotlines, but also a Dalit man and an upper-caste woman, both of whom exist on the margins of brahmanical patriarchy, even if they are differently located in terms of precarity and privilege. The film hints that Devi, whose own experiences of vulnerability have primed her for reflection, will take Shaalu's place as a partner in Deepak's life.

In holding out this prospective promise of another caste-transgressive coupledom, the film participates in what Berlant has called "cruel optimism." Like other multiplot multiplex films, this union also perhaps attempts to deliver "putatively, a more 'democratic' social imaginary."[23] In her review, Deborah Young goes a step further, declaring that "the uplifting ending paves the way for change and modernity."[24] Suffice it to say, the film's ending is suspended, suggesting that this potential cross-caste *couple-in-progress*, the harbinger of modernity, will have to contend with societal prejudice in a shining new India yet to be born. Until then, this new couple formation is left unnamed and unsculpted.

Finding Love in a Hopeless Place: Bourgeois and Dalit Love in *Article 15*

Article 15's raison d'etre has little to do with either romance or with the postmarital challenges of intimacy. In fact, the film is a well-paced police thriller that centers, albeit through a brahmanical gaze, the ignominies and violence borne out of caste in North India. The film follows Ayan Ranjan, an urbane, upper-caste police inspector, assigned to head the police headquarters in the fictional town of Laalgaon, and its neighboring villages, in India's largest state, Uttar Pradesh. At the start, Ayan brings to bear a romanticizing and patronizing lens onto the scenic hinterland: he's both spellbound by its "pollution-free" beauty, but he also mocks its "1980s Bollywood-style" gauche, feudal, antediluvian tenor. Very quickly, however, the film transitions into a noirish investigation of the kidnapping of three Dalit girls, two of whom are also raped and lynched, their bodies—following the long-standing visual economy of anti-Dalit violence—hung from a tree as exemplary lessons in retribution for insubordination against upper-caste dictates, something that also terrorizes other caste minorities into silence and submission.

Ayan's hunt for the murderer(s) and the third missing girl takes him on a journey that lays bare the predominance of caste hierarchies and upper-caste violence in rural India. Even more, it reveals the convoluted matrix of power structures—from high-ranking politicians and bureaucrats, godmen, private development contractors, doctors in government hospitals, low-ranking policemen—implicated in the perpetuation of a casteist worldview and the brahmanical oppression that accompanies it. And finally, these encounters with "the real" India unsettle Ayan's modern, metropolitan, upper-class caste-blindness,[25] as well as compel him, as a solution, to opt for a discourse that declares the paramountcy of the Indian constitution's rejection of caste-based discrimination, enshrined in Article 15.

In this scenario, focusing on the two romantic couples that occupy a relatively marginal place in the narrative schema may seem tangential to the film's own centering of caste. And yet we argue that prioritizing the couple form and romantic love as frameworks with which to read *Article 15* allows us to bring to the surface previously and usually unattended phenomena in popular Hindi cinema.

Thus Ayan and his girlfriend Aditi, and Gaura and Nishad allow us to explore, first, a couple form that is neither predicated on a linear progression toward marriage nor succumbs to postnuptial disenchantment. Second, they allow us to examine the relationship between love and politics: the implications of political incompatibility for the future of the romantic couple; the sometimes incommensurate relationship between politics and romantic desire; and, most crucially, ways in which differentially distributed political-caste-cultural-economic precarity yields a markedly varied "crises of coupledom."

And, finally, by investigating romantic love in the film, we contend with a contemporary rural spatiality as the site of desire, its interruptions, its recoveries, and its loss. More often than not, New Bollywood demonstrates a penchant for locating love in the midst of metropolitan glitz or in the endearingly quirky charms of small-town urbanism (*Dum Laga ke Haisha*, 2015). This has created a scenario in which the countryside, in general, but also especially as a space for the emergence and evolution of an amorous subjectivity, stands utterly marginalized. *Article 15*, however, encourages us to reinscribe the cinematic imaginary of the hinterland by overlaying it with the complexities of couple formation.

Ayan and Aditi's relationship doesn't follow the usual "boy meets girl, love encounters obstacles, boy gets girl"[26] narrative arc. We quickly surmise that Ayan and Aditi were college sweethearts who continue to remain each other's' confidantes, even if they "talk less, argue more" now. Aditi lives in Delhi, while Ayan has been transferred to Uttar Pradesh as the additional superintendent of police. We meet them at a stage when the joyous frisson of early love has already withered in their relationship. In fact, all the accoutrements of mainstream Bollywood's depiction of romantic love are missing from their relationship: there is no urgent plot progression toward marriage; we learn nothing about the role their respective families have played vis-à-vis their relationship; there is no obvious emotional impediment that keeps them apart. And yet their interactions indicate a definite crisis of intimacy, a crisis that comes to focus on the realities of a casteist modernity (rather than, as the New Bollywood films Gopal discusses, within the matrices of conjugality).

We are given very few insights into the root causes of Ayan and Aditi's alienation from one another. In the course of the film, however, it is their differing (initial) responses to caste (discrimination and violence) that emerges as the centerpiece around which their crisis of coupledom is enacted. Interestingly, then, even as *Article 15* makes caste violence in rural India its primary subject of representation, it investigates the phenomenon in close conjunction with the fate of a modern bourgeois couple, decoupled from matrimony. Perhaps it is precisely the dethroning of conjugality as a cinematic priority that opens the way, simultaneously, for the exposition of another form of modern coupledom, rarely explored in Hindi cinema—the long-distance couple—as well as makes room for something besides "love itself" as the central puzzle that the couple must grapple with.

In order to fully grasp the film's political vision, it's important to fathom the contours—both the form and function—of Ayan and Aditi's relationship through the nature of their conversations that transpire over calls and texts. It is true that their six long-distance (and two in-person) interactions are marginal and disconcertingly abrupt. Even so, their metronomic interruptions in the film's narrative flow determine how the film, and its protagonist, arrive at their argument about caste, marking both the progressive contours and the myopic limits of that argument. To put it another way, the film's liberal politics in acknowledging caste as an ongoing oppressive force, as well as its problematic caste politics—that the resolution to the caste question is framed within an overwhelmingly brahmanical savior complex—are borne out of, in large part, the bourgeois romantic relationship between Ayan and Aditi.

In some ways, these ritualistic exchanges with Aditi are what tether him to his urbane, bourgeois existence, something he's jarringly separated from once he gets off the multilane highway to police the dusty interiors of the Indian cow belt. Ayan's persistent need to narrate his ambient and eventful experiences to Aditi are as much about her role (however undefined) as his primary partner as about his need to administer information to a witness who shares the bourgeois sensorium through which he accesses his new spatial context, a rural habitus. Ironically, however, his uncomplicated desire to simply transfer information—about the pollution-free environs of the countryside, the rape and lynching of two Dalit girls, the role he needs to play in discovering the culprits—are all subjected to an incessant process of translation and editorializing by Aditi. She punctures his pastoral musings and compares him to the notorious "Mountbatten," the last viceroy of India, reminding him that his elite presence is as alien as that of the British in colonial India. She berates him for his willful refusal to read the lynching of Dalit girls as caste-based violence (he seems content to accept that they might be victims of honor killing by their own fathers). And she expresses frustration at his lack of self-knowledge and conviction, his proclivity for spinelessly following other people's expectations.

The mismatch between what Ayan needs and what Aditi offers, is, of course, a necessary plot device to move Ayan past his upper-class-caste misreading of his experiences. It is, in large measure, Aditi's contrary political wisdom that compels him to address the operation of caste in the case of the lynched girls. At the same time, though, the strain and dysfunction of their relationship encapsulates not only the divergence of their ideological positionality, but also the innate precarity latent in their means of communication. Shaunak Sen argues that the preponderance of cellular technologies occasioned a new narrative possibility in cinema: characters physically separated by geography could now "participate in the dramatic universe via the cellular topology."[27] While Sen draws attention to the figures of the terrorist and the unknown lover-caller, our interest lies in examining the new form of cinematic coupledom—the long-distance lovers—made possible as a result of cellular ubiquity.

Ayan contacts Aditi for all sorts of reasons and on all kinds of occasions: to report major and minor incidents; for solace or to express outrage in moments of political-professional conundrum; to seek her assistance in drawing national media's attention to the lynching case; to share the absurdly arcane, casteist things that his subordinates say. In some ways, all of Ayan's lonely, contemplative moments on screen morph into shots of him sitting in his car or office, his cellphone in hand, either calling or texting Aditi. Curiously, then, Ayan perpetually occupies a hybrid spatiality, traversing between his corporeal presence in rural India and his confessional, overwrought interiority, turned toward his lover in the city. At the same time, though, the continuous exchanges between Ayan and Aditi are marred by an inescapable potential for miscommunication. The cellular mediation upon which their relationship depends always carries the threat of contributing further to the emotive distance between them. We can never be certain how they read and interpret each other's messages, and while the voiceover of the character, speaking out loud their portion of the exchange, confirms for the audience the tonal nuances of how the communication is intended, there is no guarantee that the recipient of the message interprets it correctly. Therefore, while cellular technology enables a physical mobility and separability of the romantic couple, it also introduces a new kind of precarity of coupledom.

One episode, in particular, highlights the double strain that political differences and cellular mediation put on their interactions. A deeply shaken Ayan calls Aditi to tell her about the horrifying sight of the lynched girls; he speaks hurriedly, emphasizing how young the girls were, comparing the lawlessness of the situation to the "wild wild west." Aditi responds to his agitated angst with a morose sobriety and a moment of silence, which he misreads as her absence from the other side of the line: "hello, you there?" he asks. In this fleeting moment alone, several things become evident: the strain that technological communication puts on them, the distinctions in their emotive landscape, and the gap in their grasp of grass-roots reality. While the lynching of Dalit girls conjures for Ayan a cinematic hyperreality, far removed in time, genre, and geography, for Aditi their murder only confirms a truth about contemporary India that she already knows. Her very next words—"Last week they'd found another girl's body in Rajasthan; looked like rape, but some people were dismissing it as honor killing"—clarify why her response to Ayan's information isn't one of naive shock or disbelief; she's well-versed in the knowledge that such horrors are routine. At the same time, she draws attention to the caste and metropolitan privileges that allow cases like "Nirbhaya"[28]—of upper-caste girls raped in Delhi—to make front-page news in national newspapers, while incidents of Dalit girls raped and lynched in Uttar Pradesh and Rajasthan receive little coverage.

Ayan's response to Aditi's reality check is to become defensive and aggressive, accusing her of jumping the gun in assuming that this is, in fact, upper-caste violence against Dalits rather than intracaste patriarchal violence (a narrative the other cops are trying to establish). He goes on to reprimand her for lacking "moderation," for expecting him to be an "activist" and an academic ("I can't do a PhD on this okay"), when all he wanted was to "share this with [her]."

The final retorts exchanged between the two clinch the matter: "You want a hero, Aditi," to which she replies, "I don't want a hero, Ayan. I just want people [*log*] who don't wait around for a hero." What's fascinating is that while Ayan's jibe seems fueled by a sense of personal hurt, a long-standing sense of inadequacy of not being good or heroic enough to satisfy his politically woke girlfriend, Aditi's retort seems less fixated on the private grievances of their relationship and more concerned with how society, as a collective, functions. While he's disappointed in her as a girlfriend—for judging him, not hearing him out without challenging him—she's disappointed in him as a member of society, who has the power to impose the rule of law and bring about justice and yet will not operate with the political-ethical clarity he ought to.

In a sense, Aditi enables Ayan's foray into realities that he has, conveniently enough, remained oblivious to. Not only does she remind him of the Dalit girl's rape-lynching incident in Rajasthan, she also alerts him to the workings of caste in temporal and geographical domains that are far more proximate than he imagines: caste taboos aren't just the preserve of rural districts; "till a few years ago, even our moms would separate the maid's utensils," she tells him when he expresses disbelief at the practices of untouchability that still persevere in villages. As his girlfriend, then, she functions as a historical-anthropological archive that challenges an ahistorical, depoliticized understanding of the world he inhabits. This is why it is to her that Ayan first confesses the shame that's replaced the unmitigated pride he used to feel for his country, and it is to her that he first articulates his intention to "unmess" things, to find "new words" and "new ways" to address the "caste-war" going on in this country.

The limitless access that Ayan exercises upon Aditi's time and emotional-intellectual-political labor needs noting. Empowered by cellular technology, he contacts her while she's working from home, driving, on an early-morning jog, on the verge of leaving home; each time, not only does she abandon what she's doing to patiently attend to the wide array of his emotional and practical needs, but often also offers him insights and perspectival shifts he didn't even know he wanted or needed. The asymmetrical and gendered nature of the labor she performs goes unnoticed mostly because women's reductive function as provocateurs of male agency in cinematic narratives is utterly normalized. Aditi is less a visual spectacle and more the ethical epicenter against which Ayan must measure his benevolent brahmanical, masculine agency.

As a result, Ayan's moral imperative to do what is "right," to bring to justice the corrupt and violent machinations of the upper castes, is seemingly whittled down to a question of being inspired by his romantic love, who also doubles as his moral compass. The film tricks us into thinking that the true reward(s) of action against caste violence is the elevation of Ayan's status in the eyes of his lover, who will now look upon him with that special "sparkle" that was missing before. It is as though the real benefits Ayan accrues for catching the culprits is the reinstantiation of bourgeois coupledom, rather than the reinscription of privilege: the end of his rural stint, return to metropolitan comfort, and a pat on the back from the nation's home minister. Whether or not an upper-caste man goes against the system, more likely than not he benefits from the institutional structures within which he operates. The film encourages us to forget that.

While many reviews lauded *Article 15* for its supposedly unflinching account of the pervasiveness of caste, several also justifiably critiqued it for propagating an "upper-caste gaze,"[29] a brahmanical savior complex and spectatorship.[30] Lower-caste audiences, after all, don't need lessons in their own suffering, especially when Brahmin heroes dominate the narrative. As Pradeep Attri suggests, none of this is new to Hindi cinema: by putting a "Brahmin character in charge of telling a Dalit story,"[31] the movie prioritizes humanizing casteist behavior. While the film may, as Uday Bhatia believes, "afflict the comfortable"—the multiplex, educated audiences who feign caste neutrality and remain caste-blind—it nevertheless "robs Dalits of their agency."[32] In many ways, *Article 15* has been read as an exercise in *savarna* narcissism and self-aggrandizement, wherein both the brutalizers and liberators of Dalits are Brahmin; "marginalized voices remain marginal" in the film, but their "collective traumas" are "mined" for, ostensibly, socially responsible scripts.[33]

What's missing from these important criticisms is the vital role that bourgeois romance and coupledom play in the film's perpetuation of brahmanical interventionism and upper-caste entrepreneurialism. It is true that the film does validate Aditi's version of reality over Ayan's, in which caste violence stands indicted and punished. Nevertheless, in offering the audience a more liberal, self-aware upper-caste character (who draws the protagonist over to her version of politics), the film neutralizes an Ambedkarite politics of caste annihilation[34] in favor of a navel-gazing reformism. Even more crucially, it is upper-caste-bourgeois love that powers and sanctifies the dilution of the film's anticaste politics.

It's important to note, for instance, that Aditi's gender and class identity frame the limits of her political imagination. She is, it is true, a "New Woman," living alone in Delhi, the national capital, and, as we're informed in passing, works on "gender equality and human rights," subjects on which her articles are often published. Despite the personal and professional independence she embodies, however, the two predominant markers that characterize her leave much to be desired: First, her primary (and frankly only) responsibility in the film is curtailed by her heteropatriarchal function to spur Ayan into action. Her second characteristic feature is the upper-class context she inhabits. Each time she appears on screen, she's located within an excessively bourgeois mise-en-scène: a posh beige living room with lush pillows carelessly strewn about, the inside of a car, a manicured park, and a lavish balcony. The seamless switch between her Western and traditional sartorial attire—from a chic jogging outfit to a flowy, white *salwar kameez*—and the everyday practices and technologies she engages in repeatedly confirm her caste-class privileges. The film also renders her hyperindividuated (she's never seen with any other character or engaged in an activity that isn't immediately stalled in order to redirect her attention to Ayan) and thus she functions as the feminine, nurturing, guiding counterpart to the Brahmin hero.

In many ways, then, Aditi, and her romantic relationship with Ayan, is what determines the film's bourgeois, brahmanical rendition of the caste problem and caste solution. It appears as though the film intends for its elite audience to receive, alongside Ayan, an anticaste education through Aditi's political wisdom, as she unveils the subtle dimensions of the caste cauldron and explicates the stakes involved in battling it. But really, what occurs is that Aditi's interjections do the work of muddying the truth about caste in contemporary India and distract from the truly emancipatory routes to combat it, which would at the very least entail centering Dalits. In reminding Ayan (and the audience) about "our mothers" who "till a few years ago" practiced untouchability, the film, via Aditi, does something nefarious: It pretends to challenge an urbane, liberal smugness that projects caste atrocities exclusively onto India's rural landscape, but what it really does is precisely to reconfirm that myth by, first, allocating only "minor" (when compared to rape and lynching) caste offenses to urban settings. Second, even these are temporally and generationally distanced (these "minor" offenses were committed a few years ago, by our mothers).

This narrative, while appealing to and assuaging upper-caste metropolitan audiences, is patently inaccurate. Ashwini Deshpande argues that "India's 'Silicon Valley' cities, poster children of modern, globalizing India, temples of cutting-edge information technology," report hundreds of cases under the SC/ST Prevention of Atrocities Act (1989) each year.[35] It is reasonable to assume, Deshpande continues, that these reported cases are only the tip of the iceberg. Furthermore, the crimes reported under this act are far more egregious than what Aditi would like us to believe. Amit Thorat and Omkar Joshi's 2015 Indian Human Development Survey reveals that 27 percent of Indians continue to practice untouchability despite it being illegal.[36] Similarly, Evita Das has examined the continuing caste segregation that governs housing in most metropolitan centers in India.[37] Attri is right when he asserts that *Article 15* ignores the fact that "caste has changed its location" and now resides in top universities and medical colleges where Dalit students are persecuted, in higher courts where Dalits are rarely represented among judges. While caste in rural India may manifest itself in forms that are "easier to identify and fight," in urban settings its articulation is as potent, even if less obvious. Moreover, Aditi's progressivist assumption that millennials are somehow less casteist than their mothers' generation—an argument latent in her comment—is, unfortunately, a falsity. In an attitude survey conducted in 2016 by the Center for Study of Developing Societies (CSDS) in Delhi, along with the German political foundation Konrad-Adenauer-Stiftung, which surveyed a sample of 6,122 respondents between the ages of fifteen and thirty-four, found that the plurality (36 percent) of them were against intercaste marriages; only 4 percent had had an intercaste marriage. Thirty-nine percent of them were fond of using fairness cream; colorism, we must remember, is an integral part of casteism in India.[38] In, fact, Ravikanth Kisana notes, "When it comes to caste, there's a strange diffidence, a disquieting silence, even from model millennial progressives."[39]

What is most problematic about the film's valorization of Aditi's views on caste, then, is that despite what appears as her initial rejection of upper-caste heroism ("I don't want a hero, Ayan"), she proactively aids the cultivation of Ayan's brahmanical interventionism. Teju Cole, in the context of racism, suggests that the "white savior complex" "is about having a big emotional experience that validates privilege."[40] For the film, Ayan's political awakening, the risks he takes to see justice served, are the principal, memorable aspects of the plot, rather than the horrific murder of Dalit girls. His "coming of age" overwrites the story of a community and its oppression and resistance.

And it is Aditi who brings him to victory. Crucially, she instructs him, transferring her flawed caste analysis to Ayan as she prepares him to undertake the anticaste battle as a solitary messiah figure. And, following the lessons learned from his lover, Ayan acts alone; everyone else only implements his commands. Neither of them, in their anticaste work, think to collaborate with Dalits, or better yet, to learn from them. They don't even make the most superficial attempts at consulting Dalits over "matters that concern them."[41] In the end, then, it turns out that Aditi did, in fact, desire an action-oriented, magic-wand-wielding hero who can fix complex social problems with grand individual gestures. It's the kind of individuated heroism that denies or negates the resilience of survival, resistance, and collective mobilization that Dalits across the country enact every single day. The last time we see Ayan and Aditi together, her eyes glisten with awe, devotion and love; this is the moment that Ayan, and we, have waited for. When she finally embraces him, it is the only instance, in the entire duration of the film, that we witness romantic desire between them. The embrace not only marks the end of their crisis of coupledom, it also welcomes "home" the well-intentioned, benevolent Brahmin-savior who has finally come into his own. The success of the modern bourgeois-*savarna* love is predicated on the latter. This is why the sentimentalism of their reunion prefigures the triumphal heroism of Ayan rescuing the third, missing, Dalit girl.

If the contentions in Ayan and Aditi's romantic relationship are channeled and resolved through caste, then Gaura and Nishad's trajectory of coupledom follows a very different path: their lived experiences as Dalits throw into disarray the very possibility of romantic love. To put it differently, while caste is the occasion and site upon which Ayan and Aditi play out their bourgeois brahmanical angst, for Gaura and Nishad the all-consuming reality of caste renders impossible for them the actualization of a romantic/nuptial/postnuptial future. It's curious that a film in which romantic love is so marginal (at least on the surface) manages, nevertheless, to insert two "broken" couples into its narrative. At the same time, though, it creates a hierarchy of marginality even between them. So while Aditi and Ayan's relationship is sketched through eight quick scenes, we see Gaura and Nishad together only twice, and they're alone just once. As a result, narratologically speaking, they are doubly relegated to the margins and granted neither togetherness nor privacy.

It is impossible to know why only a tiny sliver of narrative space is conceded to Gaura and Nishad. Is the film governed by brahmanical hegemony, a lack of cinematic imagination and political will, which ensures that upper-caste stories and characters invariably dominate and which incapacitates the telling of Dalit stories? Or, as a generous reading of the film might suggest, is Gaura and Nishad's formal sidelining precisely the political statement the film wants to make, that Dalit love has little chance of thriving or surviving in a casteist society? To be clear, the two logics do not have to be mutually exclusive. At any rate, for our purposes, the question remains: why examine Gaura and Nishad's fringe, failed romance?

If a study of Ayan and Aditi's relationship tells us something about the conjoined functioning of brahmanical patriarchy and bourgeois love, or the ways in which the two coconstitute and legitimate one another, then a close examination of Gaura and Nishad's relationship is critical for at least two reasons. First, the two of them, together and separately, are the only Dalit characters assigned voice and agency. Besides them, the Dalits we encounter are mostly nameless, silent weathered faces, "poor, dark-skinned" bodies in unclean, tattered clothes or downtrodden victims of discrimination, rape, lynching, flogging, poverty.[42] Jyoti Nisha reads this as the "branding" and "stereotyping" of Dalit characters that affirms their victim status instead of validating Dalit experiences. Gaura and Nishad, on the other hand, both speak and act, and unlike their bourgeois, Brahmin counterparts, they do so from within, and on behalf of, the communities in which they are embedded. While Nishad sustains a critique of and challenge to state-sanctioned and state-perpetuated anti-Dalit violence, drawing attention also to the state's appropriation of Dalit politics, Gaura does the tenacious work of moving the state apparatus to acknowledge caste atrocities and urging it to act to protect Dalits (specifically, to find her missing sister) and bring the culprits to justice. There is, to be sure, a gendered dimension to the political labor the two perform: Nishad stands up to the state, using aggressive but nonviolent tactics to get its attention: strikes, protests, arson (that damages property but not lives). Gaura, on the other hand, pleads with the state machinery and is focused more on fighting for the family and the intimate community of her village.

Second, the representation of Dalit love is such a cinematic rarity that it must be taken seriously, even when the film itself doesn't seem to necessitate it. Gaura and Nishad, even in their state of abbreviated, collapsed coupledom—they were lovers waiting to get married until Nishad's radicalism turns him into an enemy of the state and he has to go into hiding—offer us more in terms of the delineation of Dalit love than nearly all of popular Hindi cinema before it.

But politics supersedes Gaura and Nishad's romantic relationship, converting it into a "luxury" they cannot sustain, a "choice" they must forsake. In Ayan and Aditi's case, the toll that politics takes on their relationship manifests as an opportunity for them to work out their liberal, upper-caste guilt, and in the bargain rescue their relationship. The domain of political participation, then, is a galvanizing force that offers exciting prospects for the bourgeois, brahmanical couple: the chance to combine self-congratulatory "wokeness" with the fortification of coupledom.

For Gaura and Nishad, however, political pressures operate very differently. Their relationship is held hostage to, and imposed upon, by brahmanical society, curtailing both their agency and a romantic future together. Their "decision" to forgo the relationship, then, is not really a decision at all, not one made freely by autonomous and free subjects of the nation-state, at any rate. They embody both the impossibility and the violence of having to choose between coupledom and survival, in either scenario, there can be no winners. In a sense, then, Gaura and Nishad represent another type of a long-distance couple; their bodies are not remote from one another, but they're jointly distanced from a world that cannot accommodate them. The impossibility of their togetherness marks the "long distance" that society has to travel before they can have a fair shot at a life of dignity and romantic happiness.

The fact that Gaura and Nishad exist outside the purview of upper-caste bourgeois bliss is most succinctly articulated in their inability to rely on the cellular technology that otherwise keeps the privileged long-distance couple intact. The cell phone, which offers Ayan and Aditi the means to carve out intimacy and privacy for themselves, even when they are hundreds of miles apart from one another, does not proffer any such refuge to Gaura and Nishad. A cell phone exchange between them would only become a means of surveillance by the state. This is why they use the cell phone, the classic symbol of the ubiquity of liberalization and digital modernization, not for private romantic communication, but as a weapon against the state: a means to launch a large-scale strike of Dalit workers.

We first encounter Nishad as a voice-over, relaying a message to all Dalits in the region: "You and I are invisible to them, but their lives depend on us. We work on their farmlands, we clean their shit, we deliver their babies, burn their corpses on funeral pyres. Don't beg for justice anymore. You've already begged for too long. Now, whatever work you do, just stop." Interestingly, at this point in the film, the audience is already familiar with what the voice-over means: a stand-in for, and an access into, the messages sent between Ayan and Aditi, and thus associated with intimacy, romantic entanglement, everyday communication, and difficult, personal conversations. Nishad's voice-over, however, changes this association between cellular technology and bourgeois coupledom. With his clarion call to strike—one way to make a brahmanical society recognize the gargantuan and menial nature of the labor that lower castes perform—he opens up a new potential for weaponizing the tools of elite coupledom. What would ordinarily have been a political announcement on a loudspeaker, for instance, when transferred through the cellphone morphs instead into a difficult political message infiltrating private gadgets and personal spaces; it transforms the site of privacy, individuality, and individuated romance and hails it into a political collective.

Fascinatingly, in the voice-over, Nishad's voice comes to us as a kind of "acousmatic" sound, a sound whose origin or source is not just decorporealized (as in any phone conversation), but also deracinated and impossible to locate.[43] It's the kind of sound, Steven Bruhm argues, that disorients the listener, invoking fear and awe at its phantasmic immateriality.[44] It's safe to imagine that for a predominantly urban, elite, upper-caste film audience, a Dalit leader's declaration of work cessation, especially one that comes in this auditory format, produces a double-faceted anxiety: a specter of caste-subaltern insurrection that, worse yet, cannot be named or tamed. What's noteworthy, as Sen reminds us, is that the acousmatic sound's terrifying character evaporates as soon as it is de-acousmaticized, and the voice is "resecured to the physical body"; its alienness is disrupted, and "the aural entity gets re-humanized."[45] Even though the film grants minimal space to Nishad, the space it does ascribe to him humanizes him, incontestably. Through two exceedingly powerful scenes alone, the audience is not only given a chance to align Nishad's voice with his corporeal materiality, but is also introduced to his political vision, his creative-scientific genius, his fearlessness, and the ethical compulsions that guide him. In doing so, the film manages not only to affirm his humanity—precisely the thing that upper-castes deny Dalits—but also validate his politics of Dalit liberation. Even more, the most powerful way in which the film secures the legitimacy of Nishad's personhood and his anticaste politics is through his ruminations on love, or rather love's impossibility.

Nishad articulates a distinctly Dalit love, one that treasures the simultaneous mundanity and gravity of all that is meaningful, even while it mourns the negation of these from Dalit lives. For all the film's flaws, the scene in which Nishad and Gaura meet one last time before he is gunned down by the state in a pseudo "encounter," heartbreakingly captures what Suraj Yengde in *Caste Matters* calls the "juxtaposition of possibilities and deep pain" that defines Dalit love.[46] What's really difficult about this scene is that the catalogue of things Nishad grieves aren't grand ambitions but the minute banalities of existence. He laments the brutality of a world in which the gestures of love—bringing flowers, sitting by the riverside with his lover, or staring at the moon—begin to feel like "committing a sin." Crucially, what he condemns is not love but an apolitical pursuit of coupledom; the phenomenon that is the biggest banality, the most commonplace of all occurrences, the event that lies at the heart of every film, every normative story, is subjected to scrutiny as an embodiment of self-indulgence. Coupledom, not love, is unveiled as the ultimate expression of inequitably distributed privilege. In this scene, the film, perhaps despite itself, unequivocally reveals the narcissistic limits *of* bourgeois, upper-caste love, and the violence of the limits *on* radical Dalit love.

In exploring upper-caste and Dalit relationships separately, the film also considers the operations of caste in love relationships that might be characterized as "modern," in that they are neither "arranged" nor matrimonially oriented. In his essay on India's "arranged marriage regime," Yengde does the important work of unmasking the "brutal social reality" of caste that "sits uncomfortably at the center of all romantic and marital relations in India." He exposes arranged marriages for what they are, a confirmation and securitization of caste by families that act like "cops" to ensure the "purity" of "bloodlines."[47] This endogamous insularity of caste is not, however, confined only to "traditional" formulations of love. As Kriti Budhiraja reminds us, love marriages (or nonmarital relationships) are also "wrought with all the calculations of the arranged marriage market." Upper-caste people invariably fall in love with people from their own caste background. In part, of course, this is the result of structural conditions that "ensure we only interact with people from similar backgrounds." But our notion of the "types of people" we find "attractive" are also hegemonically conditioned.[48] To be clear, the embargo on cross-caste relationships is enforced by the upper castes, who rape, murder, and lynch couples who violate this taboo. Thus the power of intercaste marriages threaten the very foundations of love—traditional or modern—in India.

Article 15 resolutely avoids imagining an equal, consensual, intercaste desire. In fact, the film gives the briefest glimpse of this radical, risky possibility only to retract and subsume it into its Brahmin savior syndrome. In *Totality and Infinity*, Emmanuel Levinas writes that the "face of the other" is powerful not as a physical, aesthetic object, but in the ethical imperative, the obligation it demands of us.[49] This is why, through an encounter with the face of the other, we discover the intersubjective enactment of responsibility. The face-to-face encounter "interrupts our free activity," produces a "discontinuity of one's inner life,"[50] and "calls us to account for ourselves."[51] The naked defenselessness of the face of the other signifies "Do not kill me"[52] and opens the possibility of dialogue. The first time Ayan sees Gaura is just such a Levinasian moment: Ayan is a tad embarrassed by the overzealous festivities organized by his subordinates for his arrival in Laalgaon. He messages Aditi about the Bollywoodesque character of this place, and when he looks up from his phone, he makes eye contact with Gaura, who along with a few other villagers is urging the police to lodge a complaint about the missing girls; one of them, as it turns out, is her sister.

Something about Gaura's face—perhaps the panic in her large eyes, its striking beauty, her intense, imperceptibly pleading expression—draws him in, and he inquires about her, only to be told "there's no problem, sir"; it's just their "usual drama" to complain about missing people, and the necessary inquiry is underway. This is a remarkable moment in how it coalesces the power dynamics at play: her gender, poverty, caste all make and mark her as available to Ayan's gaze. And yet her face exercises a power of its own, which has an immediate impact upon him. He loses track of "his inner life"—his girlfriend he was just texting, his desire to get back to the city, the joke he was cracking about the outmoded aesthetics of this place—and becomes consumed by Gaura's face. This is because the face, ultimately, "resists [his] possession" and "power"[53] and makes instead a demand upon him to recognize her anguish, to not let her, and others like her, die. In fact, its contiguity is so dramatic that, as Levinas suggests, it defies conceptualization, and our instinct is to overlook the force the other's address has on us.

Ayan tries to repel the summons of her face again when she and the missing girls' fathers arrive at his residence. Once again, he is compelled to look at her face but tries to normalize the intensity it produces in him by taking recourse to officious jargon—"Let the postmortem report [of the lynched girls] come, I'll do something"—and by starting to walk away. Gaura doesn't let him do so without making him confront the truth: she tells him about the girls demanding a negligible hike in their wages; the local construction contractor's retaliation against them (he slapped Pooja, Gaura's sister, for their audacious impertinence); and the police's refusal to forge an FIR (report) because of the contractor's affiliation with a state politician. From here on out, Ayan follows the evidentiary lead Gaura shares with him and doesn't rest, no matter what the impediments in his way, until the rapist-murderers are caught and Pooja is found.

In some ways, then, even more than the ethical injunctions from Aditi, what transforms Ayan is the "encounter" with Gaura's face: its caste, class, and gender vulnerability, but most of all the humanity it embodies. He succumbs to her tireless, persistent demand that he be accountable to her and enforce institutional and ethical responsibility toward her community.

This is why the film commits such a grave error when it concludes with Gaura folding her hands and bowing her head in gratitude to Ayan after he recovers her sister. The image of a Dalit thanking an upper-caste man, of course, undermines the film's self-espoused anticaste politics. As Ankur Pathak argues, "it reinforces the idea that the world is wronged, and righted, by *savarna* men, while everyone else exists in the shadow of their benevolence."[54] Equally problematically, it also articulates a willful denial of the literal and existential labor that Gaura and Nishad have to do—the work they do to keep up the pressure, and the amount of suffering they have to endure—to move an upper-caste man to simply do his job, recast by the film as an upper-caste man's entrepreneurial, ethical commitment to truth. The resurgence of his and Aditi's bourgeois coupledom happens on the back of the suffering faces and murdered bodies of the Dalit lovers. The film tries hard to obfuscate this reality.

Resisting Love: *Geeli Pucchi*'s Break from the Cruel Optimism of Inter-Caste Love

Neeraj Ghaywan's *Geeli Pucchi* (2021), translated as "sloppy kisses," is one of the four short films that make up Netflix's anthology *Ajeeb Daastaans*. In many ways, Ghaywan's film is an unprecedented delineation of how caste and casteism embed the very foundations of the everyday. In *Geeli Pucchi*, caste's totalitarianism is comprehensive and touches *everyone*: it governs the professional choices we make, or those that are made for us, and the modes of transport we (must) take to commute between home and work. It dictates the spaces in which we enjoy our lunch break, and with whom we share the hour. It also finds articulation in the acts of kindness and generosity extended to, or withheld from, us. And, therefore, caste inflects both the lightness of mood and the dourness of disposition with which we navigate the world. It necessitates the finding of eggless recipes for birthday cakes, affects the "stenches" we notice and the lengths we (can) go to avoid them, and affects the discourses of "hygiene" we weaponize and readily abandon when convenient. It manifests in the offenses we cause and our banal and callous attempts to paper over them. It is present in how, and how much, fear governs our ambitions, actions, speech, and even our unconscious desires; in the rituals of reproduction that we willy-nilly participate in; in the matrix of precarities that constitute us; and in the constant juggling of which vulnerability we treat as salient in which moment. And, of course, it orchestrates who we fall in love with, the conditions of love's disclosure, and the ostensible inevitability of heartbreak. The film is remarkable, then, in its capacity to lay bare the unremarkability of caste's operation.

Geeli Pucchi studies caste not just through the oppressions it hurls upon Dalits, but also through tracing and tracking the intentionally normalized and invisibilized structures of privilege it accrues for upper castes. In this film, caste doesn't enter the fray as a late-entrant villain, a third-party spoiler of fun and the joys of love. Rather, caste is the a priori, always-already present determiner of identities, behaviors, modalities, and possibilities. It works on everyone and everything; of course, *what* it does to people, to their relationship with themselves, and each other, is differently distributed and realized.

Geeli Pucchi is also committed to an exploration of the surprising directions and outcomes of caste violence. Even as it acknowledges that Dalits are the primary recipients of its viciousness, it forgoes an understanding of caste in which oppression is unidirectional, administered upon Dalits alone. Instead, the film offers a compelling account of how brahmanical patriarchy is predicated upon violating the physical and psychological sanctity of upper-caste women as well. Priya's ditsy and buoyant personality cannot mask or override what it means to be enshrined within her brahmanical, heteronormative identity as "Sharma ji ki bahu" (Mr. Sharma's daughter-in-law). She experiences the pressure tugs to fulfill caste codes from all quarters, and across a spectrum of emotional registers. Her ex-girlfriend Kavita chides her for not giving up her homosocial desires to embrace the imperatives of married life. Her family demands that she must ride a scooty, instead of walk or take a rickshaw, to and from work. Her upper-caste boss benevolently instructs her not to eat with the factory workers because it "stinks" and the factory floor is "unhygienic." Her husband coaxes her into midnight sex in the bathroom, the only privacy they can afford in a two-bedroom house with eleven residents, and his love-bombing overattentiveness convinces her to accept the irreversibility of her matrimonial and motherhood status. Her mother-in-law warns her against unseemly friendships with butch women, and guilt-bullies her into relinquishing her job for her duties as a new mother.

Importantly, each of these demands transforms Priya's corporeal existence and subjecthood into both caste system functionary and its beneficiary, a preserver and reproducer of brahmanical purity and caste hierarchy. The film, then, meticulously exposes the workings of the double-edged sword of caste by unveiling the threats, pressures, and coded violence that lace the "forms of responsibility and veneration"[55] given to *savarna* women. All requests upon their being are actually a call to order, to fall in line with the caste order. At the same time, all commandments to serve caste's dictates also interpellate, invite, and empower Brahmin women to perpetuate caste and ensure the marginalization of Dalits.

This dynamic is palpable too in the scene where Priya, as a new employee, comes to the canteen where the assembly line workers eat. Her awkward exchange with Bharti is interrupted by the arrival of a male worker (we recognize him as the man who had also harassed Bharti for not being feminine enough, in the film's opening scene). He walks over to their table, looms over their seated bodies, and creepily smiles and ogles at Priya. He starts talking to her (but loudly enough for everyone to hear), declaring that her presence at the factory is akin to the descent of a goddess in their midst. In many ways, the inseparability of his leering expression from the servility of his compliment allows the film to expose how a Brahmin woman is simultaneously the explicit object of heteropatriarchal sexual fantasy, as well as the emblem of caste purity to be worshipped and regulated. The lecherous beneficence extended to Priya, which sexualizes and venerates her in the same breath, keeps her in "place": she may be an upper-caste data operator, but she is still a woman serving the goals of brahmanical reproduction. His words celebrate Priya's arrival: despite all the "*tarakki*" (advancement) that India has made, she is the "first woman" to work in the factory, he tells us. And yet the lasciviousness of his address undercuts the sincerity of his words, because they reflect more an excitement at being able to relegate women to sexual objects in the workplace than an endorsement of women as professional colleagues. The excited acceptance of Priya as a colleague in the factory is, then, really a moment of glad-eyeing her. Priya is forever the attention of a watchful, grasping male gaze, not just on the factory floor, but also above in the managerial offices.

At the same time, the scene lets us register how the *savarna* woman's body exists, at all times, as a counterpoint against the body of the Dalit woman, in this case Bharti, the woman sitting across from Priya. The film demonstrates how the disparagement of the *savarna* woman (Priya) and Dalit woman (Bharti) are not just the outcome of the same structures of subjugation, but that their oppression is in fact entangled and coconstituted. The disingenuous lauding of the *savarna* woman is not only an insult to her, but also serves to insult Bharti. As the male coworker turns his attention away from Priya to Bharti, the layers of his insult become harder and harder to parse because they interweave between an assault upon Bharti as a Dalit, a lesbian, a butch woman, and a working-class subject.

For instance, in congratulating Priya for being the first woman to work in the factory, the male coworker deflects attention away from the discrepancies in employment along caste lines (there are hardly any Dalit workers too, despite India's "*tarakki*"). In a brahmanical world, gender trumps caste considerations as a marker of representational progress. At the same time, in welcoming Priya as the "first woman to work in the factory" he renders invisible the only woman who has, in fact, worked in the factory. This invisibilization occurs because Bharti's queer presentation marks her as a nonwoman, unavailable within heteropatriarchy. But the insult to her gender (she's not even worthy of being counted as a woman) is provoked equally by her Dalit identity and the sense of her errant sexuality. Within a casteist logic, Bharti's Dalit identity would ordinarily render her accessible for sexual violation by upper-caste men. This automatic entitlement to her as a Dalit woman, however, is interrupted by her queerness, her nonfeminine presentation, and because she's an overalls-clad worker. In his vitriol, then, her coworker denies her existence both as a (desirable-queer-Dalit) woman and as a (Dalit-queer-female) worker. And it is precisely her Dalitness and queerness that emboldens the ferocity of his attack.

The final insult against Bharti, before she loses her temper and flings water in his face, further encapsulates the slippery, messy, and coagulated nature of caste's violence and the perverse convolutions it produces as it brushes up against other social identities. The coworker says something oblique about how Bharti must rely on her own hands to "satisfy herself," a triple innuendo that invokes the idea of her hand as a penile substitute (a nightmare threat in a heterosexist universe), suggests that she must rely on her grease-ridden hands as a manual laborer working in the factory (something that detracts from her desirability as a woman), and condemns her to manual labor (because of her caste) even though she is educated enough to be a white-collar worker. He then warns Priya against staring too long at Bharti, lest she also "grow a beard on her face." The overt implication of his words relates to the misogynist fear that lesbians "infect" and "convert" women away from compulsive heterosexuality. But the threat also conjures and relies on a casteist worldview. After all, the concerns around infecting and polluting upper-caste women are integral also to the embargo on touching (or even looking) across caste lines.

This is why it matters that the film is titled "sloppy kisses": it forces us to imagine the intercaste transference of bodily fluids deemed so dangerous to upper-caste sanctity and brahmanical purity. When Bharti and Priya kiss, it is not just their bodies that threaten to self-combust with desire, guilt, and trepidation about what their act of love signifies for their (inter)personal trajectories. The amorous exchange of saliva also portends a takedown of a whole ideology and society centered around the prohibition of this possibility (between women;

between a Dalit and a Brahmin). The "sprouting of a beard" is not even the real worry here, but its appearance wouldn't be ideal either.

Geeli Pucchi, then, gives us the dizzyingly interlinked, impossible to untangle, and overwhelming complex nature of oppression. As viewers, our heads reel as we work hard to decipher who, between Bharti and Priya, is more in trouble, in which moment, and for which crime. The answers seesaw constantly: their precarities shift with every scene, but also remain consistent and permanently skewed (or are they?). The threats they face (together and individually) alter with each spatial shift. Bathrooms, bedrooms, kitchens, the factory floor, the glass office cubicles upstairs, the river bank, the street-food stall, each of these geographies unleashes a new variation in their vulnerabilities. Every interaction between them, and between them and other characters, launches a new speculation of how their precarities will map out. In one instance, it may appear that Priya and her mother-in-law are at odds in their relationship with one another: Priya is desperate to return to work, and the latter is dead-set against it. And yet in another moment, the two are in sync in terms of how they view Bharti, a Dalit woman whose ancestral knowledge of midwifery must be assumed and extracted for free, in service of producing Brahmin progeny. It is no wonder that Priya can casually commit the betrayal of sharing the secret of Bharti's caste with her mother-in-law. They may be each other's familial enemies but their caste affiliation wins out against Bharti.

And yet despite the ever-shifting terrain of power between the two protagonists, the film goes out of its way to establish a shared vulnerability between them. In one instance, the overlap in their precarities is conveyed visually through cross-fading between two scenes. We see Bharti watch a video of her and her girlfriend giggling, kissing, teasing each other. Lying in bed, watching the selfie video on her phone, Bharti tears up, overcome at the premonition of loss captured in the video itself; her girlfriend keeps telling her to stop recording (presumably to ensure the secrecy of their relationship) and makes a joke about packing her up in a suitcase and taking her to Delhi (presumably a suggestion that her girlfriend is moving away). We see Bharti in the video become solemn and melancholic at the mention of her girlfriend's departure, and she turns off the recording. The present-day Bharti finishes watching the video, puts down her phone, curls up in a fetal position, and cries. The camera, allowing her some privacy in grief, backtracks from the closeup of her face, lifts above her, and watches her side-turned body, gently sobbing in the isolation of her home.

Before we know it, however, the image changes and we find ourselves looking from midair at a different set of bodies curled up in bed. This time it is Priya sleeping on her side, being caressed by her husband into waking up to join him in the bathroom for midnight sex. Next, we see Priya pressed against the bathroom wall, her husband's bare back facing us as he repeatedly thrusts into her. If Bharti's tearing eyes were the center of focus in the previous scene, here we see the top half of Priya's face pressed against her husband's shoulder. And we detect a glazed-over impassivity, a glassy-eyed resignation at having to participate in a loveless, desireless act of intimacy. The film, then, visually matches Bharti's lonesome grief with Priya's entrapment within an overcrowded home, where she must suffer through the rituals of matrimony. If the throwback clip establishes a part of Bharti's backstory, compelling the viewer to recognize the histories of grief, loss, and vulnerability that are interlaced with her angry, scowling workplace persona, the following scene gives us the everyday violence of Priya's married sexual life as the flipside of her effervescent girlishness. In different ways, both Bharti and Priya's stories mark the impossibility of desire—of sustaining it or experiencing it—in the face of coercions imposed by normativity.

And yet, even as the film takes the time to dwell on the overlaps in Bharti and Priya's precarities, it never errs into carelessly equating them. Instead, by exploring the disjunctions in how their precarities play out, the film is able to demonstrate the hierarchies and nuances of vulnerability. It is able to offer a clear-sighted understanding of the saliency of caste as a game changer. Despite a shared gender and nonnormative sexuality, the caste disparity between Bharti and Priya ensures that their intersectional identities unravel very differently. *Geeli Pucchi*'s brilliance lies, then, in its perspicacious rejection of neoliberal feminist and pink-washed queer politics that diminish the role of caste and class in their analysis of women and queer people's lives.

This is why, in *Geeli Pucchi*, the collapse of romantic love promoted by caste produces a strikingly different affect than what occurs in either *Masaan* or *Article 15*. In these latter films, the end of the road for the romantic couples Devi-Piyush, Deepak-Shaalu, and Gaura-Nishad is ultimately a segue and setup for the possible emergence of other couples (Devi-Deepak, Ayan-Aditi) who, we are encouraged to optimistically believe, will navigate caste more successfully and ethically than their predecessors. *Geeli Pucchi*, however, unceremoniously abandons this cruel optimism about caste's surmountability by love, endlessly perpetuated like a feedback loop by mainstream Bollywood cinema. The film breaks from Bollywood's dominant genre of romantic love, and even from the dominant tendency within the subgenre of a caste-framed love story. *Geeli Pucchi* transforms the pervasive uncertainty of caste into an occasion to abandon love altogether for an exploration of something else: aromantic survival.

Furthermore, what causes the crumbling of coupledom in *Geeli Pucchi* isn't a "world-shifting" event:[56] an accidental death or state-sponsored murder. Love's victory is forestalled by the banal cruelty latent in the everyday practices of caste. In the film, romantic love totters at the altar of secrets never meant to be told, about one's caste or the unmeritocratic reasons why one lands a job. It withers at one person's subtle but timely withdrawal from interlocked hands. It distorts at the humiliation of being left uninvited into a room, or being served tea in conspicuously separate utensils. It succumbs to the everyday pressures of motherhood, thwarted ambitions, and workplace machinations. Nothing dramatic; nothing fatal; sans melodrama.

In this film, caste produces a distinct affective universe, and a nonverbal language of precarity, that do not usually appear within Bollywood's brahmanical heteronormativity and upper-caste romance. It manifests as unnamed resentments: Bharti never confronts Priya about the shift in her behavior after learning about Bharti's caste. Priya never confronts Bharti about conspiring to take over her job. There is no resolution born out of working through misunderstandings. It takes the form of strategic withholding of information: about last names and reasons for crying. Precarity manifests through somatic slippages: a tight-set jaw, angry eyes, unexpected tears, a hand held up too quickly to refuse someone's offer of food, strained laughter, a hand hovering in midair, a moment too long awaiting confirmation of someone's caste before attending to her injuries. It is expressed, most of all, through exchanged glances that confirm the reversal of power and the acceptance of vengeance in exchange for unspoken humiliations.

Geeli Pucchi, then, categorically abandons the myth of love's redemptive power. It rejects the idea that love supersedes the entrenchments of ideology and the entitlements of privilege. Even more importantly, in doing so, it opens up a new narrative arc, in which the film may be thought of less as a failure of love and more as a Dalit worker's triumph. Most readings of the film hinge on the idea that Bharti's revenge is directed against her lover Priya,[57] though they differ in their defense or castigation of Bharti's actions.[58] There is a shared understanding in these readings that the film is about Bharti's (justifiable or unjustifiable) revenge against a lover. What we want to suggest, however, is that it is inaccurate to read Bharti's surreptitious actions as revenge that pivots around romance or that is about the takedown of an ex-lover. Rather, Bharti's disillusionment with love creates the pathway for finding a crack in the sedimentations of power. The abandonment of love as a project allows Bharti to de-exceptionalize Priya, and to see and treat her as the caste functionary that she is, willingly.

In the course of their relationship Priya has proved that she is willing and eager to create dialogue across horizontal power structures and breach transgressions with those she deems her caste equals. This is why, while she thinks that Bharti's last name is "Banerjee," she tells Bharti stories about her ex-lover Kavita; confides in her about how she got her job (by leveraging her brahmanical identity and the epistemological privileges—like palm reading—it garners);

and shares the secret of her unhappiness in marriage because she is incapable of being attracted to her husband. Priya is willing to eat meat in secret though it breaks caste prohibitions, and she even invites her lesbian lover to her marital home. What Priya is incapable of, however, is engaging in dialogue and solidarity across vertical power axes. This is why she withdraws her hand from Bharti's the moment she learns about the latter's caste, and why she asks her to wait outside when she goes into her boss's office to celebrate her birthday with her upper-caste and upper-class colleagues. When they meet in private after Bharti's caste reveal in the men's locker room, Priya's affect is entirely different. She is disingenuous from the moment of her arrival, pretending that she's been looking for Bharti for a long time. She makes excuses about why she didn't feed Bharti cake, introduces a stilted formality and distance between them by referring to Bharti as "Bharti ji." And, by the end of their conversation, she seems to move in to hug Bharti, but abruptly stops herself from doing so by wrapping her arms around herself instead.

By this time, however, Bharti has already recognized and accepted the entrenchment of Priya's brahmanical identity, and she refuses to participate in Priya's pretenses. She grieves intensely and quickly. Before Priya's arrival in the locker room, we see her sitting on a bench, doubled over in anguish, crying, expressing anger and frustration. By the time Priya comes, Bharti no longer views her as a lover who has hurt her, but as a part and parcel of the system that treats her as disposable.

In encouraging Priya to embrace her role within brahmanical patriarchy, pushing her further into a matrimonial abyss by convincing her that motherhood will solve her problems, Bharti isn't simply punishing Priya-the-individual who has hurt her. Rather, she is taking on the caste-class conglomeration of upper-caste managers that keep her out. The outcome of her revenge isn't against Priya alone; it is also against the manager who had refused to give her the job to begin with, even though she was more qualified and is a more earnest and efficient worker than Priya ever was.

This is not to deny the particularly personal tonality of the revenge, laden as it is with the grief, trauma, and bitterness of love's betrayal. But to read Bharti's actions as being directed against Priya alone, and in retaliation against love's failure, is to miss Bharti's astute political understanding of how power coalesces. Her scheme isn't so much to avenge Bharti as it is the outcome of a sharp political analysis of how Priya serves and fits within a power structure. To ignore this would be to fail to recognize how the exercise of her political knowledge and agency has a multimodal resonance that extends far beyond Priya as an individual and as a piece of the caste puzzle. The second that love's exceptionalizing power is evacuated from the mix, Bharti can treat Priya as the person she herself chooses to be: an upper-caste woman working in tandem with upper-caste men to reinscribe Bharti's vulnerability and marginalization.

Geeli Pucchi is unique, then, not just for giving us the complexity of caste-borne oppression, but also because it offers us Dalit working-class agency that ends in success. Bharti now has the job that should have been hers to begin with; she has the grudging respect and admiration of her boss who now relies on her because she's an exceptional data operator who completes all her tasks before her boss has even anticipated them. Her connivance against a casteist system has brought her in. Her excellence will stabilize her within the system.

At the same time, while the film's analysis of oppression is sophisticated, precise, and fecund, its imagination of resistance and liberation is tellingly streamlined as an excessive isolationism. Scholars like Bargi have pointed out that Bharti acts like "the perfect soldier, she fights her battle, silently and secretly, all along, with dogged determination."[59] Her hyperindividualism is, of course, indicative of the litany of grievances, losses, and discriminations she has survived: a husband who left her a few weeks after a miscarriage, a woman lover who perhaps left town and reneged on the relationship, colleagues who harass her, a boss who refuses to give her the job she's qualified for, a new lover who turns out to be casteist. And yet the film's incapacity to envisage a solidaristic form of agency is characteristic of what we may call the film's "situated imagination"[60] within a brahmanical, neoliberal world.

Nira Yuval-Davis[61] suggests that imagination is "not straightforwardly a faculty of the individual but it is (also, or even primarily) a *social* faculty," in that what we imagine as possible is itself an outcome of a milieu, and not a deracinated break from it. This is why, even though *Geeli Pucchi* can give us a rare cinematic subject—the Dalit queer working-class protagonist who enjoys, by the end of the film, upward mobility and professional success—the film's imagination of how to achieve this feat is laced by and within brahmanical and neoliberal frameworks. Das points to the way in which the film regurgitates the brahmanical idea that in order to deserve equality, or activate their liberation, marginalized people "have to be exceptional."[62] This logic is intrinsic also to capitalist-neoliberal frameworks that rely on notions of meritocracy and hard work to legitimate the structures of inequality they propagate.

Similarly, even though the film is able to construct and explore a thoroughly intersectional identity in Bharti, it is unable to envisage the many dimensions of her being as nodes of connection, as opportunities for dialogue, collaboration, or solidarity. Her multilayered intersectionality become the cause for her remoteness from everyone else rather than an occasion to calibrate community with the many oppressed groups that she could belong to. The film's inability to explore the possibilities of liberation in the same robust way in which it delineates oppression is very much what constitutes it as a narrative of precarity. The siloing of being, of resistance and tactics of survival, even when suffering is shared with more and more people, is very much a symptom of the success of precarious times.

As viewers, we cannot help but wonder what a conspiratorial solidarity between Bharti and Dashrath, her Dalit friend, would have entailed and enabled? In which cinematic world would Bharti not only reject love for liberation, but also choose Dashrath as a comrade with whom to collectively seek liberation. It is true that Dashrath has internalized the fears and terrors circulated by brahmanical violence: that Dalit resistance produces lynched, burned, raped Dalit bodies. And yet, people's politics, motivations, actions change; we see that change in Bharti herself. For a while, she is willing to forgo lunch with Dashrath because her Brahmin lover wants her to join her upstairs, away from the factory floor, where they can exist in a private bubble of their own, away from everyone's prying eyes. By the end of the film, Bharti knows the deceptions and delusions that undergird love's exceptionalizing tendency. What would it take, then, for Dashrath to have a similar trajectory, an evolution of his political vision that ends in clarity about the limits of his fears and the power of supporting Bharti in her ambitions? And conversely, what kind of a narrative would be willing to explore Bharti and Dashrath as genuine coconspirators, seeking conjoined liberation. *Geeli Pucchi*, as it is configured, leaves us asking: What kind of white-collar personnel does Bharti make for those beneath her? What kind of a boss to Dashrath would she make, one who exacerbates his precarity or one who remembers their erstwhile shared precarity on the factory floor and acts accordingly?

The incompleteness of Dalit coupling in the films reminds the viewer not just of the scarcity of portrayals of lower-caste, intercaste, and Dalit love onscreen, but also of the structural impediments or the precarities engendered by neoliberal Hindutva that render impossible such romantic love. At the same time, it is important to recognize that the three films offer very different landscapes of romantic relationships and their intersection with caste. In curtailing the future of intercaste and Dalit couples, *Masaan*, *Article 15*, and *Geeli Pucchi* pose radically discrepant real and implied "solutions." *Masaan* anchors its hope for a more progressive future in proposing the possibility of yet another intercaste "couple-in-progress"; certainly their fate is yet to be determined, but the inkling of their transgressive coupledom is undeniable. *Article 15*, on the other hand, extinguishes Dalit love in favor of its determined rehabilitation and reentrenchment of bourgeois brahmanical love. *Geeli Pucchi* disinvests from love altogether and focuses on the lone Dalit worker's survival and success. While *Masaan* and *Geeli Pucchi* use their romantic "couplings" to mutually reinforce a seamless censure of caste and (hetero)patriarchal hypocrisy and prejudice,

Article 15 founders on its centering of its upper-caste couple, whose apparent nonnormativity masks conformity to tropes of male heroism and female emotional labor. These are not just "different ways" of exploring the intersection between love, sexuality, and caste, but rather, different imaginings of where love, and by proxy (as Gopal would suggest) citizenship, are located and how they are defined. The couples in crisis, and the couples in progress, that we study in *Masaan, Article 15*, and *Geeli Pucchi* represent a neoliberal nation struggling with its legacies of caste, without being able to offer collective solutions for an equitable future.

5: Sexual Precarity, Class Divides, and Neoliberal Feminism

In this chapter we read moments of interaction between women and insert class as a critical lens to examine the exclusions performed and exacerbated by neoliberal feminism in contemporary India. We study three films—*Veere Di Wedding*, *Lust Stories*,[1] and *Is Love Enough? Sir*—for how these films depict women's on-screen encounters when they transpire within and across class lines. We examine how the films attend to the interior lives of elite and nonelite women and configure their respective precarities differently. We find, perhaps predictably, that the interactions between working-class women and middle- and upper-class women are not always altercations but are usually fraught and devoid of the possibilities of cross-class feminist solidarities. What is surprising, though, is that even the breezy interactions between class-insular women friends that pass as female bonding, as in a film like *Veere Di Wedding*, do not really offer a radical politics of female solidarity. Located within neoliberal and postfeminist politics and aesthetics, the film's casual evocation of elite lifestyles, denigration of working-class women's life struggles, and the content and target of its sexual humor jeopardize a radical reworking of patriarchal and heteronormative frameworks and encourage us to settle for a future in which "women playing the same games as men do" is the only mode of radicalism or emancipation on offer.

It is important to consider the place these films occupy within the genre of "women-centric" films that have proliferated in the aftermath of the 2012 Delhi gang rape (discussed in chapters 1 and 6). In the past decade or so, Hindi cinema has demonstrated a decided investment in constructing new cinematic modalities within which to explore and experiment with women's stories and voices. A slew of mainstream and "*hatke*" films—such as *English-Vinglish* (Gauri Shinde, 2012), *Queen* (Vikas Bahl, 2014), *Parched* (Leena Yadav, 2015), *Pink* (Aniruddha Roy Chowdhury, 2016), *Anarkali of Aarah* (Avinash Das, 2017), and *Lipstick under my Burkha* (Alankrita Shrivastava, 2017), among others—have tracked women's journeys of self-discovery, focusing on issues of autonomy, consent, and sexual harassment. Other films such as *Dum Laga ke Haisha* (Use All Your Force, Sharat Katariya, 2015) or *Shuddh Desi Romance* (A Pure Desi Romance, Maneesh Sharma, 2013), forefront women's narratives within couple formation in middle-class contexts. Significantly, a new kind of female star has emerged in conjunction with these films. Actors such as Radhika Apte, Swara Bhasker, Kangana Ranaut, Taapsee Punnu, to name a few, occupy a newly opened terrain in the Hindi film industry and predominantly play the strong "new women" roles in such films.[2]

All three films discussed in this chapter were released in the same year (2018) but represent two distinct subgenres within the broad rubric of women-centric films. While *Veere Di Wedding* (henceforth *VDW*) is a shining example of a relatively new Bollywood genre, the "chick flick," *Is Love Enough? Sir* (henceforth *Sir*) and *Lust Stories* are films reliant on OTT platforms (Netflix India) for their distribution and success. Even so, all three New Bollywood and New Media texts showcase the "new woman": the predominant model of empowered womanhood that Hindi cinema has resorted to since liberalization. This figure of the postliberalization new woman is a contemporary iteration of the relationship between femininity and modernity that is situated within a trajectory with historical antecedents and lineages in the Victorian new woman, its colonial counterpart in India, and the global prototype of the modern girl from the early twentieth century.[3] In that period of sociocultural-political ferment, the new modality of womanhood that came into being was a product of the anxieties and needs of the male anticolonial nationalist elite to combat colonialist discourse around a regressive Indian culture in need of reform. Thus, as Partha Chatterjee[4] has argued, the middle-class Hindu woman came to occupy a culturally wrought position, someone who had access to education and opportunities in the public sphere but on whose shoulders was placed the responsibility of establishing the superiority of Indian spirituality and tradition. This ostensibly entitled figure was thus subject to new patriarchal injunctions, ultimately compromising her liberation and constraining her progress. Fast forward to a century later, and another distinct articulation of the "new liberal Indian woman" emerged in the contexts of upheavals caused by liberalization and the concomitant rise of the middle class and Hindu nationalism. This post-1990s figure who became iconic of a "new India"—similarly burdened with simultaneously preserving India's cultural and traditional identity while participating in global networks, surveilled for a "modernization-without-westernization"[5]—is especially characterized by a neoliberal postfeminist subjectivity, geographical mobility, a reliance on consumerism to articulate her entrepreneurialism, and sexual autonomy.

Of course, within mainstream representations of the post-1990s new woman, the poor, working, and lower-middle-class women usually remain on the outskirts of this category of newness. *Lust Stories* and *Is Love Enough? Sir* are therefore unique in their enactment of a strategic cinematic reversal. The female domestic workers, migrant laborers, and aspirational lower-middle-class young women in these films interrupt and reconfigure the easy narratives ordinarily associated with the elite new woman. Spatially and narratologically, the two films sideline the middle- and upper-class neoliberal new woman who otherwise dominates contemporary popular Hindi cinema, exemplified in a film like *VDW*. This decentering explodes the hegemonic contours of the new woman as empowered femininity and its concomitant delineation of gender-based vulnerability as represented in mainstream Hindi cinema. Placing class precarity as a primary lens unsettles all the markers of women's liberation—whether pleasure, mobility, choice, autonomy, sexual agency, consent, entrepreneurial savvy—to reveal the deep contradictions and hollowness that characterize mantras of postfeminism and neoliberal feminism in twenty-first-century India.

Often, neoliberal feminism's incongruities coalesce around sexual politics. We highlight the intricate enmeshment between neoliberal feminism and sexual politics, across cinematic genres, to draw attention to the classed character of women's sexuality in neoliberal India. On the surface, wealthy women have a casual, easy, humor-laden relationship to sex and sexuality. Most of their life's challenges revolve around the ease of access to sex, and their right to sexual agency is the one issue for which they will stake an unmitigated claim. A subtextual analysis of *VDW's* sexual politics and sexual humor, however, reveals a whole gamut of conservative sexual politics that undergirds the film's neoliberal politics. Or, to put it another way, its version of sexual humor, and its overreliance on this particular kind of sexual politics, is indicative of a hyperindividualized, postfeminist understanding of women's emancipation. It also shows how upper-class and caste power and privilege inoculates elite women to a large extent from the ubiquity of sexual harassment that minority women are subject to in contemporary India.

In *Sir* and *Lust Stories*, we see how limited it is to conceive of women's precarity as predominantly sexual precarity, an overdetermined collapse that both neoliberal and culturally right-wing discourses rely on. When sexual precarity dominates as the primary source of vulnerability for women, it sidelines class-based structural inequalities that working-class women endure, navigate, and survive. This narratological and ideological fixation on women's bodily and sexual precarity also ignores the ways in which nonelite or working-class women are exposed not only to the dangers of sexual abuse by upper-class men, but also to violence, marginalization, and exploitation by their elite female counterparts. This is the legacy of neoliberalism hijacking feminist politics.

Neoliberal Feminism and Postfeminism

While neoliberalism is a macroeconomic doctrine that entails deregulation, dismantling of social welfare programs, and the privatization of public services, scholars such as Wendy Brown, Wendy Larner, and Catherine Rottenberg, among others, have argued that, as a set of practices, neoliberalism extends its grasp upon facets of life that aren't overtly economic or related to state policies.[6] In fact, neoliberalism's impulse is to usurp all spheres of life, to become a central organizing ethic of society that shapes the way we live, think, and feel about ourselves and each other. As neoliberal rationality becomes the dominant mode of governance, it "produces subjects, forms of citizenship and behavior, and a new organization of the social."[7] In this new regime of morality, collective forms of action or well-being are eroded, and emphasis is placed on self-reliance, efficiency, and the individual's capacity to exercise his or her own autonomous choices.[8]

Rottenberg, Nancy Fraser, and Elisabeth Prugl note that with neoliberalism, feminism too undergoes an important transformation.[9] Most crucially, the neoliberal feminist subject distances herself from the political ideals associated with feminism of the 1960s and 1970s, to celebrate the wider range of choices in women's personal and professional lives that were now available to them. This disidentification with second-wave liberal feminism is borne out of a discourse that, on the one hand, relegates the feminist revolution to the past because it is assumed to have fulfilled its mission, and on the other hand holds individual women responsible for whatever inequalities that do continue to persist. Instead of challenging the social, cultural, and economic forces that produce gendered inequality, neoliberal feminism turns the matter of structural inequalities into an individual affair through the personal choices that women make.[10] A valorization of the expanded choices available to women, even if they reconfirm patriarchal hegemony, and an encouragement of the maximal articulation of these choices through "consumer sovereignty" are thus the founding principles of a postfeminist regime. It is choice per se, rather than the type of choice or the constraints under which choices are made, that is read as a sign of women's agency. Women's liberation is reduced to individual women's economic success and their ability to freely participate in cultures that previously excluded them, from pornography consumption to attendance at corporate executive board meetings.

In the Indian context, a host of scholars such as Rupal Oza, Leela Fernandes, Maitrayee Chaudhuri, and Inderpal Grewal, among others, have examined the emergence and spread of neoliberal feminist ideas since the 1990s.[11] Grewal writes, "the current phase of capitalism in India is producing a new kind of popular, cosmopolitan feminism that seems to operate differently than the feminism that many have come to associate with women's movements in India."[12]

Chaudhuri notes that it is not that the issues raised by the women's movement recede entirely. Instead, "what happens is that . . . collective ideas of women's liberation and freedom become reconfigured as essentially individual desires and goals, which the new opportunities that the growing market offered could gratify."[13] Some of the features of neoliberal feminism in India include the use of the vocabulary of, and the emphasis on, individualism, subjective desires, choice, agency, empowerment, self-monitoring and surveillance, consumerist desires, and sexual pleasure.

Interestingly, these scholars rarely use the language or framework of "postfeminism" to examine gender in liberalized India. Likewise, scholars who study postfeminism in the Global North have not taken into account the ways in which the ideological imperatives of postfeminism are relevant to the Global South. And yet for our purposes, postfeminism's individualizing logic, which downplays and depoliticizes the continuance of gendered inequality and its constitutive imbrication with consumerist notions of "choice," make it a markedly useful lens with which to think about these women-centric films.[14] In doing so, this chapter takes seriously Simidele Dosekun's contention that although postfeminism is undertheorized in non-Western contexts, it nevertheless circulates as a transnational culture and sensibility through the mediated circuits of consumer culture. Dosekun identifies postfeminism as "a neoliberal, individualistic, and consumerist discourse" that is very much pervasive in the Global South and is "potentially and variously available to globally 'scattered' feminine subjects who have the material, discursive, and imaginative capital to access and to buy into it."[15]

Veere Di Wedding

Dosekun's discussion provides an important context for a film such as *VDW*. The film's central protagonists are four young women (Kalindi, played by Kareena Kapoor; Avni, played by Sonam Kapoor; Meera, played by Shikha Talsania; and Sakshi, played by Swara Bhaskar) whose lives are fully and successfully embedded in India's neoliberal universe. The casual ease with which the film is able to give us the transatlantic hypermobility of these women, and without judgement depict a live in relationship, an interracial marriage, and premarital sex, even as it locates a "big wedding" at the heart of its plot, are testament to the film's comfort with its own neoliberal, globalized milieu. Like any good chick flick, in the course of the film *VDW*'s protagonist(s) come to terms with their life choices, overcome their psychological hurdles and self-imposed sexual embargos, and take charge of their personal relationships as they journey toward self-knowledge and self-actualization. The film raises questions about prescribed gender and sexual roles for women; it plays out the difficulties of negotiating expectations and achieving independence, emphasizes the role of female friendship, embraces consumerism, and hyperventilates about matrimonial travails (right from the decision to marry to the disappointments that accompany post-married life). The film's posters too are replete with traditional chick flick paraphernalia: they all feature the female leads in settings and sartorial styles associated with weddings, beaches, and bedrooms. In these regards, *VDW*'s chick flick status is unmistakable.

At the same time, its decidedly depoliticized engagement with these women's lives, outside the concerns of heterosexual matrimony, the sexual and consumer privileges that women enjoy, combined with the utter disparagement of and lack of solidarity with any other women besides each other, is symptomatic of the film's predominantly postfeminist rationale. The protagonists of *VDW* may be thought of as the female counterparts of the globe-trotting, luxury-holidaying men in *Zindagi Na Milegi Dobara* (2011), a neoliberal buddy road-trip Hindi film. Its vision of what women's lives entail is coopted, hegemonized, and scripted by a heteropatriarchal neoliberal worldview in which to be liberated is to act as men do: take international holidays to decompress, visit strip joints, and crack sexual jokes in which nearly all women (including working-class women) who don't meet the criteria of the "new young women"[16] that the protagonists represent are subjected to vicious and frankly sexist disparagement. This is why we argue that while it is undeniably refreshing to watch the film push back against the repressive taboos surrounding women's sexuality and desire, these are articulated only within neoliberal renditions of heterosexuality, matrimony, motherhood, and consumerism.

VDW is thus both a part of, and yet apart from, the broad genre of "women-centric" films. To different degrees, most of these postmillennial films, *VDW* included, highlight the pluralization of women's stories but also unwittingly articulate the extent to which feminism has been coopted within neoliberalism in contemporary India and Bollywood's cozy alignment with discourses of globalization. Where *VDW* stands apart from these films is the confident ease with which it embraces its postfeminist stance. Star practices too reflect on formations of "postfeminism," and it is telling that the film's main characters are played by female actors such as Kareena Kapoor and Sonam Kapoor, Bollywood royalty with an established reputation as glamour queens and social media savvy fashionistas who often espouse easy mantras of postfeminism. The film locates these characters within an abundant, affluent, hyperconsumerist, and elite milieu. In its embrace of consumerism, the idea of the self as enterprise, presenting of sexual expression as agency, and its impatience with any need for institutional or structural social change, *VDW* occupies a central place in thinking about the new modes in which feminism is being reinvented in India today.

Released in 2018 and dubbed as India's answer to *Sex and the City*, *VDW* evoked mixed responses. Surprisingly, the Indian Central Board of Film Certification (CBFC), the government regulatory body that had initially refused to release another recent film, *Lipstick under My Burkha*, for being too "lady-oriented" (i.e., containing sexual scenes centered around women), certified Ghosh's film for release without any objections with an "A" (Adults Only) film certificate rating. The Pakistan film censor board, on the other hand, banned the screening of the film for its "vulgar dialogues and obscene scenes."[17] Some responses to the film in India also denounced it for being "degrading," "decadent," and "vulgar" and for its tawdriness, frivolity, and flippant vision of women's liberation.

At the same time, there were others who lauded it as the first "feminist" film of its kind. For documentary filmmaker and critic Paromita Vohra, what saved the film "despite its flaws" is "how tenderly it regards human desire," thus making it an "effortlessly feminist" film that "release[s] a feeling of possibility."[18] Film studies scholar Anupama Kapse similarly suggested the film's feminist potential in its focus on "female pleasure [which was] at the heart of the film."[19] Pradnya Wagule incisively noted that the film was "feminist to the extent the market will allow it to be."[20] Reviewing the film for the *Ladies Finger* blog, Sharanaya Gopinathan went so as far as to say that "*Veere Di Wedding* is a feminist film in spite of the cast's assertions to the contrary."[21] Indeed, Kareena Kapoor, the film's central cast member, or at least the one with the biggest star power, was keen to distance herself, and the film, from being identified as feminist. At a promotional event for the film at which the film's coproducers Rhea Kapoor and Ekta Kapoor were also present, she asserted that while she believed in "gender equality," she "wouldn't say she is a feminist" which she worried was associated with "man-bashing."[22] In another instance, however, the film's second biggest cast member, Sonam Kapoor, seemed to take a different position, declaring, "When women say that they are not a feminist, it is very sad and ignorant."[23]

What the film's cast and crew did seem to agree on is how the frank depiction of female desire, sexuality, and friendship are rare in popular Hindi cinema, and thus *VDW* marks an important landmark. To be sure, the film is unusual in its prioritization of female friendships. As Kirin Narayan has argued with regard to folk wedding songs, more often than not it is the case that "[female] friendship [is] culturally acknowledged only when women are unmarried."[24] In contrast, *VDW* presents as paramount the friendship shared by four women, albeit each of them upper-caste and upper-class women in different transitional stages of their lives. In fact, one of the tacit ways in which female friendship is legitimated and celebrated by the film is for the salubrious influence it exerts on women's successful transition into and existence within heteropatriarchal relationships. While anxieties produced by the prospect of marriage, and within matrimony, are central to the thematic concerns of the film, female friendship does not occupy an oppositional or mutually exclusive relationship to heterosexual desire or marriage.

In this regard, the film embodies a decisive rejection of women's movements in India, especially third-wave feminism of the 1980s and 1990s, that were invested in confronting—both legally and culturally—the exploitation of women within marriage and domesticity, their physical vulnerability in public spaces, and underrepresentation in politics.[25] In fact, *VDW* stands in sharp contrast even to more contemporary articulations of feminism in urban India that have found expression in a range of campaigns (often online and youth-led) such as "Pink Chaddi" (pink underwear), "Take Back the Night," "Blank Noise Project," "Besharmi Morcha" (SlutWalk), "Pinjra Tod" (flee the cage), or the massive spontaneous protests and public events following the horrific 2012 Delhi rape.[26] What is common to these twentieth- and twenty-first-century movements is their call for a collective and intersectional addressing of women's shared experiences and precarities and a united resistance against the monitoring of their mobility and sexual autonomy.[27]

VDW, on the other hand, truncates these dimensions associated with Indian feminisms in favor of a resolutely insular, upper-class, upper-caste female corollary of what Waghule calls "bro-culture," perhaps best illustrated in "*Tareefan*" (compliments), the film's end-credits song-and-dance sequence. The film's focus on female friendship, then, is not a gateway to explore the radical possibilities of women's subjectivities, their personal and professional relationships, or their liberated futures, but a distraction that masks the dilution of the intersectional and collective capacities of feminism. In that sense, the ostensible plurality offered by the group of four friends, who really represent a class-caste and cultural homogeneity, is part and parcel of the postfeminist maneuver to normalize the prioritization of elite women's "problems" as ubiquitous and to project their rituals of consumerist pleasure seeking as the automatic model for women's liberation. Female friendship, as imagined in the film, is not, as so many reviewers suggested, an expression of gender solidarity, but rather a red herring that invites and trains audiences into a neoliberal preoccupation with interpersonal (as opposed to intersectional) relationships and upper-class lifestyles as the only legitimate modalities for women's emancipation.

The single most fundamental tenet of the neoliberal postfeminist ethic is expressed in its rejection of a collectively oriented feminist project that is concerned with how women can unite along shared affinities and struggles in favor of an individualized politics of selfhood.[28] In this reconfiguration, the inward focused feminist subject accepts full responsibility for enhancing her own well-being and self-care, lauds an entrepreneurial individualism,[29] and has little interest in a collective envisioning of social justice. In *VDW* this takes the form of utter disparagement of nearly all the women who aren't one of the four central protagonists.

When we are first introduced to the adult Avni, we find her representing the interests of a husband against his wife's alimony demands in a divorce case in a Delhi court room. What's alarming about this sequence isn't so much that she represents the interests of a man; lawyers, after all, fight all sorts of cases, even ones where their own politics aren't entirely aligned with their clients'. Rather, it's the vitriolic condemnation that Avni launches against the wife's rightful claims to her husband's money that marks this moment out as political crux of the film. Just as the camera enters the courtroom, we hear the wails of a woman (the wife) and see Avni rolling her eyes in annoyance at what is meant to be viewed as the woman's manipulative hysterics. Avni's address to the judge confirms her position: "Your Honor, what is the basis of her demand for maintenance? The fact is that she has emptied out the [jewelry] locker [safe]; she hasn't worked a single day in her life, and she has done nothing in life besides drama. She's getting what she deserves: zero. She shouldn't get even a penny." This is followed by the judge, snappily convinced by Avni's indefatigable logic, signing the divorce settlement papers that entitle the woman to nothing.

This scene helps to quickly establish the film's worldview: we are far removed from the feminist struggles of the 1970s and 1980s, both in India and globally, that fought long and hard for women's economic rights and security in marriage. Avni's speech, and the lack of protest it receives from the judge and even the wife's own lawyer (who stays silent even when the woman urges him to speak) work to quickly and efficiently—very early on in the film—assuage any audience anxieties that a film with four women will be a "feminist" film, one that entails male bashing or an exposition of women's rights. In a context when the antifeminist men's rights movement has been gaining ground in India, along with other developments such as the continuing ascension of aggressive, muscular brahmanical Hindu nationalism (that expresses itself in campaigns of Love Jihad or the war on Valentine's Day), and where there is a mainstream acceptance of the discourse that women routinely abuse antidowry and anti-sexual-harassment laws to persecute innocent men with trumped-up charges, Avni's opening speech is all the more insidious.

Even more, the scene lays the foundation for a key dichotomy between and taxonomy of women who deserve entitlements and those who don't. What's surprising, though, is that the grounds for what constitutes a "deserving woman" are fluid. While the wife is berated here for not having an independent income and for not having "worked a day in her life," later in the film Avni jumps to give her friend Sakshi—who also has no independent professional identity or income and lives off her millionaire father—legal aid to protect her financial interests in her divorce case.

Shortly after the courtroom scene, in an arranged marriage setup, Avni is paraded by her mom in front of Manish and his parents. While the two families are playing the match-making game, we hear sounds of a woman sobbing coming from a different part of the house, and Avni excuses herself from the conversation on the pretext to "check on tea." When Avni enters the kitchen, she sees her domestic help, Shanti, her face bruised, crying as she makes tea for the guests. Avni places her hand on Shanti's shoulder to turn her around, and we see the full extent of the violence that her husband, ostensibly, has unleashed on her. Avni's first words to Shanti convey sympathy but also her exasperation at the latter's circumstances: "I cannot see your black and blue face every morning along with my tea." Avni's horror at the sight of Shanti's domestic abuse injuries is accompanied by an impatience at the latter's refusal to act and leave her husband: "Uff, stop crying . . . Thank god I'm a lawyer; I'm going to get you divorced," she says, threatening also to file an FIR (a police report) against Shanti's husband.

There's much to unpack in this scene. Ostensibly, the scene lets us know that Avni is as adept at being a shrewd, no-punches-pulled kind of lawyer, as good at calling out women who fake victimhood as she is at being compassionate and using her legal expertise to intervene on behalf of a working-class woman to stop her domestic abuse. That she pays no heed to Shanti's protestations of "Nahin Didi" (no, sister) is meant to be beside the point. And yet it is significant that Avni's paternalism is blind to what the lower-class woman may herself want. This could have potentially been a moment where the similarities between Avni and the maid's situation are made visible; they are both working women (unlike Avni's friends) and they both struggle to navigate the matrimonial market and the concomitant gendered inequities that follow. Instead, in this moment, as elsewhere in the film, middle- and upper- class modern young women like Avni display female individualism at the expense of feminist politics. The film opts to establish the upper-class woman as the working-class woman's savior. It is also interesting that while victim status is granted to Shanti (as opposed to the woman in the court scene), Avni still expresses impatience at Shanti's tears, in a kind of "if you won't fix your problem, stop crying about it" way. The postfeminist rhetoric that women are responsible for fending for themselves combines, in this scene, with a neat and convenient distinction, along class lines, between those who still need access to the hard-won rights that feminism made accessible to women and those who are past the need for feminism. As Dosekun, whose work focuses on postfeminism in Nigeria, so astutely notes, "In highly inegalitarian local contexts while upper-class-women function as 'empowered' and thus no longer in need to feminism, lower-class women are seen as 'still disempowered' and in need, still, of feminism's interventions."[30]

What's most unsettling is the speed and ease with which Shanti's plight is forgotten. Avni is distracted by the news, received via text, announcing her friend Kalindi's engagement to her long-term boyfriend. Avni shrieks with joy, announcing the good news loudly to Shanti, who grins widely in response to her employer's excitement. The abrupt shift in the scene's tonality—from somber to exuberant—indicates just how incidental working-class women's predicaments really are to Avni and to the film; the forgettability of Shanti's problems is seconded by the fact that she never appears on screen again.

In fact, there are only other two contexts in which working-class women are even referenced, both times as insulting appellations. When a potential suitor Nirmal rejects Avni after she kisses him, she berates him for his double standards, saying, "You think you want a modern and independent wife, but all you really want is a *naukarani* [servant/maid] who nods her head [in agreement]." Clearly, a servant cannot be modern or independent since the sort of liberation or empowerment being envisioned here is exclusively the preserve of middle- and upper-class women like Avni and her friends. Another important moment is when we finally discover the reason for Sakshi's divorce: among the many stresses in her marriage, one is that her husband would expect her to do domestic chores (daily cooking, hosting parties, etc.) and then humiliate her for not being well-turned-out when his work friends were over. "You're looking worse than a *bai* [servant]," he tells her. When Sakshi finally reveals the acrimonious details of her marriage to her friends, in their eyes, it is this crime—of comparing her to working-class domestic help—that most condemns her husband. Avni tells Sakshi she'll help her fight her divorce case, stop her husband Vineet from blackmailing her (for having caught her masturbating) into coughing up millions because "Nobody calls my best friend a *bai*." The film then renders working-class women's lives and struggles into immemorable glitches that matter only inasmuch as they impede the postfeminist female subject's morning tea consumption; their professional identities—as domestic help—are turned into insulting appellations by the men who use them and by the women who accept them as degrading comparisons. In the postfeminist gender regime, it is far worse to be called a poor woman than a slut.

In fact, the film and its central protagonists travel a fair distance in legitimating their general displeasure at and lack of solidarity with nearly all the other women in the film (besides each other). All middle-aged or older women (mothers and aunties) are dismissed as nags (Avni's mother) or gossipy neighborhood aunties who make the lives of young, single, divorced women hard with their taunts, jibes, and snooping questions. Even the well-intentioned older women, like Kalindi's mother-in-law and Bhandari's mom (the man Avni has a one-night stand with) are rendered contemptible for their gauche and smothering mannerisms and grotesque aesthetics; they embody the aspirations of the nouveau riche, getting the markers of a globalized aesthetic terribly wrong. As a result, their taste in clothes and décor are the subject of multiple jokes in the film. Finally, Kalindi's stepmother, Paromita, is made the object of vicious ridicule: she is depicted as the stereotypically loud and pretentious Bengali woman dressed in handloom saris and silver jewelry. She is even called a "slut" or whore (*bazaroo aurat*) by Kalindi's snobbish and sexist gay uncle.

In *VDW*'s version of things, the postfeminist subject is a tricky assemblage; not every woman, simply by virtue of being a woman under a neoliberal regime, gains automatic entry into the echelons of empowered neoliberalism. In the film, it is only the central protagonists, the four friends, who check the right boxes, embody the correct cultural facets, and thus represent the right kind of femininity. Being upper-class is a requirement, of course, but not sufficient criteria (as we learn in the courtroom scene); being born rich, rather than simply marrying rich, makes for a more "legitimate" postfeminist subject, which explains why Avni offers to help Sakshi protect her (father's) financial interests during her divorce when she didn't extend the same courtesy to the woman in the courtroom scene.

Fascinatingly, the postfeminist neoliberal subject critiques patriarchy most staunchly only when it comes in the way of her exploring her heteronormative sexuality. Sexual double standards are a deal breaker for her. This is why Avni's rejection of Nirmal (on the grounds that he morally castigates her for trying to kiss him) and her journey to sexual self-confidence are some of the most central concerns of the film. In this new gender regime, "being without a husband does not mean [women] will go without men."[31] Sexual freedom is the one cause, the one ethic, for which postfeminist subjects will seemingly stake a political claim. At the same time, though, as the next section of the chapter on sexual humor will demonstrate, sexual autonomy is a privilege that only the right kind of woman—the postfeminist subject—can avail. Older women, stepmothers, daughters of unlikable aunties, are exempt from partaking in this privilege.

This is not to suggest that the postfeminist subject is perfect or inured against committing mistakes; quite the contrary, in fact. As Kalindi's dead mother's voice-over tells us, the whole film is an exposition on letting daughters and women make mistakes and learn from them. What distinguishes the four friends, however, is that they never resort to melodrama or hysterics (unlike the woman in the courtroom, Shanti, or Kalindi's mother-in-law) in the face of adversity. Remarkably, then, we don't see even one of the four characters cry;

they always maintain a dignified emotional sobriety, which singles them out as being adept at managing life's travails.

And, of course, when it all does get too much, the girls know what to do to keep calm and carry on: take a luxury holiday abroad, blow off some steam through the appropriate channels of consumerism, and return to normalcy with the renewed commitment to addressing their problems head-on.

Since female liberation in the film translates to girls playing the same games that *veeres*/bros do, the film borrows tropes from the neoliberal bromance or contemporary Bollywood male buddy road to superimpose onto its vision of what feminine choices entail and enable. The girls' trip to Thailand allows the chick flick or "*veer* romance" to further trade in hyperconsumerist spectacles in environments of urban affluence and privilege. What brings the girls' together is their ability for consumptive travel, their attitudes, and lifestyles. With a swipe of her credit card and a few clicks on her iPad, Sakshi books an extravagant trip where her female buddies (who she refers to as "bitches" in another postfeminist move of reclaiming an insulting word) can heal (or stop "giving it up" to everyone, as she puts it) after Kalindi breaks off her engagement to Rishabh, as she feels overwhelmed by the demands of his suffocating family. With an HSBC credit card, there is really nothing that money can't buy; nothing is priceless! The girls fly business class, stay at a private luxury villa, have champagne by a swimming pool, stroll on the beach in bikinis, eat crab by the ocean, smoke marijuana joints, visit strip clubs. When they end up on the dance stage, Sakshi and Meera gyrate on the poles, reinforcing the film's postfeminist moves, a sense that feminism has been "taken into account" (as McRobbie puts it).

After the vacation, the girls decide to "lean in" and are able to quickly mend the chinks that have emerged in their friendship and deal with their personal issues. It is this—their capacity to take individual responsibility of their "bad choices" (marriage phobia; obsession with getting married; sexless marriage; failed marriage and the subsequent acting out through alcohol consumption and late-night partying out of guilt for having embarrassed one's parents), and their ability to rectify their mistakes by making "good choices"—that mark them out as the only "girls" (because postfeminist culture girlifies women) deserving of the accolades that neoliberalism and postfeminism shower on its adherents. By the time the four friends return from their holiday, they have resolved their internal conflicts and we see each of them taking "action," setting in motion their entrepreneurial spirit, to fix their lives. Kalindi reconnects with her fiancé and ultimately marries him; Avni confronts her mother about the pressure the latter puts on her to get married because she has come to terms with her own sexuality unencumbered by matrimony; Sakshi finally tells her parents why her marriage ended, only to find that they are nothing but supportive of her; and,

Meera fixes her sexless marriage by initiating sex with her husband immediately after her return from the holiday with friends.

Indeed, the reclaiming of sexuality and sexual pleasure seems central in the film's postfeminist gender regime, one that is supposed to unsettle traditional insistence on female chastity and virtue. The ubiquity of sexual humor is one of the prime forms that this embrace of sexuality takes in the film. Its investment in exploring the lives of four economically privileged women, and the modes of self-fashioning and self-articulation they have access to, combined with the film's predominantly comic tenor, opens up the possibility of endless jokes, sexual innuendoes, and witticisms that these women share with each other in their attempt to voice their frustrations. Like never before, at least in popular Hindi cinema, we see young women embrace their "bad girls" status as they unabashedly plow through the audience's (and, at times, even their own) discomfort at sexually explicit humor and adamantly reinstate the sexual in their everyday lives and conversations. In some ways, then, their recourse to sexual humor may be read as an integral component of women's expressive rituals and their ordinary conversations; it could be seen as an urban-chic variant of what Gloria Raheja and Ann Gold argue, in their study of rural women's oral traditions in North India, constitutes "a moral discourse in which gender and kinship identities are constructed, represented, negotiated, and contested in everyday life."[32] At the same time, however, a closer analysis of the humor they resort to and the code switching they engage in in these "funny" moments, and the content and target of humor, leaves us with a less than satisfying envisioning of the liberatory potential of the kind of sexual humor that *VDW* puts on offer. In other words, while Raheja and Gold examine the relationship between language and gender to uncover the "creative power of women's discourse," our computational analysis of *VDW*'s sexual humor, similar to Stanley Tambiah's findings in relation to North Indian women's songs, unveils the ways in which the linguistic rebellions of the four protagonists "leave the dominant male ideology more or less intact."[33] The ostensibly subversive titillations offered by the film's sexual humor, in fact, mask an insidious normalization of, and participation in, a sexist logic conflated with entitlements of caste-class privilege.

Conventionally, sexual humor has been identified as a masculine pursuit that, as John Morreall suggests, allows men to communicate with one another without revealing anything about themselves.[34] In fact, the world of dirty jokes and bawdy humor has long alienated women. For one, in such standard jokes women exist mostly as stereotypes: dumb blondes, nagging wives, angry feminists, mothers-in-law, and sex objects. Women are thus invariably the butt of the joke in sexual humor. Second, there's a tacit pressure on "respectable" women to excuse themselves from such humor or ignore it when it occurs in their presence for fear of being judged as sexually available or promiscuous. Women who agree to listen to or tell such jokes are read as signaling their access to "fallen knowledge" and thus are read as conveying their willingness to accept a man's sexual approach.[35] At the same time, women are caught in a double bind: their unwillingness to laugh at sexual jokes is used to condemn them for having no sense of humor.

In this context, Janet Bing earmarks a useful distinction between the more mainstream sexual jokes that men ostensibly tell and what she terms "liberated sexual jokes." While the former simply violate the "taboos against talking in public about sex," "liberated sexual jokes," she writes, "are funny because they violate taboos against talking about sexism."[36] Bing's ethnographic work, in which she studies sexual jokes shared between women, crucially disrupts the assumption, shared both by common wisdom and humor scholars, that women do not tell dirty jokes. At the same time, her conclusions reveal an interesting facet that often characterizes women's sexual humor: sexually liberated jokes, in which the script shifts from the sexual to the nonsexual (the reverse setup mostly characterizes jokes that men tell) allow women to introduce difficult subjects that are hard to openly discuss, such as the unequal distribution of domestic responsibilities. In women's liberated jokes, then, it is the inferior status of women rather than the sex that is the focus of the punch line. A similar pattern can be traced in women's expressive traditions that Raheja and Gold translate: the "hidden transcripts" of stories, songs, personal narratives, and conversations they examine "at some levels serve to perpetuate gender inequalities, but they also render conceivable and may indeed sanction women's active resistance."[37]

VDW offers a fascinating test case for the analysis of women's sexual humor. We coded approximately thirty-six moments of sexual humor that were shared between the four protagonists. Our goal was to follow Bing's lead in trying to track the patterns of interaction in an all-women friend group when the topic of conversation turned to sex or when a nonsexual matter was deliberately sexualized.[38] We defined the moments of sexual humor as ones where one of the four characters says something sexual that elicits laughter from the characters on screen or is meant to produce laughter from the audience.[39] Most often, such utterances included both serious conversations and teasing one-liners about sex, masturbation, or orgasms. On a few occasions, we found that the humor entailed invoking a hypersexualized identity (for instance, women referred to as "slutty" or "*randi*") or using sexual vocabulary as an expletive ("go fuck yourself"). We coded these sexual utterances that produce laughter to reveal the following:

1) Who cracked the most sexual jokes and which character was at the receiving end of this kind of humor?
2) Do any of the four protagonists, when they tell a joke, demean any women?
3) Did the joke enable a critique of sexism or patriarchy?
4) Does the sexual humor build on a conversation that is already sexual or does it introduce a sexual angle to a previously nonsexual conversation?
5) Was a Hindi-language word used in the sexual component of the joke?

Fascinatingly, we found that it was Sakshi—the richest of the four friends, on the verge of a divorce, the most brazen in her consumption of cigarettes and alcohol, and the most gratuitously "carefree"—who cracks the maximum number of sexual jokes. Most commonly, her jokes ranged from alternately teasing Avni about her "sexcapades" (with her boss; the men she meets at her mother's behest through matrimonial websites; her one-night stands) to encouraging Avni to unabashedly pursue her sexual adventures. In total, then, Sakshi was responsible for nearly 53 percent of the sexual humor in the film.

The character who came closest to Sakshi in making sexual quips, albeit with a wide margin separating them, was Meera, a fat woman married to a white man, going through a proverbial "dry spell" ("*sookha*" as Sakshi calls it) in her marriage, on account of the travails of childbirth and postpartum weight gain, because of which she feels poorly about her body and thus can't bring herself to have sex with her "*Bechara*" (pitiable) husband, John.[40] The teenage and adult versions of Meera combined make thirteen jokes (three as a high schooler and ten in adulthood), bringing her sexual jokes to 27 percent of the total sexual jokes told by the four main characters.[41] Her humor, like Sakshi's, is also supportive of Avni's sexual rendezvous (she keeps tells Avni to "mount" Nirmal ("*tu chad ja*"), but unlike Sakshi, she makes allusions to the size of her husband's penis, speciously convincing her friends that she has a gratifying sex life ("Who can't be happy with John's john?"). Importantly, she is also the one to introduce the humor around "what masturbation is called in Hindi" ("*charam such*"), which becomes a running joke for the rest of the film. A key distinguishing factor uniting Sakshi and Meera, then, is that they are (unhappily) married. Their matrimonial status, it seems, entitles them to a certain amount of narrative space to engage in sexual humor. This entitlement, though, as our analysis demonstrates, is actually rooted in and is an attribute of a sexual politics invested in preserving the virginal sanctity of their more reputed costars.

In contrast, Avni cracks only four (11 percent) jokes, most of which are self-directed and draw attention to the ways in which her life is hemmed in by society's sexual double standards. For instance, she highlights how even though it was her boss who was married with two kids, having an affair with him made her the "*tawaif*" (tramp). Finally, Kalindi, around whom the film's central crisis revolves—she is marriage-phobic because of her childhood trauma of watching her parents' ugly fights—says something sexual *and* funny only twice in the film: the first is directed at her stepmother, Paromita (she tells her friends she wishes Paromita would go "fuck herself" rather than interfere in her wedding planning). The second time, her humor is directed at Sakshi after the latter reveals the long-awaited reason for her divorce: that she was caught masturbating by her husband. With utter incredulity Kalindi asks Sakshi to explain the course of events: "So, basically, after the fight [with your husband] you were sitting around bored, and thought you may as well jerk off?"

At first glance this disparity between those who make sexual jokes and those who don't might be attributed to the different personalities in the friend group, a symptom, perhaps, of nothing more than the varied levels of comfort with sexual humor that each character is willing to display. And yet the data is revelatory of much more. Sakshi and Meera, the two women who between them are responsible for producing, 80 percent of the sexual humor, are not just married women, but are also women whose married lives have turned out to be far from perfect, and it is around a "lack of sex" that the crisis in their matrimonial relationship is articulated and crystalized. There seems to be, then, a direct correlation that the film makes, perhaps unwittingly, between personal sexual frustrations (Sakshi resorts to masturbating with a dildo only after three months of no sex with her husband, and Meera has been in a sexless marriage for a year) and the capacity to engage in sexual humor.

Even more interestingly, however, it is telling that the burden of the film's risqué maneuvers is carried, to a disproportionate degree, by a woman who is a soon-to-be divorcee and a fat woman. What we find, therefore, is that it falls upon the two archetypal characters who have been historically maligned and treated as objects of derision and ridicule in popular Hindi cinema, to facilitate the film's gamble in pushing the boundaries of propriety as it challenges audiences to imagine the sexualized life of its female protagonists. That two of the most vulnerable character types do the majority of the work, as it were, of sexual humor, that they do the work and bear the responsibility of keeping things light even as the film undertakes the task of opening up new vistas of possibility for women in Hindi films, is very much in alignment with a postfeminist myopia about the unequal distribution of vulnerability that different women embody. It perfectly encapsulates neoliberal feminism's blindness to the incommensurate scales of emotional labor that certain women have to perform, and the risks they have to incur, in order to make their own lives, and the lives of women who are far more privileged, more livable.

Significantly, this mismatch between the work of sexual humor that the different characters undertake maps on perfectly to the hierarchy in the celebrity status of the actors who play these roles. The two junior actors—Swara Bhaskar (also known in the industry for sticking her neck out to defend liberal, secular, and feminist politics) and Shikha Talsania—who don't have much leverage or dynastic cache in the industry, produce the maximal raunchy humor in the film. On the other hand, Kareena Kapoor and Sonam Kapoor who are far more secure and ensconced in the elite echelons of the industry by virtue of their "star kids" status and their affiliations with the big film dynasties (Kareena, of course has the double buffer, as it were, of being a Kapoor and a "*begum*" through marriage to Saif Ali Khan, scion of the royal Pataudi family), rarely get their hands dirty with the dirty jokes. Kalindi/Kareena is able to remain entirely untainted by the sex talk that happens around her. She is almost never[42] on the receiving end of her friend's sexual humor, and when these conversations do happen around her, she is able to maintain an air of "I'm too cool to be perturbed or shocked, but too decorous to participate." Even though she has been in a live-in relationship with her partner for three years, there is never any conversation about her sex life, no allusions made to her desires. The film subtly but adamantly makes clear that her crisis isn't sexual, it's emotional. And therefore the film is able to create this implicit and neat divide between women who render themselves sexual through humor and those who remain virginal (even if not literal virgins) by a lack of participation in that humor. And it's important to note that the virginal status is retained for the most important character, for Kalindi and her story is set up as the film's anchoring center. In doing so, the film consolidates the most mainstream and conventional form of femininity that has dominated Bollywood thus far. But even more, in retaining her as the nonsexual center of the film, it protects the celebrity status of the actor who plays the part. Not long before the film was made and released, Kareena entered motherhood. By creating this imperceptible, yet crucial, distance between Kareena and sexual humor, the film opts to protect Kareena from charges of impropriety that would mar her status both as *begum* and mother. In doing so, however, it reinstates the gendered and sexual status quo that it ostensibly aspired and avowed to overturn in the first place.[43]

There were some other notable highlights that emerged from our coding of sexual humor in the film: in nearly 40 percent of the jokes that were cracked, women were referred to in some demeaning capacity (as in the case of the two jokes that Kalindi makes at her stepmother and Sakshi's expense), or the point of the joke was to shame the woman for her sexual choices or situation (including lack of sex). Sakshi, for instance, quizzes Avni about how she can bring herself to have sex with a man called Nirmal. In another instance, toward the end of the film, when Sakshi confronts the neighborhood aunties who have taunted her about her inappropriate nightlife, her clothes, and her return to her parental home without her husband, Sakshi's avenges her humiliation at their hands, ironically, by outing the daughter of one of these aunties for being a drug addict and shaming her for sleeping with a drug peddler. In fact, our data here may be downplaying just how derogatory the film is toward most, if not all, women that are not one of the four of them.

Furthermore, we found that only 25 percent of the jokes were, in some capacity, a critique of sexism/patriarchy/sexual double standards. Or, to frame it another way, for 75 percent of the sexual humor, the fact of sex itself was funny or the object of humor, the punch line of the joke. What this suggests is that very few jokes would qualify as what Bing considers sexually liberated jokes. Additionally, the results were in keeping with our argument that the film endorses a mindless imitation of masculine and masculinist rituals and cultures of self-expression as a model for women's liberation; and, to be fair, the title of the film itself explicitly encourages us to expect and accept this modality for women's way forward. The film not only works with the clichéd assumption that women "blow off steam" in the same way that men do, but it actually encourages it as an elixir to the array of life's problems. Sexual humor, like leisure holidays abroad, are the lessons in unrepression that these women seemed to have learned from their male cinematic counterparts.

What was especially illuminating was that 64 percent of the incidents of humor entailed the use of Hindi verbiage in the most explicitly sexual component of the joke. These included references to condoms as "*chatri*," orgasms as "*charam sukh*," fucking as "*thokna*," whining as "*randi-rona*," masturbation as "*apna haath jaggannath*." This may seem to be a curious thing to highlight, given that the entire film is in Hindi. If we consider the class background of these characters, however, the code switching to Hindi in moments of sexual humor feels incongruent within the cultural milieu the film itself contrived as an authentic rendition of upper-class women's lives. It's interesting that a film that chooses to pitch itself as giving the audience an inside view of what "real" conversations between urban upper-class girlfriends look like, and doesn't shy away from placing these women in their extremely privileged sociocultural milieu, suddenly opts out of the linguistic realism of what these moments would sound like and chooses instead to turn them into occasion for exploring, possibly, the earthiness of sex talk in Hindi. It is hard to completely understand the logic for inserting Hindi in this insistent and contrived way. Perhaps it is the film's way to making its deeply bourgeois habitus palatable and accessible to a wider audience; it could be a way of just adding to the titillation and sensationalism associated with the film. But what it also does is to turn Hindi—the language itself—into an object of humor. This is most evident when Meera shares the Hindi word for orgasm with her friends: they all giggle and practice the throaty, guttural sound that the word "*sukh*," when said right, produces. What is abundantly clear in this moment is that it isn't the reference to an orgasm that has the girls in splits, but the oddity of what it sounds like in Hindi.

What was discomforting was that these moments of sexual humor, then, become occasions for these otherwise intensely anglophilic (and quite possibly anglophone), upper class women to dabble in what might be considered "linguistic slumming." As Tejaswini Ganti in her essay about "language hierarchies in Bollywood" argues, India's linguistic terrain has shifted substantially since liberalization. Even though Hindi films today are "much more diverse and regionally specific" than "films from earlier decades," there is a corresponding "waning" of fluency in Hindi among the elite members of the film industry and Indian society more generally.[44] Language thus continues to function as a site "for the elaboration of distinction, the performance of cultural capital, and the enactment of new hierarchies."[45] The Indian super-elite today thus distinguish themselves from the aspirational middle classes by displaying a hyperfluency in "polished" English and Westernized (Americanized) accents, verbiage, and idioms ("bro," "chick flick"). While Ganti's argument draws attention to the discrepancy between the increase in "localized registers of Hindi" in film dialogues versus the "increased prevalence of English within the film industry," we want to draw attention to the treatment of Hindi within the social landscape of the film itself. As characters of a popular Hindi film, most of their dialogue is indeed in Hindi, and yet their titillated unfamiliarity with, and jocular recruitment of Hindi for its sexual slang and in moments of sexual humor, draws attention to the characters' relationship to the language, as a low-brow novelty.

This would explain why Kalindi—who we have earlier identified as virginal and whose characterization is most enveloped by the star status of the actor who plays her—never utters a sexual word in Hindi. The only two times she does produce humor, even as she toys with a sexual vocabulary, she uses explicitly English terminology: "fuck off" and "jerk off." What seems to be happening, then, is that the film treats humor as not only a way to talk about sex, but also as a way to joke about Hindi. We may even say, then, that more than any character in the film, it is Hindi that is most often the butt of the joke. And because there is an exhilaration associated with engaging in the very things we revile and disparage, we see the women enjoying their *derive* through the linguistic cultures they wouldn't ordinarily touch with a barge pole.

On January 25, 2019, Amazon Prime, India, released the ten-episode web series *Four More Shots Please*, and the show got enough traction to be renewed for a second season that was released in April 2020. The web series revolves around four upper-class female friends in Mumbai and their conversations around sexuality, desires, and marriage. The proliferation of other such cultural productions—such as the 2019 film *The Zoya Factor*, an adaptation of Anuja Chauhan's successful 2008 Indian chick lit novel, and the 2020 Netflix reality TV show *The Fabulous Lives of Bollywood Wives*—that have arrived on the heels of *VDW*'s commercial success speak to the influence of the neoliberal and postfeminist aesthetics and politics of *VDW*. These texts reinforce *VDW*'s status as an important marker in postliberalization and millennial New Bollywood's representations of femininity and feminism, one where "post-feminism and neo-liberalism coalesce in the construction of a selfhood that celebrates self-enterprise, pleasure, and sexuality, and posits them as women's empowerment."[46] Through focusing especially on the workings of sexual humor, the depoliticized presentation of women's lives, and the lack of solidarity with other women, we have situated our analysis of *VDW* in contrast to the celebratory reviews of the film that see its treatment of female desires as radical or groundbreaking. Instead, we see *VDW*—through its endorsement of entrepreneurial individualism, aspirational lifestyles, language of choice, and individual empowerment—as exemplifying a postfeminist rationale, a symptom of the co-opting of feminism in contemporary neoliberal India in which, to quote from a song in the film, "no one gives a damn" about structural inequalities or collective struggles for social justice.

The Maladies of Maids, Masters, and Madams in Mumbai in *Is Love Enough? Sir* and *Lust Stories*

Female domestic workers constitute a large part of India's enormous unorganized and unregulated sector, which is defined by irregular, casual, precarious work, that is, "employment that is uncertain, unpredictable, and risky from the point of view of the worker."[47] A 2018 report of the International Labor Organization suggests that the total share of "informal employment" is 87.8 percent in southern Asia (compared to 18.1 percent in North America), indicating the magnitude of difference in the extent of "irregular work" in the Global North and South.[48] According to official estimates, more than four million people are employed as domestic helpers in middle-class and affluent Indian homes. Unofficial estimates put that number at fifty million. Two-thirds of these workers are women.[49]

These female domestic workers are often called "maids," a word that "captures the semi-feudal and gendered dimensions of the relationship."[50] While domestic servitude[51] on the Indian subcontinent has a long history, the specifics of the contemporary conditions of servitude are structured by the new economic regime and local policies that are shaped by neoliberal forces of globalization:

uneven development, displacement, urbanization, and exponential growth of the middle classes with aspirational lifestyles. The phenomenon of "uptitling"—such as referring to maids, drivers, guards, as "staff" in upper-middle-class Indian households—is a feature of precarization under the new regime. The title inflation covers up for sterile work, and as Guy Standing explains it, "someone in a static, going-nowhere job is given a high-sounding epithet to conceal precariat tendencies."[52] The heightened vulnerability of the growing group of "expendables"—domestic workers, other working-class internal migrants from the hinterland—was painfully evident in the Indian government's disastrous management of the COVID-19 pandemic. Domestic workers found themselves becoming the target of increased surveillance and segregation, losing their livelihoods, and stigmatized as carriers of disease even as the great middle class struggled to manage households without them. Millions of internal labor migrants in low-income jobs were left stranded by the government's arbitrarily announced national lockdown, leading to widespread chaos and loss of life and livelihood. According to a news magazine report, this led to the "forced migration of at least 15 million people crisscrossing the country to get back to their homes."[53] Many of them never made it back home.

Zoya Akhtar's short film segment in *Lust Stories* (an anthology of four short films from Netflix-India)[54] and Rohena Gera's *Sir* have female domestic workers as their protagonists.[55] Akhtar's twenty-minute film features Sudha (Bhumi Pednekar), a maid with benefits who cleans and cooks for, and sleeps with, her male employer, Ajit (Neil Bhoopalam). It turns out that Ajit is simultaneously entertaining an arranged marriage with a more "suitable girl": English-speaking and upper-caste-class. Along similar lines, *Sir* explores the intimacy that develops between a live-in maid, Ratna (Tillotama Shome) and her U.S.-returned employer, Ashwin (Vivek Gomber). Both films invited strong responses, especially for their presentation of unusual subject matter: cross-class physical "intimacy" and a shift of the female domestic worker from narrative periphery to the center. While some reviewers celebrated Akhtar's *Lust Stories* as "nothing short of revolutionary" for its depiction of "a domestic worker as a sexual being,"[56] others accused it of participating in an eroticization and fetishization of the *bai* (female domestic help), "used sexually and cast aside by the man once he is engaged to someone who is equal in both caste and class."[57] Similarly, *Sir* was celebrated both as "one of the more subtly-constructed, sensitive, and realistic portrayals of love relationships"[58] and as "a story of deliberate caste-blindness and gender privilege"[59] that glorified its female protagonist's sexual harassment, thus contributing to making "life more unsafe for domestic workers."[60] We use these commentaries as provocations to explore the films' engagement with the intersection of gender and class precarities. We do this slightly differently, through focusing not just on the onscreen relationship between master and maid, but also through centralizing the encounters and exchanges between maids and their madams.

We ask: How is the notion of "mobility" (spatial/physical, social/professional) recalibrated with the centering of a female migrant worker? What might sexual "consent" mean within the context of unequal class- and gender-based power hierarchies? For working-class women, how are notions of choice or autonomy reconfigured outside of contexts of consumerism? In conclusion, we also note that even as both films offer insights into structural conditions that might render the lives of working-class women acutely and differentially vulnerable, their approach of focusing on the intimate and personal rather than the institutional, structural, and social context reveals the limits of their critique of neoliberal feminism. In the end, *Sir* remains invested in a cruel optimism in its sentimental "happy ending." In contrast, *Lust Stories* offers a more clear-eyed look at the tenacity of socioeconomic chasms that engender and reinforce precarities in contemporary India.

Both *Lust Stories* (Akhtar's segment in the Netflix anthology) and *Sir*'s unconventional content can be attributed to the films' production, distribution, and exhibition contexts. Both films were released for streaming on Netflix (although unlike *Lust Stories*, *Sir* was also released in theaters). Indeed, the entry and growth of streaming services and OTT platforms, as a natural progression of the arrival of multiplex cinema, is radically transforming the media landscape in India. In an interview, the main female lead of *Sir*, Tillotama Shome,[61] noted that *Sir* dropping on Netflix was her "first experience of the enormous power of OTT, and how it can travel into people's homes and hearts in numbers that are mind-boggling." The new media landscape has especially expanded space for women as creators, actors, and staff (mainstream Bollywood being a notoriously male-dominated industry)[62] and has created creative space for different kinds of storytelling, both in terms of experimentation with form, such as the anthology film, and delivery of more edgy content. This was especially possible because these platforms were not in their initial years subject to the state's censorship regulations in the same manner as Indian cinema was, although this situation is rapidly changing as filmmakers self-censor to avoid run-ins with Hindu nationalists, and the Ministry of Information and Broadcasting has announced stricter digital guidelines and oversight mechanisms.[63]

In popular Hindi cinema's checkered history of representation, domestic help has been both ubiquitous and marginalized, a reflection of social reality where domestic servitude is part and parcel of everyday life in India. Servants exist mostly as shadowy generic cinematic types: objects of pity and condescension, comic relief, or celebrated as Gunga Din–like simple-minded loyal servants who are eternally loyal to their sahibs. Women servants, in particular, have been presented within a duality as maternal and desexualized, or as sexualized and possessing lower-class vitality.[64] Several post-1990s films, such as *Hum Aapke Hain Koun!* (Sooraj Barjatya, 1994), *Maine Pyar Kiya* (Sooraj Barjatya, 1989), and *Kabhi Khushi Kabhi Gham* (Karan Johar, 2001), treated servants as part of one big happy (Hindu Indian) family. Their lives, the films' subtext suggested, had improved under the new regime ushered by economic liberalization. They continued to enjoy the feudal patronage of their employers, even while developing more democratic forms of camaraderie with the family's younger generation. In some rare instances, however, popular Hindi cinema has addressed the sexual precariousness of lower-class women, even if only to highlight the heroism of the bourgeois hero/heroine. In fact, one of Bollywood's most important women-centric films, *Damini* (Rajkumar Santoshi, 1993), which has acquired the status of a feminist cult classic, revolves around the eponymous upper-class woman's fight for justice for the family's maid, who dies after being gang raped by men of the family she serves. Despite extreme pressure from her husband and in-laws, and at great physical and emotional cost to herself, Damini offers testimony for the prosecution against her brother-in-law. The film has an imagination of ethics and solidarity toward working-class women, even as it enshrines the upper-class woman as the courageous truth teller and seeker of justice.

Sir and *Lust Stories* attempt to break away from these tired tropes by granting the female domestic workers primacy as characters with a coherent interiority articulated around their sexual, social, and professional desires and aspirations. These women navigate the intricacies of interclass romantic relationships and the drudgery of domestic labor with an acute self-awareness of their precarious position, while exercising their autonomy, dignity, and agency even in personally and professionally treacherous situations. They can hold nuance and contradictions, not just with regard to their own positionality, but also about their male employers. The latter are not exempt from the women's critical gaze, but neither are the women in a hurry to declare themselves passive victims, or passive beneficiaries, of their employers' attentions. In that sense, the two films flip the script: upper-middle-class characters, men and women alike, are relegated to the margins and serve as spotlighting tools to shine light on the vicissitudes and victories of working-class women's lives. The films, in giving voice to these long-neglected figures, are able to explore the complex experience of "gendered abjection, stigmatization, subordination, [and] menial labor" in domestic servitude. And, as Ambreen Hai suggests, such cultural texts unearth the ramifications of what occurs when "privilege and disprivilege" are so contiguously proximate.[65]

Sir begins with the maid, Ratna, on the move. We learn that her visit to her family (mother and sister) in the village has been unexpectedly interrupted:

she has been asked to return to the city by her employers. A class precariat, her time is not hers and she can be "recalled" for "duty" anytime without an explanation. But what stands out about the opening sequence is Ratna's remarkable spatial and geographical mobility as she undertakes the long journey from village to city. We see her riding pillion on a motorbike, in a shared taxi, bus, and local train before she walks into her place of work, an apartment in a luxury skyscraper in Mumbai. In fact, Ratna's physical mobility is reinforced variously in the film as she confidently navigates the city spaces for labor and leisure, speaking to the ways in which working-class women have always been more mobile out of necessity or choice than their upper-class and caste counterparts.

Her spatial mobility—from rural to urban and within the city—also manifests in opportunities for social mobility.[66] Sonal Sharma and Eesha Kunduri, in their study of internal women migrants engaged in domestic, home-based work, have found that for these workers "articulations of agency in terms of economic matters . . . are not independent of the social and spatial mobility options offered by city spaces but are, in fact, embedded within them."[67] Ratna is an "internal migrant" to Mumbai, a young widow from the village who has only been allowed by her in-laws to work in the city on the condition that she remit money back home to them. Ratna's spatial and geographical mobility has allowed her, as she herself tells us on multiple occasions, to escape the social death of being a young widow in rural India. It has bestowed her with a sense of economic agency for herself and her younger sister, to whom she sends money in the hope that at least she will escape the destiny of a "servant." Ratna is also an aspiring entrepreneur, wanting to start her own business as a fashion designer and have her sister manage her finances. The urban networks she forms with other working-class women like Lakshmi, another domestic worker in her building, has direct consequences for her upward mobility. It is Lakshmi who loans her money and helps her buy materials for her tailoring course. They offer each other a much-needed affective support system in the form of chats over tea in the communal spaces that the two women can occupy in their "off-time."

This emphasis on the maid's mobility allows *Sir* to diversify the viewer's conceptualization of the cinematic new woman, who is predominantly identified with the mobilities of globalization—international brands, foreign travel, and global citizenship—and identified with the glitzy spaces of liberalization (bourgeois homes, malls, multiplexes, corporate offices). It also helps the film establish the internal migrant's "right to the city" even as the gatekeepers of privilege try to deny her access to elite spaces. And it complicates an easy binary between necessity and choice. However tedious or monotonous her journeys or work might be, Ratna "chooses" to move to and work in the city since the city offers her possibilities. At the same time, the extent of her drudgery forces us to recognize the constraints under which choices are made. This blurring disrupts a shallow notion of choice as a smorgasbord of options to which a sovereign individual has unfettered access.

The film directs attention to the web of class, gender, and sexual precarity within which Ratna is located and in which she labors to maneuver as she determinedly pursues her aspirations. Ratna is in a (sexually) precarious position as a working-class single woman and live-in maid. She shares space with her male employer after his wedding is called off, and other "staff" (maids, driver, security guard) in the building are quick to notice the tricky position in which she finds herself. Of course, while the precariat class is hyperaware of Ratna's vulnerability, Ashwin's elite compatriots are utterly oblivious to the "inappropriate" possibilities that might ensue. This is both because they cannot fathom a mutual, consensual intimacy between Sir and Servant, but also because the upper-class men are exempt from suspicions of sexual coercion toward their working-class employees.

The latter is all too common in Indian households. A survey conducted by PRIA and the Martha Farrell Foundation found that 29 percent of women domestic workers experienced sexual harassment at work.[68] And yet feudal and caste-based entitlements make invisible the suffering of maids, predicated as it is on elite entitlement toward bodies of poor women. The film goes to great lengths to highlight Ashwin's gender, class, and caste privilege, which contributes to his imperviousness about Ratna's tenuous circumstances as he pursues her. Unlike his friends and family, who treat Ratna as an invisible presence when they aren't snubbing or humiliating her, Ashwin is kind and generous to Ratna. All his interactions with her end with a polite "thank you," the classic marker of a U.S.-returned-yuppie who has adopted the mannerisms of the global neoliberal elite (as opposed to the Old World feudal rich), without any real material understanding of class politics. Ashwin represents the "new man" of neoliberal India, someone who wears pale pink shirts, is urbane and suave, displays a cosmopolitan persona, seems sensitive and in touch with his emotions, professes enlightened and egalitarian values, has close female friends, cares about environmental sustainability, pursues an unconventional career as a writer rather than joining his father's business. He presents a new kind of benevolent upper-class patriarchy: entitled and well-meaning but ignorant. His progressiveness extends only to the miniscule socioeconomic milieu to which he belongs.

He remains incognizant about the gender and class precarities for someone like Ratna. As Sanchita Dasgupta notes in her review of the film, "He is unwilling to put her needs first, showing no recognition of the difficult situations he subjects her to."[69] This becomes painfully obvious after he kisses Ratna (and she returns the kiss) and asks her to go out on a date with him. Ratna reminds him that they will become a laughingstock, to which he passionately responds, "I don't care." It never strikes him to consider Ratna's desires or "cares." She has to spell it out for him: "I care about it, Sir." For him, it is only the roadblocks he would encounter in dating a lower-class woman that matter. Her challenges and insecurities in such an encounter are beyond his ken. This is clear on another occasion when Ashwin puts Ratna in a compromising position with the other servants, jeopardizing her "honor" (as she puts it). Ratna confronts him, and to his protest that he does not see her "as a servant," retorts, "No matter what you feel or say, I'm your servant in the end." Ratna's insistence on the material realities that undergird the power differential between them operates as an exhortation for Ashwin to check his privilege and recognize her precarity. His privilege keeps him from acknowledging and recognizing the high stakes of romantic, sexual transgression for Ratna. In fact, because of Ashwin's advances, Ratna has to leave her job, which pushes her further into socioeconomic precarity. She has to move in with her sister and brother-in-law in an overcrowded one-room accommodation in a chawl with shared bathrooms.

The film also pays attention to the enormous emotional labor that Ratna must perform, even for a seemingly sensitive metrosexual male with a liberal mindset. She shops, cleans, and cooks for him. But it is the unpaid emotional labor that Ratna expends on her male employer that is most telling of what class and gender precarity demands of her. Arlie Russell Hochschild's important work on "emotional labor" categorizes it as the invisible and silent work where an employee has to project a requisite demeanor, suppress her own emotions, and artificially induce different emotions to do her physical work and evoke an appropriate emotional response from a customer or employer.[70] Throughout the film, we see how Ratna is emotionally attuned to her employer, anticipating his needs and shielding him, all the while laboring to keep her own feelings of exhaustion, exasperation, disappointment, anger, fear, and desire in check. Ratna shares her life story (how she was widowed at the age of nineteen after only four months of marriage) to pull Ashwin out of his doldrums and emphasize that life is worth living. In another instance, she thoughtfully moves wedding gift boxes that arrive for him, as she can see that he's still wallowing about the cancellation of his wedding. All he can do is joke weakly: "At least I got gifts even though I didn't get married," a response that is completely oblivious to Ratna's emotional perspicacity or how the huge gift boxes will overcrowd Ratna's small "servant's quarter." Ashwin's interactions with Ratna cast suspicion on his myriad reasons for abandoning Sabina, his intended, at the wedding altar: she cheated on him, he didn't love her enough, she was a romantic while he isn't, and, of course, he couldn't "be the guy who makes her give up her dreams [of romance]." Most importantly, he muses that he had felt obliged to get engaged to Sabina because she had supported him through the difficult time when his brother passed away. Wallowing in self-centered ennui, Ashwin remains unaware of the extractive nature of his relationships with women. His gender and class privilege renders him incapable of the reciprocity of emotional caregiving required in an egalitarian relationship.

In the same vein, the brief encounters between Ratna and the various elite new women in the film also throw into stark relief how class privilege (and precarity) manifests in interclass interactions between women. Whether it is Sabina (Aswin's ex-fiancée), Ankita (Ashwin's friend, a fashion designer), or the nameless young woman Ashwin meets at a bar, much like in *VDW*, it is their sexual desire that is centralized, both as a defining feature of their agency and as that which is the cause of complications in their lives. For example, Sabina has a "fling" before her marriage to Ashwin that results in the marriage being called off, Ankita invites herself to a party to Ashwin's apartment because she fancies him, and a young woman at a bar "checks out" Ashwin with frank desire before having a one-night stand with him. This open articulation of desire and sexual autonomy is a manifestation of class privilege and not as easily available as a mode of expression for Ratna, whose livelihood and aspiration are threatened when her master shows (sexual) interest in her. The film thus brings attention to the ways in which New Bollywood's women-centric films about elite new women, which frame the discourse of sexuality as the primary source of vulnerability for women, sideline class-based considerations of structural inequalities that render working-class women's lives multiply vulnerable to exploitation.

This fascination with women's sexual privilege or precarity also ignores the ways in which nonelite women are exposed not only to the dangers of sexual harassment by upper-class men, but also to violence and marginalization by their elite female counterparts. The condescension with which the upper-class woman treats the working-class woman is especially evident in the scenes with Nandu, Ashwin's female friend.

Nandu is presented as a professional young woman whose temper is as short and tongue as sharp as her blunt bob, when she talks to and about "the help." She snaps at Ratna for interrupting her conversation with Ashwin ("can't you see we're talking?"), and is enraged that "her" "bloody maid" didn't show up for work again, something that has caused her much convenience, as she has to make lunch for her husband (one can't of course miss the sad-and-delicious irony here). This illustrates how neoliberal feminism props up the gendered infrastructure of care work as aspirational, professional women outsource care work. In another scene in the film, at a party at Ashwin's mother's house, Nandu does not so much as glance at Ratna as she picks up an hors d'oeuvre from the tray that Ratna is carrying. For the elite new woman, the help either exists as a punching bag to vent frustrations; to lubricate, with culinary delights, upper-class fraternizing; or to enable her professional pursuits by managing her home and domestic chores. The maid of course cannot be seen as a fellow working woman with aspirations and dreams; instead, the madam draws a distinction between herself and the maid that shores up her own classed, classist new woman identity and ultimately the neoliberal capitalist project.

But even as *Sir* takes the cosmopolitan English-speaking elite to task for their insensitivity, it ultimately redeems and celebrates them as liberal and enlightened saviors and tutors of the working-class woman. In a brief appearance, Sabina (Ashwin's jilted ex-fiancée) offers her postfeminist, neoliberal mantra—the emphasis on individualism, choice, agency—to Ratna: "This is the city, not the village. . . . Here, you build your own life, and play by your own rules." Like Avni in *VDW*, who is annoyed at her crying maid who's being abused by her husband, Sabina has little patience with the idea of a woman as victim who cannot manage her own life. Anyone can claim public space, life, and success and deal with forms of inequality with resilience, confidence, a get-up go-get attitude, the right positive disposition. Ratna thus has an epiphany, and, as she narrates in a phone conversation with her poor sister (who's "poor" not because of rural poverty due to neoliberal government policies or uneven growth and development, but because she's still stuck in a culturally regressive rural environment), it suddenly dawns on her that, "I can be whatever I want."

If Sabina offers Ratna a lesson about leaning in and reinventing herself, another "madam" (Ankita) saves the day by offering her a job as a tailor. It feels doubly insulting, as well as telling of the inequality of access and opportunity, that Ratna is grateful to have this chance for employment from a woman who has behaved abominably toward her in the past. In a previous scene at the start of the film, Ankita unleashes her ugly fury at Ratna, whom she calls a "moron" when Ratna accidentally breaks a glass and spills red wine on her dress. Ankita threatens to deduct the damages from Ratna's salary to teach her a lesson and set her "straight." Ankita's verbal violence directed toward Ratna ("moron") mirrors Nandu's ("bloody maid"). What is especially disturbing is that Ankita's threat reveals her perfect awareness of the working-class woman's economic precarity and weaponizes it against her. Meanwhile, her opacity to her own entitlement and bourgeois privilege is jarring. Moments before this incident, Ankita had been complaining to a male friend about the patriarchal mindset of Indian men, who are threatened by her financial success and scared to pursue romance or marriage with her. Even as Ankita's insecurity does not compare to Ratna's very real class and gender vulnerability, her own (real and perceived) experience of gender marginalization presents an opportunity, an inroad into developing intersectional networks of solidarity with others, like Ratna, who are oppressed.

Instead of drawing connections and engaging in political critique and collective struggle to change society, however, the elite woman creates distance and classed distinctions that aids the neoliberal project by legitimizing hierarchical relationships and gendered socioeconomic inequalities. While Ankita does offer Ratna a job after finding her tailoring and craftsmanship up to the mark, this appears less a gesture of cross-class fellowship with another working woman based on common ground, and more a favor done for a friend, a fellow cosmopolite, in lieu of a real apology.

In the end, the film betrays its neoliberal impulse, both in how it refuses to vilify the cosmopolitan elite (new man or woman) for its blindness to class privilege and systemic constraints and in the way its ending reinvests in the cruel promises of neoliberalism: the notion that expanded choices and golden opportunities are available to anyone with individual grit and talent. Thus the possibility exists that the maid may outgrow her "tailoring" ambitions and become a fashion designer, find equal footing with the master and marry him, and live happily ever after. In this, the film echoes the promise of enterprise as a way out of precarity for the poor that we see in films such as *Sui Dhaaga* discussed in chapter 2, albeit here it is a working-class woman who is set on the path to self-fashion her future.

In contrast to *Sir*'s "feel good" ending, Zoya Akhtar's short film in *Lust Stories*, which centralizes a maid in a sexual relationship with her employer, ends on a less sentimental and starker note.

Akhtar's short is the second chapter of the four-film anthology, all of which, in one way or another, center female characters and their sexual desires. Together, the films disrupt and discard "Bombay cinema's conventions of family drama and its rules about the representation of sexuality."[71] Akhtar's film stands out from the rest in concentrating its narrative on a working-class woman as its main character. Sudha, a young maid, works for a young male bachelor, Ajit, who lives and works in Mumbai. The main action of the film involves the arrival of Ajit's parents from Meerut (a smaller city in North India), who are on a mission to finalize an arranged marriage for their son, which they successfully complete by the end of the film when Ajit is betrothed to a young woman, Aparna.

Since the film is invested in presenting "middle/upper-class scenes of domesticity from the perspective of a female servant,"[72] the film uses many closeups that maintain a tight focus on the female domestic worker as it limits the action of the film to the indoors. We see nothing of Mumbai, where the film is set. All through the film, Sudha barely speaks, but the camera and the light stay on her. Most of the dialogue and events that transpire in the film are filtered through Sudha's expressive face that registers a range of feelings. Since the film presents the domestic from the point of view of the help, it spotlights

Sudha's painstaking labor that she carries out day after day. We see her broom and mop floors, prepare tea, wipe the kitchen counters, wash the dishes, rinse and dry clothes on the rack, etc. In addition, she provides sexual services to her male employer.

The film deliberately begins with playing with the viewers' assumptions. On the soundtrack, we hear heavy panting and moaning before we see a man and woman having sex in a bedroom. We assume that it's a couple, lovers, in the throes of passion; there's nothing to suggest otherwise. Both get to be on top, both seem satiated as they consummate their desire. Afterwards, the man steps into the shower, asks for a towel, and the man and woman engage in brief playful postcoital banter. We still assume that they're a couple. If a frank expression of sexual desire is a hallmark of the postliberalization new woman, then this young woman qualifies as one.

The next moment sweeps the rug from under our feet as the woman squats and picks up a rag to mop the floor. They may be "lovers," we realize, but she is a servant and he is her employer. This is not a relationship of (social) equals; he is, in fact, on top, as the opening shot suggests.

This power differential between the elite and the precariat is not invisibilized by the film. It directs our attention to the casual indignities that the working-class woman is subjected to by the middle and upper classes. We see the hypocrisies of middle-class Indians whose small-mindedness is on full display in how it shows its appreciation for the help. For instance, Ajit's parents, who otherwise praise Sudha for being a good servant who has kept the house in order and taken "good care" of their son, decide to offer her one packet of snacks (because two seems excessive!) and leftover *mithai* (sweets) as compensation. Another "madam" rewards her maid with damaged hand-me-down clothes while extracting maximum labor from her. Discardable clothes for the disposable maid.

It is this harsh truth that Sudha's glance knows when she sees Ajit's intended for the first time. It is as if Sudha has been anticipating this moment all along, even as she might've entertained a different outcome in her wildest dreams. From the moment Sudha looks at Aparna (English-speaking, fair-skinned, tall, slim, dressed in a virginal pale pink kurta) enter the apartment with her parents, who hope to secure a good match for their daughter, she recognizes the inevitable script that is about to play out. The air in the one-bedroom apartment has the tension of a taut rubber band as both sets of parents engage in middle-class small talk while Ajit and Aparna withdraw to the bedroom to talk. This tension is conveyed by Sudha, her face and her movements, as she goes about preparing and serving tea and snacks to the visitors. The film directs our attention to the precarity of the working-class woman through her silence, which expresses the emotional labor she is required to undertake. Thus she can seethe with anger but can never express it; she has to go about doing her chores as she is commanded to, maintaining the required subservient and "happy servant" demeanor. And she has to endure the pain of seeing the man she has been sexually intimate and vulnerable with not only treat her as invisible but also subject her to the humiliation of witnessing his low-key flirtation with another woman on the same bed where they have sex.

The maid's silence in the workplace contrasts with the madam's vocalization of the hardships she faces in her profession. For instance, Aparna has no hesitation in complaining about the marginalization of women in the technology industry. Aparna, the girl who codes, tells Ajit about her boss and gender discrimination through microaggressions at work, and she also accuses him of patriarchal assumptions: "You guys always think we girls can't program." Ajit listens sympathetically but jokes that he can't take her seriously since she's still programming in "Perl," a computer programming language whose heyday has passed. He delegitimizes her professional concerns and uses her complaint as an occasion to flirt with her, playing on the homonym and telling her that "pearls" (jewelry) look great on her. "Carnivorous" Ajit has Men's Needs (a nod to Arundhati Roy's *The God of Small Things*) that need to be satisfied. As he tucks her hair behind her ear and lets his hand linger, Aparna, acting like a coy and respectable prospective bride, tells him to "stop." And he does. Of course, it does not take a major leap of imagination to know that Sudha's consent would've meant little to Ajit; her compliance, and her silence due to her class-gender precarity, is guaranteed. What choices did Sudha have? What would any accusations or show of anger have meant for her reputation, current employment, or further employability?

The last shot of *Lust Stories* offers a stark contrast with that of *Sir*. It leaves us staring at the elevator that has taken Sudha and a fellow maid down to the ground floor to exit the building after a day's work. *Sir*, by contrast, ended with Ratna taking Ashwin's call from the terrace of the luxury building in which he lived, and addressing him, for the first time, by his first name. As Ratna looks down, the glistening world beneath her feet, several new prospects open up for her, as she and Ashwin can finally explore a relationship as equals. She is no longer his employee; he's moved to the United States, and a relocation there promises more democratic possibilities for starting afresh. By contrast, Sudha knows the dismissive symbolism of the box of *mithai* (sweets) she leaves with: a meager compensation for all the domestic and sexual labor she performs for the son who's wedding engagement is being celebrated.

Sudha leaves the apartment without exchanging any words with Ajit and waits for the elevator to arrive. The camera, focusing on the door behind her, tricks us into hoping that Ajit will come after her and offer some version of consolation or apology. The film, however, participates in no such deflections from the violence of what has transpired. Instead, another maid walks out of a neighboring apartment and starts chatting with Sudha as the two wait for the elevator. She shows Sudha a beautifully embellished kurta her madam has given her. Sudha's gaze moves to the tear in the piece of clothing, confirming that this grand gesture is really a hand-me-down. The other woman quickly glosses over the obvious: "It's no big deal; I'll get it darned and wear it to my sister's wedding." With a curious smile on her face, Sudha decides to join in the excitement about the kurta, agreeing that her friend will look great in it. Next, she brings out the box of sweets that her employer's mother had given her and offers it to the other woman, who gleefully partakes of it, encouraging Sudha to do the same. Sudha, continuing to smile, takes a piece out and eats it. It is hard to decipher the meaning of her cryptic expression. The smile indicates the recognition of common ground between her and the other maid: both leaving the homes in which they work with little, paltry tokens of bourgeois gratitude, which are more insulting than genuine or generous. The smile, perhaps, signals a recognition of the grossness of "madams and sirs," and operates as an opting out of a hurt response to Ajit's callousness toward her. In this moment, she seems to recognize that whether the "gifts" come as sexual or sartorial favors, what really defines bourgeois treatment of maids is extraction and exploitation. The elevator finally arrives, the two women enter it, the door closes, and the camera stays back, watching the grill door of the elevator. The narrative offers no spin, no hope to dilute this ugliness of reality that ensues in Mumbai's high rises.

6: Politics and Political Agency in the Age of Precarity

The interminable insecurity bred by neoliberalism disrupts both the possibility and success of progressive collective mobilizations. Its insistent logic of "There Is No Alternative" (TINA) fosters a habitus of financial, psychological, affective, and relational contingency, producing a chilling effect on our capacity to stake a claim in alternative politics. The itinerancy of both professional and personal realms reduces our capacity to rally together and demand a better world. Survival and individual upward mobility replace the desire for building a shared vision and thinking and acting jointly. We've discussed this at some length in chapter 1. In this final chapter, we turn our attention to another political outcome of a culture that breeds precarity: the ascendancy of authoritarian populism.

In order to do so, we study two categories of films. The first encapsulates middle-class and elite responses of outrage to complex political questions: development and corruption in *Shanghai* (2012) and *No One Killed Jessica* (2011), respectively. Second, we focus on the genre of "cop films" by analyzing *Simmba* (2018) and *Sooryavanshi* (2021) for how they tackle national anxieties around rape and terrorism. Shetty's films, we argue, are textbook articulations of the present conjuncture, in which neoliberal Hindutva relies on the strongman figure for its success. Significantly, therefore, while overtly the four films engage the key issues of development, corruption, terrorism, and rape, what they reveal is an entire gamut of subterranean ideologies and institutionalized practices upon which the politics of neoliberal Hindutva rest. These include everything from middle-class activism that champions an antipolitics and disparages the poor, fueling a politics of *ressentiment* to mobilize disenfranchised subaltern classes, the role of the media, the dismantling and minimalization of democratic institutions and fantasies of individuated solutions, the promotion of extrajudicial vigilante mechanisms, the recruitment of gender politics to further right-wing causes, an intensification of the precarity of religious minorities, and the art of turning national precarities into entrepreneurial occasions.

We read the four films together to examine political outcomes in a culture that breeds precarity. If the other chapters are organized around social identities (caste, class, religion, gender), then this chapter delves into how identities are mobilized politically. The films in this chapter have diverse industrial and production contexts that impact aesthetics and content. Thus, *Shanghai* and *No One Killed Jessica* as multiplex films geared toward urban audiences and the blockbuster "cop films" *Simmba* and *Sooryavanshi* all offer a distinct expression or manifestation of political agency in response to political "corruption." *Shanghai*'s dystopian presentation of the inefficacy of any kind of resistance contrasts with *No One Killed Jessica*'s triumphant celebration of middle-class political agency. Both films, however, display a skepticism of traditional democratic avenues for redress that dovetail with the neoliberal tendency of disaffection with all politics. In comparison to these films, in *Simmba* and *Sooryavanshi*, the political agent and agency that is valorized is the culture of impunity in law-enforcement machinery embodied in the muscular, masculinist vigilante cop. In these films, the state and cop are aligned with authoritarian values.

We study these four films for their grammar of politics, for how they accommodate neoliberal Hindutva's imagination of politics, for how they spotlight and construct precarious citizens. We investigate these films for their distortion of facts, their strategic deployment of discourses to disaggregate shared precarities. Following neoliberal Hindutva's dictate, these films convert political issues that ought to become grounds for rallying people together into occasions for widening social, economic, religious rifts. The solutions they proffer as resistant responses against the condition of precarity are inadequate, dishonest, distracting, and authoritarian. The agents of change condoned are inevitably upper-middle-class or authoritarian individuals. It is their political tenor and tendency that are validated. Concomitantly, those condemned are the poor and the religious minorities. Their agency is qualified as grotesque, futile, self-serving, and antinationalist.

Although the tenor of the films is distinct, what resonates across all the seemingly disparate films is how their political stances ultimately coalesce into a capitulation to the status quo by being unable to offer any viable antineoliberal political alternatives. Together, the juxtaposition of these varied cinematic texts reveals the limits of the ways in which Hindi cinema has imagined political agency in response to precarity.

Shanghai: Authoritarianism and the Politics of *Ressentiment*

Shanghai captures a critical juncture in the nation's relationship to its postliberalized self and illuminates Bollywood's imagination of politics under neoliberalism. The film subtly encapsulates the contradictory, competing sociopolitical impulses produced by neoliberalism that India witnessed in the 2010s: the middle class's exasperation with liberalization's half-empty promises, distortedly articulating itself through anticorruption campaigns; subaltern disaffection against inequities exacerbated by liberalization, usurped and mobilized to forward neoliberal Hindutva's cause. In *Shanghai*, these real-world phenomena are explored with nuance, through mapping predictable political contestations and surprising affective affinities. The film was released around the same time as the emergence of the Aam Aadmi Party (that we discuss in chapter 1) and two years before Prime Minister Narendra Modi's first electoral victory in 2014. Remarkably, the film gives eerie expression to this important political cusp: it presents a pre-Modi national context that had embraced neoliberalism's jargon of development and enshrined faith in its expanded middle class. Simultaneously, the film offers a premonitory cinematic articulation of what the normalization of nationalist political jingoism and neoliberal fervor entail: a conflation that has come to a head in India in the post-Modi era. In that sense, the film enables us to recognize the overlaps between neoliberalism and Hindutva's strategies of mobilization.

Shanghai presents its audiences with a wide gamut of political players: the officialdom of high-end politics (politicians, bureaucrats, multinational corporations) as well as the grimy foot soldiers (lower-rung party workers, small-time crooks, mercenaries) who operationalize the everyday violence necessary for the actualization of neoliberal landscapes. We also meet the small but steadfast group of left-wing intellectuals, activists, and political agents who resist neoliberalism's onslaught. Proshant Chakraborty[1] rightfully credits the film for conceptualizing the horizontal and vertical workings of the state, for elaborating on its multilevel field of operation, and for acknowledging how the margin, and its precarious inhabitants, function in tandem with the center. Recruiting and weaponizing them is at the heart of how the state reproduces its power and legitimacy. Even more compellingly, the film curates a visual archive to capture neoliberalism's enlistment of emotion as a key component of its success. In framing neoliberalism through its emotive charge and affective logics, the film captures the reverie and revelry associated with the inchoate promises of mobility embedded in the creation of world-class cities and special economic zones.

The narrow streets and chowks of Bharatnagar, the fictional city in North India where the film is set (only two hours away from Delhi, we are told), are forever congested by raucous processions celebrating the transformation of Bharatnagar into "India Business Park" (IBP). Night and day, party workers and supporters of Jan Mukti Morcha (JMM) take to the streets and dance to the ceaseless sound of drums, publicly exhibiting their jubilation at the arrival of this economic development project to their town. The irrepressibly festive mood on the ground is counterposed by the tenuousness of the coalition between JMM and the state's ruling party, Rashtriya Pragati Dal (RPD) that has made IBP possible. The hushed, secretive phone calls between party leaders, the untraceable orders to eradicate all those who consciously object or unwittingly stand in the way of IBP's successful implementation, and the ever-proliferating number of murdered corpses that pepper the film's progression, confess to the neoliberal agenda's surprising fragility. In *Shanghai*, manic bodies and frenetic soundscapes do the crucial work of naturalizing neoliberalism's arrival by ensconcing it in hypervisible public pleasure. The insistent publicness and aggressive joyfulness also mask the self-serving motives and violence that constitute the groundwork for legitimating neoliberalism.

These bodies on the line, recruited to ease the free flow of capital—whether through their celebratory zeal or recourse to violence—invariably belong to working-class, subaltern men (mostly) and women. Class elites observe them, for the most part, from the cocoon of their air-conditioned cars or from the across the erected platforms from which they give speeches to crowds of *aam junta*. The film makes us register the disdain and contempt with which bourgeois men, even on different ends of political spectrum, view sweaty, gyrating lower-class bodies. On different occasions, both Dr. Ahmadi—the left-wing academic activist based in New York who arrives in Bharatnagar to protest IBP—and Krishnan, a senior bureaucrat entrenched in the political establishment, also ideologically and professionally committed to neoliberal development projects, find themselves stuck in traffic jams caused by the pro-IBP processions. And both Ahmadi and Krishnan are exasperated by the interruptions and delays in the movement of their respective vehicles. Ahmadi's irritation and anger at the throng of men dancing in the middle of a street may be, in some measure, laced with disbelief at their political naïveté and delusion about the good that corporate capital will bring. Even so, he and Krishnan articulate a shared affective distance and a patronizing annoyance toward the underclasses.

While Ahmadi might view them as mindless sheep, all too easily interpellated by neoliberal purposes and right-wing political machinations, Krishnan's attitude toward them condenses the more mainstream middle-class response of wanting to cleanse and gentrify the spaces they move through: he wants his driver to "blow the horn" so the milling crowd gets out of the way of his car. He is frightened and appalled when one of party workers throws himself onto the hood of the car, hurling abuses and threats at the driver. The man's aggressive entitlement to public spaces is read as a sign of the lumpen proletariat having become too unruly and emboldened as a result of social fluctuations and democratic political license. What men like Krishnan, and perhaps most of the film's middle-class audience, would prefer is for the bodies that build world-class cities to remain invisible, or at the very least not assert their presence through rowdy interruptions that block the way of elite bureaucrats sitting in the back seats of their chauffeur-driven cars, making their way back home from work.

In many ways, our reading differs from Šarūnas Paunksnis's excellent analysis of *Shanghai.* Paunksnis suggests that the film appropriates and neutralizes dissent, perpetuates the myth that "the system corrects itself," and endorses the middle-class's imagination of itself as saviors who can weed out the "bad apple" or corrupt politicians.[2] In doing so, he rightfully argues, it leaves untouched a root cause analysis of inequity, oppression, and systemic change. Here, however, we focus on how the film dismantles the grandiose self-fashioning of the elite middle-classes and yet falls back on the idea that intervention by middle-class individuals is most likely to have an impact upon an inequitable system. As a result, the film invests most of its energy in exploring the capacities and limits of its middle-class characters to create meaningful political shifts. And while underclass characters occupy a substantial portion of the film's narrative and its affective and aesthetic landscape, their political agency is construed as invariably misdirected and pathetically ineffectual; they're reduced to pawns working against their own self-interest and all too easily quashed by the cruel and callous maneuvers of those in power.

Like Banerjee's other films such as *Khosla Ka Ghosla* (2006) and *Oye Lucky!, Lucky Oye!* (2008), *Shanghai* too is unique in its complex rendition of middle-class consciousness and ideological inclinations. But its most striking feature is how little faith it expresses in the possibility of change altogether. And this is where our conclusion differs from Paunksnis's. In the end, the vision for the future that *Shanghai* leaves us with is not the false hope that the system can fix itself; rather, the film ends with a dystopic death knell pronouncing the impossibility of anything improving, ever. The corrupt, murderous, self-profiting politicians like Desh Naik and Madam ji, the chief minister, can be halted in their nefarious schemes. But there's always another opportunist waiting in the wings, and this time it's someone from the liberal side of the political divide. The film willy-nilly fixates on the middle class as the beacon of any meager hope, and then goes onto abandon hope altogether. It is not just the appropriation of dissent, but the utter irrelevancy and inefficacy of dissent that signals *Shanghai*'s subtextual politics, thus demonstrating a disenchantment with all politics, a peculiarly neoliberal tendency.

Shanghai offers an intriguing spin on the Indian new middle class, as embodied in Krishnan's character. Leela Fernandes and others have argued that in a postliberalization context, this class has come to represent "an idealized national standard of living" that other social groups can and must aspire to and "potentially achieve through the practices of consumption."[3] Similarly, Arvind Rajagopal suggests that this class's "newly legitimated right to consume" makes them the rightful successors of the speedily declining developmentalist regime that dominated the Nehruvian socioeconomic vision of India.[4] Interestingly, however, Krishnan's middle-classness does not first and foremost articulate itself through gratuitous or overt consumerism. It is true that his air of efficiency is very much constituted by his consumer accessories; the rimless glasses, expensive watch, and the immaculate suits that he's always dressed in all express a material and psychological ease in the world, no matter what professional challenges he might endure. And yet the defining feature of his middle-class identity lies elsewhere, not rooted in identifying him as a consumer.

In some ways, his exceedingly calm, self-contained, unsmiling officiousness aligns him much more closely with the old middle class that first emerged in the colonial context and rose to enjoy immense power in the Nehruvian period. Embedded as they were in circuits of nonaristocratic privilege "through involvement in civil service, educational institutions, shared discourses on law, etc.,"[5] they came to oversee the developmental state. Krishnan, then, carries the gravitas of a class that has always been important and that continues to be even after liberalization, spearheading the nation's reconfiguration albeit along a different economic-ideological axis. This is a class that since postcolonial Independence shaped the subconscious and the grammar of politics in India.[6]

Through Krishnan's character, then, the film gently explores the middle class as an embodiment of authority, with a longer history, that is not reducible to its newfound purchasing power in a free-rein marketplace. Krishnan's whole being pulsates with what Pierre Bourdieu would classify as "taste" and an ostensibly seamless enculturation within everyday practices that reproduce power through the accumulation of different kinds of capital: material, social, cultural. His bourgeois habitus is upheld by his close networks with powerful people and opportunities. He shares a casual intimacy with, and enjoys mentorship from, other senior bureaucrats like Mr. Kaul (the chief minister's principal secretary), and with "Madam" chief minister herself who asks after his pregnant wife and offers him praise for his discretion in the inquiry in Ahmadi's death. He can charge into police stations and demand that senior police officers comply with his investigation. The promise of a foreign posting in Stockholm and a seat on the board of an international corporation are dangled before him in exchange for his commitment to seeing through the government's development projects. The source of his capacity to enact change, to *feel* and *be* agential, is thus wrapped up in a complex set of factors: his class and professional identity; upper-caste brahmanical masculinity (he wears a *janeyun,* sacred thread that Brahmin men wear); Westernized presentation; and in the hard-working, meritocratic, rule-abiding persona that he exudes.

At the same time, the film undertakes a complex examination of the limits of Krishnan's capacity for enacting real change. It takes immense, if subtle, pleasure in diluting the air of superiority and the agentic aura that Krishnan exemplifies. He can pretend to set aside his own grudges against Ahmadi (who had disrupted the last development project that Krishnan was heading) and direct an objective inquiry into the political activist's fatal accident. But he—and we—quickly learn that his individual commitment to fairness and truth have little bearing on how things transpire. The inquiry is a sham, and he has been chosen to lead it precisely because he has ingratiated himself as a reliable operative of the state. Every step of the way, he encounters both banal and significant obstacles that confirm the vagaries, absurdity, and impossibility of the task he has been assigned. *Shanghai* slips into rare moments of humor to puncture Krishnan's self-assured propriety. He is assigned dusty, cobwebbed, furnitureless rooms in which to conduct the inquiry, spaces that instantaneously desanctify the grandiosity of his claim that he's been sanctioned by the chief minister herself to do this work, a refrain he pathetically keeps repeating in order to be taken seriously.

The film carefully shows us how the pseudo-procedures of governmentality undermine Krishnan's authority and capacity to do right. But it also spends time deromanticizing Krishnan as the complicit functionary of the state that is now impeding his bureaucratic professionalism. Krishnan is no hero. On the contrary, we often see him act like a coward, screaming pitifully for his domestic help to save him when crises ensue. On two occasions—when a Molotov cocktail is thrown into his house by people trying to intimidate him to stop the inquiry into Ahmadi's death, and when Shalini and Jogi bang on his door in the middle of the night, begging for shelter against goons sent by JMM—Krishnan's response is to wail for his servant to intervene and manage the situation. He doesn't want to ruffle the feathers of people above him in the hierarchy; he readily complies with the chief minister's instructions to shut down the inquiry. He is compelled to act ethically only when irrefutable evidence stares him in the face, when precarious bodies intrude into his home and confront him with truth about the political conspiracy to assassinate Ahmadi, a conspiracy that taints not just the obviously corrupt Desh Naik, but also his much revered, sophisticated political patron "Madam," the chief minister.

So why then does Krishnan act against the corrupt politicians he serves? What moves him to challenge his bosses and expose their profit-seeking murderousness? It is important to distinguish Krishnan's anticorruption maneuver from Ahmadi's critique of the neoliberal state for its desire to create gated communities on lands appropriated from poor people. It is critical that we do not read a political-ideological shift in Krishnan's change of heart. Even by the end of the film, what he objects to is not the forceful eviction of indigent, working-class families from their *bastis*. As Satish Deshpande argues, "the middle class is the class that articulates the hegemony of the ruling bloc."[7] Krishnan does not separate himself from this ruling bloc. Instead, it is another dimension of his middle-classness that compels him to take political action to disrupt the status quo. He is, and remains to the end, fundamentally convinced about the aptness of neoliberalism's development project. He only distances himself from the immorality of its implementers: the corrupt politicians who supersede the laws of the market with their own profiteering. As Fernandes suggests, in India "neoliberalism as *doxa*" has resulted in liberalization being presented as "a natural, apolitical process of unleashing the power of the market and diminishing the role of the state. This doxa in turn construes all forms of distributive politics as not only inimical to the efficiency of the market, but as venal and self-interested."[8] Krishnan's anticorruption morality, then, conflates distributive politics with self-serving politicians who redirect capital into their private coffers. He exemplifies the classic middle-class discursive device, where the critique of corruptions in welfare implementation is reassigned as a critique of welfare itself.[9]

In this logic, neoliberalism goes scot-free. The precarity it produces is treated as exceptional: the murders are the problem, not the dislocation of hundreds and thousands of poor people; and the game of politics is blamed for not letting the market sort out sociopolitical-economic fluctuations. Krishnan's actions, then, endorse a demand for the state's further withdrawal, leaving neoliberalism's implementation in "the hands of technocrats" and "far away from the messy world of politics."[10]

Curiously, while the film affords a skeptical glance toward Krishnan's bureaucratic myopia, it confirms its own antipolitics by treating all politics—whether that of political leaders or the collective politics of subordinated groups—as debased and criminal. Men like Bhaggu and Jaggu—hired as mercenaries by JMM to execute Ahmadi—constitute the bottom of the pyramidical hierarchy of corrupt politics. The film's own middle-class gaze becomes apparent in the way it treats Bhaggu's aspirational self and political subjecthood. Bhaggu is giddy with delight at the prospect of IBP's arrival, because in exchange for his services to Desh Naik and JMM he will get to learn English and work in a pizza restaurant. Empowerment under neoliberalism is invariably cast as self-improvement, and Bhaggu seems to have all too readily internalized the lesson. He imagines himself protected by "powertoni," given immunity for his actions through his "patronage networks" with the politician and other higher-up party workers (like Damle).[11] The mindless mania with which he follows the party line—vandalizing bookshops that carry copies of Ahmadi's book, dancing with feverish excitement during the street processions, wildly participating in the riots organized by JMM to protest Krishnan's report accusing Desh Naik of conspiring to kill Ahmadi—attests to his unquestioning investment in the political party and its nefarious leader as the means for fulfilling his aspirational goals. He is willing to do everything asked of him: "If you say, I will cut off my head and bring it you," he tells Damle.

What is unacceptable to him, however, is to be asked to stay away from his patron: "Do not tell me not to come here [the Morcha celebration, where Desh Naik is milling around with his supporters] . . . do I need permission to come to Deshji's temple?" Bhaggu's mistake lies in trusting politicians, in treating a human being, rather than the neoliberal market, as his god. Inevitably, he is dispensed with, with as much ease as all others who stood in the way of Desh Naik and the chief minister's plans. The last glimpse we get of Bhaggu is of him face down in the street, blood oozing out of his face and body, cast aside as a pawn by the very people who exploited him.

Jaggu, his companion, on the other hand, is motivated by fear. He is the more timid, melancholic assassin, with a defeatist air, dolefully following the instructions of those much more powerful than he (including Bhaggu, his friend). When Shalini (Ahmadi's political comrade and romantic partner) finally learns that Jaggu, the man arrested for driving the truck that mowed down Ahmadi, is the husband of Gauri, her domestic help, she has a hysterical, irate response. Shalini beats Jaggu, hitting him repeatedly with a metal *thaali*. Her words to him display her utter incomprehension at his actions: "How can you people just kill another human being?" He begins a response but is cut short: "You beat me so much in front of my own daughter. It's because you are 'big' people. . . . Desh Naik is even 'bigger'."

Even though it is Jogi who interrupts him from completing his thought, commanding him to talk straight and not waste everyone's time with his self-pity, this moment marks the film's own lack of interest, beyond the superficial, in understanding the complexity of motivations that drive men like Bhaggu and Jaggu. Their actions are framed as determined purely by aspirations of mobility or fear of the powerful.

There is no deeper analysis of the way in which neoliberalism itself has exacerbated these contexts of inequity and fantasies of escape from disenfranchisement. There is no serious engagement with the "politics of resentful aspiration"[12] that men like Bhaggu are mobilized for and encouraged to misdirect their anger at academics, or activists like Ahmadi, or other working-class people like Jogi (as in the film), or even religious minorities (as in real life in contemporary India). Ajay Gudavarthy would describe Bhaggu as an embodiment of the "the age of anger," displaying "ressentiment": "a combination of resentment and sentiment—which, in a sense, is a mix of envy, humiliation, and powerlessness"[13] produced when the neoliberal state abandons people to either the "hierarchical collectives of the local" or to the "facelessness of the global."[14] *Shanghai* allows us to register the way that Bhaggu's anger and Jaggu's fear are mobilized by and for a corrupt politics. It spends little time, however, in examining the marginalization and alienation of a neoliberal national order that make them susceptible to be recruited for such mobilization in the first place: their historical, ideological, and political alienation in contemporary India.

Bad politics, and by extension all politics, is rejected as the culprit for people's misery. There is no imagination of a radical, progressive collective that can be effectively sustained in the realm of politics. Even the group of people led by Ahmadi dwindles to an oddly paired twosome of Shalini and Jogi, resorting to whistleblowing as political intervention. The anti-IBP political movement, if there ever was one, is relegated to cinematic sidelines and rendered ideologically forgettable. A left-wing political activist's murder might be a tragedy worth investigating and exposing, but a deep exploration of the politics he espouses is not. Contemporary Bollywood cinema's inability to give weight to an antineoliberal politics is a marker of the cinema of precarity, which itself is a rendition of the failure of radical political alternatives under neoliberalism. This is also what Paunksnis calls "one-dimensional cinema," where critiques of the current state of affairs function only to further consolidate the status quo and do not offer any truly disruptive or viable alternatives.

Nevertheless, *Shanghai* touches upon a variety of morbid symptoms of neoliberal precarity. Most of all, it formulates a keen and prefigurative insight into the mechanics of mass mobilization under Modi's India. Although there is no categorical identification of Desh Naik as a leader of the Hindu right, the emotions he invokes in his constituents is premonitorily indicative of the mobilization strategies that the Modi-led BJP successfully deployed to "suture together a broad social base, represented as 'the people,' through the creation of an aspirational identity."[15] The film illustrates the inclusiveness of right-wing populism. Desh Naik is the quintessentially strong leader whose holograms, hoardings, and other political gimmicks produce a sense of direct, nonmediated rapport between him and his followers. His authoritarianism elicits a cruel aspiration in his base: people surrender themselves to his whiplash whims, switching like zombies between states of ecstatic celebration and volatile vandalism, burning the city down at the slighted suggestion of an insult to their leader. His followers also exhibit reactionary aspirations, deflecting their own disempowerment onto other marginalized social groups through street violence and vigilante justice.

Desh Naik, like his real-world predecessor, embodies what Priya Chacko calls "marketized Hindutva," a conjoining of neoliberal economic approaches and Hindu nationalism.

No One Killed Jessica: New Politics of the New Aam Aadmi

Released in January 2011, *No One Killed Jessica* (henceforth *NOKJ*) offers an "interpretation"[16] of a real-life event that transpired on the night of April 30, 1999, at a party at the Tamarind Court Café (Keno's in the film) in South Delhi. Thirty-four-year-old model Jessica Lall was murdered by Siddhartha Vashishta (better known as Manu Sharma), part of the capital city's brat pack and the son of a wealthy and influential politician (former union minister Venod Sharma). Manu Sharma shot Lall after she refused to serve him and his friends drinks after the last call. What was as an open-and-shut case—more than three hundred eyewitnesses, among them prominent Delhi elite, were present at the scene of the crime—turned out to be a long, drawn-out, and messy court case that lasted more than seven years as witnesses turned hostile and evidence was tampered with, resulting in an acquittal of the accused on February 21, 2006, by the Delhi High Court (the highest court after the Supreme Court). This decision unleashed public anger and outrage and resulted in "one of India's most rigorous public protests and media campaigns"[17] that demanded that Sharma be rearrested and charged with the crime. The concerted effort involved street demonstrations, candlelight vigils, text message campaigns, and email petitions,[18] and it was one in which English-language print and broadcast media played a prominent role. This mobilization by the middle classes led to a retrial of the case on a fast-track basis. And on December 18, 2006, the High Court announced its verdict that found Sharma guilty of murder and sentenced him to life imprisonment.

Gupta's crime thriller, titled after the provocative headline from the popular English-language daily, *The Times of India*,[19] the day after the initial acquittal, revisits the incident. The first half of the film focuses on the murder of Jessica and the futile fight, both in and out of the courtroom, of her sister Sabrina Lall to ensure that Jessica's murderer is sentenced, while the second half of the film focuses on the fierce journalist Meera Gaity's successful campaign to get justice for Jessica. The film thus combines "documentary as well as fictive elements" to narrate the case from a "perspective in which corporate news media form an alliance with an increasingly disenchanted Delhi youth and thus together represent an emerging counter power vis-à-vis a deeply corrupt political elite and judiciary."[20]

No One Killed Jessica presents a distinct articulation and validation of middle-class politics as they emerged at the end of the first two decades of neoliberal reforms. The post-1990s period saw the rise of an assertive and aspirational new middle class, the primary addressee of the new consumer-oriented economy that followed the reforms. Much has been written about this new Indian middle class that has been called India Shining or India Rising: its size, definition, demographic, character, aspirations and preoccupations, and especially its exponential growth as it has come to dominate public discourse and imagination in the post-1990s period. Because the heterogeneous and internally differentiated character of this class makes it difficult to define precisely, scholars have suggested other productive ways of thinking about it, especially how the middle class as a social construct has come to perform important ideological work and how this ideological role also distinguishes new middle-class politics.[21]

NOKJ delineates both the ascendancy of the professional, urban, English-speaking section of the middle class, as this subgroup usurps the category of the universal citizen or *aam aadmi*, and delineates the class's response to real or perceived precarity by launching anticorruption protests against the state and its institutions. This middle class is set apart as the only class to be reckoned with; other groups—whether politicians or high-ranking officers or the poor—are to be disciplined or led by the enlightened and entitled middle-class agent, as it will school them into the right kind of politics and causes. The film especially shows the power of this "hegemonic class . . . to shape the subconscious, the grammar of politics."[22] And, as the film reveals, the ideas that middle-class politics seizes upon, while presented as serving "public interest," are an antipolitics that contribute to the hollowing out of state institutions.

Significantly, in its presentation of middle-class politics, *NOKJ* marks a shift from how they are depicted previously in popular Hindi cinema, especially in the 2006 cult classic of youth revolt, *Rang De Basanti* (Color Me Saffron, Rakeysh Omprakash Mehra, henceforth *RDB*), even as this film serves as an important precursor and intertext. The hugely popular *RDB* first articulated the power and legitimacy of aggressive middle-class politics and inspired real-life social movements against corruption, including the mobilization around the Jessica Lall murder case (which is referenced in the film). Both *RBD* and *NOKJ* were produced under the banner of UTV, a major production house that emerged in the 2000s, and focused "a new kind of cinema" that successfully blended Bollywood-style entertainment with "concerns of the middle classes";[23] not surprisingly, both films did well with multiplex audiences. In *RDB*, a group of carefree and disillusioned college friends are inspired to make change as they participate as actors in a film about India's anticolonial revolutionaries. The friends undergo a political awakening once they lose a friend (a pilot in the air force) in a plane crash caused due to a technical malfunction that could have been avoided if it weren't for the callous negligence of corrupt politicians. They protest his death by organizing a candlelight vigil at India Gate (a war memorial in New Delhi), which has since become the prime site of protest among urban and middle-class youth, also featuring in *NOKJ*. *RDB* played a central part in creating a "politics of symbolism" that's taken on "such a vigorously fetishized character," and how "Candlelight processions, human chains, and silent marches à la [*RDB*] [have come to be] identified uncompromisingly as elite praxis now."[24] This has been called the "RDB syndrome" that produced "flash activism," a "temporary social mobilization around a particular civic issue."[25] *RDB* is thus undoubtedly an important suggestive intertext for *NOKJ*.

NOKJ, however, strikes a different note as it explores a nonmasculinist and nonfatal form of middle-class service to the nation. Toward the end of *RDB*, the radicalized male youth are declared terrorists and gunned down by the state (the army and police, in an excessive use of force) for hijacking a radio station to air their message to the nation's youth; ironically, their message to the youth, before they die, is to inspire them to serve their country and effect change by joining the civil services and occupying government positions. These youth are of different faiths (Hindu, Sikh, Muslim), classes (mostly middle class, but one of them is a millionaire's son), and even political leanings (one of them is involved in the student wing of a Hindu right-wing party). *NOKJ* makes no such painstaking attempts at assembling a "utopian microcosm" or secular nationalism and renders invisible these other social identities to establish the hegemony of a small segment of the middle class as the class that represents (i.e., portrays, speaks on behalf of, acts as the representative of) the people.[26]

More than idealism or disillusionment, what characterizes this professional middle class with cultural capital is an entitlement and a bias toward action, an impatience with the slow deliberations of democratic processes to solving political problems. It demands speedy redressal of its grievances. This middle class does not engage in armed struggle or martyrdom to confront the abuse of political power within institutional structures, but instead deploys specific strategies and class-specific weapons in its arsenal—such as its command over communication media technologies—to take back the nation from corrupt politicians and other political representatives. The film captures this moment of new forms of political culture emerging through the increasing media-ization of politics as well as the influx of private capital in the media domain, which allowed the middle class to redefine the terms of democratic politics.

In an interview with the news agency Reuters, Gupta, the director of *NOKJ*, noted that his film "is about the 10 percent of India which is good, as opposed to the 90 percent which is bad and that we crib about every day." He further argues that the Justice for Jessica campaign "really showed that there is so much power that the educated middle class wields, if only they would harness it."[27] Herein lies the crux of the matter. The director's tellingly curious statement makes it clear that the film treats the 10 percent as the 90 percent, making the middle-class minority stand in for the nation's representative majority. He also makes it clear that the film and the campaign it showcases is a celebration of the politics and activism of this "good" 10 percent or the "educated middle class," which is lauded as the *aam aadmi* of India, rather than a class with particular politics and motivations that align them with and within neoliberal Hindutva.[28]

Thus, Sabrina Lall and Meera Gaity and their ilk—urban, professional, English-educated, equipped with social, educational, and cultural capital—become "representative citizens"[29] rather than an extremely small minority in India. These representative citizens are also resurrected as enlightened and pedagogically responsible for educating the rest of the country about civic and democratic virtues, an ideological role that the middle class had claimed for itself after independence and that transformed in the context of liberalization. It is their activism, the film purports, that will fix the corruption of politics and invigorate it.

In doing so, the film endorses the "increasing disdain for the role of the state and politics" held by the dominant fraction of the middle class.[30] While high politics is aligned with corruption-as-villainy, "heroism" rests with the English-educated professional middle class. The crisis of high politics is presented through a malaise-ridden state and a dishonest political establishment. In the course of the film, we see police officers and witnesses bribed and intimidated, and Sharma's politician father wield influence to effect a "not guilty" verdict for his errant son, compelling a lesson for the middle-class citizenry to stay vigilant against corruption. The corrupt political elite constitutes an internal threat to the nation, and Jessica becomes a martyr in the war against corruption just like the soldiers at Kargil who are fighting an external enemy. This analogy is established toward the beginning of the film through the intercuts between a martyred soldier's body covered in an Indian flag (in the 1999 Kargil war with Pakistan) and Jessica succumbing to her gunshot wounds in the ambulance.

Even the Delhi commissioner of police does the bidding of the political higher-ups. He gaslights Sabrina into thinking she's being "paranoid" when she asks him if witnesses are being intimidated or bought. Instead, he asks her to "relax" and put her faith in the system: "Prosecution has handed the case to the investigating officers. We have to trust them, and you have to trust us." Traditional democratic institutions and the discourse of official politics are inadequate and feeble, endemically corrupt, and fail to deliver solutions. It is thus left to the new middle class to step in, take matters into their own hands, and deploy nonelectoral means to effect social and political change. Or handle efficiently whatever gets in the way of achieving their aspirations and hegemony.

The egregious blatancy of political corruption is captured early in the film when Meera's boss (Gaurav Capoor) asks her to cover the story of Jessica's murder trial. Meera is not interested in the story and presumptively dismisses it as a trial whose outcome is certain: "He's not going to get away [with it] . . . C'mon Gaurav, even Hindi movies don't show politicians as villains anymore." This is a telling comment about both the changed landscape of Hindi cinema, which historically enjoyed a penchant for featuring unscrupulous politicians, and the diminished significance and authority of the state functionaries deemed weak and ineffectual in postliberalization India. Meera, of course, is proved wrong about the damage that even politicians made redundant under neoliberalism can cause to matters dear to the middle classes.

If corrupt politicians and high-ranking police officers are subjected to critique, the snobbish and insular members of the upper middle class are also taken to task. In fact, the film skewers them as self-seeking and superficial. The caricatured (female) socialites come in for special censure. For instance, the owner of Keno's, Mallika Sehgal (based on the entrepreneur-socialite Bina Ramani), is portrayed as a spineless and simpering pathetic woman who is more interested in savoring her rich and moist chocolate cake in a fancy restaurant than reassuring Sabrina that she will identify the culprit during the trial. Similarly, in the police station, a socialite, not wanting to get entangled in the messy murder case, lies confidently to the investigating police officer, N. K., that she had left the club at midnight, before the crime happened. Proud of being a member of the transnational globetrotting Indian elite, she lets it be known that she had to leave the party early since she had to pick up her husband who was returning from a business trip in Singapore. Her navel-gazing disconnectedness from reality, and from the working conditions of the vast majority of the country, are made amply clear as she complains about the heat in the police station: "It's too hot in here. How do you people work? Can you please turn on the AC?," while drinking from her bottled mineral water. This woman's use of phrase "you people" to refer to the inspector and his colleagues suggests her affective and ideological investment in the sociocultural and economic distance between her and them. This is an important dimension of the film because it demonstrates the heterogeneity of the Indian middle class and focuses its critique only on an elite segment or the socialites, and the high-ranked officers and politicians.

On the other hand, the working classes—the servers, Shankar and Dharam, who are eyewitnesses to Jessica's murder—are not only shown to have little political agency and motivation, but they are also presented as opportunists. Dharam reassures Sabrina that he will tell the truth in court, but he also asks her for money saying that he's in need. Sabrina, desperate and decent, gives him money and justifies what is essentially a bribe as he's "the poorest and most vulnerable" of all the eyewitnesses. But he turns out to be an unprincipled double-crossing opportunist who extracts money from both parties, sells himself to the highest bidder, and thus refuses to do the right thing by identifying the murderer.

Sabrina is therefore subjected not only to the abuses of the political elite but is also at the mercy of class subalterns. This sets up the professional middle class as the persecuted class, overshadowing even Shankar's articulation of subaltern precarity. When Shankar says, "I want to do the right thing, but I am poor. Back in the village, I have a wife and two little kids. . . . Try to understand my [*majboori*] plight," Sabrina, instead of recognizing embedded power relations between them, or her class privilege and his subaltern precarity, and extending solidarity to him, insists that her *majboori* (her uphill battle to get justice for her sister in the face of corruption) is greater and trumps his class precarity. In some ways, then, the film's subalterns are shown to be clear-eyed pragmatics in their assessment of the trickiness of the situation. They too will negotiate a price tag on their participation in middle-class causes. In this, they are different from the wider middle class, which will rise from its apathy-ridden slumber and protest the denial of justice for Jessica. Their goals are entirely self-serving; they are *majboor*: powerless, constrained, incapable of action, and thus of no help to the middle classes.

In a sense, the film mirrors what is true about Indian polity under neoliberalism: The poor who continue to be excluded from civil society place their faith in electoral politics. New political actors from previously subordinated groups have entered the domain of official politics and taken up leadership roles in central and state governments. In response and in contrast, the middle class has withdrawn from electoral politics, devalorized party politics, state welfarism, and the public sector even as they benefit from its services. Increasingly, as John Harris and others have noted, it turns to civil society as the domain for its self-assertion, and middle-class activism has become one of its defining features.[31] Thus, while in terms of its political character, the middle class has generally been apathetic and complacent, it has engaged in collective action that is highly guided by its narrow, class-based self-interests, which has deeply unsalutary effects for poor and marginalized groups. Even as it claims for itself a progressive and enlightened role in creating a public sphere and safeguarding public interest (as opposed to special interest), middle-class protest politics on the ground often betray socially illiberal and exclusionary tendencies aimed at protecting or consolidating their own interests.[32]

No One Killed Jessica showcases this "new politics," variously referred to as middle-class protests or "elite revolts," where the media, as part of civil society, especially plays a significant role. In the film, in a further undercutting of formal democratic politics, it is "television news media rather than political representatives who are seen as being more proximate to the lives of ordinary citizens."[33] The outraged journalist serves as a vocal mouthpiece of the desires, anxieties, and agendas of the new middle-class politics. Meera is incensed that "justice has been denied" and forges ahead to expose the injustice with the support of a whole private corporate network behind her. In spectacular fashion, she organizes "sting operations" and staged interviews to expose the rot in the system. She goes on TV and raises questions about the police, the government, and the legal system.

Meera offers a new model for engaging crisis: she persists and, crucially, her fervor mobilizes other people like her, that is, a segment of the middle class, to fight what is rotten in the Indian state. At her behest, the TV network launches the "Justice for Jessica" campaign, to which the middle class responds overwhelmingly. The campaign fuels public outrage and draws affective responses from the middle class (in living rooms, malls, cinema halls, girls' hostels, TV showrooms, etc.) as they watch the coverage; they experience a "political awakening" and call in to the network, send SMS (text) messages, blog, show up for street protests and silent marches. The signs that the protesters hold up—"Remove the system"—provide an insight into their antipolitics. The campaign becomes the middle class's platform to vent their disenchantment and frustrations, and we hear a litany of disaffections against the state and its institutions. People from across the nation, from different metropolitan regions, and from across the religious spectrum, call in to share their disillusionment: "Police, government, law and order are mere words in this country." Ordinary people, they tell us, have nowhere to go for justice when the police and the courts betray them.

This middle-class activism is what, the film argues, constitutes the true essence of a "Shining" India. The "India Shining" campaign was first used in the BJP's 2004 election campaign as a slogan to celebrate the phenomenal growth rate of the Indian economy. At the time, although the BJP government didn't come to power, the refrain became closely associated with the middle-class's neoliberal aspirations. The film confirms the belief that "Rising India" is not just about the economic performance of the middle class or the nation claiming "its rightful place as an international superpower." Even more significantly, it is premised on middle-class politics.[34] Meera's voice-over informs the viewer that the Jessica Lall case was a "*shine hone waale India ke history ka ek milestone.*" Meera's words carry a double meaning: In one reading, the case is "a key milestone in the history of Shining India." But, even more accurately, it is "a milestone that will make the country shine [in the future]." India shines and will shine because of the candlelight vigils of the middle class, an enlightened group whose activism creates a civil society that will reform, or so the promise goes, the state and politics at large.[35]

There is also no mistaking this class's patriotism and pride, and we see strident and casual assertions of middle-class nationalism in Meera's responses to events relating to national sovereignty, which resonate with Hindu nationalist rhetoric. The middle class's hawkishness is evident in Meera's response after she reports on the story of India's release of three terrorists to save the lives of hundreds of hostages (referencing the 1999 hijacking of an Indian Airlines flight by a Pakistan-based terrorist group); she lets her personal opinion be known to her boss. "Ours is a soft state. Why does the Indian government always give in?"[36] While this comment is meant to reinforce Meera's reputation as a fearless journalist, it also registers the middle class's hardline stance and aggressive politics that advocates for more "stringent" and effective measures to root out what it sees as "societal ills" and counter any external and internal threats. Such a stance has also caused this class to support a "strong" and "decisive" leader like Modi on matters pertaining to national interest, as well as to advocate and approve of authoritarian state practices such as the death penalty for rapists, as we show in a discussion of the cop film *Simmba* in this chapter.

Similarly, Meera's voice-over at the beginning of the film provides an important insight into the easy and pervasive jingoism among the middle class. The voice-over connects the destiny and rise in fortunes of the nation and the middle class. Meera narrates that at the turn of the millennium, after its successful second round of nuclear tests (in Pokhran, Rajasthan, in 1998), just as India was knocking on the doors of the elite club of global nuclear superpowers to be let in, she had finally, after knocking on the doors of various networks, found employment as a reporter for a news channel. Her search (middle class) for employment is compared to the nation's place in the global power structure. The narration has a triumphant ring to it as it mentions India's achievement of nuclear capability under the BJP-led government, where nuclear capability was associated with self-reliance, self-esteem, and international prestige. Meera's matter-of-fact confident, celebratory tone echoes the India Shining middle class's overwhelming support for the government-financed nuclearization of the country, a program that had less to do with actual security threats to the nation than with the symbolism of muscular nationalism associated with it, which is supposed to remedy the middle-class's sense of injury of India (and itself) being denied membership or recognition as a global power.[37] There is a displacement of precarity from the poor—who would benefit more from access to basic material resources than to nuclear power—to the middle class. Rupal Oza argues that the tests "functioned as a way to solidify the tenuously held coalition government led by the BJP and to displace concerns about India's loss of economic control [after structural reforms] by reviving India's military strength."[38] Furthermore, as Oza notes, the widespread popularity of the tests was also "symptomatic of a political shift that indicated greater receptivity of the Hindu nationalist vision of the country."[39] *NOKJ*'s invocation of the tests captures yet another key dimension of contemporary Indian middle-class political imagination.

Khakee Encounters: New Bollywood's Cop Films

It might seem counterintuitive to study cop films for their articulation of collective politics and political agency. The figure of the cop, after all, operates as a representative of the state, and embodies its coercive ideology and practice. He exemplifies both the everyday, mundane practices of the state—maintaining law and order to ensure the smooth functioning of societal grids—as well as its crisis-management avatar when he protects the nation-state under duress. And yet, in the history of Hindi cinema, time and time again the police officer has converted his intimacy with official power into subaltern agency, advancing the rights and welfare of the dispossessed, the silenced, and those without political will or agency. The cop, by virtue of his proximity to, and embedment within, state apparatuses is the vehicle par excellence of juridical, legal processes. At the same time, his capacity to reject legal authority, prompted by frustrations at the state's ineptness, marks him as a curiously liminal character, one who remains bound by (and to) a moral-ethical jurisprudence, even when he commits acts that are extrajudicial and outside the bounds of constitutional frameworks. In fact, when the state is morally corrupt, inefficient, or dysfunctional, the cop's recourse to illicit legality is what represents the purest embodiment of what his professional responsibility *ought* to entail.

Hindi films have long familiarized us with the cinematic trope of the cop who resorts to extralegal means to render "justice." The quintessential cop film of the 1970s is *Zanjeer* (Chains, 1973), a film about an honest police officer who has to work outside institutional frameworks (since they're either corrupt, weak, or loophole-ridden), to avenge both his family's murder and to bring criminals (smugglers, corrupt politicians, underworld/mafia dons) to justice. *Zanjeer* also introduced to the public the powerful cinematic figure of the "angry young man" who represented "subaltern anger," or the disaffection of the dispossessed urban working-class precariat. Against a background of massive sociopolitical upheaval and crisis of faith in governmental and legal institutions, this angry young man as cop came to be synonymous with the superstar Amitabh Bachchan, who "lash[ed] out at a system of social injustice,"[40] offering "antiauthoritarian fantasies of resistance"[41] and heralded "the arrival of populism on the national arena."[42] The cop as the "angry young man" thus combines state authority with the moral authority of the common man. As a state official, he is armed with the skills to navigate state machinery but also with the power to reject and disrupt its monopoly over demarcations of right and wrong. He can weaponize his own state-sanctioned power against the state but can also discover and recover nonstatist methods of resistance. He is both the ideal state functionary and the ideal citizen.

The interlink between the police and politics—politics both as ideology and as official channels of the state's operation—is thus rendered explicit in every cinematic rendition involving cops. The cop in every role—whether as the comic-relief constable, the corrupt officer, the honest, earnest boss, the revenge-seeking vigilante cop turned rogue—offers us the occasion to trace a popular, bottom-up perception of the relationship between the state and its citizens. This figure also offers us a commentary on politicians, state policies, and rhetoric surrounding national development, national security, and legal enforcement. This is why several scholars have read the various iterations of the cop figure (and cop films) over the decades as responses to shifts in the Indian political landscape and the concomitant shifts in attitudes toward the state. M. K. Raghavendra, for instance, suggests that every time the Indian state was seen to have weakened or worsened—in the 1960s after the 1962 Sino-India War, or in the 1980s as a result of Indira Gandhi's emergency years, or as in the aftermath of economic liberalization in the 1990s, seen as withdrawing from its own institutions—disenchantment with the state was reflected in the portrayal of the police as having lost moral authority or as weak or impervious to legality, respectively.[43]

At the same time, however, as Raghavendra argues elsewhere, "The police have consistently represented the authority of the State in the Hindi film."[44] And thus even when the cop acts against the state, he is in fact endorsing a utopic idea of how the state *should* act. This is why, for M. Madhava Prasad, the joke that in classical Hindi cinema (of the 1960s) "the police always arrive late" on the scene after the hero has already beaten up the villain and neutralized his threat is not reducible to "a satire on the incompetence of the police." Instead, the police's delayed arrival enables the state's "feudal system of justice" to play its part. The police must wait their turn to bring criminals to justice because premodern modalities too play a part in the reinstatement of law and order and in the enactment of justice in the modern state. The police's tardiness, then, functions as an encoded endorsement of the "final alliance" between the feudal and the modern "sites of power," both of which "retain their separate identities" but also operate with an interwoven interdependence in the postcolonial state.[45] The official channels of legality allow vigilante forces and impulses to have the first go.

In the end, however, vigilantism, including the cop's extrajudicial rage, must relent to the reassertion of the "legal state" in the form of the police arriving to put any remaining criminals behind bars or the hero offering himself up to the state (*Meri Awaz Suno*, Hear My Voice, 1981). There is, in the end, a "reluctant[ance] to accept the vigilante fully or to allow him unambiguous sanction."[46] The films ultimately invoked the state (via the police) as the final bastion of legitimate authority and recalibrated anger toward the state as renewed faith in the reform of its institutions (police, judiciary, administration) whose inefficacy or corruption had paradoxically spurred the hero's vigilantism in the first place.

Anustup Basu[47] deploys Achille Mbembe to study the proliferation of the "encounter trope" in films since the 1990s as a more contemporary manifestation of the conflation between the modern and the feudal. These films instate a logic where weakly mediated "government bureaucracies, a nominal civil society, and ineffectual or naïve media" demand the perverse mixing of "capital or technology with new medievalisms." The "encounter"—the colloquialism used to describe the extralegal killing of enemies of the state (usually terrorists, sometimes rapists)—is thus the secret practiced in open daylight. It is the "degree zero of metropolitan order," an "act of clearing," the state of exception that allows the everyday to exist and thrive. Without the police's capacity and willingness to cross the borders of legality and "encounter" monsters who deserve extermination, the realm of human activity and human rights would not exist. The "constitutional pieties of the state" can come into being, therefore, only because the cop is illicitly authorized to suspend them.

As Arunima Paul reminds us, however, the figure of the cop has not always represented this quasi-conflictual, semicompetitive relationship with the state, where he embodies both its legal authority and a resistance to its failures. Paul discusses two post-1990s cop genres of the "national cop film" and the "provincial cop film." In these post-liberalization renditions of the cinematic cop, the cop is the perfect instantiation of the state's will to modernization and postcolonial development.[48] In this, these films, she argues have an older lineage and share something in common with the "five year plan hero" of the 1950s. According to Sanjay Srivastava, this figure found expression on screen as a middle-class masculinity that adhered to the ideals of patriotism, mobility, modernity, technocratic governmentality, and a self-sacrificing investment in national good.[49] His capacity for delayed gratification and distance from mindless consumerism established him as the model for emulation and revival about five decades later in films like *Sarfarosh* (Patriot, 1999, John Matthew Matthan), *Khakee* (Rajkumar Santoshi, 2004), and *Black Friday* (Anurag Kashyap, 2004), released after liberalization. Paul suggests that the "national cop" retains the "developmental mandate for an educated and qualified middle-class hero as a figure of reason and transformation who transcends the suffering (family trauma) as well as pleasures of the self (consumerism)."[50] This national cop travels across variously recalcitrant geographies—those scarred by communal disharmony, militancy, insurgency, or terrorism—and his ultimate responsibility, as Paul argues, is to bring to submission these contested territories, to subsume and redevelop them within the bounds of nationalism and neoliberalism.

If bourgeois urbanity and elite educational backgrounds are the hallmark of the national cop, then the "provincial cop film," set in the hinterland, disrupts the hegemonic, elite metropolitan understanding of the nation in crisis, by adopting a different lens than the one utilized by the national cop, to understand issues of correction, justice, governance, and political action. By delving into provincial dystopia, disaffection, and dissent, these films, Paul notes, show rampant corruption in law enforcement and highlight an inequitable polity and brazen power hierarchies. In their climactic depiction of "a mobilized provincial public adopting vigilantist modes of political action," films like *Shool* (Lance, Eeshwar Nivas, 1999), *Gangaajal* (Holy Water, Prakash Jha, 2004), and *Aakrosh* (Outrage, Priyadarshan, 2010) evoke an impasse constituted by neoliberal anxieties about a "failing" developmental state and electoral democracy, as well as suspicion of mass political action."[51] As we will show, this impasse finds renewed expression in the new cop-franchise films.

One of the biggest trends in postmillennial popular Hindi cinema has been the emergence (or re-emergence) of genres related to law and order and homeland security. 2010's biggest box-office hit was *Dabangg* (Abhinav Singh Kashyap), a supercop film about a Robinhood-esque policeman with a complicated moral code (he is corrupt in that he takes bribes, but only from the bad guys; and he looks out for the little guy). The film's huge success led to two sequels (*Dabangg 2*, Arbaaz Khan, 2012; *Dabangg 3*, Prabhu Deva, 2019). A slew of police procedural films and shows have also appeared on OTT platforms such as Netflix and Prime, including *Delhi Crime* (2019), *Aranyak* (Wild, 2021), *Dahaad* (Roar, 2023), *Kathal* (2023), and *Indian Police Force* (2024). Another conglomeration of prominent cop films has been directed by Rohit Shetty, who has created a shared "cop universe," a cinematic franchise that focuses on larger-than-life Hindu cop heroes. Films in the franchise include *Singham* (2011), *Singham Returns* (2014), *Simmba* (2018), and *Sooryavanshi* (2021).[52]

In the next section, we study two films from Shetty's cop universe, *Sooryavanshi* and *Simmba*. In many ways, these films encapsulate New Bollywood's distinctly political mood—of unabashed nationalism, Islamophobia, and upper-caste Hindu patriarchal majoritarianism—as it engages older, longstanding political questions and debates. These films tackle issues of terrorism and rape, respectively, two issues that have occupied, and continued to occupy, the most rhetorically charged valence both in India's public sphere and within Hindi cinema. What they (and the cop film genre more broadly) enable us to see is the renewed investment in the figure of the police officer as a political agent, acting on behalf of the state *and* the people. Here, then, is the rub: For the most part, over the decades, the cinematic cop's crisis entailed a hard choice, to represent the state and win over the people through his technocratic zeal or to serve the people by going against an apathetic state. Precarious times, however, yield new political configurations.

Sooryavanshi and *Simmba* share features with previous cinematic renditions of the cop even as these are reconfigured in the contemporary political moment. Thus the angry young man figure is reworked in the figures of Simmba and Sooryavanshi. Simmba is not a traumatized orphan (although he is an orphan) or disaffected antiestablishment figure. He is more a buffoonish, self-gratifying cop who eventually transforms into a roaring lion against the lackadaisical institutions of the state to avenge sexual violence against women. His campy buffoonery doesn't quite disappear; it is just amalgamated and repurposed within the patriarchal, protectionist, masculinist logic of the state (and its people). Simmba doesn't have to step out of the state to annihilate the rapists, but to properly *step into* his state-sponsored role as its functionary. Similarly, the brooding masculinity of the angry young man is remodeled in *Sooryavanshi* as Soorya's unapologetic ethnonationalist masculinity. But he too, outside of his professional identity as a cop, is a bumbling man, incapable of getting anyone's name right or fulfilling the responsibilities of a husband.

In both instances, far from practicing self-denial or shunning consumerist desires like the cops of yore committed to a developmentalist state, both films feature flamboyant cops and revel in consumer cultures, whether of Ray-Ban sunglasses, shiny SUVs, high tech, and superior weapons as they tackle threats to national security or economic prosperity. What is perhaps most striking about these new cop films is how custodial violence, extrajudicial vigilante justice, and the "encounter" occupy less the space of secrecy or a state of exception and rather operate as normalized, foregone, and matter-of-fact occurrences sanctioned by the state. Finally, not only is the vigilante cop not at odds with the state, the vigilante publics that goad the cop's extrajudicial justice grant to his actions an ethical responsibility and legitimation. This then creates a harmony between cop, people, and the state to reveal a consensus around authoritarian populism that provides the edifice of the neoliberal Hindutva state.

In an article, Sanjay Srivastava suggests that during the 2014 general election, Narendra Modi's campaign and the pre-prime-ministerial discourse that surrounded him "significantly focused upon his 'manly' leadership style: efficient, dynamic, potent, and capable of removing all policy roadblocks through sheer force of personality."[53] This was in sharp contrast to his "*majboor*" (pathetic and helpless) predecessor's government run by the "impotent" Manmohan Singh and controlled by the *ma-bete* (mother-son) duo of the Gandhi family

(Sonia and Rahul Gandhi).[54] Modi's rise in the era of digital media has much to do with building an image of omnipotent masculinity promoted through both his physicality and aggressive policy shifts that caste aside a predecessor who was deemed hamstrung (by "policy paralysis" in media discourse). Modi's willingness to attract attention to his physicality with references to his taut, fifty-six-inch broad chest has become a synecdochic signifier for a *mazboot* (strong) government that can take on terrorists with as much aplomb as it can deal with issues of housing, sanitation, health insurance, and LPG cylinders. His unabashedly self-indulgent consumerism—ultraexpensive suits and accessories, elite air travel—contribute to a Hindu masculinist typology that is aggressively self-reliant and able to solve national problems while fulfilling personal ambitions of upward mobility. Modi's lineage, from tea seller at a train station to the nation's most powerful man, unafraid to exercise his power to inure both the nation and himself against attacks, is then perfect fodder for Bollywood's dream machine. The figuration of the state in the cop genre amplifies this Modi-like potency. In this cop universe, a euphoric-celebratory public casts aside cumbersome institutions and judicial processes as niceties that delay and deny the gratification of instant justice.

The cops in Shetty's cinematic franchise represent this fantasy of authoritarian populism: strongman leaders, governed by a neoliberal, entrepreneurial commitments, can perform the unthinkable. They can create an absolute political-ideological consensus between the nation-state and its people. Cop films like *Sooryavanshi* and *Simmba* present an incisive articulation of authoritarian populism in India "that combines strongman leadership, strident ethnonationalism, populist strategies, and elements of neoliberalism."[55] They glorify the culture of impunity in law enforcement machinery and valorize the muscular Hindu vigilante cop as the patriotic savior of the nation and its women. In the films, panics around rape and terrorism, respectively, thus serve to "win for the authoritarian closure the gloss of popular consent."[56]

In studying these films, we come to learn something about how cops operate as agents of neoliberal Hindutva, exacerbating the precarity experienced by women and religious minorities (primarily Muslims) in contemporary India. These films reveal new structures of consent formation mobilized via the figure of the police officers. Simmba and Soorya, the cop protagonists of the two films under consideration, are perpetually recruiting on- and off-screen publics into the authoritarian logics they embody. Through cinematic strategies of the "voice-over," for instance, communities within the films, as well as the audiences watching the films, are absorbed into statist, authoritarian master narratives. Incredibly, however, there is a clear separation of subaltern bodies into those who are inducted on the side of the cop as worthy of protection (Hindu women) and those who are exempted from inclusion and left to their own narratological and political devices (Muslims). This demographic-identitarian segregation is predicated on the cop's obfuscation and subsumption of antiauthoritarian politics, where legitimate unrest is perpetually neutralized through the neoliberal politics of cooption and coercion. In that sense, these cop films mark an instructive moment in the evolution of the genre, and offer us sites to trace the contours of the citizen-state's interface with the nation's changing polity, divided along idealized and dystopic provincial representations.

"No Arrest. No Long Cases. Justice on the Spot": Simmba Encounters the Rapists

The third film in Shetty's cop universe and a remake of the 2015 Telegu hit film *Temper*, *Simmba* is about the eponymous orphan and corrupt cop (Sangram "Simmba" Bhalerao) who is only interested in filling his coffers with bribes. This until his conscience is aroused: a young woman he develops brotherly affection for (Aakruti Dave) is fatally gang-raped by the brothers (Sada and Giri) of a local criminal drug lord (Durva Ranade). The conscience of the sleeping lion (Simmba translates as lion) awakens. He dons his khakee police uniform and roars with vengeance to kill the two rapists in a staged encounter in his police station. *Simmba* thus belongs to the subgenre of the postmillennial "encounter films" in which cops "encounter" or commit extralegal killings to deliver "justice" by riding the social landscape of those deemed criminals.[57]

What is especially remarkable about *Simmba* is how it manipulates and instrumentalizes Akruti's rape, and the politics and discourses around it, to build consensus across multiple, disparate constituencies—judges, politicians, cops, middle-class men and women, young and old—to condone aggressive, muscular, individuated solutions to women's gendered, sexual precarity. The final solution—kill the rapists—is presented as the will of the people who appoint (and anoint) the cop as a strongman leader and their political representative. The cop executes their wish in a context where both the people and the police are frustrated by the constraints and failures of democratic institutions. Vigilante justice becomes their only alternative.

The film's opening makes its political stance explicit through the Godlike voice-over, soaring above the wail of sirens, as a procession of jeeps screech to a halt outside a police station. The voice-over tells us that "Two encounters have happened. While these encounters are unofficial, this is the first honest deed that the officer-in-charge of this station has done." This loaded, opening exposition, does important political work to determine how the audience should make sense of what has happened. On the one hand, the choice of the words "first honest deed" critique Simmba's erstwhile corrupt actions (he was, until recently, a shameless bribe-taking cop). But the voice-over's ultimate force lies in its declaration that the encounter, "while unofficial," was an "honest deed." The narration ostensibly sets up "honest" in tension with "unofficial," but the tension is precisely what brings legitimacy to "encounters" as police practice. Indeed, the encounters are "unofficial" in that they're undertaken by a cop who's working outside sanctioned judicial processes and bureaucratic channels. However, the word "honest"—with all its attendant associations of fair, good, just, right—establishes for the viewers the legitimacy of the extrajudicial act. Importantly, audiences and fans would easily recognize the voice-over as belonging to Singham (Bajirao Singh), the super cop from the inaugural film of Shetty's cop-universe franchise. Singham, played by Ajay Devgn, is already established as a cop whose self-righteous zeal lends even more moral weight to the endorsement of vigilante justice.

If the opening with Singham's voice frames and overdetermines how we read Simmba's actions, the film itself is an illustration of *how* Simmba operates as he marshals vigorous support for authorizing an "unofficial-honest deed" of murdering rapists. His vigilantism might be outside the bounds of legality, but it is not without process. It may not follow legal routes, but it does adhere nevertheless to systematic, ritualized protocols. The film lays out the contours of these extrajudicial systems of justice in the age of authoritarian populism. This is not mayhem, but an alternative rationality and set of intentional practices that accompany the worldview.

It's fun and games in the first forty-five minutes of the two-hour and thirty-nine-minute film, which establish Simmba as a rogueish cop without a conscience. He is flamboyantly dishonest in his dealings. The main lead, Ranveer Singh, hams it up as he plays, with cartoonish gusto, a feisty orphan-turned-cop who makes no bones about his chosen profession: he became a cop "to make money, and not to be Robinhood and help others." We see him outcrook the crooks and outswindle unscrupulous businessmen with his own crass corruption. Simmba becomes a cop because he wants "power"; it is precisely the authoritarian nature of law enforcement that draws him to this calling.

So enmeshed is his subjectivity with his occupation, his personhood and corporeality with that of the state, that he has "police" tattooed on his bulging forearm, which, on numerous occasions, he proudly flexes and flaunts. Simmba is literally the "strong arm" of the state. Even though his tattoo is a nod to Vijay's iconic forearm tattoo—"*Mera Baap Chor Hai*" (my father is a thief)—in *Deewar*, Simmba's persona is far removed from that of the angry young man. As a policeman, he is nothing like the haunted, desperate cop in *Zanjeer*. Simmba's tattoo does not signify a traumatized and scarred body or bespeak a history of shame and helplessness, as it does in *Deewar*. It is not a forcible branding that is a "signifier for marginality and social displacement" or of existing "outside the pale of the family."[58] Simmba's tattoo is a marker of pleasure and pride, of just how unmitigatedly he revels in being a cop, and how glad he is to exist as an extension of the state. Melodramatic excess rather than physical restraint defines his relationship to his profession. Unlike the angry young man version of the cop, he has no skepticism toward "the rituals of the family/nation,"[59] hegemonic institutions that exact more than their pound of flesh. Instead, Simmba invests in an indiscriminate familialization of the body politic that he polices. The orphan-turned-vigilante-cop turns the nation into his family and forges a familial relation with every person he meets.

With the rape of a young woman, the film's tenor shifts from comedy to action and social drama. This turning point is anticipated in an exchange between Simmba and Nityanand Mohile, an ethical head constable whom Simmba supervises. After Simmba strong-arms an ordinary and helpless middle-class man into signing off his home (property and land) at a reduced price to a corrupt corporator, Mohile berates Simmba for "betraying his duty." While Simmba has previously ignored Mohile's withering looks, this time he loses his patience with Mohile's accusations and snaps back: "You're accusing me like I raped someone." In the film's ideological schema, rape is the worst crime. Duping old men out of their property and cozying up to land sharks doesn't compare and doesn't even deserve any verbal chastisement. As the film progresses, we come to learn that the adequate punishment for rape is the termination of life. This exchange, which precedes Aakruti's assault and murder, provides an insight into how the film is interested in "muscular masculine celebrations of Maratha chauvinism and patriarchy," which are more "insulted by rape" than anything else.[60]

Through Aakruti's gang-rape and death, *Simmba* invokes implicitly but also names explicitly the gruesome 2012 Delhi rape case and the discourses surrounding it.[61] Simmba co-opts the fears and anxieties associated with rape to drum up support for his own violent, masculinist, authoritarian populist agenda. Women's gendered and sexual precarity is not an occasion to address structural issues, but an opportunity to forward a conservative ideological stance that legitimizes coercive and exclusionary state practices. Historically, as feminist scholars (such as Lata Mani in the context of sati in colonial India)[62] have noted, women's bodies have been used as the ground or site on which other debates are staged; ultimately, women's voices are silenced to support other ideological stances and political agendas. This film is no exception in that the violence committed against a woman's body offers provocation to build consensus for unconstitutional and undemocratic delivery of justice.

The film steadily builds momentum toward normalizing its argument about how rapists should be dealt with. It harnesses and manipulates how the discourse around rape permeates through different sites and spaces: in public protests and vigils, in the economic realm, within households, and in the courtroom. The film performs multiple forms of appropriation of disparate ideologies articulated as distinct modalities of resistance—civic unrest, women's anger, parental insecurity, patriarchal protectionism—and melds them all into one to produce a singular meaning and outcome. The film thus does the important ideological work of mobilizing a "fractured public . . . through profoundly modern calls for civic participation, into violence and into condoning violence."[63]

The film's politics continue to reveal themselves in how it presents the protests and candlelight vigils that follow in the wake of Aakruti's rape and death. First, protest is presented as something that the middle class does, as it stands in for "the people," and thus the poor and working class is entirely absent from participation and investment in the cause. In fact, one of the kids (Chhotu) who is speech-impaired and who was a key eyewitness in the Aakruti case turns "hostile" and disappears. The poor are thus either rendered mute witnesses or can't afford principles and can be easily bought. The class precariat, and class precarity, are "cinematically cleared"[64] while middle-class voices are amplified. Second, the focus is on middle-class outrage, and what is amplified is their bloodthirsty, regressive demand for capital punishment for the rapists. The film spotlights protest signs that are held by middle-class young men and women: "Hang the rapist or we riot"; "Hang all the rapists. We want justice"; "There is no place for a rapist in society." None of the protest signs demand legal reform or legislative changes to address gender-based violence.[65] The film has nothing to say about socioeconomic precarity, and its relationship to gendered violence, produced by neoliberal capitalism in India.

Third, since the film is invested in enshrining the cop as the ultimate agent of justice, the cops join and support these protests, rather than trying to disperse the crowds. This is a far cry from how the police operate in India in the context of public protests. In fact, those protesting Pandey's 2012 rape were met by the state's draconian reaction: curfew was imposed in some parts of the city, and protestors were hosed down, lathi-charged (struck by wooden batons), and teargassed by the Rapid Action Force units of the police.[66]

What the film does dial up is the rhetoric of the need to protect *Bharat ki betiyaan* (daughters of the nation).[67] It is critical to note that the nation is specifically invoked as "Bharat," which is the word to connote "India" that the Hindu Right prefers to use. Christophe Jaffrelot sees the increasing use of "Bharat" instead of "India" an expression of the saffronization of the public sphere. In a statement made during an interview on a major news network after the 2012 rape, Mohan

Bhagwat, the leader of the Hindu right-wing Rashtriya Swayamsevak Sangh (RSS) organization, suggested that "Such crimes [of rape] hardly take place in Bharat, but they frequently occur in India."[68] In Bhagwat's worldview, Bharat is associated with the "virtues" of a traditional idyllic Hindu nation, while India signals the "vices" of modernity or secularism, etc. And the crimes of "India" must be prevented from occurring in Bharat through the protection of its chaste and virginal women (read: Hindu women).[69] The strategic invocation of *Bharat ki betiyaan* provides an insight into how the film's patriarchal-protectionist and nationalist-populist message work together to disempower women.

In the courtroom, Simmba appeals to the female judge, reminding her that she, too, like the victim, is a *Bharat ki beti*. His address positions her not as a public official or a professional working woman, but as mother and daughter. Conveniently, the judge is swayed and grants another hearing date to the prosecution. Even more, when the rapists' mother takes the witness stand, this judge castigates her, blaming her for her sons' deviancy: they wouldn't be rapists if it weren't for her faulty upbringing. Here the film transfers the responsibility for women's precarity onto women in the legal field to bring the violent men to justice, and to women as mothers to raise men who are not rapists. Importantly, then, the male vigilante steps in to deal with the rapists, when all the women in public, professional, and domestic spheres fail to fulfill their responsibilities.

The *Bharat ki beti* discourse also resonates with the Modi government's Beti Bachao, Beti Padhao (save the girl child, educate the girl child) campaign. In one scene, Nandini Mohile propels Simmba into action: "the daughters of the country are getting educated but who will save them from the monsters." Her exhortation is a tacit endorsement of Modi's campaign launched to address female feticide.[70] It encourages families to stop treating their daughters as a liability and give them a good education. That is what will enable them to maximize their "capacity to become virtuous market citizens" and be empowered to serve their family and nation. Simultaneously, though, Nandini's words mark the limits of what the government can do: it can't protect women from monstrous men who interrupt their emergence as prospective neoliberal subjects. Hence the need for an "*eda*" cop to rectify the challenge of monstrous men who pose a physical threat to women's emancipation. At the same time, the narrative of "monstrous men" does not acknowledge systemic operations of patriarchal power and masculine privilege, and it also sidetracks the other, everyday obstacles that stand in the way of women's education. After all, we must not forget that Aakruti's father, with his lower-middle-class salary, is barely able to pay for her education to become a doctor. Women's aspirations encounter many more roadblocks tied to the neoliberal economy besides rapist men. The film makes no room for this conversation.

A closer look at the 2012 Delhi rape case, from which the film borrows heavily, enables us to observe the extent to which *Simmba* evacuates the wider neoliberal context that fuels such violence against women. Jyoti Singh Pandey was the daughter of an airport worker who came from a family of agricultural workers; she was the first in her family to have a professional career. She was enrolled in a physiotherapy course and, to pay for her education, she was working nights at an outsourcing firm, helping Canadians with their mortgage issues.[71] On the night of her fatal sexual assault on December 16, 2012, in South Delhi, she was returning home with a male friend after watching a late-night show of *The Life of Pi*. On the private bus they boarded, he was beaten up and she was brutally raped by five men, all friends of the bus driver. Jyoti succumbed to her injuries a few days after the attack. The event sparked mass anger and nationwide protests and international attention and censure, resulting in the establishment of five fast-track courts to deal with issues of sexual violence against women. The Justice Verma Committee, a special commission of legal experts, was formed to recommend changes to the laws pertaining to gender-based violence. While one of the perpetrators allegedly committed suicide in jail, the High Court sentenced the remaining four others to capital publishment, and the seventeen-year-old minor was sentenced to three years in a reform facility.

The film makes a few critical and telling changes in its fictionalized dramatization of this incident. In the film, like Jyoti, Aakruti is a young female Hindu (medical) student who is gang-raped and murdered. The film, however, attempts a "sanitization" of the victim's profile, and she is presented as the ideal *Bharat ki beti*, the kind of gendered subject who can be valorized within the politics of neoliberal Hindutva. The film takes pains to establish Aakruti, always dressed in modest "Indian" clothes, as a chaste Hindu woman. Her goodness, purity, virtue, innocence, and diligence are repeatedly emphasized. This is what makes her an uncomplicated recipient of the audience's sympathy. This is why her nocturnal activities are assiduously reframed by the film. Unlike Jyoti, Aakruti is out at night not for recreational activities, but to teach street kids. She is raped and murdered not while she's out with a male friend, but as punishment for discovering that the Durva and his brothers are using street children as drug mules. Ironically, women as neoliberal subjects—aspirational, educated, hard-working, successful—must still be desexualized in order to qualify as sympathy-worthy cinematic subjects. Jyoti, as a modern, mobile woman, could easily be read as deserving of her lot. In an interview, Mukesh Singh, one of her rapists, maintained that a "decent girl wouldn't [have been] out at night." In the misogynist worldview he represents, "A girl is far more responsible for rape than a boy. . . . Housework and housekeeping is for girls, not roaming in discos and bars at night, doing wrong things, wearing wrong clothes."[72] The film cleverly sidesteps these contradictions in neoliberal India's public sphere by disassociating the rape victim from any threatening markers of modernity.

In another divergence from the 2012 case, the film establishes both Aakruti and her perpetrators as middle-class, in contrast to Pandey and her perpetrators, who, as internal migrants from the rural to urban center, represent aspirational India. This alteration of class location has the effect of erasing the complex intersections of gender and class inequalities or precarities present in the 2012 incident. As Tithi Bhattacharya has noted, gender violence and misogyny need to be contextualized against the promises of neoliberal capitalism in India and its failures, which are managed by the deflection of frustrations and resentments of one oppressed and aspirational group (working-class men) upon another precarious segment of the population (working-class and lower-middle-class women).

Simmba has nothing to say about these messy politics in which neoliberal economics intermesh with traditional forms of patriarchy and Hindutva ideologies. Instead, it mobilizes the moral economy of patriarchal nationalism. Overall, then, the distortions in the film have the effect not only of valorizing a certain type of female subject who appeals to the conservative gender values of the Hindu nationalist-authoritarian populist project but also of marginalizing or erasing the larger socioeconomic context and contradictions resulting from the adoption and failure of neoliberal reforms. The wide and complex arena of the neoliberal nation is in fact distilled and shrunk to a tiny locality: a *dhaba* (eatery) and the police station across from it.

The interpellation of women in the endorsement of violent vigilante justice, with the cop as political agent, reaches an escalation in the *dhaba*, where multiple women, young and old, traditional and modern, gather and speak up. Thus while Aakruti's death silences her voice, the film does not silence women's voices in general. Rather, its insidiousness lies in how it makes the middle-class Hindu women speak: loudly, angrily, and in unison to support a politics of individuated, retributive, vigilante violence as the solution to women's sexual precarity. Whether it is the rape victim herself, the female court judge, Simmba's love interest (Shagun Sathe), the head constable's daughter (Nandini Mohile), or the home minister's daughter, women are incessantly recruited and willingly offer themselves up as *Bharat ki betiyaan*. Their response is homogeneous, and they accept a patriarchal, protectionist lens, thus negating the history of feminist activism around sexual violence in India, including the unprecedented mass protests after the 2012 rape. These women conveniently delegitimize themselves as political agents and gladly accept the mantle of political provocateurs who urge men to act on their behalf.

Simmba goes to each one of them to solicit their opinion, and in every instance they give him the permission and the encouragement to become an agent of change by acting "unofficially." As Simmba asks these women what they feel each time they encounter news of rape, and what they think should happen about Aakruti's case, they are resoundingly unanimous in their demand that the rapists be killed. Their demand perfectly echoes the language and ideology of the candlelight vigils and public protests that also espoused a lethal solution to the rapists: "They don't deserve to live. Just kill them"; "They should be castrated in public." The film, then, becomes an archive of women's perspectives. Importantly, their perspectives are not mismatched at all. When official avenues fail, the unofficial recourse to justice becomes linear and coherent. No complications or contradictions muddy the waters. And, ironically, the unofficial pathway becomes the gateway for dominant Hindutva ideology to surface and take precedence. These women may emerge from different walks of life, but their voices and opinions arrive at a shared crescendo that reiterates and legitimizes a vigilante, authoritarian politics. With every confirmation Simmba receives from the women, he pats his gun, resting in a holster around his waist. The gun, as a phallically loaded object, becomes an apt vehicle of choice for vengeance and to reinstate a protectionist-patriarchal masculinity.

Despite the heavy overlaps, the film insists that Simmba's masculine self-positioning stands in sharp distinction to the patriarchal violence of the rapists. In fact, on two different occasions, Simmba mocks the rapists' masculinity in the police station. He enlists female cops to beat the perpetrators. He taunts the men to dare to rape these women, while the latter snicker and snort in response to Simmba's goading of the men. The scene of the female cops slapping and beating up the men with their bare hands is oddly reminiscent of violent public action, or mob lynching episodes, which in contemporary India have been largely directed against the poor, Dalits, and religious minorities. The scene, then, participates in the normalization of "vigilante publics" and their "spectacular violence."[73] As Shakuntala Banaji argues, a violent, fascist public consciousness is the "necessary base for state fascism." This scene recruits women as participatory agents of vigilante violence.[74]

Later, when he's preparing to stage the encounter, Simmba taunts the rapists for their "impotence," their inability to do anything when the women cops beat them up and other civilian women witnessed their emasculation. Nothing, Simmba tells them, can be more humiliating. All these insults to their "*mardaangi*" (manhood) have the desired effect: the rapist brothers lash out, and Simmba shoots them in "self-defense." As they are shot, the image of Aakruti appears in soft focus, in white, smiling, and signaling her approval of vigilante vengeance.

As Stuart Hall notes, authoritarian populism is distinguished by its ability "to construct around itself an active popular consent."[75] The film manufactures consent for cop vigilante justice, presented as a necessary, moral, and rightful circumvention of the law. In contrast to the angry young man films of the 1970s in which the angry cop was celebrated as a figure of antiestablishment populism, here the cop functions to serve a right-wing establishmentarian populism.

Of course, Simmba goes scot-free for these extrajudicial killings because, by the end of the film, there is a strikingly single note sounded as the assembled bloc—of ordinary middle-class people, the state (judges, politicians), the cop—condones Simmba's actions. Singham (the original cop hero from Shetty's film franchise, and whose voice-over the film opens with) returns at the end of the film. He is appointed by the home minister as a "neutral officer" in an SIT (special investigation team) inquiry to investigate the veracity of Simmba's claim that he killed the rapists in self-defense. Predictably, Singham is not all that "neutral," and he too gives his stamp of approval to Simmba's extralegal methods: "No arrest. No long cases. Justice on the spot." This is the new way under neoliberal Hindutva.

The overburdened justice system cannot deliver, and hence police brutality—not recognized or acknowledged as such—is necessary for a swift dispatch of justice. The film's populist consent depends on the failures of the system to stoke public distrust and contempt for institutions.[76] Importantly, unlike "classical fascism," authoritarian populism "entails a striking weakening of democratic forms and initiatives, but not their suspension."[77] The film ratifies this qualification: the state (through the home minister) does play a role, albeit a feeble one. He shows little regard for constitutional reforms or the legal system and processes. And therefore the state assists in its own peripheralization. It self-sabotages its predominance, thus enabling the vigilante cop to usurp its authority as the people's representative. There is no tension between the police, the politicians, the people (the middle classes). Everyone's on board with the new sidebar judicial order in which a paternalist vigilante cop operates as a brutal state executioner. Such a man is hailed as a fearless leader and a protector of women's virtue.

Homeland (In)securities: *Sooryavanshi*

Sooryavanshi follows predictable plot points: the threat of another terrorist attack looms large in present-day Mumbai. The antiterrorism squad (ATS), led by the protagonist Soorya (played by Akshay Kumar), spends its time tracking down the forty "sleeper terrorists" that infiltrated India from Pakistan a decade and a half ago and the six hundred kilos of RDX that has been hidden in India since 1993 (the year of the first major bomb blasts in Bombay). The film is action-packed from the get-go; all detective work is absurdly quick and always yields successful results. The film has its fair share of SUV entourages speeding down highways, helicopter chases, bazaar brawls between terrorists and the police, and averted bomb blasts. All of this transpires to the beat of an aural landscape that's come to be associated quintessentially with Shetty's cop franchise: the name of the cop-protagonist is turned into a hypnotic incantation that plays in the background to the action sequences. And the chanting of the hero's name is overlain with the sound of sirens and drums, creating a background score that's akin to a euphoric public celebration during a Hindu festival.

Indeed, ATS officer Soorya is godlike: the high-angle frontal shots through which he's introduced compel us to savor his impeccable physique, his easy corporate-golfer aesthetic of aviator sunglasses and cargo pants, the reverential status he enjoys from his subordinates who are in awe of his leadership but also share an intimate bonhomie with him; they feel comfortable enough to tease him about his minor flaws (he forgets and confuses everyone's names, including the names of criminals, his colleagues, and his own wife). The film's generic narratology is matched, then, by its template use of the body of the male superstar: larger than life and basking in adulation that he receives both on- and off-screen.

In many ways, there is nothing new here. The way Akshay Kumar as Soorya swallows up the film's visual landscape is reminiscent of Hindi cinema's enshrinement of fantasies of a fearless, dynamic, and erotic masculinity ever since the emergence of the angry young man in the 1970s. And yet there is a critical difference. Amitabh Bachchan as the angry young man was a one-of-a-kind actor, corporealizing a new on-screen articulation of discontentment. As Samir Dayal suggests, "Bachchan's muscular elegance" could only be "aspirational, belonging to a fabulous and fabulist manhood, in reality inaccessible to most spectators." Bachchan's embodiment of wrath that signified the frustrations of an entire post-Nehruvian generation was thus expressed through a "nonrepresentative representation of Indian masculinity"; it exceeded any "correspondent referent of Indian masculinity."[78] Akshay Kumar as the cop hero, however, signifies a whole brood of men, a franchise-nation of martial patriots, "*ede policewale*" (slightly crazy cops)[79] played by Hindu actors who, in the Hindi film industry, exemplify an alternate universe to the monopoly of the Khans—that we discuss in chapter 1—and on-screen announce the death knell to terrorists and rapists. If the angry young man marked a cinematic adjacency to the gentle, urbane, encultured masculinity of Nehruvian postcoloniality, the Sooryavanshis, Simmbas, and Singhams denote the new national, aspirational mainstream. They are slightly funnier and a tad more accessible and personable than their main man, the ultimate strongman,[80] Prime Minister Modi, in whose shadow they follow and whose version of ethnonationalist masculinity they work overtime to normalize and popularize.

Sooryavanshi assumes and addresses an audience with whom it shares insider knowledge and consensus about how much India has suffered because of terroristic violence. The film begins with a disembodied voice-over giving us a synoptic history lesson of bomb blasts in the country since the early 1990s. Everyone conversant with Bollywood star texts and Shetty's cop universe recognizes the absent body of Ajay Devgn as the somber, officious recounter of this history. Devgn is, after all, the actor who plays Singham in the first superhit installment of the cop franchise. Devgn's auditory slippage from his own film to another film in the shared cinematic universe smooths the way for an easy, automatic transfer of ideologies between the filmic universe and its real-world counterpart as well. When actors and characters across films share a particular narrative, the audience is also encouraged to imagine itself as coinhabiting the same, all-encompassing worldview and interpretive framework. Ultimately, the giving of information—about terroristic events over the past three decades and how the Indian state has curtailed terroristic activities—is not about giving the audience new information at all. It is about jogging certain memories of national trauma that should never be forgotten, and it is about interpellating audiences into normative scripts about the state and its enemies. In the guise of telling them what they already know, the film in fact perpetuates a vociferously linear account of what needs to be remembered and believed.

There's a telling moment in the film: A Mr. Nayar from the Intelligence Bureau arrives from Delhi to warn the ATS team in Bombay about the likelihood of another terrorist attack. Addressing an audience of politicians, bureaucrats and policemen, all gathered around in a boardroom, he says: "As you all know, after Section 370 was scrapped in Kashmir, it has become impossible for terrorist organizations like Lashkar to create animosity between the people of our country, or to infiltrate and send arms and ammunition into India."

Through this utterly casual and passing reference, the film turns what was an extremely controversial and contested decision by the Modi government—to revoke a constitutional provision of autonomy granted to Kashmir—into an occasion for establishing a community of shared wisdom. The "*jaisa ki aap sab jaante hain*" (as you all know) in the same breath confirms for the audience the obviousness of the motivation for scrapping Article 370, as well as the success of the enterprise: that it was all about the management of terrorist infiltration, and that it has in fact yielded exactly what was anticipated. The offhand manner of conveying this information gives the audience a remarkably innocent and incontestable rationalization for the Indian state's drastic measure of changing its constitution. It also nudges the viewer to accept that *this* is the version of explanations that they should all *already know*. The film works hard to establish that everyone within the film, and those watching the film, are all on the same page. Devgn's auditory documentary-esque summaries of the dates and sites of terrorist attacks, which are then repeated later in the film by Soorya as well, is one means of achieving this continuum and ubiquity of knowledge about key political events that have shaped the trajectory of the nation today.

This unrelenting pervasiveness of the state's master narrative produces a serious consequence: the figure of the cop, unlike his angry young man predecessor, is no longer in competition with the state to fulfill the responsibilities that the state has reneged on. Rather there is a perfect synchronicity and collaboration between the two; there is no room for frustration with or criticism of the state. In fact, even when the cop acts illicitly, it is never without state sanction but in anticipation of state permission that is always already guaranteed. Early on in the film, Kabir Shroff, the joint commissioner of police, asks the chief minister to come to the ATS headquarters late at night. Upon his arrival, the minister is given an update about the whereabouts of a Pakistani insurgent—Riyaaz Hafeez—who has been hiding out in Jaisalmer, Rajasthan, pretending to be a hotelier for the past fifteen years. We see Shroff and the politician with their backs to us as they stare at multiple screens flashing with images of places and people under surveillance by an array of uniformed (female) officers sitting in the room. The central screen has an image of two dead bodies covered with white sheets lying on the ground. The "investigation of these two suspects," we learn, has led the police to Hafeez's whereabouts. The paucity of details surrounding the death of these "suspects" is astounding. After the barrage of information that the audience has been given, via Devgn's voice-over at the start of the film (excruciating details about terrorists in India and Pakistan and their nefarious plans), the film barely pauses to let us register the death of these two men, who have most likely been "encountered" as terrorist suspects. Even the chief minister does not ask any questions about them; the cop's word is the final word. He determines our response to death, frames certain bodies as victims of the nation and certain others as disposable, relevant only as information or for the evidence they generate about other things and people that really matter.

The chief minister instructs Shroff to send his team to Jaisalmer immediately and "arrest the bastard." Without a moment's hesitation, Shroff responds, "I'm sorry, Sir, but we couldn't wait to get permission." The minister had been unreachable while in a three-hour flight, and Shroff went ahead and took the unilateral decision to send his team to hunt down Hafeez. Once again, Shroff receives no objections, no questions. Clearly, then, the cop's actions, even without official approval, are in line with what the state already wants. The cop is the mechanism for pre-emptive promptness, not a vehicle for overcompensatory amendments against the state. He only hastens state operation. And because of his ability to anticipate the state's actions, even before the state knows that it needs to act, the state always emerges as efficient and successful at combating its enemies. The implicit subtext is that this is a new phenomenon: in 1993 they might not have been able to pre-empt the twelve bomb blasts in Bombay. But today, with Article 370 in place and the free rein given to the police, the state will not only rectify its past mistakes (for example, letting terrorists like Bilal Ahmad escape to Pakistan), but it will also halt new terroristic possibilities.

And this is because the state is willing to go that extra mile. They'll do whatever it takes: physical torture, psychological warfare, intimidation, humiliation of suspects. In each instance, state machinery encourages the police to both act before consent (by assuming its eventual arrival) and, where necessary, act without consent. So when Soorya tells his boss, Shroff, that the only way to get Kadar Osmani (another terrorist in India) to start talking is to "humiliate" him using an "unofficial" strategy, because beating and torturing him are not doing the trick to "break" him, Soorya gets exactly what he needs from him boss: a confirmation to go ahead. This authorization, however, is given without ever saying the word "yes." Instead, it comes in the form of a refusal to say "no." In response to Soorya's request for the license to violate the law, Shroff mock chides him: "Oh yes, like you've never done anything till now without my permission." Without a categorical "yes," Shroff lets Soorya know that the field of possibilities for dealing with terrorists is wide open, and that the state's endorsement to break rules can be tacitly assumed. Even more, the disregard for protocols protecting human rights is turned into an open secret and a matter of mirth; all the subordinates witnessing Shroff and Soorya's interaction snicker at this exchange between the two senior police officers. The shared joke operates at multiple levels: it testifies to collective humor at Soorya's pretense of seeking permission; at Shroff's fake irritation about Soorya not following rules; at the delicate balance performed in the routine of seeking and granting (un)official clearance; and at how in-step the two cops are even in the moment when they're discussing stepping out of line. They each know the role they need to play to sidestep the law together. There is no rift, only the smoothest continuum between the state, top-ranking police officers, their underlings, and the audience that is in on the joke.

But a successful moment of humor rests upon the exclusion of someone's body and subjecthood; the joke is predicated on someone's elimination from insider status and their consequent response of nonlaughter. Muslims do not laugh in *Sooryavanshi*. They are, instead, angry, taciturn, vengeful, and petulantly committed to watching "India burn." The film enacts a very different approach to the Muslim question than a film like *Gully Boy*. In the latter, the current "condition of Muslims" in India is tackled as a single throwaway sentence. Otherwise, the film steers clear of a commentary on national politics and the ascendency of Hindutva ideologies. *Sooryavanshi*, however, takes on the challenge of explicitly spelling out "*Musalmaano ka haal*" (the situation Muslims are in).

It does so, first and foremost, by leaving Muslims to tell their own story of trauma. Anti-Muslim riots never make it into the national narrative. The historical background relevant to the film begins with the violence endured by the country in 1993, with the Bombay bomb blasts, not with the post-Ayodhya riots in 1992, in which more than two thousand Muslims died in Bombay alone. The film enforces a jarring severing of two intimately connected moments of violence and insists on starting history where the political culpability of Islamic terrorists (and their sympathizers) begins. The film's historiography is fully aligned with a Hindutva timeline. What happened to Muslims during the riots is something that the Muslim terrorists are left to recount; the film, and the nation it depicts, have no interest in anything else.

In some ways, the film is rare for how unequivocally it lays bare the politics of associating terrorists and Muslims, a key political tactic used by the Hindu right to justify its Islamophobia and to intimidate and delegitimate Indian Muslims as political agents. When Soorya reaches the Muslim *mohalla* to arrest Kadar Osmani, a Lashkar and ISIS-supporting politico-religious leader, a Muslim crowd gathers to protest his arrest. Addressing a *maulvi* (Muslim priest), Soorya offers a litany of Osmani's crimes—misleading young boys in the name of religion and sending them off to Syria to fight for ISIS, etc.—as evidence for why his arrest is necessary. But the "dialogue" with the Muslim community, the willingness to address and engage them, and offer a detailed explanation for the police's actions, is not an exercise in assuaging people's unrest or their suspicion of the police. It is, rather, the segue to a threat: "If, after knowing all this [about Osmani], you still continue to support him, then the whole community can be blamed." Soorya categorically warns Muslims that they are themselves responsible for being labeled unpatriotic, antinational, and untrustworthy because of who they ally with. But that's not where the threat ends: if they don't comply, then "another 1993-type of situation can occur," and "neither you nor we want that," Soorya reminds them.

At the start of the film, Devgn's disembodied voice-over had left out any mention of the anti-Muslim riots of 1992 to cleave the country's suffering (because of the blasts) from the suffering Muslims underwent in the 1992 riots. In this instance, Soorya's evasion (of leaving out any mention of the riots) achieves a different end. The warning about history repeating itself ("*1993-jaisa mahaul*") cloaks an unspoken threat of anti-Muslim riots. No Muslim can remember the Bombay blasts without remembering the riots that preceded them. When Soorya mentions the blasts, the riots linger just under the surface of his words and return as phantasmagoric reminders of what Muslims should fear. Orchestrated riots: always denied, always deployed. Soorya's warning, however, goes yet a step further. He pleads with the *maulvi*, "as one Indian to another," to "let him do his job," otherwise he'll have to bring in the Central Reserve Police Force (CRPF), India's paramilitary force to manage internal national security. Tipping his hat to Muslims as compatriots just masks the final thread of the warning, that the federal state's coercive apparatus is at the cop's beck and call. Needless to say, the *maulvi* instructs the crowd to back down. Whether it's the fear of being branded a terrorist, attacked in a riot, or taken out by special armed forces is hard to say. But the subtle intensification of the pressure to relent is decidedly hard to miss or ignore.

The story of Muslim precarity is left to the meager and unreliable narrative capabilities of the "bad" Muslims, and, predictably, they come up short at convincing the audience (or the characters in the film) of the authenticity of Muslim vulnerability. The film works hard to present political grievances by Muslims as malicious distortions and exaggerations of the truth. So Osmani's words, "You know what the condition of Muslims in this country is?" are negated when a retired Muslim policeman, Naeem Khan (who just happens to be visiting the police station) reminds Osmani of his grubby origins: he was a petty thief before he donned the garb of a pious man. Osmani is, of course, shamed into silence by the "*tewar*" (temper) of real "*Hindustani Musalmaan.*"

Another tactic for disqualifying the validity of protest from Muslims is to suggest that their civil rights were never really violated. The "unofficial" technique of humiliation that Soorya uses to get Osmani to talk about his terroristic affiliations is to bring the latter's wife and daughter into the police station and pretend to torture them. They are taken into a room adjoining the one in which Osmani is strung from the ceiling, their mouths covered so that they can't make a sound, and two female police officers fake screams in response to the sound of pseudo-belt-lashes, to make Osmani believe that the women in his family are being tormented. There is no real damage and, therefore objections to police brutality against religious minorities are unwarranted.

In this scene too the film takes recourse to humor to dislodge attention from the horrific nature of what is transpiring on screen. Instead, we are pushed to laugh at the absurdity of the erotic, sexualized screams that the female cops produce. Soorya reprimands his women colleagues for confusing torture for "Kamasutra" and for not faking Muslimness convincingly enough: one of the women cops uses the Sanskritized word "*pitaji,*" instead of the Urdu word "*abboo,*" as she calls out to the "father" Osmani to save her. There is much to unpack here: The film's gender politics are obvious in its use of women to create sexual humor. And its gendered ethnonationalism is on display because it reinforces the normalcy of patriarchal protectionism; even a terrorist will succumb to the horror of his women relatives being violated. Or perhaps it suggests that Muslim men are especially susceptible to the pressures of wanting to protect their women's honor. The scene also articulates a subtle castigation of Urdu as a language associated with terrorists and with the griminess of fake torture and bad porn. Most critically, the scene of simulated torture is used to make us unsee real torture on screen: Osmani hanging by his arms from the ceiling of a prison cell, and his wife and daughter being gagged into silence. And it does the trick to falsify our memory of real-world ideologies and incidents in which the Hindu Right advocates and deploys the use of sexual and physical violence against Muslims.[81]

There is one exception, where the film grants an iota of sympathy for the distress that Muslims have endured. When the police catch up with Bilal Ahmad, who has returned from Pakistan to set in motion the next terrorist attack in India, he threatens to take his own life before being subjected to the ignominy of being hanged like a "spectacle." With his gun to the temple, he describes his motivation for turning to terrorism. He tells Soorya that his house was scorched and that his wife, children, and father were burned alive during the 1992 riots: "I still hear their screams twenty-seven years later." There does seem to exist a momentary possibility of empathy that the film allows the viewer to feel for Ahmad: we see the flashback sequences, which ostensibly stand in for glimpses of Ahmad's memory, of a mansion engulfed in flames. This visual assemblage, however, is distinctly minimalist compared to the long newsreel, archival footage we're shown every time bomb blasts by Islamic terrorists are brought up in the film. Then we see a sequential collage of photographs: collapsed buildings, chaos and catastrophe in public spaces, dead and injured bodies strewn everywhere. In contrast, the images of a burning house do not produce the same affective tenor. So even when there is a basic visual repertoire offered to produce sympathy for the victims of communal violence, it is no match for the hyperbolic cinematic arsenal through which the impact of terroristic violence is represented.

During the conversation, Soorya does acknowledge that "what happened" to Ahmad "was wrong." He even urges Ahmad to remember that India "*tumhara bhi hai*" (India is yours too). But these words of commiseration are sandwiched between strategies of dismissal that once again invalidate Ahmad's grief and anger. "What about the blasts you organized out of revenge?" is the first comeback that Ahmad receives from Soorya. "What happened with you was wrong, but you also took thousands of innocent lives." This rejoinder is particularly poignant because, as a young man, Soorya had lost both his parents in the blasts. "If I wanted," he continues, "I could take out all my anger [*bhadaas*] on you right now." And then comes the clincher: "But that time has passed" and Ahmad needs to forget, to move on: "*aage badhna hoga*."

Herein lies the film's ultimate treatise on the management of political discontent and psychological trauma because of sectarian state politics. The answer to terrorism lies in one's capacity to "move on," to repurpose trauma, as Soorya has done, toward the higher end of protecting the nation. Ahmad, and by extension the Muslim community's failure, lies in their inability to be entrepreneurial with their pain, in their incapacity to convert pain into productivity. This is the neoliberal spin on ethnonationalism. This idea is re-enlisted at the end of the film, when Simmba arrives on the scene (to give Soorya support in taking down the terrorists), and with his classic earthy humor reminds the terrorists that their activities hurt the economy, affect tourism, impact the entertainment, sports, and art industries.

If terrorism jeopardizes the smooth flow of capital, then the terrorist is the equivalent of a bad venture capitalist, who misrecognizes the sagacity of the avenues of his investment. Instead of devoting his energies in and to the nation, he detracts from the nation. He is unable to get over structural traumas and deal with them as individual familial loss. Rather than nationalizing his trauma, he insists on traumatizing the nation. The Muslim terrorist is thus the psychologically stunted, mentally unwell melancholic, brooding over the communal past, when the security state has opened up an exciting neoliberal future. The Ahmads, Osmanis, and Hafeezes refuse to enter the technofinancial global order that would free them from the oppressiveness of Muslimness and allow themselves to be, as Basu puts it, "subsumed and extinguished into an overall civic religiosity of neoliberal market structures."[82]

What this narrative does is to invent the Indian Muslim as "an entity that is at once pathological and infantile,"[83] and therefore, after all is said and done, pathetically ineffectual. In the same breath that the film collapses Muslim with terrorist, it also disassociates terrorists from the possibility of success. The Indian state and police, we learn, will always forestall political antagonism from religious minorities. The film reinforces the idea that any politics that is misaligned with ethnonationalist outcomes is doomed to self-combustion. This is why Ahmad unwittingly self-sabotages the terrorist plan by insisting on going to visit his mother's grave in Bombay, even though he is repeatedly warned against this kind of sentimental foolishness. Predictably, he is recognized at the graveyard, caught, and must take his own life. Thus, despite decades of "progressive underdevelopment, and disenfranchisement of entire Muslim communities,"[84] Muslims are deemed incapable of even proper, or properly terrifying militant political expression. As terrorists, they are not only devoid of good politics, they are devoid of politics altogether, or of a political future that is not entirely subsumed within a majoritarian nationalist paradigm. Without threatening nudges, reminders, and rejoinders from the Hindu cop, outdated traumas, foiled plans, and familial fixations are all they're capable of.

Ajay Gudavarthy argues that this narrative structure, in which the malfunction of Muslim unrest is always a given, always scripted into the story from its very inception, offers audiences "many comforts," especially when neoliberal reforms have expanded the realm of uncertainty and insecurity in everyday life.[85] The predictability of these narratives is premised on the knowledge that Muslims are the "safest enemies to have in India": they are a numerical minority (only 15 percent of the nation's population, while Hindus constitute 80 percent of India), socially backward, and economically marginalized. And yet positing Muslims as the stable, unified enemy allows an authoritarian populist state, and its cultural texts, to generate a unified Hindu identity that can forever exist in a quasi-panicked, quasi-celebratory state, fearful of Muslims but rejoicing in their guaranteed vanquishment. In the end, what this produces is a cinematic universe in which all erstwhile idealism of communal harmony, even if it only once existed at the discursive-cultural-cinematic realm, is permanently laid to rest. What is normalized, in lieu of it, is a popular politics of pragmatism:

> From an imagination of overcoming conflict, we are reconciled to the fact that conflict is an everyday reality and that we will live with these conflicts for a long time to come. . . . The state that was forced to speak a social democratic language now, under populist regimes, has given voice to the views that we used to hold all through only in the private realm. The state has also accepted that conflicts are going to stay unsolved to become our lived reality.[86]

In this scenario, the cop, as a state functionary, becomes *the* vehicle of pragmatism. He brings a middle-class Hindutva drawing-room version of politics out into the open, embodies and encourages a rampant disregard for a politics of justice or equity, and moves to evacuate a politics born out of disenfranchisement and suffering to kneel at the altar of an impervious state, or worse, a state that is proactively vindictive.

Epilogue

America Ferrera's iconic speech "It is literally impossible to be a woman," in Greta Gerwig's blockbuster summer 2023 hit *Barbie* opened floodgates in popular culture conversations, in the United States and around the globe, about the inordinate and contradictory pressures that operate on women to embody a stable, satisfying, and palatable femininity. Women, Ferrera's character Gloria tells us, are condemned to inhabit liminal and untenable spaces. Their relationship to their bodies, behavior, and emotions; to power, money, professional and maternal identity; to their sexuality; to other women and to men, are all organized around the expectation to walk an impossibly thin line and any inevitable wavering is subject to harsh castigation. This "rigged system" is not even something women are allowed to complain about. Critically, what Ferrera's speech leaves unnamed is the "system" itself that produces this perpetual state of vulnerability for women. Although patriarchy is the automatically assumed culprit, her list of grievances, as our book has shown, are better understood through the conjunction between patriarchy, capitalism, and neoliberal (white) feminism that the speech strategically eclipses, all systems that, in fact, coalesce in Barbie as commodity, Barbie as a "doll just representing women," and *Barbie* as film that champions both capitalist commodity fetishism and a confident arrogance about its ability to compositely "represent" all women. Thus, in a predictable legerdemain, the film converts an embodiment of privilege (white, thin, blonde, hyperfeminine woman) to stand in for a broad swathe of diversity in femininity. The film's encouragement of the shift from *Barbie* (a singularity) to *Barbies* (an embracing of plurality) seemingly accommodates the idea of Barbie as something that can endlessly proliferate to encompass every type of woman (Black, Brown, sexy, butch, grungy, presidential, aeronautical etc. etc.). But this move really masks something else that is important to note: the film promotes the encapsulation and distillation of all difference into a marketable brand. It distracts attention away from the Western white "OG" template of femininity as a site of privilege and often as source of oppression for several other demographic identities, and it offers a multicultural celebration of *all* women, who are all, as it turns out, ultimately one, a commodity marketed and sold for profit. The film's solution, then, is not much different from the problem Ferrera was identifying to begin with. In having a Brown, Latina actor/character make this speech in defense of women's rights, but really in defense of everything that Barbie represents (even with an all-inclusive do-over), the film tries to reconcile yet another impossibility.

In this global order, progressive politics (of feminism, for instance, as in the case of Ferrera's speech), hijacked by neoliberal identity politics and self-administering solutions, thrive alongside a resurgence of regressive, neoconservative, embittered, extremist, masculinist, and authoritarian politics. The banal violence and mediocrity of this latter political tendency is profoundly captured in a particular scene from a Bollywood film *Pati Patni Aur Woh* (2019; Husband, Wife, and Her). Notably, the scene's adjacency to Ferrera's speech produces an uncanny effect. The lament of the main character, Chintu Tyagi, about the difficulties facing the ordinary middle-class Indian man (read Hindu, upper-caste) operates with the same mechanics as Ferrera's speech: a listing of the "arenas of impossibility" that men must traverse:

> Who am I? I am a middle-class Indian man. The Indian middle-class male. So, whether I get sunstroke or loose motions [diarrhea], no one gives a damn. I am the unfortunate bull that toils all day and yet sometimes goes to sleep with no results. If I show some concern for my mom, the wife calls me a mamma's boy. If I show some affection to my wife, then in my mother's eyes, I'm a henpecked husband. If I move to a big city, I destroy tradition. And if I stay back in a small town then I'm the enemy of development. If I pay my taxes honestly then I'm broke. And if I don't pay them, I'm a thief. If my wife works, I am an opportunist. If she doesn't work and sits at home then I'm sexist. If I ask my wife for sex, then I'm a beggar. If I turn down my wife for sex then I'm a persecutor. And if I find my way into somehow having sex with her, then I'm a person with bad morals.

So much of Tyagi's (Kartik Aaryan) frustrated vent session with his closest friend Fahim Rizvi (Aparshakti Khurana) categorically focuses on women and their refusal to be satisfied or appreciative of men's drudgerous efforts. Mothers and wives are the primary cause of his grievances, making endless material and emotional demands on his time, wallet, and sanity. Tyagi's speech follows from a scene in which his wife complains about their mediocre life in a small town ("We are made for the clubs and restaurants of Delhi, not the cantonment of Kanpur"), demanding a more ambitious and go-getting spirit from her husband. This sequencing further fixes women and their limitless and impossible-to-meet standards as the source of tension in men's harried lives.

Counterposing Ferrera's and Tyagi's speeches helps us register the overlaps in the narrative strategies operating in global discourses and in India's domestic preoccupations. It also allows us to recognize the copresence of neoliberal logics with a neoconservative turn (in this case, men's-rights-type politics). We have elaborated on both these elements throughout this book. What is also common to the two speeches is that privilege masquerades as disempowerment. Here a distractive politics of *ressentiment* overtakes reality, thus allowing a Hindu, Brahmin, middle-class man to articulate a politics of subalternity, no less to his truly precarious interlocutor, his Muslim friend Fahim. In a frightening scene toward the end of the film, in what is treated as a moment of levity set up to tickle the audience, a policeman threatens to "encounter" Fahim if he continues his antics (expectedly, his friend Tyagi, who is the real instigator of the antics, is not subjected to the same intimidation).

We also want to draw attention to how Tyagi's speech mishmashes complex and deeply political, public questions into purely interpersonal ones (his speech is really about trying to legitimate his desire to commit adultery). Class, labor, alienation, urban migrancy, taxes (all associated with the big questions that confront men) are treated as sites of interpersonal frustration rather than as domains of interjection and imposition by the political economy. The ethical and legal implications in marital rape are evacuated and replaced by the anxiety of being accused of having "bad morals." Even the total personalization of political, public questions doesn't lead to a heightened or improved commitment to relationality. Instead, the masculine and misogynistic fortifies itself into a solipsistic centrality; all others (particularly women) are treated as impingements to its happiness and success. Tyagi adamantly avoids framing his complaints as political critiques. He weaponizes his disgruntlement into a distorted victimhood and severs the possibility of compassion or empathy for the other. His rant mishmashes all-too-common middle-class banalities about the defunct "state of affairs today" with sexual entitlements that are reminiscent of an incel rationality. Although a comic variant, Chintu Tyagi and his casually Islamophobic milieu fit in perfectly with the more toxically masculinist, vengeful, and hyperxenophobic worlds represented by the men in Sandeep Reddy Vanga's films *Kabir Singh* (2019) and *Animal* (2023).

The central aim of this project has been to explore how Hindi language cinema of the past two decades or so has grappled with a complex national conjuncture in which neoliberalism and Hindutva work in tandem, bringing their divergent narratives into resonance with one another. Reading these together has enabled us to observe that their ostensibly accidental overlaps are, in fact, strategic convergences that orchestrate and yield a shared, mutually beneficial, and predatory politics of precarity. This "cinema of precarity," in the Indian context, offers a strikingly different set of interpretive, affective, and political interventions from those found in postliberalization films of the 1990s and early 2000s. Each chapter of the book focuses on some dimension of the techniques by which the vulnerabilities and aspirations produced under one regime often function as mobilizing grounds for the other.

In a key methodological commitment to tracing repetition, as trope and as mode of analysis, we trace over and over again the insidious maneuvers by which aspirations and their failures, in love, enterprise, spatiality, identity, and politics, are weaponized by the politics of Hindu nationalism. In doing so, we surface the affective foundations of contemporary India's authoritarian populism and religiously right-wing politics. The attention to repetition also reveals Hindi cinema's relationship to precarity as a frustration-inducing condition, something that requires an ad nauseum revisitation in the hope of finding an out from an untenable situation. Simultaneously it exposes the lure of the myths dangled by neoliberalism and majoritarian politics. In replaying and repeating these myths as the solution, the films also participate in the re-entrenchment and reproduction of a cruel optimism. The films overprescribe the givenness of the world as is (there is no alternative), encourage impossible-to-attain promises for the self to thrive, distort one's relationship to the other, and create a disinvestment in collective aspirations for a democratic and just world. We spend time analyzing, with a critically compassionate lens, the various agents—individuals, institutions, and the state—who instigate, perpetuate, or resist neoliberal Hindutva. Our interest has been both in the material and the emotive infrastructures of precarity, its structural processes and its methods of subjectivization. This analysis has enabled us to unfurl other difficult questions: Who benefits (in fantasy and in reality) from this state of precarity? Or who (all) does the cinema of precarity serve and how?

In some ways, Shah Rukh Khan's 2023 blockbuster *Pathaan* offers an ineluctable evidencing of our book's central argument: Hindi cinema today reveals a foundational paucity in imagining and articulating a nonprecarious world. Even when the films are critical of the exploitations under neoliberalism or the violence of majoritarian identity politics, even when they hark back to older templates of cinematic progressivism, they end up reinscribing structures that further cement precarious conditions for the poor, religious minorities, and neighboring nationalities. Furthermore, *Pathaan* compels a particularly unsettling dimension of the silences and censorships induced under neoliberal Hindutva. The film encapsulates to a heightened degree the shifts in the nature and scope of cinema as social critique and political intervention in the age of popular authoritarianism.

The near-euphoric affective and political investment in *Pathaan* and its paratexts is impossible to explain outside the context of the thanatotic violence that characterizes Modi's India. So many commentaries testified to how the film's frantic pace, plot twists, aesthetic lushness, global flow, and moments of sexual, secular, jocular irreverence felt like a thunderbolt, punctuating the morbid avalanche of crises that has engulfed India's past decade. As we discuss in the first chapter, this continual barrage and routinization of manufactured catastrophes is what Berlant has called a state of "crisis ordinariness," which in India is unmitigatedly part and parcel of the current government's ethnonationalist Hindutva project. In this scenario, *Pathaan* seemed to tap into a widespread visceral, even if inchoate, desire to experience something—anything—that wasn't hijacked by the terror of an exclusionary, intimidating state. Its seemingly old-world, secular nationalist worldview felt like an antidote, a reprieve effect, holding out permission to its viewers not only to be unabashedly entertained, but also to entertain something other than the fear, uncertainty, and vulnerability experienced by millions suffering under the hegemony of sectarian politics.

Pathaan's release and reception within this larger setting of precariousness—for religious minorities, the future of the film industry, and for SRK's own star text—all of which the film manifests and manages, is why we read it as an instantiation of postmillennial Bollywood's "cinema of precarity." It is understandable, particularly in India's current censorial political climate, why *Pathaan*'s subtle jabs against authoritarianism, jingoistic nationalism, and communal ideologies make it an unusual and innovative cinematic and political intervention, despite its cliché genre elements. And yet, in keeping with the limitations of mainstream Bollywood's engagement with neoliberal Hindutva, the film's diagnosis of what needs intervention is inadequate, and its interventionist apparatus is counterproductive. It uses all the accoutrements of a neoliberal image economy (think globetrotting mobility, jet-setting lifestyles, glitzy hotels, sexy bodies, monster automobiles) and the neocolonial "big-brother" rationality of a hypermilitarized, surveillance-driven, paranoid security state to make an argument about religious tolerance and a nationalism grounded in compassion.

The contradiction aside, what we want to draw attention to is the film's political imagination, which, unlike what others have suggested, we do not see as a harking back to some 1950s–1960s benign nationalism (if there ever was such a thing at all). On the contrary, *Pathaan*'s world is very much a postliberalization, post-Pokhran universe, in which a flexing Indian state sits resolutely in the global superpower hot seat. The film objects only to the distortions caused to this aspirational fantasy by what Hindutva does to its domestic minorities (of course Kashmiri Muslims are exempt even from this objection). The film, then, asks us to participate in an illusion captured by this equation: Nuclear power nation + neoliberal economy – Hindutva = good nationalism or nationalism for all. And what is so disingenuous about this fantasy equation is that for a film that is so self-aware about its cinematic legacy, history, and present-day state of politics, it ignores that there is no such thing, and never has been in India, a postliberalization history divorced from Hindutva politics. In fact, the trajectories of the two have been intertwined from the get-go; they literally and discursively cocreated and sanctioned one other, in fact using Bollywood to inseparably nestle the two together in the nation's collective consciousness. Unlike aging superstars, who can make dramatic comebacks, there can be no "comeback" of a template of nationalism that never existed to begin with.

SRK's postrelease press conference, in which he compared Deepika Padukone, himself, and John Abraham to the iconic Amar, Akbar, and Anthony, doubled down on the nostalgic allure of a less toxic, secular nationalism. In the analogy, the three real-life actors become champions, embodying and renewing the cinematic promise of religious compatriotism encapsulated in Manmohan Desai's film *Amar Akbar Anthony* from the late 1970s. But nostalgia is a perilous journey. Despite the radical potential of this avowal, we want to draw attention to two factors that reveal something rotten and inadequate at the heart of the analogy, both in terms of what the analogy says about *Pathaan*'s engagement with present-day realities, and the idyllic myth of secular India constructed by Bollywood. While it is true that a Hindu star actor (Deepika) is involved in this brave cinematic trespass against Hindutva ideology, it is also telling that Hindu main characters are almost entirely absent from the screen. In the fictional worlds that *Pathaan* conjures, it is narratologically and politically too dicey to write proactive Hindu characters who are committed participants in the project of rebuilding a secular India. The screen, it seems, can no longer accommodate such characters or commitments. This risky work on the screen must be left to religious minorities. SRK's invocation of Desai's film obfuscates this strategic maneuvering that frankly allows *Pathaan*, the film, to exist and circulate in the world, and governs its script, plot, and the identities of the characters who execute it.

But there is an even deeper crisis at the heart of the promise that *Amar Akbar Anthony* held out, even fifty years ago. It is that the three main characters from diverse religious identities are, in the end, in the last instance, at their point of origin, all Hindus by birth. The film's secular world, then, is really an assimilationist fantasy, even if a particularly delightful and gentle one. This logic relies on the slippery, tacit conflation between "we are all one because we are all Indian," with "we are all one because we are all [ultimately] Hindu." We cannot forget that the other end of spectrum of this benign fantasy is the RSS vision of the nation, which, as the Mohan Bhagwat tells us, is achievable through the "Ghar Wapsi" project: to reconvert and reclaim all non-Hindus back into the fold of Hinduism. Pathaan's origin story—that he was an orphan left at the steps of a cinema hall, reclaimed, and renamed by his adoptive Afghani mother—when reread through this (we'll admit) ungenerous light, begins to occupy an unstable pedestal. It functions, then, less as a defense of difference, for Hindus and Muslim alike, to the right to life, dignity, and citizenship, and becomes more an insistence on sameness that is distilled down to the normative as the basis for those rights. Instead of a radical move, Pathaan's orphanhood becomes a subliminal placative exchange. The skeptics can accept Pathaan as heroic, not because he is Muslim, but because he may not, after all, be Muslim at all. Beneath his Afghani appellation may lie a Hindu origin story. Awkwardly, then, in the very process of normalizing the idea of nationalist Muslims, the film ends up performing and participating in an insidious correlation.

This is why we think that *Pathaan* undoes so much of what it hopes to achieve. We're inviting and initiating an analysis of the film that isn't caught between a wide-eyed celebration of the film or an angry dismissal of its betrayals, though perhaps the film deserves both. Instead, in reading the film as an example of "cinema of precarity" we are identifying its structures of resistance and exploring the reasons for why they amount to so little. As we have argued in this book, one of the things we find in common in films of the past decade is that, for the most part, they are strident articulations of precarities that define the present—whether real or imagined—but are unable to offer radical or realizable solutions or exits out of them, even as they scramble for those solutions. This capacity to name the precarious present without laying a stake or direction for a secure future, is a characteristic defining feature of the "cinema of precarity."

There is, however, one exception to this broad-scale tendency that we identify: something different happens when it comes to the Muslim story. Let's pose this differently: How does *Pathaan* tackle or forward the long-standing "Muslim question" that has haunted popular Hindi cinema since Independence? As we have discussed in chapter 3, so many scholars—Ira Bhaskar and Richard Allen, Kalyani Chadha and Anandam Kavoori, Anand Vivek Taneja, Mukul Kesavan, Fareed Kazmi, Maidul Islam, and Aravind Unni, among others—have tracked Bombay cinema's changing relationship to the "Muslim question." They have traced the Islamicate cultures and roots of Hindi cinema, parsed through the many tropes of Muslimness, and unraveled the structures of marginalization that Muslims and the spaces of their inhabitancy are subjected to onscreen. *Pathaan*, we argue, along with films like *Gully Boy*, marks a new milestone in the history of the "Muslim question." These films create sympathy for and investment in male Muslim protagonists, and even grant them freedom from terroristic determinism (which, we know, has regulated so much of the Muslim presence in contemporary Hindi films). But these films are unable to really name the wider political precarization of Muslims in India. Which raises another question: How do we engage and resist the thing we do not name?

In chapter 3, we demonstrated how *Gully Boy*, in the name of "normalizing" its Muslim characters, de-exceptionalizes what is in fact a new moment in Indian polity of the state's explicit adoption of a Hindutva-promoting agenda and its active flaming of anti-Muslim sentiment. In *Pathaan*, too, the perils of nostalgia, we identified earlier, work hand in hand with what we might call "liability of unnaming," this new tendency in even progressive films to leave unnamed the politics of Hindutva, against which they hope to posit new ways of knowing, being, and believing. So what happens to the purported politics of *Pathaan* when it refuses to categorically name the ideological enemy it contests?

Just to clarify, we understand these films' survival strategy of leaving unnamed the authoritarian, fascistic politics they counter. But we think it is just as important to explore the repercussions of this unnaming. For one, it immaterializes the Muslim question. The fanaticism of Islamophobia looms large; it becomes the ether, the air the films breathe, and it functions as the atmosphere in which they are produced, to which they respond. But the atmosphere does not manifest in a corresponding material reality onscreen. It is a secret that dictates so much of how these films congeal, but no one can speak it. This produces a sense of *impresence*, a contestation of ideas and worldviews conjured through invocations, hints, jokes, and gestures, without reference to the concrete stake anchored in the material consequences that the anti-Muslimness of BJP's India produces. We won't go into this here in an extended way, but there is a connection to be made between this larger immaterialization of Muslim precarity and the way in which Kashmir and the abrogation of Article 377 is reduced, or immaterialized, to a plot point.

To be clear, within contemporary cinematic oeuvre, not everything difficult and challenging in today's India is subject to this etherization. For instance, many films do name and show the exacerbation of inequities along class, caste, and gender lines, along rural, periurban, and urban divides. SRK's *Jawan* (Soldier, Atlee Kumar, 2023), for instance, which has shot past *Pathaan*'s box office numbers, itself does a remarkable job of emphatically addressing the unequal distribution of wealth, the exploitation in debt economies, the corruption in public health care, the grotesque workings of crony capitalism, all matters that hit close to home for the current political dispensation. But the Muslim question is decidedly missing from the long litany of economic and social issues that *Jawan* addresses head-on. And so we find ourselves in this bizarre situation where on the one hand, *Pathaan*, the film that is invested in the reconstruction of a secular India, cannot name the context that produces the high urgency for the project, and on the other we have *Jawaan*, which can name so many ills of the present moment but steers clear of addressing Hindutva Islamophobia as one of them. The result, then, is that there is no film able to venture an account of the coproduction of anti-Muslimness and dysfunctions of a neoliberal state. Or, to put it another way, perhaps *Pathaan* allows us to register the limits of neoliberal stardom as an adequate foil to religious authoritarianism.

The film, even in its apparent political risk taking, is a testament of what happens to culture and cultural artifacts when neoliberal precarity is hijacked by strident religious authoritarianism. We conclude with our reading of *Pathaan* to demonstrate what in India today are the sharp limits of what can and cannot be said, to show the fixities of representational stereotypes even when films attempt to expand and problematize them, and to acknowledge that the "Muslim question," perhaps more than any other social problem, marks the hard boundaries that remain the toughest to engage and navigate in Modi's India. As the country enters a third electoral term under his leadership in 2024, we anticipate that this will continue to be a central question that will haunt the fate and future of the nation.

14. Henry Giroux, "The Terror of Neoliberalism: Rethinking the Significance of Cultural Politics," *College Literature* 32, no. 1 (Winter 2005): 1–19.

15. Pramod K. Nayar, "Mobility and Insurgent Celebrityhood: The Case of Arundhati Roy," *Open Cultural Studies* (2017): 47; and "Purity, Precarity, and Power: Prayaag Akbar's *Leila*," in *Representations of Precarity in South Asian Literature in English*, ed. Om Prakash Dwivedi (Cham, Switzerland: Palgrave Macmillan, 2022), 145.

16. Francesco Sticchi, *Mapping Precarity in Contemporary Cinema and Television* (New York: Palgrave Macmillan 2021), 4.

17. Sticchi, *Mapping Precarity*, 5.

18. Samanth Subramanian, "When the Hindu Right Came for Bollywood," *New Yorker*, October 17, 2022.

19. Isabelle Lorey, *State of Insecurity: Government of the Precarious*, trans. Aileen Derieg, with a foreword by Judith Butler (New York: Verso, 2015), 6.

20. Berlant, *Cruel Optimism*, 198.

21. Lisa Rofel, *Desiring China: Experiments in Neoliberalism, Sexuality, and Public Culture* (Durham, NC: Duke University Press, 2007), 15.

22. See Vassilis Tsianos and Dimitris Papadopoulos, "Precarity: A Savage Journey to the Heart of Embodied Capitalism," *Transversal* (October 2006).

23. Judith Butler, *Precarious Life: The Powers of Mourning and Violence* (London: Verso, 2004).

24. Butler, *Precarious Life*, 18–21.

25. Butler, *Precarious Life*, 7.

26. Jan Bremen, "A Bogus Concept?" *New Left Review* 84 (Nov/Dec 2013).

27. Since the eighteenth century, the entrenchment of capitalism as the authoritative regime, and its corresponding bourgeois-liberal hegemony, have yielded an unprecedented commodification of the natural environment (land) and human society (labor), dictating that self-interest emerge as the guiding principle of the laissez-faire doctrine. Crucially, the success of this epistemic shift required self-governing from each individual. Building on Michel Foucault's theorization of biopolitics, Lorey (*State of Insecurity*) writes that Western man had to "learn to develop a relation to himself that is creative and productive, one in which it is possible to shape one's 'own' body, life and self, and thus also one's 'own' precariousness" (26). Thus the management of capitalism's wide-ranging dispersal of precarity is turned into an individualized concern. As Lorey astutely observes, these techniques of self-governance not only do the work of mythologizing "possessive individualism" (in the way that Macpherson uses it) and strengthening "fantasies of mastering one's 'own' precariousness," they also segregate us and dissolve our ties to others (38).

28. Lorey, *State of Insecurity*, 38.

29. Jonathan Parry, "Introduction: Precarity, Class, and the Neoliberal Subject," in *Industrial Labor on the Margins of Capitalism*, ed. Chris Haan and Jonathan Parry (New York: Berghahn Books, 2018), 2.

30. Eva Mazierska, ed. *Work in Cinema: Labor and the Human Condition* (New York: Palgrave Macmillan, 2013), 9.

31. Richard Seymour, "We Are All Precarious: On the Concept of the Precariat and its Misuses," *Patreon*, June 5, 2020, https://www.patreon.com/posts/we-are-all-on-of-37918050

32. Lorey, *State of Insecurity*, 39.

33. Herbert Marcuse, *One Dimensional Man* (London: Routledge and Kegan Paul, 1964).

34. Parry, "Introduction: Precarity, Class, and the Neoliberal Subject," 3.

35. Berlant, *Cruel Optimism*, 192.

36. Brett Neilson and Ned Rossiter, "From Precarity to Precariousness and Back Again: Labour, Life, and Unstable Networks," *Variant* 25 (Spring 2006): 10.

37. Randy Martin, *The Financialization of Daily Life* (Philadelphia: Temple University Press, 2002).

38. Sticchi, *Mapping Precarity*, 10.

39. See Carlo Vercellone and Alfonso Giuliani, "An Introduction to Cognitive Capitalism: A Marxist Approach," in *Cognitive Capitalism, Welfare and Labour: The Commonfare Hypothesis*, ed. Andrea Fumagalli, Alfonso Giuliani, Stefano Lucarelli, and Carlo Vercellone (Abingdon: Routledge, 2019), 13, 23.

40. Kapur and Wagner, *Neoliberalism and Global Cinema.*

41. David Harvey, *A Brief History of Neoliberalism* (New York: Oxford University Press, 2007).

42. Jean-Claude Barbier, "A Comparative Analysis of 'Employment Precariousness' in Europe," paper presented at the Economic and Social Research Council's seminar, "Learning from Employment and Welfare Policies in Europe," Paris, March 15, 2004, http://www.cee-recherche.fr

43. Parry, "Introduction: Precarity, Class, and the Neoliberal Subject," 3.

44. Lorey, *State of Insecurity*, 11.

45. Seymour, "We Are All Precarious," n.p.

46. See Gilles Deleuze and Félix Guattari, *A Thousand Plateaus: Capitalism and Schizophrenia*, translation and foreword by B. Massumi (Minneapolis: University of Minnesota Press, 2005), 492; and Félix Guattari, *The Three Ecologies*, translated by I. Pindar and P. Sutton (London: The Athlone Press, 2000).

47. Ritu Vij, "The Global Subject of Precarity," *Globalizations* 16, no. 4 (2019): 510.

48. Sticchi, *Mapping Precarity*, 11.

49. Seymour, "We Are All Precarious," n.p.

50. Guy Standing, *The Precariat: The New Dangerous Class* (London: Bloomsbury, 2011), 9, 12.

51. Parry, "Introduction: Precarity, Class, and the Neoliberal Subject," 29.

52. Parry, "Introduction: Precarity, Class, and the Neoliberal Subject," 29.

53. Sticchi, *Mapping Precarity*, 10.

54. Parry, "Introduction: Precarity, Class, and the Neoliberal Subject," 16.

55. Frederic Jameson, "Future City," *New Left Review* 21 (May-June 2003), http://newleftreview.org/II/21/fredric-jameson-future-city

56. Wendy Larner, cited in Nandini Gooptu, ed., *Enterprise Culture in Neoliberal India: Studies in Youth, Class, Work, and Media* (London: Routledge, 2013).

57. Henry A. Giroux, "Protesting Youth in an Age of Neoliberal Savagery," *E-International Relations*, May 20, 2014, https://www.e-ir.info/2014/05/20/protesting-youth-in-an-age-of-neoliberal-savagery/

58. J. Gilbert, "What Kind of Thing Is 'Neoliberalism'? *New Formations: A Journal of Culture/Theory/Politics* 80, no. 80 (2013), cited in Jeremy Vachet, *Fantasy, Neoliberalism and Precariousness: Coping Strategies in the Cultural Industries* (Bingley, UK: Emerald Group Publishing, 2022), 10.

59. Byung-Chul Han, "Why Revolution Is No Longer Possible," *Our World*, November 3, 2015, https://ourworld.unu.edu/en/why-revolution-is-no-longer-possible

60. Giroux, "Protesting Youth in an Age of Neoliberal Savagery."

61. Standing, *The Precariat.*

62. Martin Bak Jørgensen, "Precariat—What It Is and Isn't–Towards an Understanding of What It Does," *Critical Sociology* 42, no. 7–8 (2015): 959–74.

63. Michael Hardt and Antonio Negri, Declaration (Argo-Navis, 2012), 29.

64. Hardt and Negri, Declaration, 103.

65. Sarah Jaffee, "Post-Occupied," *Truthout*, May 19, 2014, https://truthout.org/articles/post-occupied/

66. Stanley Aronowitz, "Where Is the Outrage?" *Situations* 5, no. 2 (2011): 26.

67. Anton Jager and Arthur Borriello, "Is Left Populism the Solution," *Jacobin* (2019).

68. Colin Barker, Gareth Dale, and Neil Davidson, *Revolutionary Rehearsals in the Neoliberal Age* (Chicago: Haymarket Books, 2021).

69. For a critique of Standing's work from the view of the Global South, see Ritu Vij, "The Global Subject of Precarity," *Globalizations* 16, no. 4 (2019): 506–24.

70. Standing, *The Precariat*, 1.

71. Standing, *The Precariat*, 7–8.

72. Standing, *The Precariat*, 13

73. Standing, *The Precariat*, 24–25.

74. Standing, *The Precariat*, 10.

75. Standing, *The Precariat*, 24.

76. Standing, *The Precariat*, 131.

77. Standing, *The Precariat*, 17.

78. Lorey, *State of Insecurity*, 2.

79. Lorey, *State of Insecurity*, viii.

80. Lorey, *State of Insecurity*, 26.

81. Lorey, *State of Insecurity*, 70.

82. Lorey, *State of Insecurity*, 26.

83. Rebecca Prentice, "From Dispossessed Factory Workers to 'Micro-entrepreneurs': The Precariousness of Employment in Trinidad's Garment Sector," in *Industrial Labor at the Margins*, ed. Chris Hann and Jonathan Parry (New York: Berghahn Books, 2018).

84. Judith Butler, "'What would it mean to think that thought?': The Era of Lauren Berlant," *The Nation*, July 8, 2021, https://www.thenation.com/article/culture/lauren-berlant-obituary/

85. Giorgio Agamben, *The Coming Community*, trans. Michael Hardt (Minneapolis: University of Minnesota Press, 1993), 64–66.

86. Agamben, *The Coming Community*, 192.

87. Berlant, *Cruel Optimism*, 1.

88. Berlant, *Cruel Optimism*, 10.

89. Herbert Marcuse, "Aggressiveness in Advanced Industrial Society," in *Negations: Essays in Critical Theory* (Boston: Beacon Press, 1968), 256.

90. Berlant, *Cruel Optimism*, 11.

91. Berlant, *Cruel Optimism*, 199.

92. Butler, *Precarious Life*, xii.

93. Butler, *Precarious Life*, xiv.

94. Butler, *Precarious Life*, 20.

95. Butler, *Precarious Life*, 26.

96. Butler, *Precarious Life*, 20.

97. Butler, in Jasbir Puar, "Precarity Talk: A Virtual Roundtable with Lauren Berlant, Judith Butler, Bojana Cvejić, Isabell Lorey, Jasbir Puar, and Ana Vujanović," *TDR* 56, no. 4 (Winter 2012), Precarity and Performance: Special Consortium Issue, 163–77.

98. Butler in Puar, "Precarity Talk," 173.

99. For this section, we draw upon our previously published works, Megha Anwer and Anupama Arora, eds., *Bollywood's New Woman: Liberalization, Liberation, and Contested Bodies* (New Brunswick, NJ: Rutgers University Press, 2021); and "Of Women, Gay Men, and Dead Cats: The Precarity of Neoliberal Aspirations," *Critical South Asian Studies* (forthcoming *Critical South Asian Studies*, 2023).

100. Raka Ray and Amita Baviskar, eds., *Elite and Everyman: The Cultural Politics of the Indian Middle Classes* (New Delhi: Routledge, 2020), 2.

101. Leela Fernandes, "Rethinking Globalization: Gender and the Nation in India," in *Feminist Locations: Global and Local, Theory and Practice*, ed. Marianne de Koven (New Brunswick, NJ: Rutgers University Press, 2001), 147–67; and Rupal Oza, *The Making of Neoliberal India: Nationalism, Gender, and the Paradoxes of Globalization* (New York: Routledge, 2006).

102. Rajni Kothari, *Growing Amnesia: An Essay on Poverty and the Human Consciousness* (Delhi: Viking, 1993).

103. Ray and Baviskar, *Elite and Everyman*, 3.

104. Jyotsna Kapur, "An 'Arranged Love' Marriage: India's Neoliberal Turn and the Bollywood Wedding Culture Industry," *Communication, Culture & Critique* 2, no. 2 (2009), 232.

105. Anwer and Arora, *Bollywood's New Woman*.

106. Meheli Sen, "'It's all about loving your parents': Liberalization, Hindutva and Bollywood's New Fathers," in *Bollywood and Globalization*, ed. Rini Bhattacharya Mehta et al. (London: Anthem Press, 2010), 146.

107. Ashish Rajadhyaksha, "The 'Bollywoodization' of the Indian Cinema: Cultural Nationalism in a Global Arena," *Inter-Asia Cultural Studies* 4, no. 1 (2003): 32.

108. Šarūnas Paunksnis, *Dark Fear, Eerie Cities: New Hindi Cinema in Neoliberal India* (New Delhi: Oxford University Press, 2019), 8–9.

109. For a brief discussion of the relationship between the Indian state and cinema till the 1990s, see Tejaswini Ganti, *Bollywood: A Guidebook to Popular Hindi Cinema* 2nd edition (NY: Routledge 2013), 22–36.

110. Rajadhyaksha, "The 'Bollywoodization' of the Indian Cinema."

111. Tejaswini Ganti, *Producing Bollywood: Inside the Contemporary Hindi Film Industry* (Durham, NC: Duke University Press, 2012), 4.

112. Gopal, *Conjugations*.

113. Tejaswini Ganti points out that, "It is no surprise that it was a BJP government that granted industry status since the party's support base is heavily drawn from petty traders and small businessmen who comprise the vast distribution, exhibition, and finance apparatus for Hindi filmmaking." Tejaswini Ganti, *Bollywood: A Guidebook to Popular Hindi Cinema* 1st edition (New York: Routledge 2004), 51.

114. Monika Mehta, "Globalizing Bombay Cinema: Reproducing the Indian State

and Family," *Cultural Dynamics* 17, no. 2 (2005): 135–54; Meheli Sen (2010); Roshni Sengupta, "From Nationalism to Hindutva: Bollywood and the Makings of the Hindu Diasporic Woman," in *Shifting Transnational Bonding in Indian Diaspora*, ed. Ruben Gowricharn (New York: Routledge, 2020).

115. Mehta, "Globalizing Bombay Cinema," 142.

116. See Vanita Shastri, "The Politics of Economic Liberalization in India," *Contemporary South Asia* 6, no. 1 (1997). The percentage of people living below the poverty line went from a bit more than 50 percent in 1977 to less than 23 percent in 2004.

117. Ajay Gudavarthy, *India After Modi: Populism and the Right* (New Delhi: Bloomsbury India, 2021).

118. Jisha Menon, *Brutal Beauty: Aesthetics and Aspiration in Urban India* (Evanston, IL: Northwestern University Press, 2021), 6.

119. Christophe Jaffrelot notes that "The 'saffronisation' of the public sphere finds expression in many different ways [. . .] the beef ban, new laws against conversion, the use of 'Bharat' instead of 'India' and the chanting of Bharat Mata ki Jai (if you don't you're 'anti-national'), because of the 'Hinduisation' of the names of streets and villages, because also of the rewriting of history textbooks and the public articulation of beliefs presented as scientific because they emerge from Hindu antiquity." Edward Anderson and Christophe Jaffrelot, "Hindu Nationalism and the 'Saffronisation of the Public Sphere': An interview with Christophe Jaffrelot," *Contemporary South Asia* 26, no. 4 (2018): 479.

120. Edward Anderson and Arkotong Longkumer, "'Neo-Hindutva': Evolving Forms, Spaces, and Expressions of Hindu Nationalism," *Contemporary South Asia* 26, no. 4 (2018): 371.

121. After all, the flagrant flouting of civil liberties under the Emergency (1975) and the deadliest pogroms against the Sikh minority (1984) took place under the Congress Party that ruled the nation for the majority of its post-Independence existence.

122. During the 2004 general elections, the BJP had campaigned on what among media and urban elites was widely touted as the winning slogan of "India Shining," a phrase meant to connote economic prosperity and celebrate the claimed elevation of the country into an internationally marketable brand. Despite the failure of the slogan to deliver (the BJP did not return to power) and the scathing critique the campaign received, "India Shining" has survived as a catchword that trumpets India as an emerging global power within a corporate vision of life.

123. Butler, *Precarious Life*, 34.

124. Lorey, *State of Insecurity*, 4.

125. The National Crime Records Bureau (NCRB) reported that suicides in the farming sector accounted for 7.4 percent of the total suicides in the country, resulting in deaths of 5,957 farmers and 4,324 agricultural laborers. https://economictimes.indiatimes.com/news/politics-and-nation/ncrb-data-shows-42480-farmers-and-daily-wagers-committed-suicide-in-2019/articleshow/77877613.cms?from=mdr

126. "India Budget Focuses on Tax Relief and Spending Boost," BBC, Feb. 1, 2023. https://www.bbc.com/news/world-asia-india-64462343

127. Gudavarthy, *India After Modi*.

128. Priya Chacko, "Gender and Authoritarian Populism: Empowerment, Protection, and the Politics of Resentful Aspiration in India," *Critical Asian Studies* 52, no. 2 (2020): 205.

129. Pankaj Mishra, "Welcome to the Age of Anger," *The Guardian*, December 8, 2016, https://www.theguardian.com/politics/2016/dec/08/welcome-age-anger-brexit-trump

130. Anderson and Jaffrelot, "Hindu Nationalism."

131. "Love Jihad" is the specter of Muslim men marrying Hindu women in an act of conquest. "Ghar Wapsi" is the idea of converting persons of non-Hindu faiths to Hinduism. So-called "gau-rakshaks" (or "cow protectors") are Hindutva vigilantes who vow to protect the sacred Hindu cow from the Muslim butcher and Dalit tanner. "Triple-talaq" refers to the Hindu right's desire to impose a Uniform Civil Code.

132. Anderson and Jaffrelot, "Hindu Nationalism," 474.

133. Snigdha Poonam, *Dreamers: How Young Indians Are Changing their World* (Cambridge, MA: Harvard University Press, 2018).

134. Anderson and Jaffrelot, "Hindu Nationalism," 468.

135. Butler, *Precarious Life*.

136. Megha Anwer, "Three Photographs, Six Bodies: The Politics of Lynching in Twos," *Kafila*, May 16, 2016, https://kafila.online/2016/06/05/three-photographs-six-bodies-the-politics-of-lynching-in-twos-megha-anwer/

137. Anderson and Jaffrelot, "Hindu Nationalism," 475.

138. Angana Chatterji, "Remaking the Hindu/Nation: Terror and Impunity in Uttar Pradesh," in *Majoritarian State: How Hindu Nationalism Is Changing India*, ed. Angana P. Chatterji, Thomas Blom Hansen, and Christophe Jaffrelot (New York: Oxford University Press, 2019), 402.

139. Susan Banki, "Precarity of Place: A Complement to the Growing Precariat Literature," *Global Discourse* 3, no. 3–4 (2013): 450–63.

140. See "Citizenship Amendment Bill: India's New 'Anti-Muslim' Law Explained," *BBC News*, December 11, 2019, https://www.bbc.com/news/world-asia-india-50670393

141. For more, see Citizens Against Hate-India's report on anti-Muslim hatred and discrimination since 2014; https://www.ohchr.org/sites/default/files/Documents/Issues/Religion/Islamophobia-AntiMuslim/Civil%20Society%20or%20Individuals/CitizensAgainstHate.pdf

142. See Asim Ali, "What If This Is the Hindu Rashtra?" *The Wire*, July 24, 2019, https://thewire.in/communalism/hindu-rashtra-india-constitution

143. See the introduction of Anwer and Arora, *Bollywood's New Woman*, for a description of this figure of the postliberalization new Indian woman.

144. Tithi Bhattacharya, "India's Daughter: Neoliberalism's Dreams and the Nightmares of Violence," *International Socialist Review* 97, https://isreview.org/issue/97/indias-daughter/

145. Kalpana Wilson, Jennifer Ung Loh, and Navtej Purewal, "Gender, Violence, and the Neoliberal State in India," *Feminist Review* 119 (2018): 1–6.

146. In a recent example, under the auspices of the Unlawful Activities Prevention Act (UAPA) wielded in the name of national security, student activist leaders—Asif Iqbal Tanha (of Jamia-illia) and Devangana Kalita and Natasha Narwal (of the women's collective *Pinjra Tod* that questioned sexist rules, restrictions, and moral policing in women's hostels in Delhi)—were arrested for their connection to the 2020 northeast Delhi riots around the anti-CAA protests.

147. Wendy Brown, *Undoing the Demos: Neoliberalism's Stealth Revolution* (Princeton, NJ: Princeton University Press, 2015).

148. Arundhati Roy, "I'd Rather Not Be Anna," *The Hindu*, August 21, 2011, https://www.thehindu.com/opinion/lead/id-rather-not-be-anna/article2379704.ece

149. Apoorvanand, "By Playing Hindutva Politics, AAP Is Stirring Up Trouble," *Scroll India*, February 16, 2021, https://scroll.in/article/987022/apoorvanand-by-playing-hindutva-politics-aap-is-stirring-up-trouble

150. Anand Teltumbde, "The Neoliberal Revolution," *Countercurrents*, August 30, 2011, https://countercurrents.org/teltumbde300811.htm

151. Irfan Ahmad, "Shaheen Bagh Protest Challenges BJP Govt's Brand of Populism, Is Generative of New Vision of Democracy," *First Post*, January 30, 2020, https://www.firstpost.com/india/shaheen-bagh-protest-challenges-bjp-govts-brand-of-populism-is-generative-of-new-vision-of-democracy-7976271.html

152. Shirin M. Rai, "India: From Populist Nationalism to Popular Constitutionalism," *Open Democracy*, July 21, 2020, https://www.opendemocracy.net/en/openindia/india-populist-nationalism-popular-constitutionalism/. For the meanings of the Shaheen Bagh protest, read also Shuddhabrata Sengupta, "The Garden of Freedom," *Caravan Magazine*, February 2, 2020, https://caravanmagazine.in/politics/lessons-that-shaheen-bagh-teaches-us-about-citizenship

153. Arjun Appadurai, "Three Observations from India's Past to Contextualize the Present Struggle," *The Wire*, January 10, 2020, https://thewire.in/politics/india-citizenship-amendment-protests-struggle-observations-from-the-past

154. Navyug Gill, "A Popular Upsurge Against Neoliberal Arithmetic in India," *Aljazeera*, December 11, 2020, https://www.aljazeera.com/opinions/2020/12/11/a-popular-upsurge-against-neoliberal-arithmetic-in-india

155. Ajay Gudavarthy, "Neoliberalism Is Killing the Very Idea of Citizenship in India," *Quartz India*, September 3, 2019, https://qz.com/india/1700542/neoliberalism-is-killing-the-very-idea-of-citizenship-in-india/

156. Giroux, "Protesting Youth in an Age of Neoliberal Savagery."

157. Gudavarthy, "Neoliberalism Is Killing the Very Idea of Citizenship in India."

158. Sanjay Srivastava, "'Sane Sex,' the Five-Year Plan Hero and Men on Footpaths and in Gated Communities: On the Cultures of Twentieth-Century Masculinity," in *Masculinity and Its Challenges in India: Essays on Changing Perceptions*, ed. Rohit K. Dasgupta et al. (Jefferson, NC: McFarland, 2014).

159. Sudesh Mishra, "Yahoo! Shammi Kapoor and the corporeal stylistics of popular Hindi cinema," *Continuum: Journal of Media and Cultural Studies* 26, no. 6 (2012): 818.

160. Shrivastava, "'Sane Sex,' the Five-Year Plan Hero and Men on Footpaths and in Gated Communities," 41.

161. Shrivastava, "'Sane Sex,' the Five-Year Plan Hero and Men on Footpaths and in Gated Communities," 43.

162. Aravind Unni, "Reading the 'Muslim Space' in Bombay (Mumbai) through Cinema," *Mumbai Reader* 15 (2015), Urban Design Research Institute, 183–205, http://www.udri.org/portfolio-items/mumbai-reader-15/

163. According to other figures, the population of Dalits is 20 to 25 percent of the total population. Priyali Sur, "Under India's Caste System, Dalits Are Considered Untouchable," *CNN*, April 16, 2020; Karan Deep Singh, "With Stories of her Oppressed Community, a Journalist Takes Aim at the Walls of Caste," *New York Times*, March 6, 2023.

164. Suraj Yengde, "Dalit Cinema," *South Asia: Journal of South Asian Studies* 41, no. 3 (2018): 503–18.

165. Nivedita Menon notes that "Rajput's death has been mobilized as part of a larger Hindutva campaign to purge the Bombay film industry of (or to tame)—the Muslims who dominate it; its regrettable tendency towards cultural syncretism; and most importantly, the voices in the industry that have been strongly speaking up against the politics of Hindu Rashtra since 2014." See Nivedita Menon, "Hindu Rashtra and Bollywood: A New Front in the Battle for Cultural Hegemony," *South Asia Multidisciplinary Academic Journal* 24/25 (2020).

166. We are grateful to the anonymous reviewer who encouraged us to incorporate the "nepotism debate" in the wider precarity that pervades the popular Hindi film industry.

167. Aatish Taseer, "Can Bollywood Survive Modi," *The Atlantic*, 2021, https://www.theatlantic.com/magazine/archive/2021/07/can-bollywood-survive-modi/619008/

168. Subramanian, "When the Hindu Right Came for Bollywood."

169. Swapnil Rai, *Networked Bollywood: How Star Power Globalized Hindi Cinema* (Cambridge: Cambridge University Press, 2024), 229.

170. A contemptuous term for a person with liberal, secular, left-wing political views.

171. https://boldoutline.in/akshay-kumar-officially-breaks-the-khan-monopoly.html; https://www.bizasialive.com/ajay-devgn-feels-khans-monopoly-in-bollywood-will-end-soon/

172. Radhika Raghav, "Power, Privilege, and Paradox: Understanding Ranveer Singh's Sartorial Fame and the (Un)Making of the New Millennial Masculinity in Contemporary Indian Society," *Critical Studies in Men's Fashion* 7, nos. 1–2 (2020): 177–98.

173. Kuhu Tanvir, "Snapshots of Bollywood Masculinity in the Age of Hindutva," *Special Affects*, May 1 2014, http://www.fsgso.pitt.edu/2014/05/snapshots-of-bollywood-masculinity-in-the-age-of-hindutva/

174. Sreya Mitra, "From 'Angry Young Man' to 'Benevolent Patriarch': Amitabh Bachchan, Bollywood Stardom and the Remaking of Post-Liberalization India," *South Asian Popular Culture* 18, no. 1 (2020): 63–77.

175. "I-T raids on Anurag Kashyap, Tapsee Pannu in Phantom Films Tax Evasion Probe," *Hindustan Times*, March 3, 2021, https://www.hindustantimes.com/india-news/it-raids-on-anurag-kashyap-tapsee-pannu-in-phantom-films-tax-evasion-probe-10-points-101614777138689.html

176. "'*Padmaavat*:' Fringe Outfit Announces Bounty on Deepika Padukone's Nose," *NDTV*, January 25, 2018, https://www.washingtonpost.com/world/2021/03/14/india-netflix-amazon-censorship/, https://www.ndtv.com/kanpur-news/padmaavat-fringe-outfit-announces-bounty-on-deepika-padukones-nose-1804401; and "'Slap in the face of trolls': Saif, Kareena Bashed for Naming Second Son Jehangir; Fans Laud Couple for Not Bowing Down to Hatred," *Free Press Journal*, August 10, 2021, https://www.freepressjournal.in/viral/slap-in-the-face-of-trolls-saif-kareena-bashed-for-naming-second-son-jehangir-fans-laud-couple-for-not-bowing-down-to-hatred

177. "Deepika Padukone: Bollywood Star Questioned in Sushant Singh Rajput Investigation," *BBC News*, September 26, 2020, https://www.bbc.com/news/world-asia-india-54232634

178. Priya Satia, "Aryan Khan and the Right-Wing's Disdain for Bollywood's Portrayal of Progressive Ideals," *The Wire*, October 29, 2021, https://thewire.in/rights/aryan-khan-bollywood-anti-colonial-hindutva

179. Apoorvanand, "From the Targeting of Shahrukh Khan's Son to Urdu, at Play Is Insecurity of the Hindutva Mindset," *The Wire*, October 24, 2021, https://thewire.in/communalism/from-the-targeting-of-shahrukh-khans-son-to-urdu-at-play-is-insecurity-of-the-hindutva-mindset Read also Pratap Bhanu Mehta, "What Is the Harassment of Aryan Khan Really About?" *Indian Express*, October 27, 2021, https://indianexpress.com/article/opinion/columns/aryan-khan-harassment-drugs-case-7590556/; and Pallavi Paul, "Aryan Khan and India's Addiction to the Drug Called Majoritarianism," *The Wire*, October 25, 2021, https://thewire.in/society/aryan-khan-and-indias-addiction-to-the-drug-called-majoritarianism

180. Paromita Vohra, "Phir Bhi Dil Hai Hindustani: Shahrukh Khan as the Symbol of Indianness," *Outlook India*, November 1, 2021, https://www.outlookindia.com/magazine/story/entertainment-news-phir-bhi-dil-hai-hindustani-shah-rukh-khan-as-the-symbol-of-indianness/305119

Chapter 2

1. Nandini Gooptu, ed., *Enterprise Culture in Neoliberal India: Studies in Youth, Class, Work, and Media* (London: Routledge, 2013).

2. Tomas Marttila, *The Culture of Enterprise in Neoliberalism: Specters of Entrepreneurship* (Vol. 87) (New York: Routledge, 2013).

3. Pierre Dardot and Christian Laval, *The New Way of the World: On Neoliberal Society* (London: Verso, 2014).

4. Martilla, *Culture of Enterprise.*

5. Colin Gordon, "Governmental Rationality: An Introduction," in*The Foucault Effect: Studies in Governmentality*, ed. Graham Burchell, Colin Gordon, and Peter Miller (Chicago: University of Chicago Press, 1991), 1–51.

6. Mitchell Dean, "Rethinking Neoliberalism," *Journal of Sociology* 50, no. 2 (2014): 150–63; Helen C. Williams, Katrina Pritchard, Maggie C. Miller, and Cara Reed, "Climbing to Freedom on an Impossible Staircase: Exploring the Emancipatory Potential of Becoming an Entrepreneur-Employer," *International Small Business Journal* 39, no. 5 (2020): 424–49.

7. Christina Scharff, "The Psychic Life of Neoliberalism: Mapping the Contours of Entrepreneurial Subjectivity," *Theory, Culture & Society* 33, no. 6 (2016): 107–22.

8. Jonathan Schapiro Anjaria and Ulka Anjaria, "The Fractured Spaces of Entrepreneurialism in Post-Liberalization India," in Gooptu, *Enterprise Culture in Neoliberal India*, 202–17.

9. Anjaria and Anjaria, "The Fractured Spaces of Entrepreneurialism."

10. Madhavi Murty, *The Stories That Bind: Political Economy and Culture in New India* (New Brunswick, NJ: Rutgers University Press), 4.

11. Sanjay Shrivastava, "Modi-Masculinity: Media, Manhood, and 'Traditions' in a Time of Consumerism," *Television & New Media* 16, no. 4 (2015): 332.

12. Candice West and Don Zimmerman, cited in Praseeda Gopinath and Pavitra Sundar, "Introduction: Masculinities," *South Asian Popular Culture* 18, no. 1 (2020), 1–10.

13. Amrita De, "Situating Right-Wing Populisms and Revisiting the Men and the Boys under the Neoliberal Turn," *Boyhood Studies* 13, no. 2 (Winter 2020): 105–16; Nancy Lindisfarne and Jonathan Neale, "Masculinities and the Lived Experience of Neoliberalism," in *Masculinities Under Neoliberalism*, ed. Andrea Cornwall, Frank G. Karioris, and Nancy Lindisfarne (London: Zed Books, 2016).

14. Andrea Cornwall, Frank G. Karioris, and Nancy Lindisfarne, eds., *Masculinities Under Neoliberalism* (London: Zed Books, 2016), 9.

15. Purnima Mankekar, "'We are like this only:' Aspiration, Jugaad, and Love in Enterprise Culture," in Gooptu, *Enterprise Culture in Neoliberal India*, 27–41.

16. Raymond Williams, *Marxism and Literature* (Oxford: Oxford University Press, 1978), 133–34.

17. Jamie Peck and Alex Tickell, "Conceptualizing Neoliberalism, Thinking Thatcherism," in *Contesting Neoliberalism: Urban Frontiers*, ed. Helga Leitner, Jamie Peck, and Eric S. Sheppard (New York: Guildford Press, 2007), 27.

18. Lilly Irani, *Chasing Innovation: Making Entrepreneurial Citizens in Modern India* (Princeton, NJ: Princeton University Press, 2019).

19. Michel Foucault, "What Is Enlightenment?" *The Foucault Reader*, ed. Paul Rabinow (New York: Random House, 1984), 39.

20. Marttila, *The Culture of Enterprise.*

21. Jeremy Vachet, *Fantasy, Neoliberalism and Precariousness: Coping Strategies in the Cultural Industries* (Bingley, UK: Emerald Group Publishing, 2022).

22. Mankekar, "We are like this only."

23. Herbert Marcuse, *One Dimensional Man* (London: Routledge and Kegan Paul, 1964).

24. See Vachet, *Fantasy, Neoliberalism and Precariousness*; Martilla, *The Culture of Enterprise*; Irani, *Chasing Innovation*; and Thomas J. Catlaw and Gary S. Marshall, "Enjoy Your Work! The Fantasy of the Neoliberal Workplace and its Consequences for the Entrepreneurial Subject," *Administrative Theory and Praxis* 40, no. 2 (2018): 99–118.

25. Sonal Jha, "Unbecoming Men: The Masculinity Crisis of the Bollywood Hero," *Third Text* 36, no. 3 (2022): 287.

26. Irani, *Chasing Innovation.*

27. Williams, et al., "Climbing to Freedom on an Impossible Staircase."

28. Vachet, *Fantasy, Neoliberalism and Precariousness.*

29. Jha, "Unbecoming Men," 281.

30. David Harvey, *A Short History of Neoliberalism*, cited in Jha, "Unbecoming Men," 281.

31. Šarūnas Paunksnis, *Dark Fear, Eerie Cities: New Hindi Cinema in Neoliberal India* (New Delhi: Oxford University Press), 6.

32. Dibyesh Anand, "Anxious Sexualities: Masculinity, Nationalism and Violence," *British Journal of Politics and International Relations* 9, no. 2 (2007): 257–69.

33. Mahalakshmi Mahadevan, "Engendering Familial Citizens: Serial Viewing among Middle-Class Families in Urban India," http://web.mit.edu/comm-forum/legacy/mit8/papers/Mahadevan_paper.pdf

34. Santanu Chakrabarti, "Banal Nationalism and Soap Opera" (PhD diss., Rutgers: The State University of New Jersey, 2012), https://www.proquest.com/docview/1284157920/previewPDF/DF313577A95F44FFPQ/1?accountid=13360

35. Paunksnis, *Dark Fear, Eerie Cities*, 6.

36. Raewyn Connell (2005), cited in Cornwall, *Masculinities Under Neoliberalism*, 9.

37. Cornwall, *Masculinities Under Neoliberalism*, 9.

38. Gooptu, *Enterprise Culture*, 13.

39. Irani, *Chasing Innovation*, 4.

40. Irani, *Chasing Innovation*, 5.

41. Ravinder Kaur, "The Innovative Indian: Common Man and the Politics of *Jugaad* Culture," *Contemporary South Asia* 24, no. 3 (2016): 324.

42. Gooptu, *Enterprise Culture*, 13.

43. Kaur, "The Innovative Indian."

44. Kaur, "The Innovative Indian," 323.

45. Murty, *The Stories That Bind*, 120.

46. Jeb Sprague and Sreerekha Sathi, "Transnational Amazon: Labor Exploitation and the Rise of E-Commerce in South Asia," in *The Cost of Free Shipping: Amazon in the Global Economy*, ed. Jake Alimohamed-Wilson and Ellen Reese (London: Pluto Press, 2020), 50–65.

47. Gooptu, *Enterprise Culture*.

48. Gooptu, *Enterprise Culture*, 11.

49. Mankekar, "We are like this only."

50. Gooptu, *Enterprise Culture*, 16.

51. These schemes, meant to encourage domestic manufacturing and turn India into a global manufacturing powerhouse, have not yielded successful results, especially in the garments industry. See "India Economy: Seven Years of Modi in Seven Charts," *BBC*, June 22, 2021, https://www.bbc.com/news/world-asia-india-57437944

52. Priya Chacko, "Paternalism, Neo-liberalism and Hindutva Civilizationalism," *International Affairs* 99, no. 2 (2023): 559.

53. Chacko, "Paternalism," 553.

54. Chacko, "Paternalism," 564–65.

55. Chacko, "Paternalism," 552.

56. Cited in Anjaria and Anjaria, "The Fractured Spaces of Entrepreneurialism," 197.

57. Shrivastava, "Modi-Masculinity," 331.

58. Shrivastava, "Modi-Masculinity," 336.

59. Shrivastava, "Modi-Masculinity," 336.

60. Suvij Sudershan, "The Economic Life Behind *Eeb Allay Ooo!*" *Spring: A Magazine of Socialist Ideas in Action*, March 6, 2021, https://springmag.ca/the-economic-life-behind-eeb-allay-ooo. That shining light on contemporary labor relations is a prominent goal of Vats's film is reinforced in another scene in *Eeb Allay Ooo!* where a journalist reports a story from outside a politician's house: "after months of unrest, disgruntled contractual sanitation workers registered their protest by throwing garbage in front of the Deputy Mayor's house." This marginal story provides a brief glimpse into the possibility of political action and resistance of the precariat against their exploitative working conditions.

61. Isabelle Lorey, *States of Insecurity: Government of the Precarious*, trans. Aileen Derieg, with a foreword by Judith Butler (New York: Verso, 2015), 11.

62. Guy Standing, *The Precariat: The New Dangerous Class* (London: Bloomsbury, 2011).

63. Megnaa Mehtta, "The Quintessential Prey," *Himal Southasian*, July 21, 2019.

64. Sanjay Parikh and Geetanjoy Sahu, "Has the Judiciary Abandoned Environment for Neoliberalism?" *Economic and Political Weekly (Engage)*, https://www.epw.in/engage/article/has-judiciary-abandoned-environment-neoliberalism; Manisha Rao, "Reframing the Environment in Neoliberal India," *Sociological Bulletin* 67, no. 3 (December 2018): 259–74.

65. Anjaria and Anjaria, "The Fractured Spaces of Entrepreneurialism," 195.

66. Dipankar Sarkar, "An Interview with 'Eeb Allay Ooo!' Director Prateek Vats," *Vague Visages*, July 29, 2020, https://vaguevisages.com/2020/07/29/an-interview-with-eeb-allay-ooo-director-prateek-vats/

67. Sarkar, "An Interview with 'Eeb Allay Ooo!' Director Prateek Vats."

68. Amita Baviskar and Raka Ray, eds., *Elite and Everyman: The Cultural Politics of the Indian Middle Classes* (New Delhi: Routledge, 2011), 22.

69. Jostein Jakobsen and Kenneth Bo Nielsen, "Bovine Meat, Authoritarian Populism, and State Contradictions in Modi's India," *Journal of Agrarian Change* 23, no. 1 (January 2023): 110–30.

70. Eliza Griswold, "The Violent Toll of Hindu Nationalism in India," *The New Yorker*, March 5, 2019.

71. Dipankar Sarkar, "An Interview with 'Eeb Allay Ooo!' Director Prateek Vats," *Vague Visages*, July 29, 2020. https://vaguevisages.com/2020/07/29/an-interview-with-eeb-allay-ooo-director-prateek-vats/

72. Butler, *Precarious Life*, xiv.

73. Jacobsen and Nielsen, "Bovine Meat, Authoritarian Populism, and State Contradictions in Modi's India"; Sushmita Chatterjee, "Beefing Yoga: Meat, Corporeality, and Politics," in *Meat: A Transnational Analysis*, ed. Sushmita Chatterjee and Banu Subramaniam (Durham, NC: Duke University Press).

74. Yamini Narayanan, *Mother Cow, Mother India: A Multispecies Politics of Dairy in India* (Stanford, CA: Stanford University Press, 2023), 13.

75. Sarkar, "An Interview with 'Eeb Allay Ooo!' Director Prateek Vats."

76. Raka Ray, "The Politics of Masculinity in the Absence of Work," *Oxford Development Studies* 49, no. 4 (2021): 311–23; Madhavi Gupta and Pushkar, "Why India Should Worry About Its Educated, But Unemployed, Youth," https://gdc.unicef.org/resource/why-india-should-worry-about-its-educated-unemployed-youth

77. Rakesh Kalshian, "Anger of the Jobless Youth," *DownToEarth*, May 15, 2018, https://www.downtoearth.org.in/news/economy/anger-of-the-jobless-youth-60440

78. Interview with Vikash Singh, "Kanwariyas Need to be Seen Beyond Being Merely a Cause of Traffic Snarls and Disruptions," *Scroll India*, July 30, 2017, https://scroll.in/article/845068/interview-kanwariyas-need-to-be-seen-beyond-being-merely-a-cause-of-traffic-snarls-and-disruptions. See Vikash Singh, *Uprising of the Fools: Pilgrimage as Moral Protest in Contemporary India* (Stanford, CA: Stanford University Press, 2017).

79. Snigdha Poonam, "Shiva's Band of Men: Into the World of the Kanwariyas," *Hindustan Times*, July 24, 2017.

Chapter 3

1. Arvind Unni defines the Muslim space as a space of marginalization and underdevelopment, inhabited primarily by Muslims. Cinematically, this space is associ-

ated with a proximity to the railway tracks, red-light district, defunct textile mills, and spatial and ontological distance and alienation from the rest of the city (3–4). Aravind Unni, "Reading The 'Muslim Space' in Bombay (Mumbai) through Cinema," *Urban Design Research Institute, Mumbai. Mumbai Reader*, 183–205.

2. Partha Chatterjee, *The Politics of the Governed: Reflections on Popular Politics in Most of the World* (New York: Columbia University Press, 2004), 649.

3. This section draws upon this previously published article by Megha Anwer, "Cinematic Clearances: Spaces of Poverty in Hindi Cinema's Big Budget Productions," *The Global South* 8, no. 1 (Spring 2014): 91–111, 93–97.

4. Igor Krstić, *Slums on Screen: World Cinema and the Planet of Slums* (Edinburgh: Edinburgh University Press, 2016), 2.

5. Chatterjee, *The Politics of the Governed*, 135.

6. Ashis Nandy, *The Secret Politics of Our Desires* (New Delhi: Oxford University Press, 1998), 2.

7. Nandy, *The Secret Politics of Our Desires*, 2.

8. Nandy, *The Secret Politics of Our Desires*, 2.

9. Nandy, *The Secret Politics of Our Desires*, 3.

10. Chawl is the Bombay term for densely crowded multifamily tenements for low- and lower-middle-income groups.

11. Ranjani Mazumdar, *Bombay Cinema: An Archive of the City* (Minneapolis: University of Minnesota Press, 2007), xx.

12. Amrit Gangar, "Chalchitra/Chawlchitra: The Representation of Mumbai's Chawls in Hindi Films," in *The Chawls of Mumbai: Galleries of Life*, ed. Neera Adarkar (Delhi: ImprintOne, 2011), 89, 91.

13. Gangar, "Chalchitra/Chawlchitra," 93–94.

14. Gangar, "Chalchitra/Chawlchitra," 90.

15. Gangar, "Chalchitra/Chawlchitra," 95.

16. Mazumdar, *Bombay Cinema*, 110.

17. Mazumdar, *Bombay Cinema*, 110.

18. Mazumdar, *Bombay Cinema*, 115.

19. Mazumdar, *Bombay Cinema*, 111.

20. Mazumdar, *Bombay Cinema*, 112.

21. Mazumdar, *Bombay Cinema*, 118.

22. Alan Gilbert, "The Return of the Slum: Does Language Matter?" *International Journal of Urban and Regional Research* 31, no. 4 (2007): 702–3.

23. Akhil Gupta, *Postcolonial Developments* (Durham, NC: Duke University Press, 1998), cited in Leela Fernandes, "The Politics of Forgetting: Class Politics, State Power and the Restructuring of Urban Space in India," *Urban Studies* 41, no. 12 (2004), 2416.

24. Leela Fernandes, "The Politics of Forgetting: Class Politics, State Power and the Restructuring of Urban Space in India," *Urban Studies* 41, no. 12 (2004), 2416.

25. Fernandes, "The Politics of Forgetting," 2425.

26. D. Asher Ghertner, "Analysis of New Legal Discourse Behind Delhi's Slum Demolitions," *Economic and Political Weekly* 43, no. 20 (May 17–23, 2008): 62–63.

27. Kalyani Menon-Sen and Gautam Bhan, *Swept Off the Map: Surviving Eviction and Resettlement in Delhi* (Yoda Press, 2008); Gautam Bhan, "'This Is No Longer the City I Once Knew:' Evictions, the Urban Poor and the Right to the City in Millennial

Delhi," *Environment and Urbanization* 21, no. 1 (2009): 127–42; Ghertner, "Analysis of New Legal Discourse."

28. Ghertner, "Analysis of New Legal Discourse," 60; Fernandes, "The Politics of Forgetting," 2421.

29. Ghertner, "Analysis of New Legal Discourse." 64. Earlier, judicial activism did not hold slum dwellers responsible for their unhygienic living conditions and instead held builders and bodies like the DDA (Delhi Development Authority) accountable for failure to provide adequate sanitation and other services in the *bastis* (lower-class colonies). Now, however, the courts lay the entire moral and aesthetic responsibility of destroying public land and civic life on the shoulders of the poor. The resurgence of the "polluting poor" discourse thus allows the courts to hold the poor culpable and punishable through eviction and the demolition of slums.

30. Old Delhi is called the "walled city."

31. Gautam Bhan, "This Is No Longer the City I Once Knew," 128.

32. Solomon J. Greene, "Staged Cities: Mega-Events, Slum Clearance, and Global Capital," *Yale Human Rights and Development Law Journal* 6 (2003); 163.

33. Fernandes, "The Politics of Forgetting," 2417.

34. Bhan, "This Is No Longer the City I Once Knew," 128.

35. Fernandes, "The Politics of Forgetting," 2416.

36. Rajni Kothari, *Growing Amnesia: An Essay on Poverty and the Human Consciousness* (New Delhi: Viking, 1993).

37. Shakuntala Rao, "The Globalization of Bollywood: An Ethnography of Non-Elite Audiences in India," *Communication Review* 10, no. 1 (2007): 66.

38. Anwer, "Cinematic Clearances," 91–111.

39. Ira Bhaskar and Richard Allen's *The Islamicate Cultures of Bombay* identifies four different cinematic taxonomies produced around "Islamicate" cultures: the Muslim historical film (about Urdu poets and Mughal emperors; *Mughal-e-azam*, 1960, and *Jodha Akbar*, 2008, are prime examples), the Muslim Courtesan film (*Umrao Jaan*, 1981), the Muslim Social, and the New Wave Muslim Social (*Saleem Langde Pe Mat Ro*, 1989). "Islamicate" does not refer to Islam qua a formal religion per se, "but to the social and cultural complex historically associated with Islam and the Muslims, both among Muslims themselves and even when found among non-Muslims." Ira Bhaskar and Richard Allen, *Islamicate Cultures of Bombay Cinema* (New Delhi, Tulika Books, 2009), 44–64.

40. Mukul Kesavan, "Urdu, Awadh, and the Tawaif: The Islamicate Roots of Hindi Cinema," in *Forging Identities: Gender, Communities, and the State*, ed. Zoya Hasan (New Delhi: Kali for Women, 1994), 244–57.

41. Anand Vivek Taneja, "Muslimness in Hindi Cinema," *Seminar* (2009), https://www.india-seminar.com/2009/598/598_anand_vivek_taneja.htm

42. Kalyani Chadha and Anandam P. Kavoori, "Exoticized, Marginalized, Demonized: The Muslim 'Other' in Indian Cinema," in *Global Bollywood*, ed. Anandam Kavoori et al (New York: New York University Press, 2008), 136–38.

43. Johnny Walker was the screen name of the Muslim comic Badruddin Jamaluddin Kazi who was the quintessential funnyman of 1950s–1960s films. It was common at the time for Muslim actors to take on Hindu names to gain "universal" audience acceptance, a tradition that continued until as recently as the 1990s. The actor Mehmood deserves an important mention here as well; he typically played the crass,

awkward, quasi-grotesque buffoon and friend to the central protagonist. Unlike Johnny Walker, though, he did not adopt a Hindu screen name.

44. Syed Ali Mujtaba, "Bollywood and the Indian Muslims," *Indian Muslim News and Information* (2006); Maidul Islam, "Imagining Indian Muslims: Looking through the Lens of Bollywood Cinema," *Indian Journal of Human Development* 1, no. 2 (2007): 403–22; Faiza Hirji, "Change of Pace? Islam and Tradition in Popular Indian Cinema," *South Asian Popular Culture* 6, no. 1 (2008): 57–69.

45. Chadha and Kavoori, "Exoticized, Marginalized, Demonized," 139.

46. Fareed Kazmi, "Muslim Socials and the Female Protagonist: Seeing a Dominant Discourse at Work," in *Forging Identities: Gender, Communities, and the State*, ed. Zoya Hasan (New Delhi: Kali for Women, 1994), 239–40.

47. Islam, "Imagining Indian Muslims," 404. In this overall context, *Garam Hawa* (Scorching Winds) (1973) stands out as the one film that seriously attempts a complex and sympathetic "inside" documentation of the lives of Muslims who refused to migrate to Pakistan.

48. See for instance a recent film such as *Secret Superstar* (Advait Chandan, 2017) for yet another iteration of the cruel, sadistic Muslim patriarch.

49. In the city of Ayodhya, Uttar Pradesh, the land on which the Babri Masjid (mosque) stands, is a disputed site. The land is considered especially sacrosanct because it is supposed to be the birthplace of the Hindu deity Ram. For many decades, the Ram Janmabhoomi (the land on which Ram was born) movement led by the Hindu right-wing party, the Bharatiya Janta Party (BJP), and its sociocultural wing, the Vishwa Hindu Parishad (VHP), rallied for the destruction of the Babri mosque and for the building of a Hindu temple on the site. On December 6, 1992, a large mob (which included several high-profile party members of the BJP) demolished the mosque. The incident resulted in communal tensions and riots across the country, including the 1992 riots in Bombay. In 2019, the Supreme Court of India declared a landmark verdict and ordered the disputed land to be handed over to a trust to build the Ram Janmabhoomi temple. The court also directed the government to give the Sunni Waqf Board five acres of land in another location to build a mosque. On January 22, 2024, the Ram temple inauguration or consecration ceremony was held.

50. Chadha and Kavoori, "Exoticized, Marginalized, Demonized," 141.

51. Sumita S. Chakravarty, "Fragmenting the Nation: Images of Terrorism in Indian Popular Cinema," in *Cinema and Nation*, ed. Mette Hjort and Scott MacKenzie (London: Routledge, 2005), 214.

52. Ultimately a surefire certification of allegiance is obtainable by the Muslim only by himself ceasing to be, that is, by offering to lay down his life in the hunt for "bad" coreligionists. In that sense the Indian Army grenadier Abdul Hamid, who, braving relentless fire and shelling in full-body self-exposure and armed only with a gun, singlehandedly destroyed three attacking Pakistani Patton tanks in the 1965 India-Pakistan conflict before being himself blasted by a fourth, would stand as an ideal and duly mythified real-life exemplar of the desirable. The Hamid legend in fact represents a myth of impossibility, for it automatically excludes the unspectacular if honest and hard-working average Muslim citizen by trumpeting just how much would be required of an Indian Muslim—nothing less than self-annihilation in the task of exterminating other less savory "Muslims"—to receive a full vote of confidence.

53. Mozzie is a derogatory slang epithet for a Muslim. This colonial "heritage" (the word used to be invoked by the British Raj) continues to inflect contemporary communal parole.

54. In films such as *Fanaa* (Annihilation, Kunal Kohli, 2006) and even in a recent film like *Raazi* (Agreement, Meghna Gulzar, 2018), Kashmiri Muslim women prove themselves as good Muslims and loyal Indian citizens who put their nation over everything else by killing (directly or inadvertently) their own Muslim husbands.

55. Manisha Sethi, "Cine Patriotism," *SAMAR: South Asian Magazine for Action and Reflection* 15, http://www.samarmagazine.org/archive/articles/115

56. Undoubtedly, the raving success of *Gadar: Ek Prem Katha* (Anil Sharma, 2001) is significant above all because the film undertakes to perpetuate loudly and raucously—at demagogy pitch—the claim that Pakistanis hate India. *Gadar* is also the example par excellence of a subgenre of the Bombay "masala film," one in which the Muslim patriarch is positioned as an evil fanatic standing bigotedly in the way of cross-border lovers. *Gadar*, however, is not alone in forwarding this oppressive stereotype of the Pakistani male, and even such purportedly "secular" films as *Veer Zaara* (2004) apparently find it difficult not to draw upon the ethno-profiled figure of the Muslim father, who is contrasted unfavorably with the "good" (Hindu) Indian parents.

57. For a discussion of recent films and Muslim stereotyping, see Nandini Ramnath, "Muslim Stereotyping in Hindi Films," *Scroll India*, September 20, 2021, https://scroll.in/reel/1005662/muslim-stereotyping-in-hindi-films-we-cannot-allow-ourselves-to-forget-what-constitutes-us

58. Ritanjan Das, Nilotpal Kumar, and Praveen Priyadarshi, "Producing Multiple 'Others': Spatial Upheaval and Hindutva Politics in Urban India," *Contemporary South Asia* 29, no. 4 (2021): 514–31.

59. Ghazala Jamil, *Accumulation by Segregation: Muslim Localities in Delhi* (Oxford: Oxford University Press, 2017); D. Asher Ghertner, *Rule by Aesthetics: World-Class City Making in Delhi* (Oxford: Oxford University Press, 2015); Anasua Chatterjee, *Margins of Citizenship: Muslim Experiences in Urban India* (London: Routledge, 2017); Laurent Gayer and Christophe Jaffrelot, eds., *Muslims in Indian Cities: Trajectories of Marginalisation* (New York: Columbia University Press, 2012).

60. Hem Raj vs. Commissioner of Police, judgement, 1999, cited in Menon-Sen and Bhan, *Swept Off the Map*, 6.

61. Fernandes, "The Politics of Forgetting," 2420.

62. Astha Rajvanshi, "How India's Bulldozers Became a Vehicle of Injustice," *Time*, August 11, 2023, https://time.com/6303571/how-bulldozers-became-a-symbol-of-anti-muslim-sentiment-in-india/

63. Qtd. in Thomas Blom Hansen, *Violence in Urban India: Identity Politics, "Mumbai" and the Postcolonial City* (Delhi: Permanent Black, 2001), 76.

64. The parallels with Hitler's virulent attacks against the Jewish population are not coincidental. Bal Thackeray professed himself a great admirer of Hitler for the latter's ability to oust antinationals from Germany (Hansen, *Violence in Urban India*, 86).

65. Arjun Appadurai, "Spectral Housing and Urban Cleansing: Notes on Millennial Mumbai," *Public Culture* 12, no. 3 (2000): 649.

66. Rashmi Varma, "Provincializing the Global City: From Bombay to Mumbai," *Social Text* 22, no. 4 (2004): 66.

67. Appadurai, "Spectral Housing," 630.

68. Hansen, *Violence in Urban India*, 7.

69. Appadurai, "Spectral Housing," 644.

70. Hansen, *Violence in Urban India*, 122.

71. Ranjani Mazumdar identifies a new cinematic trend in Bollywood where the city is recognized as being "cluttered with evidentiary details" and *everything* is marked and arranged as "information." Ranjani Mazumdar, "Terrorism, Conspiracy and Surveillance in Bombay's Urban Cinema," *Social Research: An International Quarterly* 78, no. 1 (Spring 2011): 143–72.

72. A Hindu restaurant owner is arrested for his friendship with a Muslim terrorist suspect, but it turns out that he had no part in the bombings. Even so, terrified and traumatized by police brutality he kills his wife, infant, and himself. The Muslim suspects arrested, on the other hand, are always guilty, obdurate, and incapable of being guilted or intimidated into suicide.

73. Teresa Castro writes, "If the term 'topophilia' does not cover all the implications of the film's topographic fascination, it can nonetheless offer a way of addressing cinema's fascination and sustained commitment to exploring the specificities of place." Teresa Castro, "Mapping the City through Film: From 'Topophilia' to Urban Mapscapes," in *The City and the Moving Image: Urban Projections*, ed. Richard Koeck and Les Roberts (Basingstoke: Palgrave Macmillan, 2010), 144–55.

74. Castro, "Mapping the City through Film," 154.

75. Qtd. in Castro, "Mapping the City through Film," 147.

76. This is the kind of argument made by films like *Kurbaan* in which even upper-class Muslim men turn out to be terrorists.

77. Those who cannot be found in the *bastis* have, in all probability, fled to Dubai. The film barely concerns itself with the hunting down of these men.

78. Although a little later in the film he does precisely that: He tells journalists that the police can show no regard for questions of human rights violations because they are not dealing with ordinary criminals. These men are Jehadis who believe they've done the right thing. In fact, no amount of torture, including the chopping off of their fingers, will make them talk. Only humiliation will do the trick.

79. Ananya Jahanara Kabir, "The Kashmiri as Muslim in Bollywood's 'New Kashmir Films,'" *Contemporary South Asia* 18, no. 4 (2010): 373–74.

80. Translated in English as "drift," *dérive* suggests an unstructured, unplanned journey through an urban space, a "technique of hastily passing through varied environments" or ambiances (Guy Debord, cited in Castro, "Mapping the City through Film"). The concept emerges out of the work of the Situationist theorist Guy Debord and relates to "psychogeography," which believes that the architecture and geography within which we move subtly impacts and directs our movement but also our emotional landscape. Debord describes psychogeography as "the study of the precise laws and specific effects of the geographical environment, consciously organized or not, on the emotions and behaviour of individuals" (cited in Castro). Joseph Hart calls it "the whole toy box full of playful, inventive strategies for exploring cities . . . just about anything that takes pedestrians off their predictable paths and jolts them into a new awareness of the urban landscape." Joseph Hart, "A New Way of Walking," *UTNE-MINNEAPOLIS* (2004): 40–43.

81. The slum is where Aamir is forced to go by the anonymous phone caller, the

terrorist mastermind, who has kidnapped Aamir's family and is using them as leverage to get Aamir to do his bidding.

82. Hart, "A New Way of Walking."

83. In effect, of course, the Godfather complex is based on this logic and dialectic: a penurious, weak, and underfed don or protector-patriarch of a beleaguered minority group is a contradiction in terms; the don must of necessity have access to the things his dependents lack and desperately need, above all, power and muscle, but also a measure of economic means.

84. Asim Siddiqui, "Why You Don't Admire SRK in *Raees*," *Rediff*, February 7, 2017, https://www.rediff.com/movies/column/why-you-dont-admire-srk-in-raees/20170206.htm

85. Kriti Sonali, "Raees vs Kaabil: BJP leader Kailash Vijayvargiya targets Shah Rukh Khan, supports Hrithik Roshan," *Indian Express*, January 25, 2017, https://indianexpress.com/article/entertainment/bollywood/raees-vs-kaabil-bjp-leader-kailash-vijayvargiya-hits-out-at-shah-rukh-khan-supports-hrithik-roshan-see-pic-4486464/

86. Tuhin A. Sinha, "Raees Is Entertaining, But Here Are My Problems With It," *Swarajya*, February 4, 2017, https://swarajyamag.com/blogs/raees-is-entertaining-but-here-are-my-problems-with-it

87. Rachel Saltz, "Review: Shah Rukh Khan as 'Raees,' a Villain but Still a Do-Gooder," *New York Times*, January 26, 2017, https://www.nytimes.com/2017/01/26/movies/raes-review-shah-rukh-khan.html

88. Omar Ahmed, "'Chariot of Fire': Genre Slippages, Iconographic Agitation and Ideological Subversion in SRK's *Raees*," *Studies in South Asian Film and Media* 9, no. 2 (2019): 116.

89. "Large-Scale Misuse of TADA by Police in Gujarat," *India Today*, https://www.indiatoday.in/magazine/investigation/story/19910315-large-scale-misuse-of-tada-by-police-in-gujarat-814201-1991-03-15

90. Parvis Ghassem-Fachandi, "The Hyperbolic Vegetarian: Notes on a Fragile Subject in Gujarat," in *Being There: The Fieldwork Encounter and the Making of Truth*, ed. John Borneman and Abdellah Hammoudi (Berkeley: University of California Press, 2009), 80.

91. Sushmita Chatterjee, "Beefing Yoga: Meat, Corporeality, and Politics," in *Meat: A Transnational Analysis*, ed. Sushmita Chatterjee and Banu Subramaniam (Durham, NC: Duke University Press), 101.

92. Chatterjee, "Beefing Yoga," 107.

93. Ornit Shani, "Bootlegging, Politics and Corruption: State Violence and the Routine Practices of Public Power in Gujarat (1985–2002)," *South Asian History and Culture* 1, no. 4 (October 2010), 502.

94. Shani, "Bootlegging, Politics and Corruption," 494.

95. Susan Banki, "Precarity of Place: A Complement to the Growing Precariat Literature," *Global Discourse* 3, no. 3–4 (2013).

96. See Omar Ahmed's essay for a different close reading of this sequence as issuing a challenge to Hindutva iconography.

97. Ghassem-Fachandi, "The Hyperbolic Vegetarian."

98. Sudhavna Deshpande, "The Consumable Hero of Globalised India," in *Bollyworld: Popular Indian Cinema through a Transnational Lens*, ed. Raminder Kaur and Ajay J. Sinha (New Delhi: Sage Publications, 2005), 186.

99. Praseeda Gopinath, "'A feeling you cannot resist': Shah Rukh Khan, Affect, and the Re-scripting of Male Stardom in Hindi Cinema," *Celebrity Studies* 9, no. 3 (2018): 309.

100. "His Name Is Khan (And It's One You Might Know)," *NPR Morning Edition*, February 11, 2010, https://www.npr.org/templates/story/story.php?storyId=123589668

101. Soutik Biswas, "What the Backlash against Aamir Khan Tells Us about India," *BBC News*, November 25, 2015, https://www.bbc.com/news/world-asia-india-34918431

102. Kailash Vijayvargiya (@KailashOnline). Twitter, January 21, 2017, 10:44 a.m., https://twitter.com/KailashOnline/status/822832221794877440. See also Kriti Sonali, "Raees vs Kaabil: BJP Leader Kailash Vijayvargiya Targets Shah Rukh Khan, Supports Hrithik Roshan," *Indian Express*, January 25, 2017, https://indianexpress.com/article/entertainment/bollywood/raees-vs-kaabil-bjp-leader-kailash-vijayvargiya-hits-out-at-shah-rukh-khan-supports-hrithik-roshan-see-pic-4486464/

103. A host of economists have discussed the failure or limited effects of the demonetization move to achieve its stated goals. Amartya Lahiri, "The Great Indian Demonetization," *Journal of Economic Perspectives* 34, no. 1 (Winter 2020): 55–74; Vivek Kaul, "Why Modi's Currency Gamble Was Epic Failure," *BBC*, August 30, 2017.

104. Angshukanta Chakraborty, "India Has Finally Made Shah Rukh Khan a Muslim," *DailyO*, December 13, 2016, https://www.dailyo.in/politics/shah-rukh-khan-raj-thackeray-raees-bollywood-indian-muslims-srk-pakistani-actors-mahira-khan/story/1/14533.html

105. Zafar Agha, "'Operation Bollywood' Is Designed to Saffronise the Industry and Ensure It Falls in Line," *National Herald*, September 29, 2020, https://www.nationalheraldindia.com/opinion/operation-bollywood-is-designed-to-saffronise-the-industry-and-ensure-it-falls-in-line

106. See special issue on *Pathaan*, in *New Cinemas: Journal of Contemporary Film* (forthcoming 2024).

107. For a discussion of *Gully Boy* and its staging of rap and hip-hop cultures, see Sangita Gopal, "Relocating Bollywood: Gully Boy and the Worlds of Hip-Hop," in *ReFocus: The Films of Zoya Akhtar*, ed. Aakshi Magazine and Amber Shields (Edinburgh: Edinburgh University Press, 2022).

108. Irfan Ahmad and Santosh Mehrotra, "No Respite from Poverty for Muslims," *The Hindu*, November 6, 2018, https://www.thehindu.com/opinion/op-ed/no-respite-from-poverty-for-muslims/article25429598.ece

109. Maria Thomas, "Indian Muslims Have the Least Chances of Escaping Poverty," *The Quartz*, September 24, 2018, https://qz.com/india/1399537/indian-muslims-have-the-least-chances-of-escaping-poverty/

110. Ruhi Tewari and Abhishek Mishra, "Every Second ST, Every Third Dalit & Muslim in India Poor, Not Just Financially: UN Report," *ThePrint*, July 12, 2019, https://theprint.in/india/every-second-st-every-third-dalit-muslim-in-india-poor-not-just-financially-un-report/262270/

111. "Shoot the Traitors," Human Rights Watch, https://www.hrw.org/report/2020/04/09/shoot-traitors/discrimination-against-muslims-under-indias-new-citizenship-policy

112. Rana Ayyub, "Narendra Modi looks the Other Way as New Delhi Burns," *Time*, February 28, 2020, https://time.com/5791759/narendra-modi-india-delhi-riots-violence-muslim/

113. Other sources: Lindsay Maizland, "India's Muslims: An Increasingly Marginalized Population," Council on Foreign Relations, July 14, 2022, https://www.cfr.org/backgrounder/india-muslims-marginalized-population-bjp-modi; https://freedomhouse.org/country/india; Sameer P. Lalwani and Gillian Gayner, "India's Kashmir Conundrum: Before and After the Abrogation of Article 370," United States Institute of Peace, August 5, 2020, https://www.usip.org/publications/2020/08/indias-kashmir-conundrum-and-after-abrogation-article-370; Kanchan Chandra, "The Roots of Hindu Nationalism's Triumph in India," *Foreign Affairs*, September 11, 2019, https://www.foreignaffairs.com/articles/india/2019-09-11/roots-hindu-nationalisms-triumph-india; K. Alan Kronstadt, "India: Religious Freedom Issues," Congressional Research Service, August 30, 2018, https://crsreports.congress.gov/product/pdf/R/R45303; Jeffrey Gettleman et al., "Under Modi, a Hindu Nationalist Surge Has Further Divided India," *New York Times*, April 11, 2019, https://www.nytimes.com/2019/04/11/world/asia/modi-india-elections.html; "This Is What the Modi Sarkar Has Done to Indian Muslims," *The Wire*, July 8, 2020, https://thewire.in/communalism/this-is-what-the-modi-sarkar-has-done-to-indian-muslims; "In Secular India, It's Getting Harder to Be Muslim," *CNN*, November 20, 2019, https://www.cnn.com/2019/11/19/asia/india-muslim-modi-intl-hnk/index.html;

114. Soumya Shrivastava, "Zoya Akhtar Explains Why Vijay Raaz's *Gully Boy* Character Deserves Sympathy: 'He's operating out of fear,'" *Hindustan Times*, April 21, 2020, https://www.hindustantimes.com/bollywood/zoya-akhtar-explains-why-vijay-raaz-s-gully-boy-character-deserves-sympathy-he-s-operating-out-of-fear/story-YTR1I8vRSNU3hFoDd71ufP.html

115. Damini Rajendra Kulkarni, "Appropriation and Articulation: Mapping Movements in *Gully Boy*," *Cinergie—Il Cinema E Le Altre Arti* 9 no. 17 (2020).

116. Igor Krstić, *Slums on Screen: World Cinema and the Planet of Slums* (Edinburgh: Edinburgh University Press, 2016).

117. Ranjani Mazumdar, "The Mumbai Slum: Aerial Views and Embodied Memories," *Mediapolis: A Journal of Cities and Culture* 4, no. 3 (November 1, 2019), https://www.mediapolisjournal.com/2019/11/the-mumbai-slum/

118. Mazumdar, "The Mumbai Slum."

Chapter 4

1. There are however rare occasions when caste has made an appearance and been accounted for in Hindi films, and within these socially conscious films the trope of intercaste love is deployed to tackle the scourge of "untouchability." For instance, three films from the 1930s–1950s—*Chandidas* (Nitin Bose, 1932), *Achuut Kanya* (The Untouchable Girl, Franz Osten, 1936), and *Sujata* (The Well Born, Bimal Roy, 1959)—all feature the travails involved in cross-caste coupledom. And, while surprisingly not all of these films end in tragedy, all the films espouse "a liberal humanist worldview (couched in melodramatic excess)" (Vijay Mishra, *Bollywood Cinema: Temples of Desire* (New York: Routledge, 2002), 20) within a "pastoral-sentimental" lens that romanticizes the Dalit, sanitizes untouchability, and sidesteps "a materialist critique of untouchability" by refusing to "delineate the structural violence" (Sangita Gopal, *Conjugations: Marriage and Form in New Bollywood Cinema* (Chicago: University of Chicago Press, 2011), 34–35) to which Dalits are subject. The transgressive potential of exoga-

mous coupledom is thus contained in these films. Some of the few other Indian films that have engaged intercaste love or relationships are *Ankur* (Shyam Benegal, 1974), *Chauranga* (Bikas Ranjan Mishra, 2014), and *Sairat* (Nagraj Manjule, 2016). For a discussion of *Sujata*, also see Sumita Chakravarty, "National Identity and the Realist Aesthetic: Indian Cinema of the Fifties," *Quarterly Review of Film and Video* 11, no. 3 (1989): 31–48.

2. bell hooks, *All About Love: New Visions* (New York: William Morrow, 2000).

3. Lauren Berlant, *Cruel Optimism* (Durham, NC: Duke University Press, 2011).

4. Jyotsna Kapur, "An 'Arranged Love' Marriage: India's Neoliberal Turn and the Bollywood Wedding Culture Industry," *Communication, Culture & Critique* 2, no. 2 (2009): 227.

5. Gopal, *Conjugations*, 17.

6. Gopal, *Conjugations*.

7. Gopal, *Conjugations*, 18.

8. "'If you're making a film for yourself, don't expect an audience': *Masaan* Director Neeraj Ghaywan," Scroll.in, July 18, 2015, https://scroll.in/article/742119/if-youre-making-a-film-for-yourself-dont-expect-an-audience-masaan-director-neeraj-ghaywan

9. Gopal, *Conjugations*, 126.

10. Gopal, *Conjugations*, 136.

11. Suvadip Sinha, "Vernacular Masculinity and Politics of Space in Contemporary Bollywood Cinema," *Studies in South Asian Film and Media* 5, no. 2 (2014): 132. In an interview, Ghaywan reflects on the depiction of the small town in Indian cinema: "Many films mock small towns and small cities, they are depicted from an outsider and urbanite point of view. But when we wanted to make *Masaan*, the intention was to tell the story from an internal viewpoint." Ghaywan, "'If you're making a film for yourself, don't expect an audience.'"

12. Gopal, *Conjugations*, 141.

13. Peggy McIntosh, "White Privilege: Unpacking the Invisible Knapsack," *Peace and Freedom Magazine*, July/August, 1989: 10–12, https://nationalseedproject.org/Key-SEED-Texts/white-privilege-unpacking-the-invisible-knapsack

14. The naming of Deepak's family's domicile, Harishchandra Ghat, is important as it invokes the story of King Harishchandra (who is mentioned as an ideal and truthful king in the Hindu scriptures, the *Puranas*, and the epic, *The Mahabharata*) and the Matanga Kanyas (girls from an untouchable family). In this story, the king refuses to marry the girls when they express that wish since as an upper-caste man, he cannot enter into a "polluting marriage" with a lower-caste girl. Vizia Bharati and Y. S. Alone, "Vilifying Dalit Women: Epics and Aesthetics," in *Dalit Feminist Theory: A Reader*, ed. Sunaina Arya and Aakash Singh Rathore (London: Routledge, 2020), 118.

15. Alain Badiou, *In Praise of Love* (New York: The New Press, 2012), 68.

16. Badiou, *In Praise of Love*, 16.

17. Badiou, *In Praise of Love*.

18. When Dalit leader and intellectual B. R. Ambedkar wrote about intercaste marriage as a central element in the "annihilation of caste" (in his speech of the same title), he was bringing attention to sexuality as the linchpin of caste, and the centrality of endogamy—the practice of marriage within the caste group or community—in the reproduction of caste. Importantly recognizing caste as a social and biological ordering where ideas of purity and pollution were central to maintaining caste boundaries,

Ambedkar saw intercaste marriage as "dissolving" caste through the "fusion of blood." Anupama Rao writes that Ambedkar's views on the constitutive relationship between caste and sexual and gender regulation had larger implications that laid bare the complex workings of the sexual economy of caste. Anupama Rao, *The Dalit Question: Dalits and the Politics of Modern India* (Berkeley: University of California Press, 2009).

19. As Ghaywan notes, "The kind of small city or town we have shown in the film [*Masaan*] is the kind that has malls and multiplexes, a place where the internet is thinning the divide."

20. Prem Chowdhry, "'First our jobs, then our girls': The Dominant Caste Perceptions of the 'Rising' Dalits," *Modern Asian Studies* 43, no. 2 (March 2009): 453.

21. Suraj Yengde, "Why Neo-liberal Capitalism Failed Dalit Enterprise," *The Print*, July 25, 2019, https://theprint.in/pageturner/excerpt/why-neo-liberal-capitalism-failed-dalit-enterprise/266446/

22. "Sangam" refers here not just to the "confluence" of the two major rivers of the Gangetic planes—Ganga and Yamuna—but also to the "union" of lovers.

23. Gopal, *Conjugations*, 145.

24. Deborah Young, "*Masaan*: Cannes Review," https://www.hollywoodreporter.com/review/masaan-cannes-review-797795

25. For more on caste-blindness, read Dhamma Dharshan Nigam, "To Your Caste Blindness," *Round Table India*, March 9, 2019, https://roundtableindia.co.in/index.php?option=com_content&view=article&id=9601:to-your-caste-blindness&catid=119:feature&Itemid=132

26. Gopal, *Conjugations*, 15.

27. Shaunak Sen, "'It's Ringing Again': Cellular Ambiguities in Hindi Cinema," *Bioscope: South Asian Screen Studies* (2013): 162.

28. Aditi is referring to the horrific gang-rape of a young woman (problematically referred to as "Nirbhaya" in the press) in New Delhi on December 16, 2012, that garnered international censure and attention.

29. Harish Wankhade, "An Upper Caste Gaze," *The Indian Express*, July 16, 2019.

30. Jyoti Nisha, "Indian Cinema and the Bahujan Spectatorship," *Economic and Political Weekly (Engage)* 55, no. 20 (May 16, 2020), https://www.epw.in/engage/article/indian-cinema-and-bahujan-spectatorship

31. Pradeep Attri, "Dalits Don't Need Upper-Caste Saviors," *Huffington Post*, June 26, 2019. https://www.huffpost.com/archive/in/entry/article-15-dalits-upper-caste-saviours_in_5d131e47e4b04f059e4c1093

32. Dilip Mandal, "Ayushmann Khurrana's *Article 15* Wants You to Believe Caste System Came from Outer Space," *The Print*, June 30, 2019, https://theprint.in/opinion/ayushmann-khurranas-article-15-wants-you-to-believe-caste-system-came-from-outer-space/256291/

33. Ankur Pathak, "Ayushmann Khurrana's Article 15 Is One Brahmin Hero Away from Being a Great Film," *Huffington Post*, June 28, 2019, https://www.huffingtonpost.in/entry/article15-review-ayushmann-khurrana_in_5d15fdoee4b03d61163a2646

34. In "Annihilation of Caste," Ambedkar wrote, "[T]urn in any direction you like, Caste is the monster that crosses your path. You cannot have political reform, you cannot have economic reform, unless you kill the monster."

35. Ashwini Deshpande, "The Ugly Reality of Caste Violence and Discrimination in Urban India," *The Wire*, December 17, 2011, https://thewire.in/caste/ugly-reality-caste-violence-discrimination-urban-india.

36. https://ihds.umd.edu/sites/ihds.umd.edu/files/publications/papers/ThoratJoshi3.pdf

37. Evita Das, "Caste Isn't Just Confined to Rural India, It's Also Part of Our Urban Reality," *The Wire*, April 22, 2019. https://livewire.thewire.in/personal/caste-isnt-just-confined-to-rural-india-its-also-part-of-our-urban-reality/

38. These are only a few, among many, indicators of the rise and continuance of a neoconservatism in India's youth. The survey also revealed that 20 percent of them believed that it was not right for women to work after marriage, that men were better leaders than women, that higher education was more important for men than women; a whopping 27 percent believed that wives should *always* listen to their husbands.

39. Ravikant Kisana, "Progressive Millennial Indians, Let's Talk about Why We Never Talk about Caste," *BuzzFeed*, June 23, 2016, https://www.buzzfeed.com/ravikantkisana/our-caste-shaped-blindspot

40. Teju Cole, "The White-Savior Industrial Complex," *The Atlantic*, March 21, 2012.

41. Cole, "The White-Savior Industrial Complex."

42. In the film, the character of Jatav might appear to be a bit of an exception to this, but he's still defined by his passivity: "he might not do what's right, but he won't do wrong either."

43. Michel Chion, Claudia Gorbman, and Walter Murch, *Audio-vision: Sound on Screen* (New York: Columbia University Press, 1994).

44. Steven Bruhm, "Cell Phones from Hell," *South Atlantic Quarterly* 110, no. 3 (2011): 610.

45. Shaunak Sen, "'It's Ringing Again': Cellular Ambiguities in Hindi Cinema," *Bioscope: South Asian Screen Studies* (2013): 166.

46. Suraj Yengde, *Caste Matters* (New Delhi: Penguin, 2019).

47. Suraj Yengde, "Apartheid in Fancy Dress: Against India's Arranged Marriage Regime," *The Baffler*, April 2020, https://thebaffler.com/salvos/apartheid-in-fancy-dress-yengde

48. Kriti Budhiraja, personal correspondence.

49. Emmanuel Levinas, *Totality and Infinity (Pittsburgh: Duquesne University Press, 1969).*

50. Levinas, *Totality and Infinity*, 57.

51. Levinas, *Totality and Infinity*, 198.

52. Levinas, *Totality and Infinity*, 84.

53. Levinas, *Totality and Infinity*, 197.

54. Pathak, "Ayushmann Khurrana's Article 15 Is One Brahmin Hero Away from Being a Great Film."

55. Sharmila Rege, "Brahmanical Nature of Violence Against Women," in Dalit Feminist Theory, 111.

56. Berlant, *Cruel Optimism*.

57. "*Geeli Pucchi* Is a Story of Revenge Served Cold," *Daily O*, April 4, 2021, https://www.dailyo.in/variety/ajeeb-daastaans-geeli-pucchi-konkona-sensharma-neeraj-ghaywan/story/1/34509.html. In an interview with Sinha, the lead actor who plays Bharti, Konkona Sensharma says that that the film "is a revenge story, but it is a revenge that you can understand. Bharti has tried everything to get what she rightfully deserves. She has a degree, she is a hard worker, she asked for a raise but she never got any of

that, she was denied all this repeatedly. There are too many barriers, too many hurdles that she has to overcome. She had to resort to other measures."

58. Bargi, for instance, critiques the film for championing Bharti's capacity to sidestep vulnerability and instrumentalize "personal emotions for the sake of a position in the factory." This, according to Bargi, makes her a "repulsive" and "frightening" subject, incapable of soliciting empathy. Pallavi Paul, on the other hand, celebrates the film for its depiction of a queer Dalit woman's "vivid and luminous rage" who, by the end of the film, "no longer aspires for inclusion," and instead "cunningly reconfigure(s) . . . an access route towards . . . emancipation." Drishadwati Bargi, "When the Functional Is Political Is Personal: Witnessing the Many Battles of Geeli Pucchi's Bharati Mandal," *Dalit Camera*, April 27, 2021, https://www.dalitcamera.com/4414-2/; Pallavi Paul, "Neeraj Ghaywan's *Geeli Pucchi* Paints a Brilliant Blue Expanse of Emancipation," *The Wire*, April 25, 2021, https://thewire.in/film/neeraj-ghaywans-geeli-pucchi-paints-a-brilliant-blue-expanse-that-emancipates

59. Bargi, "When the Functional Is Political Is Personal."

60. Nira Yuval-Davis, "Dialogical Epistemology: An Intersectional Resistance to the 'Oppression Olympics,'" *Gender and Society* 26, no. 1 (February 2012): 46–54.

61. Yuval-Davis, "Dialogical Epistemology."

62. Das, "Caste Isn't Just Confined to Rural India, It's Also Part of Our Urban Reality."

Chapter 5

1. We are focusing on one film segment (directed by Zoya Akhtar) from this 2018 film anthology. Another instalment of the anthology, *Lust Stories 2*, also featuring four short films, was released in 2023.

2. For the distinct performance politics and self-fashioning that different female actors embody in the Bollywood film industry, see the introduction to Megha Anwer and Anupama Arora, eds., *Bollywood's New Woman: Liberalization, Liberation, and Contested Bodies* (New Brunswick, NJ: Rutgers University Press, 2021).

3. For a longer discussion of Bollywood's new woman, See Anwer and Arora's introduction to *Bollywood's New Woman*, 1–24.

4. Partha Chatterjee, "Colonialism, Nationalism, and Colonialized Women," *American Ethnologist* 16, no. 4 (Nov. 1989): 622–33.

5. Rajeswari Sunder Rajan, *Real and Imagined Women: Gender, Culture and Postcolonialism*. London: Routledge, 1993.

6. Wendy Brown, *Undoing the Demos: Neoliberalism's Stealth Revolution* (New York: Zone Books, 2015); Catherine Rottenberg, "The Rise of Neoliberal Feminism," *Cultural Studies* 28 no. 3 (2014): 418–37.

7. Brown, *Undoing the Demos*, 37.

8. Wendy Larner, quoted in Rottenberg, "The Rise of Neoliberal Feminism," 421.

9. Nancy Fraser, "Feminism, Capitalism, and the Cunning of History," *New Left Review* 56 (March-April 2009): 97–117; Elisabeth Prugl, "Neoliberalising Feminism," *New Political Economy* 20, no. 4 (2015): 614–31.

10. Rottenberg, "The Rise of Neoliberal Feminism," 20.

11. Rupal Oza, *The Making of Neoliberal India: Nationalism, Gender, and the Paradoxes of Globalization* (New York: Routledge, 2006); Leela Fernandes, ed., *Feminists*

Rethink the Neoliberal State (New York: New York University Press, 2018); Inderpal Grewal, *Transnational America: Feminisms, Diasporas, Neoliberalisms* (Durham, NC: Duke University Press, 2005); Maitryee Chaudhuri, "Gender, Media, and Popular Culture in a Global India," in *Routledge Handbook on Gender in South Asia*, ed. Leela Fernandes (London: Routledge 2014), 145–59.

12. Grewal, *Transnational America*, 31.

13. Chaudhuri, "Gender, Media, and Popular Culture in a Global India," 146.

14. Rosalind Gill, "Post-postfeminism? New Feminist Visibilities in Postfeminist Times," *Feminist Media Studies* 16, no. 4 (2016): 610–30; and "The Affective, Cultural and Psychic Life of Postfeminism: 10 Years On," *European Journal of Cultural Studies* 20, no. 6 (2017): 606–26.

15. Simidele Dosekun, "For Western Girls Only? Post-feminism as Transnational Culture," *Feminist Media Studies* 15, no. 6 (2015): 966.

16. Angela McRobbie, "Post-feminism and Popular Culture," *Feminist Media Studies* 4, no. 3 (2004): 262.

17. "*Veere Di Wedding* Banned in Pakistan Over 'Vulgar Dialogues'; Here Is Why Trolls Are Calling it 'Karma,'" *Indian Express*, May 31, 2018, https://indianexpress.com/article/trending/this-is-serious/veere-di-wedding-pakistan-ban-kareena-kapoor-sonam-kapoor-twitter-reactions-5198369/

18. Paromita Vohra, "Wedding of the Year," June 10, 2018, https://www.mid-day.com/articles/paromita-vohra-wedding-of-the-year/19504159

19. Nadim Asrar, "Hot and Bothered: India's Answer to *Sex and the City* Stirs Debate," *Aljazeera*, June 13, 2018, https://www.aljazeera.com/indepth/features/hot-bothered-india-answer-sex-city-stirs-debate-180612115615871.html

20. Pradnya Wagule, "*Veere Di Wedding* Has a Problem: Its Bro-Culture," *Feminism in India*, June 4, 2018, https://feminisminindia.com/2018/06/04/veere-di-wedding-feminist-film-review/

21. Sharanya Gopinathan, "Why *Veere Di Wedding* Is a Feminist Film Despite Kareen, Sonam, and Cast's Assertions to the Contrary," *The Ladies Finger* (blog), https://www.firstpost.com/entertainment/why-veere-di-wedding-is-a-feminist-film-despite-kareena-sonam-and-casts-assertions-to-the-contrary-4496153.html

22. "I believe in equality, not a feminist: Kareena Kapoor," Press Trust of India, May 23, 2018, https://www.wionews.com/india-news/entertainment-i-believe-in-equality-not-a-feminist-kareena-kapoor-139254.

23. "Sonam Kapoor Took a Dig at Her 'Veere' Kareena Kapoor for Saying She's 'Not a Feminist,'" *Wion*, May 28, 2018, https://www.wionews.com/india-news/entertainment-sonam-kapoor-took-a-dig-at-her-veere-kareena-kapoor-for-saying-shes-not-a-feminist-140436

24. Kirin Narayan, "Birds on a Branch: Girlfriends and Wedding Songs in Kangra," *Ethos* 14, no. 1 (1986): 47.

25. See the following on the Indian women's movement: Radha Kumar, *The History of Doing* (New Delhi: Kali for Women, 1983); Nivedita Menon, ed. *Gender and Politics in India* (New Delhi: Oxford University Press, 1999); and Kalpana Kannabiran, "Feminist Deliberative Politics in India," in *Women's Movements in the Global Era*, ed. Amrita Basu (Boulder, CO: Westview Press, 2010), 119–56.

26. The "Pink Chaddi" campaign (2009) refers to the campaign where a group who called themselves "The Consortium of Pubgoing, Loose, and Forward Women" asked

people to send a gift of *pink chaddi* (underwear) to right-wing Hindu fringe activists (Sri Ram Sena) on Valentine's Day as a way to protest the moral policing of women; "Besharmi Morcha" (or SlutWalk, 2011) contests the double standards around sexuality; the "Blank Noise" project (2005) takes on public and street sexual harassment (or eve-teaching as it is known in India); and "Pinjra Tod" (2016) contests gender discriminatory policies in hostels. For a discussion of some of these contemporary expressions of feminism in India, see Ratna Kapur, "Pink Chaddis and SlutWalk Couture: The Postcolonial Politics of Feminism Lite," *Feminist Legal Studies* 20 (2012): 1–20; and Alka Kurian, "Decolonizing the Body: Theoretical Imaginings on the Fourth Wave Feminism in India," in *New Feminisms in South Asian Social Media, Film, and Literature: Disrupting the Discourse*, ed. Sonora Jha and Alka Kurian (New York: Routledge, 2017), 15–41.

27. Dalit feminists have pointed out the historical caste-blindness and exclusions of the Indian women's movement. See essays in Sunaina Arya and Aakash Singh Rathore, eds, *Dalit Feminist Theory: A Reader* (London: Routledge, 2020).

28. R. Claire Snyder-Hall, "Third-Wave Feminism and the Defence of 'Choice,'" *Perspectives on Politics* 8, no. 1 (2010), 255–61.

29. Shelley Budgeon, "Individualized Femininity and Feminist Politics of Choice," *European Journal of Women's Studies* 22, no. 3 (2015), 303–18.

30. Dosekun, "For Western Girls Only?," 967.

31. McRobbie, "Post-feminism and Popular Culture," 262.

32. Gloria Raheja and Ann Gold, *Listen to the Heron's Words: Reimagining Gender and Kinship in North India* (Berkeley: University of California Press, 1994), 1.

33. Stanley Tambiah, "Bridewealth and Dowry Revisited," *Current Anthropology* 30, no. 4 (1989): 418.

34. John Morreall, qtd. in Warren St. John, "Seriously, the Joke Is Dead," *New York Times*, Sunday, May 22, Section 9, 11–12.

35. Peter Farb, *Word Play: What Happens When People Talk* (New York: Bantam, 1974), 96.

36. Janet Bing, "Liberated Jokes: Sexual Humor in All-Female Groups," *Humor: International Journal of Humor Research* 20, no. 4 (2007): 338.

37. Raheja and Gold, *Listen to the Heron's Words*, 26.

38. There are two exceptions here. In our coding we include two occasions when the sexual joke is not between the four characters, but involves an exchange between Avni and her mother, in one case, and between Sakshi and the neighborhood aunties, in the other. We have, however, chosen to include these occasions of sexual humor because they transpire in contexts where the other friends are in the vicinity, just not present in the scene. These two moments might be interesting instances to think about how the presence of friends, even when not visible, emboldens women in the friend group to take verbal liberties with probing and domineering elder women.

39. There is one moment that does not elicit laughter on screen and yet is meant to lighten a serious, conflictual moment between the friends. This is when the friends get into a fight in the aftermath of Kalindi's disastrous engagement ceremony and start saying hurtful things to each other, and Meera says to the other three "*Guys, ye randi-rona band karo. Let's go home and have a drink*" ("Guys, stop whining like sluts.")

40. The implication is that he's pitiable because he must endure sex with a fat woman or because he is being deprived of sex because of his wife's corporeal insecurities.

41. Meera is the only one who eagerly talks about sex when we are first introduced to the protagonists as teenagers. There is a difference in the tenor of her eagerness to talk about sex and in the way that Avni, for instance, talks about it. While Avni simply declares her decision to have sex with her high school boyfriend, Arjun, on graduation day, Meera demonstrates the slightly exaggerated enthusiasm, about sex-related matters, of a girl, who, by virtue of being unattractive and controlled by her conservative father, is unlikely to find easy access to opportunities for being sexually active.

42. There is one exception to this: During dance rehearsals for Kalindi's *sangeet*, she and her fiancé walk away hand in hand, and Sakshi yells after them for taking off, yet again, to make out.

43. Avni is sexualized but in a naive way; she's sexual, but an innocent. She's someone who falls in love too easily and her mistake is her eagerness to find a man.

44. Tejaswini Ganti, "'No One Thinks in Hindi Here': Language Hierarchies in Bollywood," in *Precarious Creativity: Global Media, Local Labor*, ed. Michael Curtin and Kevin Sanson (Oakland: University of California Press, 2016), 120.

45. Ganti, "No One Thinks in Hindi Here," 120.

46. Chaudhuri, "Gender, Media, and Popular Culture in a Global India," 152.

47. Arne L. Kalleberg, "Precarious Work, Insecure Workers: Employment Relations in Transition," *American Sociological Review* 74, no. 1 (2000): 2.

48. Cited in Ritu Vij, "The Global Subject of Precarity," *Globalizations* 16, no. 4: 510.

49. "Coronavirus: How India's Lockdown Sparked a Debate over Maids," BBC News, May 6, 2020, https://www.bbc.com/news/world-asia-india-52529922

50. Otso Harju, "Women and Maids: Perceptions of Domestic Workers, Housework and Class among Young, Progressive, Middle- to Upper-Class Women in Delhi," *Working Papers in Contemporary Asian Studies* no. 55 (2017), Centre for East and South-East Asian Studies, Lund University.

51. In their seminal work on domestic servitude in India, sociologist Raka Ray and anthropologist Seemin Qayum define a "culture of servitude [as] one in which social relations of domination/subordination, dependency, and inequality are normalized and permeate both the domestic and public spheres," distinctively different from other market/labor relations because it "inhabits the private, intimate space of the home and domestic life." Raka Ray and Seemin Qayum, *Cultures of Servitude: Modernity, Domesticity, and Class in India* (Stanford, CA: Stanford University Press, 2009), 3, 192.

52. Guy Standing, *The Precariat: The New Dangerous Class* (London: Bloomsbury, 2011).

53. "Precarious Transitions: Mobility and Citizenship in a Rising Tower," *Economic and Political Weekly* 56, no. 7 (February 13, 2021), https://www.epw.in/engage/article/precarious-transitions-mobility-and-citizenship

54. A second instalment of *Lust Stories*, with four short films, was released on June 29, 2023.

55. What makes *Lust Stories* especially fascinating is that it is directed by an A-list director—Zoya Akhtar—someone whose films have focused mostly on the jetsetting cosmopolitan lifestyles of the elite (*Zindagi Na Milegi Dobara; Dil Dhadakne Do*), although she has made films focusing on characters in a less privileged milieu (*Gully Boy*). Meanwhile, *Sir* is an Indo-French collaboration, produced by Inkpot Films

(Brice Poisson and Rohena Gera), and coproduced by Ciné-Sud Promotion. Directed by Rohena Gera, the film had its World Premiere at the 71st International Cannes Film Festival in 2018, in the Critics Week competition section, making Gera the first woman filmmaker to bag the Gan Foundation Award for distribution. Similarly, in conjunction with the rise of multiplex films and streaming platforms, a new kind of female star has also emerged. Indeed, the "star texts" of the actors who play the lead female characters in both films (Bhumi Pedneker and Tillotama Shome) have been associated with "*hatke*" or diasporic films. Shome is best known for portraying the maid, Alice, in Mira Nair's crossover film *Monsoon Wedding* (2001), and her filmography is full of other "off-Bollywood" films and Indo-Western collaborations (*A Death in the Gunj*, 2017; *Nayantara's Necklace*, 2015; *Qissa*, 2013). Pednekar shot into the spotlight with her debut role in the 2015 *Dum Laga Ke Haisha*, where she played a confident fat woman, a role that confronted dominant body and beauty standards in neoliberal India. With its middle-class small-town focus, *Dum Laga Ke Haisha* is also an example of a *hatke*/multiplex film that demonstrates New Bollywood's decided investment, in the past decade or so, in constructing new cinematic modalities within which to explore and experiment with women's stories and voices, venturing beyond elite contexts. Akhtar and Gera's films, however, stand out within this growing corpus of women-centric films for their focus on the working-class urban woman or female domestic helper.

56. Poulomi Das, "*Sir* Joins Small Canon of Films Challenging Bollywood's Classist, Formulaic Depiction of Domestic Workers," *The Swaddle*, November 18, 2020, https://theswaddle.com/bollywood-classism-domestic-workers/

57. "Sir, Is Love Enough?: Sexual Harassment at Work Packaged as a 'Sweet Love Story,'" *Women's Web*, 2021. https://www.womensweb.in/2021/01/sir-is-love-enough-not-romance-sexual-harassment-at-work-unsafe-jan21wk3sr/

58. Ipshita Nath, "Netflix's Sir: The Indian Audience's Fascination With The Rich-Man-Loves-Poor-Girl Trope," *Feminism in India*, January 20, 2021, https://feminisminindia.com/2021/01/20/sir-netflix-film-analysis-review/

59. Sanchita Dasgupta, "Analysis of *Sir* (2018): Blatant Invisibilisation of Caste Privilege," *Feminism in India*, January 27, 2021, https://feminisminindia.com/2021/01/27/sir-2018-movie-analysis/

60. "Sir, Is Love Enough?: Sexual Harassment at Work Packaged as a 'Sweet Love Story.'"

61. "Tillotama Shome On *Sir* And How She Built Her 20-Year-Long Career," *Film Companion*, January 20, 2021, https://www.filmcompanion.in/interviews/bollywood-interview/sir-movie-netflix-tillotama-shome-on-how-she-built-her-20-year-long-career/

62. Srishti Behl Arya, Director, India Original Films, Netflix, "We are happy to report that we are pretty close to 50% in terms of employee ratio even in India. We've had a great run in the movies as well. For 2020–21, 50% of our creators are either female producers or female directors. Across films and series, 50% of the protagonists were women;" Karishma Upadhyay, "The Women at Netflix," *The Hindu*, March 11, 2021, https://www.thehindu.com/entertainment/movies/the-women-at-netflix/article61927886.ece

63. Niha Masih, "India Is the Next Big Frontier for Netflix and Amazon. Now, the Government Is Tightening Rules on Content," *Washington Post*, March 14, 2021, https://www.washingtonpost.com/world/2021/03/14/india-netflix-amazon-censorship/

64. "Ramu Kaka" was the cliché male servant of Hindi cinema of the 1970s and 1980s. Some examples of films with this servant figure include *Amardeep* (1979) and *Khoon Bhaari Maang* (1988). Other films that feature the female domestic worker in hapless, sexualized, or maternal roles include *Aradhana* (1969) and *Damini* (1993) among other films.

65. Ambreen Hai, "Motherhood and Domestic Servitude in Transnational Women's Fiction: Thrity Umrigar's *The Space Between Us* and Mona Simpson's *My Hollywood*," *Contemporary Literature* 57, no. 4 (Winter 2016): 508.

66. Sonal Sharma and Eesba Kunduri, "'Here, We Are Addicted to Loitering': Exploring Narratives of Work and Mobility Among Migrant Women in Delhi," in *Land, Labour, and Livelihoods: Indian Women's Perspectives*, ed. Bina Fernandez, Meena Gopal, and Orlanda Ruthven (Palgrave Macmillan, 2016), 197–216.

67. Sharma and Kunduri, "Here, We Are Addicted to Loitering,'" 204–5.

68. PRIA Gender Team, "*Sexual Harassment of Domestic Workers at Their Workplaces*," October 2, 2020, Social Publishers Foundation, https://www.socialpublishers foundation.org/knowledge_base/sexual-harassment-of-domestic-workers-at-their-wo rkplaces/

69. Dasgupta, "Blatant Invisibilisation of Caste Privilege."

70. Cited in Hai, "Motherhood and Domestic Servitude in Transnational Women's Fiction," 508.

71. Monika Mehta, "Reflections on *Lust Stories*: Online Distribution and the Production of Female Sexual Agency," *Lust Stories: A Dossier, Film Quarterly* (April 15, 2019).

72. Mehta, "Reflections on *Lust Stories*."

Chapter 6

1. Proshant Chakraborty, "The Poetics and Politics of 'Progress' in Neoliberal India," *Studies in South Asian Film and Media* 12, no. 1 (2012): 19–34.

2. Šarūnas Paunksnis, "One-Dimensional Cinema: India's New Imaginary Spaces," *Economic and Political Weekly* 49, no. 17 (April 26, 2014_: 118–22.

3. Leela Fernandes, *India's New Middle Class: Democratic Politics in an Era of Neoliberal Reform* (Minneapolis: University of Minnesota Press, 2006), 32.

4. Arvind Rajagopal, *Politics After Television: Religious Nationalism and the Reshaping of the Indian Public* (Cambridge: Cambridge University Press, 2008), 3.

5. Henrike Donner and Geert De Neve, "Introduction," in *Being Middle Class in India: A Way of Life*, ed. Henrike Donner (London: Routledge, 2011), 2.

6. Amita Baviskar and Raka Ray, eds. *Elite and Everyman: The Cultural Politics of the Indian Middle Classes* (New Delhi: Routledge, 2011).

7. Satish Deshpande, *Contemporary India: A Sociological View* (New Delhi: Penguin Books, 2003), 139.

8. Leela Fernandes and Patrick Heller, "Hegemonic Aspirations: New Middle-Class Politics and India's Democracy in Comparative Perspective," *Critical Asian Studies* 38, no. 4 (2006): 509.

9. Ajay Gudavarthy, *India After Modi: Populism and the Right* (New Delhi: Bloomsbury India, 2021).

10. Fernandes and Heller, "Hegemonic Aspirations," 510.

11. For an excellent discussion of Bhaggu and his conceptualization/use of "powertoni," see Chakraborty, "The Poetics and Politics of 'Progress' in Neoliberal India."

12. Priya Chacko, "Gender and Authoritarian Populism: Empowerment, Protection, and the Politics of Resentful Aspiration in India," *Critical Asian Studies* 52, no. 2 (2020): 204–25.

13. Gudavarthy, *India After Modi.*

14. Gudavarthy, *India After Modi.*

15. Chacko, "Gender and Authoritarian Populism."

16. The director of the film, Raj Kumar Gupta, said in an interview that "The film is my interpretation of the events." https://indianexpress.com/article/news-archive/web/no-one-killed-jessica/

17. Ritesh Mehta, "Flash Activism: Civic Justice Catalyzed by a Bollywood Film," *Transformative Works and Cultures* 10 (2012), https://journal.transformativeworks.org/index.php/twc/article/view/345

18. Mehta, "Flash Activism."

19. Vinay Sitapati notes, "A good place to gauge what India Shining is thinking at any given point is through the pages of *The Times of India*. Since the world's largest English-language daily prides itself in its commercial acumen, it is nimbly in sync with the aspirations of India Shining. *The Times of India* is also the mirror to the way mainstream English-language newspapers are headed. Whether it is the campaign to bring 'Justice for Jessica' or 'India against Corruption' exemplified by the Anna Hazare movement, India's media and film industry increasingly mirror the anxieties of India Shining." Vinay Sitapati, "What Anna Hazare's Movement and India's New Middle Classes Say about Each Other," *Economic and Political Weekly*, July 23, 2011.

20. Nadja-Christina Schneider, "Medialised Delhi: Youth, Protest, and an Emerging Genre of Urban Films," *South Asia Chronicle* 3 (2013): 99.

21. Regarding the size of the Indian middle class, a range of statistics have been offered, from 3 to 25 percent of the population. Rachel Dwyer ("Zara hatke ('somewhat different'): The New Middle Classes and the Changing Forms of Hindi Cinema," in Henrike Donner, ed., *Being Middle Class in India*, London and NY, Routledge 2011, 185–86) notes that "India's middle class is widely agreed to number some 100 million people or 10 per cent of the total population, but another figure is four million households or 25 million people." Leela Fernandes estimates the class to be "a burgeoning 250-million" (*India's New Middle Class*, xiv). Amita Baviskar and Raka Ray suggest that "With the broadest definition of the middle class in India, it is estimated that the top 26 per cent of Indian households belong to this income group" (*Elite and Everyman*, 2). Thus, wealth, income, occupation, etc. are slippery indicators to calculate the precise size or definition of the middle class, and who belongs or not within it.

22. Baviskar and Ray, *Elite and Everyman*, 19.

23. In doing so, they work both as "mainstream" and as "multiplex films." Although *NOKJ* boasts of big stars (such as Rani Mukherjee who plays Meera, and Vidya Balan who plays Sabrina), it was made on a smaller budget and focused on niche issue that resonated only with a small metropolitan/urban, middle-class, English-speaking audience, the class it addresses and celebrates. Dwyer, "Zara hatke ('somewhat different'), 197.

24. Nandini Chandra, "Young Protest: The Idea of Merit in Commercial Hindi Cinema," *Comparative Studies of South Asia, Africa and the Middle East* 30, no. 1 (2010):

122. Also, in her essay, Aarti Wani notes how the political awakening of the youth in the film is blinkered; for instance, "They do not notice that farmers, tribals, and workers are daily protesting and struggling to protect their livelihoods from an onslaught of the state and private corporations. They do not become aware of the deep divide in the country between the handful rich and the poor majority." Aarti Wani, "Uses of History: *Rang De Basanti* and *Lage Raho Munnabhai*." https://mronline.org/2007/02/12/uses-of-history-rang-de-basanti-and-lage-raho-munnabhai/

25. Ritesh Mehta, "Flash Activism: Civic Justice Catalyzed by a Bollywood Film," *Transformative Works and Cultures* 10 (2012), https://journal.transformativeworks.org/index.php/twc/article/view/345

26. Fernandes and Heller delineate three basic strata within the middle class. They define "the dominant fraction" as one that "consists of those with advanced professional credentials or accumulated cultural capital who occupy positions of recognized authority in various fields and organizations" ("Hegemonic Aspirations," 500).

27. Shilpa Jamkhandikar, "Bollywood Relives Model Murder that Transfixed India," *Reuters* (January 5, 2011). https://www.reuters.com/article/us-india-bollywood/bollywood-relives-model-murder-that-transfixed-india-idUKTRE7041H420110105

28. Fernandes, *India's New Middle Class*, xv.

29. The film establishes Sabrina as a regular person, for instance, by showing the means of transportation that she uses, which include the rickshaw, local bus, and the metro. Even the way she appears and dresses and appears—glasses, loose shirts, no makeup, hair up in a ponytail—all work to emphasize her averageness.

30. Fernandes and Heller, "Hegemonic Aspirations," 510.

31. John Harris, "Middle-Class Activism and the Politics of the Informal Working Class: A Perspective on Class Relations and Civil Society in Indian Cities," *Critical Asian Studies* 38, no. 4 (2006): 445–65.

32. There is, of course, a diversity in middle-class activisms even as they are all middle-class-driven and tend to lean illiberal; some examples, besides the Justice for Jessica campaign, include Narmada Bachao Andolan; India Against Corruption (Anna Hazare); Fight the Filth campaign in Mumbai; opposing reservation, or affirmative action, for Other Backward Classes in education and jobs; demanding capital punishment for rape; the use of Public Interest Litigations against informal settlements; protesting the Master Plan guideline to regularize illegal commercial establishments (most of which are operated by low-income residents); and so on.

33. Sokhmani Khorana, "*Peepli Live* and *No One Killed Jessica*: Remediating the 'Bollywoodization' of Indian TV News," *Image of the Journalist in Popular Culture Project* 6 (Fall 2015); 82.

34. Baviskar and Ray, *Elite and Everyman*, 3.

35. Baviskar and Ray, *Elite and Everyman*, 3.

36. Amitav Ghosh, *Countdown* (New Delhi: Ravi Dayal, 1999).

37. Ghosh, *Countdown*.

38. Rupal Oza, *The Making of Neoliberal India: Nationalism, Gender, and the Paradoxes of Globalization* (New York: Routledge, 2006), 106.

39. Oza, *The Making of Neoliberal India*, 104.

40. Ranjani Mazumdar, *Bombay Cinema: An Archive of the City*. (Minneapolis: University of Minnesota Press, 2007), 1. For more on the angry young man, read Fareeduddin Kazmi, "How Angry Is the Angry Young Man? 'Rebellion' in Conventional

Hindi Films," in *The Secret Politics of Our Desires: Innocence, Culpability and Indian Popular Cinema*, ed. Ashis Nandy (London: Zed Books, 1998), 134–56.

41. Samir Dayal, *Dream Machine: Realism and Fantasy in Hindi Cinema* (Philadelphia: Temple University Press), 70.

42. M. Madhava Prasad, *Ideology of the Hindi Film: A Historical Construction* (Oxford: Oxford University Press, 2000), 158.

43. M. K. Raghavendra, "A Renewal of Faith: *Dabangg* and its Public," *Economic and Political Weekly* 46, no. 6 (Feb 5–11, 2011): 33–35.

44. M. K. Raghavendra, *Seduced by the Familiar: Narration and Meaning in Popular Indian Cinema* (New Delhi: Oxford University Press, 2012), 130–32.

45. Prasad, *Ideology*, 95–96.

46. Priya Joshi, *Bollywood's India: A Public Fantasy* (Philadelphia: Temple University Press), 48.

47. Anustup Basu, "Encounters in the City: Cops, Criminals, and Human Rights in Hindi Film," *Journal of Human Rights* 9, no. 2 (2010): 175–90.

48. Arunima Paul, "Unraveling Countrysides: Provincial Modernities in Contemporary Popular Indian Cinema" (PhD diss., University of Southern California, 2014).

49. Sanjay Shrivastava, *Passionate Modernity: Sexuality, Class, and Consumption in India* (New Delhi: Routledge, 2018), 99.

50. Paul, "Unraveling Countrysides."

51. Paul, "Unraveling Countrysides."

52. The success of cop films has in turn also spawned other related subgenres tackling law enforcement and national security (such as spy and detective films). One of India's biggest production houses, Yash Raj Films (YRF) has churned out blockbusters in its "spy universe" franchise, focusing on RAW agents (referring to the foreign intelligence agency of India, its Research and Analysis Wing): *Ek Tha Tiger*, 2012; *Tiger Zinda Hai*, 2017; *War*, 2019; *Pathaan*, 2023.

53. Sanjay Shrivastava, "Modi Masculinity," *Television & New Media* 16, no. 4 (April 2015): 331.

54. Shrivastava, "Modi Masculinity," 331–38; and Jyotrimaya Tripathy, "The Character of Modi's Masculinity," https://indiachapter.in/index.php?/user/article/2/2/69

55. Chacko, "Gender and Authoritarian Populism," 219.

56. Stuart Hall, "Authoritarian Populism: A Reply," *New Radical Review* I/151, June 1, 1985, https://newleftreview.org/issues/ii151/articles/stuart-hall-authoritarian-populism-a-reply

57. Basu, "Encounters."

58. Ranjani Mazumdar, "From Subjectification to Schizophrenia: The 'Angry Man' and the 'Psychotic Hero of Bombay Cinema,'" in *Making Meaning in Indian Cinema*, ed. Ravi S. Vasudevan (New York: Oxford University Press, 2000), 245.

59. Mazumdar, "From Subjectification to Schizophrenia," 246.

60. Akshaya Kumar, "Cinema and its Spatial Predicates: Landscapes of Debt in Search of Justice," *Jump Cut: A Review of Contemporary Media* 60 (Spring 2021).

61. On December 16, 2012, a twenty-three-year old woman, Jyoti Singh Pandey, was gang-raped and left to die by the side of the road in Delhi; the brutal nature of the event sparked nationwide protests. The name of the raped young woman in *Simmba*, Aakruti, resonates with Jagruti (means awakening), which was one of the symbolic

names (in addition to Nirbhaya) that Jyoti was given by the media to "honor" her, before her father made the decision to reveal her name.

62. Lata Mani, *Contentious Traditions: The Debate on Sati in Colonial India* (Berkeley: University of California Press, 1998).

63. Shakuntala Banaji, "Vigilante Publics: Orientalism, Modernity and Hindutva Fascism in India," *Javnost—The Public (Journal of the European Institute for Communication and Culture)* 25, no. 4 (2018): 335.

64. Megha Anwer, "Cinematic Clearances: Spaces of Poverty in Hindi Cinema's Big Budget Productions," *The Global South* 8, no.1 (Spring 2014): 91–111.

65. A survey in India found that "over half the population preferred extrajudicial actions by the police to legal action." Roshni Chakraborty, "Sanctioning Abuse," *Harvard International Review* (Fall 2020): 65.

66. Krupa Shandilya, "Nirbhaya's Body: The Politics of Protest in the Aftermath of the 2012 Delhi Gang Rape," *Gender and History* 27, no. 2 (August 2015): 467.

67. "India's Daughter" was the title of a controversial 2015 documentary made by Leslee Udwin on the 2012 rape case. It featured interviews with one of the convicted rapists and his lawyer and was banned in India.

68. Cited in Shandilya, "Nirbhaya's Body," 472.

69. Of course, this sort of construction both leaves non-Hindu women out of the category of Indian women even as it silences how poor women, Dalit women, and non-Hindu women are disproportionately subject to sexual assault and other forms of violence.

70. "Beti Bachao: Government's Efforts to Eradicate Female Infanticide and Sex-Selective Abortion Are Inadequate," *Economic and Political Weekly (Engage)*, November 22, 2019, https://www.epw.in/engage/article/beti-bachao-eradicate-female-infanticide-violence-against-women-girls-abortion

71. Tithi Bhattacharya, "India's Daughter: Neoliberalism's Dreams and the Nightmares of Violence," *International Socialist Review* 97, https://isreview.org/issue/97/indias-daughter/

72. Damien Gayle, "'A Decent Girl Wouldn't Be Out at Night," *Daily Mail*, March 2, 2015, https://www.dailymail.co.uk/news/article-2975989/A-decent-girl-wouldn-t-night-says-one-men-convicted-gang-rape-left-Indian-girl-dead.html

73. Banaji describes how the fascist consciousness that pervades these "vigilante publics" is "in turn, a necessary base for state fascism." The vigilante publics and their "spectacular violence" "can at once be endorsed and disavowed by the state, whose purposes are furthered through participatory violence" ("Vigilante Publics," 335).

74. Here, one needs to mention a grotesque case of life imitating *Simbaa's* fictional narrative in the widely publicized 2019 Hyderabad police's extra-judicial killing of the men who gang raped a young veterinarian, allegedly when they visited the crime scene to recreate it. While this episode in the nation's recent history of macabre rape-murder crimes and the extra-judicial killings as shocking, what was even more disturbing was the celebratory wave of public support for the cops, much like the description in *Simmba* that publicly legitimizes state vigilantism as justice. See, "Hyderabad case: Police kill suspects in rape and murder of Indian vet" (BBC, December 6, 2019). https://www.bbc.com/news/world-asia-india-50682262

75. Stuart Hall, cited in Wynn Coates, "The Language of Authoritarian Populism," *Los Angeles Review of Books*, (November 1, 2021).

76. In her review of the film, Nandita Singh notes that the "premise, plot and even the dialogue of *Simmba* sounds a lot like a 2 hour 45-minute-long justification of Yogi Adityanath's 'Encounter Pradesh.' If the system doesn't work, *Thok do* (shoot them)." Nandita Singh, "Ranveer Singh's Simmba Is Everything That Is Wrong With This Country," *The Print*, December 28, 2018, https://theprint.in/opinion/ranveer-singhs-simmba-is-everything-that-is-wrong-with-this-country/170391/

77. Stuart Hall, cited in Coates, "The Language of Authoritarian Populism."

78. Dayal, *Dream Machine*, 71.

79. Singham calls cops like himself and Simmba "ede policewale" who aren't afraid to engage in encounters to rid the nation of sexual predators, criminals, and terrorists.

80. Gudavarthy, *India After Modi*.

81. In 2019, Sunita Singh Gaur, leader of the BJP's Mahila Morcha, is reported to have said that "There is only one solution for them (Muslims). Hindu brothers should make a group of 10 and gang rape their (Muslims) mothers and sisters openly on the streets and then then hang them in the middle of the bazaar for others to see." Gaur was subsequently expelled from her post. https://thewire.in/communalism/bjp-mahila-morcha-leader-says-hindus-should-gangrape-muslim-women-gets-expelled

82. Basu, "Encounters."

83. Basu, "Encounters."

84. Basu, "Encounters."

85. Gudavarthy, *India After Modi*.

86. Gudavarthy, *India After Modi*.

Index